Media Power, Media Politics

Media Power, Media Politics

Second Edition

Edited by Mark J. Rozell
and Jeremy D. Mayer

ROWMAN & LITTLEFIELD PUBLISHERS, INC.
Lanham • Boulder • New York • Toronto • Plymouth, UK

ROWMAN & LITTLEFIELD PUBLISHERS, INC.

Published in the United States of America
by Rowman & Littlefield Publishers, Inc.
A wholly owned subsidary of
The Rowman & Littlefield Publishing Group, Inc.
4501 Forbes Boulevard, Suite 200, Lanham, Maryland 20706
www.rowmanlittlefield.com

Estover Road
Plymouth PL6 7PY
United Kingdom

British Library Cataloguing in Publication Information Available

Library of Congress Cataloging-in-Publication Data Available:

ISBN-10: 0-7425-6067-8 (alk. cloth)
ISBN-13: 978-0-7425-6067-3 (alk. cloth)
ISBN-10: 0-7425-6068-6 (alk. paper)
ISBN-13: 978-0-7425-6068-0 (alk. paper)
eISBN-10: 0-7425-6395-2
eISBN-13: 978-0-7425-6395-7

Printed in the United States of America

♾️^{TM} The paper used in this publication meets the minimum requirements of American
National Standard for Information Sciences—Permanence of Paper for Printed Library
Materials, ANSI/NISO Z39.48-1992.

Contents

Introduction

Media Power, Media Politics

Jeremy D. Mayer

Welcome to the second edition of *Media Power, Media Politics*. Updating a book like this is essential because, as you will learn from the pages that follow, the manner in which politics and the media interact is undergoing a fundamental, revolutionary change. Some of these changes were anticipated in the first edition (2003), but we have asked our returning authors to emphasize how these changes have affected their topics, and we have chosen several new authors, in part because of their deep understanding of the American media's evolving nature.

It is also worth noting how much American politics itself has changed since the previous edition, and how large a role the media played in many of those changes. The 2004 presidential campaign of Howard Dean demonstrated for the first time that the Internet could be a truly powerful tool for raising awareness and funds on the road to the White House. Although Dean's effort was ultimately unsuccessful, it anticipated the tremendous growth in Internet campaigning seen in the 2008 presidential race. The 2004 presidential campaign also showed the continuing—and perhaps intensifying—influence of negative media campaigns, as John Kerry's presidential hopes went down in part due to brilliant negative ads produced by both the official George W. Bush campaign and the 527 group Swift Boat Veterans for Truth. And, at this writing in early 2008, the most watched ad of the 2008 presidential campaign was created for Internet distribution by a lone Barack Obama supporter, an unprecedented example of how the Internet empowers individuals. These are only some of the many political events that demanded an updated look at the way the media shape our democracy as they report on it.

We are also excited about some new features in the second edition. We have added brief exercises for professors and students to consider as class assignments. We believe these exercises will give you innovative and original ways in which to apply and explore the ideas discussed in many of the chapters. Several of these activities allow you to pose and answer your own questions about media politics, using empirical research that you guide and conduct. You will also find interviews with veterans of the media and political worlds, who will provide real-world commentary on the changes described by our academic authors.

MEDIA POLITICS, MEDIA HISTORY

The ability to engage in complex communication has been seen as a key point of separation between humans and other species, such as apes and dolphins.[1] While many animals communicate—and some have been shown to be capable of using names or even emitting specific warning calls for different predators— as far as we know, only humans use grammar and syntax.

Humans also have a monopoly on complex political interactions. Many social species experience power struggles among group members seeking dominance, but the size of the group, the length of the struggle, and the terms of conflict could not be more different from the human experience. Even if monkeys and wolves have a primitive form of politics, they do not have political systems worthy of the name.

Obviously, these two human advantages over other species are linked. It is impossible to conceive of politics more complicated than a tribal fistfight without complex language in which to discuss the issues. Even hunter-gatherer societies, which dominated prior to the emergence of agriculture, needed a language to discuss such topics as threats from other tribes, hunting strategies, and primitive religious beliefs. The development of our political systems has often been shaped by developments in communication technology.

For most of human history, political systems operated using oral communication. Oral political systems were limited in size, complexity, and permanence. A decision made at one time could not be reexamined in detail unless the memories of participants were trusted. Writing, as distinct from printing, emerged approximately five thousand years ago.[2] While some sizable empires did emerge without writing, they had a distinct disadvantage when they met competing groups that did possess writing. Writing allowed for larger economic endeavors and more specialized governmental organization.

But writing without printing was limited in impact. While vast imperial political systems such as the many dynasties of ancient China or the Roman Empire survived for centuries using only oral and limited written communication, any type of democracy was limited to a single city or tiny republic.

Monarchy, in all its varieties, remained dominant around the world when politics was mostly experienced in the spoken word. Democracy without printing presses could only take place by bringing as many citizens as possible into a single room and allowing them to debate directly. This is certainly one reason why so many early democracies were absorbed by larger empires that were able to amass larger armies.

The invention of the printing press by Johannes Gutenberg in the fifteenth century was therefore essential to the creation of the modern large democratic state. Gutenberg's first impact was felt in religion, as millions of Christians began to read the Bible in their native languages for the first time, sparking the Protestant Reformation. But today we can see that it was in the political world that a greater change eventually occurred. Communication scholar Neil Postman believed modern democracy was made possible by the development of the "typographic mind": In other words, the printing press changed the nature of cognition itself, and thus politics.[3] Postman argued that America was the first nation founded on print, on the ability of humans to communicate complex ideas over great distances. Without the printing press, you do not have a Declaration of Independence circulating around the rebellious colonies, rallying the public to seek independence. Nor do you get a Thomas Paine, who, at least as much as Thomas Jefferson, brought the public to desire independence and then stiffened the support for the American rebellion when it appeared that Britain would win the war. There were great orators of the Revolution, such as Patrick Henry, but without the printing press the impact of their words would have been limited to only those present at their speeches.

What was true of the United States was true of all subsequent democracies until the arrival of broadcast media. Print made possible the increasingly complex political systems of the nineteenth century. Did broadcast media damage democracy, as some, such as Postman, have argued? You will see elements of that ongoing debate in the pages that follow.

It is not a coincidence that the greatest challenges to democracy emerged in the twentieth century, cunningly using broadcast media such as radio and eventually television, as well as motion pictures, to further their aims. The new forms of oppressive political systems, including communism, fascism, and totalitarianism, were examples of what communication scholars called *propaganda systems*. In propaganda media systems, the state or its allies run all media, and the messages are uniform. Some scholars called this model of communication the *hypodermic needle theory*, in the sense that once you were injected with the state's propaganda, it could change your worldview because there were no other sources of information.[4]

This control of information makes the official media more powerful. Nonetheless, resistance media developed simultaneously to challenge state-run propaganda. One of the keys to the overthrow of the Soviet empire was the circulation of samizdat publications, underground writings by prominent dissidents that gave information directly counter to the dominant Soviet media.[5] Tyrants today hold onto television stations as keys to their power. When NATO forces led by the United States were seeking to defeat the Serbian government of Slobodan Milošević during the conflict over Kosovo, they eventually had to bomb the television infrastructure even though it was technically a civilian target. Western analysts believed that support for the neofascist Milošević would decline if his people were not receiving constant televised propaganda about the evils of the West.

Thus, throughout the long stretch of human history, the dominant form of communication in a period has greatly affected the nature of its politics. The same idea said through a different medium will not be the same when received. Consider the American political system of today as compared to the system at the time of America's founding. When the Founding Fathers were debating the new Constitution's merits, they engaged in spirited and highly complex debates in the pages of the nation's newspapers. Today, these arguments are collected in the *Federalist* and *Anti-Federalist Papers* (you can find them online with a simple Google search). These short essays were immensely influential in what was, in essence, the debate that determined whether America would be one nation. How would such a debate take place today? The dominant medium of modern politics is probably television, although the Internet is more influential among the elite. And when America chooses a president or decides whether to adopt national health care, the most important arguments are made on television, in thirty-second ads or in short seven- to fifteen-second sound bites by our leaders.

Is it possible to say something knowledgeable or meaningfully about the Constitution in a thirty-second television ad? Could even one of the *Federalist Papers* of James Madison or Alexander Hamilton be summarized effectively in thirty seconds of sound and image? The idea is ludicrous. Television might be able to cover the core ideas of one aspect of the constitutional debate in a half-hour documentary, but who would watch it? Television news has been called *infotainment* because it necessarily must mix information and entertainment. Making complex constitutional debates entertaining would challenge even Steven Spielberg. The nightly newscasts make that attempt every night as they simplify, glamorize, and sensationalize complex political developments at home and abroad. As Postman observed, "A news show . . . is a format for entertainment, not for education, reflection or catharsis."[6]

Television, of course, has done a number of marvelous things for politics. It has brought the citizens closer to their leaders, in the sense that we can see them up close and arguably get an idea of their personalities in a way that has never before been possible for citizens of democracies since the rise of large republics. It has also allowed people who cannot read to learn about politics more completely than at any time in history. For the illiterate, television and radio have brought them into the political discussion. And at times of national tragedy and crisis, television, with its vivid immediacy, brings the nation together more rapidly and perhaps more completely than print ever could. At moments such as the 9/11 terrorist attacks, a picture is worth ten thousand words, at least in terms of emotion and impact. Whether television was a good medium for encouraging careful cogitation and analysis of the appropriate responses to 9/11 is doubtful in the extreme, as anyone could glean from watching commentators on Fox News or CNN in the aftermath of the attacks.

Today, however, television's brief era of dominance is nearing its end. The authors in this book acknowledge the rapid rise of a new medium, the Internet, which threatens to absorb all prior media into its endless expanse. As newspaper readership and broadcast news viewership decline rapidly, more and more Americans are getting their news online. After fighting briefly against this change, most major news outlets have joined up. You can read *The New York Times* online and then watch clips from the NBC Nightly News. Even movies and songs are now increasingly available online. How is that "political"? Beyond the fact that many songs and movies are deeply political, the mere fact that citizens do not need to leave their homes to enjoy more and more types of entertainment may have political consequences. Those who seldom venture out into public spaces for entertainment and shopping may be less supportive of taxes and spending on infrastructure. In these and a thousand other ways, changes in the methods of communication have important and often unforeseeable consequences. We cannot say for certain what the Internet will do to American politics, although, in our final chapter, we do speculate on where the trends are heading. All we can say now is that the Internet holds the potential to make fundamental alterations in the nature of governance, campaigns, and the relationship between political elites and everyday citizens. In fact, more than any other medium in history, the Internet threatens to alter the definition of citizenship itself. By breaking down barriers between nations, by bringing news and personal views of foreigners into American homes with an immediacy never seen before, the Internet is changing what it means to be a citizen of a nation and a resident of the world.

AMERICAN MEDIA POWER

The role of the media in American politics has been a subject of much study in the last thirty years. Oddly enough, this was not true in the first seventy years of American political science. Early on, from 1900 to 1940, political scientists focused on constitutional questions and institutions of government. Some realized that newspapers and radio were important, but they lacked a vocabulary with which to discuss the media's impact and the data with which to analyze it. A few European thinkers, such as Walter Benjamin, did begin to analyze what the impact of radio and movie technology would be on society, and journalists such as Walter Lippmann became increasingly aware of the influence of their craft on political outcomes.[7] But overall, the attention of scholars was focused far from media. Even political behavioralism (the attempt to apply rigorous social science methodology to the study of politics) in its early days, from 1940 to 1970, failed to include the media as a major area of interest. Within political science, the belief was prevalent that the media had "minimal effects" on politics.[8] First, scholars believed it was very difficult for the media to change the minds of voters. This idea was best captured by one of the great early behavioralists, Paul Lazarfeld: "[T]he mind erects high tariff barriers to alien notions."[9] Lazarfeld and others conducted studies in which voters seemed unaffected by the views of newspaper editorials and the like, tending to stick with their preexisting beliefs. Second, voters were unlikely to consistently expose themselves to media with which they deeply disagreed. This idea was perhaps easier to believe when most major American cities and even many minor ones had at least two newspapers, one targeted at Democrats and the other at Republicans. A committed partisan could easily avoid reading editorials from the other side. Third, studies by scholars such as Phil Converse discovered that voters had remarkably little information about politics as well as inconsistent views on political issues.[10] In such a low-information environment, voters seemed much more likely to follow group identities such as union membership or partisan loyalty rather than new information learned from the media.

However, communication scholars in fields as diverse as journalism, business, English, linguistics, and rhetoric began to include political communication in their studies. And a few political scientists bucked the trend within the discipline and began to apply rigorous analysis to the impact of the media. Among these early luminaries were scholars such as Michael Robinson, Tom Patterson, Doris Graber, and Lance Bennett. The more the media were studied, the more they loomed as a vital part of America's politics. The study of media politics began to grow in popularity.

It may not be accidental that at the same time scholars began examining the media with newfound vigor, partisans of the left and in particular on the right were wondering about the power of journalists. At least since the 1964 Republican National Convention, many Republicans and conservatives have believed that the major media outlets and individual journalists are opposed to their political aims. In part this was because, at the time, the national media were headquartered on the East Coast, and the Goldwater Republicans were almost uniformly suspicious of large, wealthy East Coast institutions such as CBS, NBC, and the *Washington Post*. But studies eventually confirmed that there was much truth to the idea that most national reporters leaned Democratic and liberal, particularly on social issues such as abortion and civil rights.[11]

Significantly later, a number of leftist activists and scholars made counterclaims about media bias. Noam Chomsky, among many others, accused the media of blindly following the lead of the American establishment in foreign policy and ignoring genocides and crimes by America's allies.[12] Others suggested that since the national media were increasingly corporate, they were unlikely to give fair coverage to rights of workers, national health care, free trade, and other economic issues.[13]

On the campaign trail, the media loomed larger and larger in the race for the presidency. Tom Patterson, in his seminal book *Out of Order*, argued that the media had largely replaced the party elites in the candidate selection process because of the advent of the primary system.[14] During the convention era, nominees were selected by party bigwigs. But after 1968, voters were asked to choose nominees in low-turnout primaries and caucuses in different states on different days. These contests empowered the media, who determined whether a win was actually a "win" by setting the expectations game. The media could give momentum to one candidate and refuse to cover another. This largely unchecked power demonstrated yet again the importance of studying the media. Scholars such as Larry Sabato also examined whether the overall negative tone of the media, with its emphasis on scandal and personal failings, was having a negative impact on Americans' views about politics.[15]

WHAT'S IN THE SECOND EDITION

Today, as the scholars in this volume demonstrate, media power is among the most important topics political scientists examine. Any introductory textbook on American politics that does not include a section on the media is incomplete, and any sustained analysis of Congress, the presidency, American foreign policy, interest groups, state politics, or public opinion that omits the media is inadequate. The media matter—in ways that are often surprising and subtle. This volume is part of the ongoing attempt by scholars to document and analyze how our national political systems are affected by and respond to our media. We begin this book with a section on the media and its relationship to the major institutions of America's national government: the presidency, Congress, and the courts.

Most scholars of American politics acknowledge that the power of the presidency in the twentieth century grew far beyond the scope envisioned by the authors of our Constitution. For most of American history, Congress was the dominant branch in policymaking, except in wartime. When Woodrow Wilson, then a professor, wrote his influential 1888 book on American politics, he titled it *Congressional Government*, because it was Congress then that guided policy, much more so than the president. Ironically, it was perhaps the presidency of Woodrow Wilson, along with Theodore Roosevelt, that first showed how the mass media would strengthen the presidency in its relationship to Congress and to the public at large. There are many reasons for the growth of executive power, including the massive increase in the size of the military and the dominant role of America's diplomacy in the post–World War II world, but surely the mass media's emphasis on the presidency over Congress is one of the most important.

In their chapter, "The Presidency and the News Media," Jeffrey Crouch and John Anthony Maltese demonstrate how changes in technology, alterations in the organization of the White House bureaucracy, and the evolution of presidential media strategies have all contributed to the increase in presidential influence through the media. In a detailed comparison of the media presidencies of George W. Bush and his predecessor, Bill Clinton, the authors demonstrate how, regardless of party or ideology, presidents today must constantly evaluate their media strategy and impact. Using an enlarged White House staff, modern presidents can control their message throughout the federal bureaucracy more effectively than at any time in history. Presidents are often judged today by how effectively they get their "message of the day" out to the media, or around the media directly to the public. Crouch and Maltese raise important questions about what this new media environment means for presidents and for the future of America's executive branch.

The rise of the mass media enhanced the power of the president in the twentieth century, and simultaneously diminished the power of Congress. In chapter 2 Mark J. Rozell and Richard J. Semiatin explain that the media fail to do justice to the functions of Congress and tend to emphasize scandal and conflict. In comparison to the executive branch, which is able to present a much more unified message, Congress is diffuse and disorganized, tending to send negative messages about itself through the media. While few presidents attack their own branch, many members of Congress depict the national legislature negatively in their speeches and ads. And, as the authors point out, the nature of the legislative process is unappealing, particularly on television. In the vision of the Founders, Congress was intended to occasionally slow down—if not stop—popular but misguided proposals. The media do a very poor job of explaining why lengthy inaction may often be wiser than rash haste. In the age of the Internet, though, members of Congress are increasingly able to speak directly to the voters if they can drive traffic to their congressional and campaign Web sites. Still, this has not yet created a positive media environment for Congress as an institution. Americans still tend to dislike Congress much more than they do the president, even while expressing approval for their own representative or senators.

Our next chapter examines the press's relationship with the least known of the three branches of government: the judiciary. In "Press Coverage of the United States Supreme Court," Vincent James Strickler and Richard Davis argue that while the media spends the least amount of time covering the judiciary, the courts tend to be treated well by the media in comparison with the other branches. The few journalists who cover the Supreme Court beat have a tendency to feel almost protective toward the Court. They do not, in any case, report much about personalities and scandals. This may also be because historically the members of the court have been very media shy. Not only are oral arguments held away from video cameras, but the justices also conduct their ultimate deliberations in complete secrecy. They even force their clerks to sign nondisclosure agreements, legally binding them to silence about what they see and hear at the Court. Even more so than Congress, the judiciary is daunting in its complexity. As a consequence, the broadcast media may cover as few as 8 percent of Supreme Court decisions in any given year. The thousands of verdicts and decisions made by federal district and appeals courts receive almost no coverage at all. When the media do cover the courts, our authors find, the quality of the coverage is disappointing: "In sum, reporting about the Court is meager, superficial, often inaccurate, and almost entirely focused on the Court's work product."

This is a harsh verdict, perhaps, but the authors provide several examples. When the Supreme Court chooses not to hear a case, it is often reported as a decision in favor of one of the litigants, when in fact there has been no ruling. The distinction may appear minor to someone who is not a lawyer, but it is vital to understanding the nature of the judicial process. In defense of the reporters, though, our authors note that most justices on the Supreme Court make little effort to directly explain their decisions even in the cases they do decide. The justices tend to let their lengthy decisions speak for themselves, placing reporters in the role of interpreters for the mass public. Strickler and Davis argue that working the Supreme Court beat is more similar to covering Buckingham Palace or the Vatican than it is to covering the White House or Congress. The Court remains aloof from the American public, by design of the Founders, and this aloofness is still reflected in the way it is covered in the media.

Another look at the way the media covers court matters is the topic of chapter 4. In "The Gatekeeping Power of the Media as Illustrated in Its Coverage of Civil Rights and Liberties," Nina Therese Kasniunas argues that citizens and scholars must remain vigilant about the way the media exercise their filtering power. Because the mainstream media are still the primary agenda setter for the citizenry, their gatekeeping power is both impressive and worrisome: "The media's most insidious power is the ability to control what gets reported and whose voice is heard in that story."

In studying how the media covers civil liberties, the chapter outlines how much more attention civil liberties has received in the post-9/11 environment. However, while much has changed from 1999 to 2006 in terms of frequency of stories about terrorism, wiretapping, habeas corpus, and other matters that touch on individual freedom, one constant has remained: the media's reliance on a single interest group for authoritative commentary on civil liberties—the American Civil Liberties Union (ACLU). Kasniunas's research shows that before and after 9/11, broadcast and print journalists tended to include ACLU opinion in the vast majority of stories about civil liberties. Who is more powerful: the Supreme Court or the ACLU? Based on the infrequent coverage of Supreme Court decisions regarding individual freedom compared to numerous references to the ACLU in nearly every civil liberties issue, the media seem to have selected the ACLU. How did an unelected, unappointed group become so dominant? Is this healthy in a democracy? This type of media bias, in which disorganized and independent media outlets all seem to go to a single source, is far more worrisome than simple left- or right-wing bias, according to Kasniunas. The media may also tend to cover those issues the ACLU finds to be vitally important.

The Internet may offer a partial solution to this conundrum. By analyzing citizen attention to a controversial civil rights incident in Alabama, Kasniunas shows that YouTube and blogs provide a way around the media's gatekeeping. Although most of America noticed the Jena Six debate only when it broke into the mainstream media, on the Internet it had been a gathering storm for months. On topics as obscure as civil liberties in a small southern town, the Internet offers citizens a chance to challenge the ACLU's media-awarded status as the arbiter of what is important in American civil liberties, according to Kasniunas.

Much of what government does occurs within the vast and typically anonymous institutions of the executive bureaucracy. A very small percentage of our population interacts directly with presidents, members of Congress, or the Supreme Court. They do receive checks from the Social Security Administration, mail from the U.S. Postal Service, and tax refunds (or audits) from the Internal Revenue Service. How the media treat these activities helps determine how citizens feel about "government" as a whole, and in our fifth chapter, Jan Vermeer highlights some of the paradoxes of media's coverage of the bureaucracy. Most Americans are satisfied by their interactions with specific departments of our federal and state governments, yet they have an overall negative impression of government bureaucracy. Vermeer looks at several explanations. First, the media have an obvious bias for newsworthiness. When a bureaucracy does its job well, there is typically no news. But when there is malfeasance, incompetence, or scandal—that makes headlines. Vermeer contrasts the media's coverage of the Federal Emergency Management Agency's (FEMA) inept response to Hurricane Katrina with its much more competent response to earlier hurricanes. The former was the subject of worldwide media attention, while the latter was a small part of the human story of the hurricanes. Which is more typical of FEMA's performance as a whole? Vermeer also notes that the media tend to cover conflict: in particular, conflict with a close proximity to the media's readers and viewers.

Bureaucracies are not passive recipients of media coverage. They regularly engage in media strategies through their public information officers. Different bureaucracies adopt different postures toward the media. Some, such as America's intelligence agencies, simply avoid the media as much as possible. Most, however, see the media as vital conduits for communication with the citizenry. When the Department of Agriculture issues a recall of contaminated spinach, for example, it requires the cooperation of the media. Finally, most bureaucracies engage in public relations outreach to the media. A bureaucracy such as the National Aeronautics and Space Administration (NASA) needs the media to maintain its popularity with the American people. If the agency loses its positive public image, it will be politically weakened and could be vulnerable to budget cuts from Congress and the executive. In that sense, media relations can be a matter of life and death for a department or agency.

The media and the federal bureaucracy are far from the only players in the game of garnering the public's attention. Many interest groups monitor specific federal agencies and then use the media to publicize actions they disagree with. Federal and state politicians also frequently use the hot glare of the media's spotlight in their attempts to alter bureaucratic behaviors and policies. Vermeer notes how, even when such attempts are unsuccessful, they tend to put a political leader in a very favorable light, as a challenger to a heartless and faceless bureaucracy on behalf of honest constituents. This is yet one more reason why the bureaucracy may have such a negative image in America—it benefits politicians to portray them in that manner. In the end, Vermeer concludes that little is likely to change in the depiction of the bureaucracy as a cumbersome and inefficient entity.

In chapter 6, Tari Renner and G. Patrick Lynch look at another little-studied aspect of American media politics: the way state and local governments interact with the media. In "A Little Knowledge Is a Dangerous Thing," the authors explore how paid and unpaid media are part of the story of modern state politics. Scholars have paid little attention to state media politics, in part because the media seem to pay less attention to state institutions and actors. Yet in the midst of this "Swiss cheese journalism"—in which the gaps are larger than the substance—Renner and Lynch find important changes and impacts. The amount of money spent on paid media in state elections is growing exponentially. In the absence of media coverage of state politics, parties and politicians are buying time on television to speak directly to the voters.

But why is there so little coverage about state politics, when there has been a resurgence of policymaking at the state level in such matters as welfare and education? First, state boundaries tend not to follow neatly the media market outlines, so few local stations cover an entire state, and even fewer have viewers in only one state. Second, the national media tend to cover state and local politics only when there is a sizable scandal or a major national disaster. When a governor is on the national news, it usually means she is in trouble—or her state is.

Vast changes in the corporate structure of the media also help explain the absence of good coverage of state politics. In the past, newspapers were often locally owned and edited, and many cities had two or three of them. Now, newspapers, radio and television stations, and national networks tend to be owned by large conglomerates. Editorial decisions about the most important state media are often made by people who don't live in the state. The profit motive has also forced metropolitan newspapers to cover more entertainment and living "news" at the expense of state politics.

State politicians have begun to respond to this environment, becoming far more aggressive in their marketing to state media. To some extent, newspapers have improved their coverage of local politics by "zoning," or including sections in the paper directed at particular counties or regions that are distributed only in those areas. But for the foreseeable future, our authors conclude that state leaders and institutions will continue to be comparatively ignored by the media, particularly the national media.

In her chapter, "Political Parties and the Media," C. Danielle Vinson analyzes how the media and shifting election laws have shaped the political parties in modern America. Twenty years ago, scholars began to argue that the media had played a large role in the decline of American political parties. The rise of candidate-centered campaigns was in part a media-created phenomenon. Vinson shows how the parties have used the media to mount a comeback. Although recent changes in campaign finance laws were expected to result in far fewer party ads in campaigns, in fact the parties have run almost as many ads as they did before. The vast majority of the ads have been negative, and parties have been able to craft similar messages in districts across the country when the national mood calls for it. Party leaders in Congress have adroitly used unpaid media, such as the Sunday talk shows, to attempt to mold a coherent national message as well. Indeed, Vinson argues that party leaders have supplanted traditional congressional power centers, at least in the eyes of the media: "[O]ver time, party leaders have made up a growing proportion of the efforts by members of Congress to go public, and today on major issues, they are usually more prominent than committee chairs."

The leaders of the Republican National Committee (RNC) and the Democratic National Committee (DNC) have become far more prominent in the national media than they were previously. Media savvy in an RNC or DNC chair is no longer just a positive attribute; it is an essential component of the job. Under recent chairs, both parties have expanded their presence on the Web, particularly in outreach to young voters. The media still have at least one large blind spot: third parties. Representatives of such parties almost never get coverage in the American press. Is the press simply accurately assessing the reality of the weakness of such parties, or are they in effect creating it by keeping the American people ignorant of the policy proposals of these parties?

The power of the Democratic and Republican parties in American public life is unlikely to dissipate. The news media, and their shifting coverage, have at times changed the way these historic institutions interact with the public—and indeed with each other—but they remain stubbornly entrenched at the heart of the nation's politics, and thus analysis of the relative strength and the tactics of the two parties remains a fixture of news coverage in America.

Parties are groups organized primarily to win elections. And during the long and indeed nearly endless presidential campaign season in America, the media pay far more attention to the horse race than to the ongoing governing process. In the next chapter, "Presidential Elections and the Media," Mary E. Stuckey and Kristina E. Curry argue that most prior studies of the media's role in presidential elections have been negative. Stuckey and Curry provide a far more balanced look than the prior studies at how the media inform Americans about candidates, platforms, and polls. They attack the idea that there was ever a golden age in which campaigns were substantive and issue based, and fairly and completely reported by newspapers. Television may have many negative effects on American politics, but they look most negative when examined against a false history of "clean" politics in the past.

The authors also point out that blaming the media for the rise of candidate-centered elections may be putting the cart before the horse in terms of causality: "Candidate-centered campaigns have contributed to the fragmentation and lack of coherence that characterizes our national politics, and that makes those politics more difficult for citizens to assimilate and understand. The more confusing politics becomes, the more necessary are the media as interpreters."

The highlight of the chapter is a comparison of the presidential elections of 2000, 2004, and the early months of the 2008 campaign. Much of what is established truth about the media politics of those years is challenged in these brief comparisons. The authors do not, for example, agree that by 2004 television was far more important than newspapers in the coverage of the election. Newspapers remain relevant and powerfully shape the national understanding of events. In the end, the authors conclude that the greatest impact of the media on presidential campaigns is not to trivialize, cheapen, sensationalize, or darken with negativity. Rather, journalists' most dominant function is to winnow out the minor candidates, and in this way reduce the choices presented to the voters. There are troubling aspects to this conclusion, but it is far from the negative depiction common in most discussions of the media's role in elections in America.

Just as the media have been seen by many to have had a baleful influence on campaigns, interest groups have often felt that the media unfairly depicted them as hostile special interests. In "The News Media and Organized Interests in the United States," Ronald G. Shaiko highlights the antagonistic yet increasingly symbiotic relationship between interest groups and the media. Changes in the way Congress operates have made special interests far more interested in gaining press coverage. Today, interest groups often have to convince members of Congress that their issues have broad grassroots support, which usually means using the media to get their message out to citizens. Modern lobbyists can talk to Congress indirectly, using "outside" strategies in which the media is both the conduit through which the group contacts the general public and the source of news back to Congress about any demonstration of the public's affection for the group and its stance.

Why would the media let themselves be used this way? As much as journalists still promulgate the negative stereotypes about lobbyists and lobbying, thanks to budget cutbacks in the increasingly profit-driven mainstream media, journalists depend on them for stories and information. Shaiko proposes a new rule to describe how the media relate to interest groups: "[I]nterest groups and lobbyists have influence in inverse ratio to media competence." When journalists know very little about an issue and lack the skill or time to educate themselves, they can easily fall prey to a clever media campaign devised by an interest group. Rather than challenging an interest group's press release, investigating its claims, and contacting opposing groups, it is easier to simply report what the group has sent out.

Interest groups have aggressively stepped in as media consolidation has reduced the ability of media outlets to pay for real journalism. Shaiko writes of video news releases (VNRs), which offer television news stations prepared content that they can air with little or no alteration. VNRs offer a significant cost savings for television stations, but deceive viewers into thinking they are watching objective journalism. Our own government has also recently been caught placing taxpayer-financed VNRs in the media, as well as surreptitiously paying columnists to support government policies. The presidential administration may be one of the biggest "interest groups" trying to spin the media, as the White House increased payments to private public relations firms from $39 million in 2000 to $88 million in 2004.

Philanthropic foundations are other unusual interest groups trying to influence media coverage. Shaiko shows how their donations to public broadcasting often come with strings attached, such as requiring that the money be spent on coverage of a particular issue. While most of us might feel better about a nonprofit giving money to a public broadcasting unit than, say, Exxon paying CBS to give positive coverage to the petroleum industry, it remains a source of potential bias. Is National Public Radio (NPR) less likely to do an exposé on problems at philanthropic foundations, given that much of their funding comes from that sector? Ultimately, Shaiko worries that the media will continue to fall for spin from interest groups of all kinds unless it somehow recovers its core competencies in reporting.

Chapter 10 examines how the media use polling to measure and report public opinion. Stephen K. Medvic and David A. Dulio argue that any given poll can either report on the contours of public opinion about a subject or person or become news itself. When does a poll become more than simply an attempt to take the pulse of the country? When the results are unusual or new enough that they become a story in themselves? This unfortunately creates a negative incentive for news organizations sponsoring or using polls: A poorly worded question can look like a sudden shift in public attitudes, which is very newsworthy.

Polls have become stunning in their ability to accurately predict election outcomes, and the methodology for accurate prognostication is improving all the time. Yet the media use of polls may never recover from the debacle of the exit polls of 2000 in which the crucial state of Florida was awarded erroneously to Al Gore, then to George W. Bush—and then to no one. The authors show the special challenges exit polls present and give the little-understood details of how the Florida polling and reporting got it so wrong. But exit polls remain essential to election reporting. Although networks trumpet the predictive power of exit polls as the most important feature, their explanatory power is the more important function, because exit polls are a vital method for understanding why the election went a certain way. Exit polls, and polling in general, are going to be part of election coverage for the foreseeable future. The media have to become better at using polls and at providing enough information so citizens can benefit from poll reporting.

One aspect of the modern media system that is obvious to even a casual observer is how small the world has become thanks to new communication technology. A hundred years ago, the continents were linked only by inefficient telegraph communication, and news leaked out of foreign countries in dribs and drabs over a period of days. In "The New Bully Pulpit: Global Media and Foreign Policy," Maryann Cusimano Love shows how the media are truly international today, and have direct influence on foreign policy here and abroad. Some believe the influence has been largely for the good, since at the very moment the media are spanning the globe, the number of democracies worldwide has never been higher. Demonstrators against Soviet oppression in Eastern Europe believed Western media coverage would ensure their safety and their eventual success. However, others see the media as a baleful influence on foreign policy in America. The *CNN effect* means that decision makers face a time crunch to make fast decisions about issues that touch Americans emotionally. Others argue that the media have forced a schizophrenic foreign policy on the nation by calling for one policy and then failing to support it. In this view elites, who used to have more power in foreign policy than in domestic policy, have been prevented from offering coherent and difficult solutions. Skeptics question both views—perhaps the media are not strong enough to alter most foreign policies for good or ill. On the other hand, Cusimano Love points out that perceptions *are* power in this instance: If the media are believed by elites to shape public attitudes about foreign policy, elites will behave as if this were true and act accordingly.

One of the ways in which elites have sought to limit the influence of the media on foreign policy is through restrictions on the media during wartime. Many in the foreign policy and military establishments believed that unfair, inaccurate, and biased reporting of the war in Vietnam contributed to America's defeat in that war. In order to control what images and stories the media sent out about the first Gulf War, the media were tightly limited in what they could see and to whom they could talk. Press disdain for these techniques led to further changes, and in the wars in Afghanistan and Iraq, reporters were "embedded" with military units in a way that gave them a much closer look at operations than they had in the Gulf War.

But the media's job in wartime does not begin with the first shot in battle. The media's failure to find out that many in the intelligence community believed Saddam Hussein had no weapons of mass destruction and no meaningful contacts with al-Qaeda contributed to the successful launch of the war in Iraq. The difficulties facing the media in reporting on foreign policy at home and abroad are vast and growing larger. After numerous budget cuts and consolidations, fewer journalists are around to translate complex foreign situations into meaningful news.

One of the most complex foreign policy challenges the United States faces today is the threat of global terrorism. In "The Central Role of Media and Communication in Terrorism and Counterterrorism," Brigitte L. Nacos outlines how modern terrorists not only seek coverage for their violent acts from the media, but actually operate their own media broadcast networks and Web sites. Even video games are a method of communicating to potential terrorists and their supporters, and the Internet gives terrorists the ability to get their message out to potential followers and supportive populations without being filtered through and edited by the mainstream media.

Still, the mainstream media remain vital to the success of terrorism, because of their control over access to the majority of the population in the West. Extremists rely on the media to report violent deeds so that more people become aware of their cause. Nacos points out that they carefully plan the timing and locations of their attacks to maximize press coverage. Journalists face a tough decision whether to interview terrorists and give them legitimacy and coverage or turn down an interview that is certainly newsworthy and would get the public's attention. Yet by treating the videotaped statements of Osama bin Laden and other terrorists as at least as important as those of legitimate national leaders, do the media exacerbate the problem of terrorism?

The media can also make mistakes in covering counterterrorism responses by national leaders. Nacos argues that the traumatizing impact of terrorist acts like 9/11 can make the media temporarily forget its role as a watchdog on the accuracy of statements made by government officials: "In the American setting, most news media became the carriers of propaganda messages by the Bush administration and its supporters in the Congress and elsewhere that directly or indirectly linked Iraq's ruler to al-Qaeda and the 9/11 attacks, while ignoring completely or mostly that there was no credible evidence for such claims." Because the current war on terror is in great measure a war about communication between terrorist groups and governments, the media must be sensitive to its great responsibilities as a gatekeeper.

But perhaps the Internet offers new hope for getting foreign news? After all, nothing has made the world smaller than Web sites linking citizens from all over the world to each other with shared interests and content. The final chapter explores the good and the bad about the Internet for American media politics. Rising faster than any previous medium, the Internet threatens to absorb all other media into its broadband maw. What will American politics look like when the dominant method of communication is the Net? On the positive side, ordinary citizens will face fewer barriers than at any other time in modern history to creating political content that attracts readers and changes minds. The creative energy of tens of thousands of anonymous individuals can be harnessed by "wiki" technologies in ways that were unanticipated even a decade ago. The Net could also allow for more participation in politics, through donations and through Web activism. But a host of negatives are already visible. The filterlessness of the Internet will allow rumors and half-truths to jump directly into the nation's consciousness. And candidates today are under almost constant surveillance, knowing that the smallest gaffe or misstatement could be uploaded to YouTube by any hostile individual. What is perhaps most impressive about the Internet is how rapidly it is evolving and growing. Whether this evolution will favor the positive trends or create new negatives is currently unknowable.

Taken together, these thirteen chapters paint a broad portrait of American media politics at the end of the first decade of the twenty-first century. Once a neglected topic, the role of the media in influencing political behavior and institutions has become one of the key areas of academic analysis. Numerous organizations exist to evaluate the political impact of the media and to ferret out evidence of journalistic bias. No one doubts the importance of the media anymore. Understanding the role of the media is a necessary component of American political studies today.

NOTES

1. Jared Diamond, *The Third Chimpanzee: The Evolution and Future of the Human Animal* (New York: Harper Perennial, 1992/2006), 141–67.

2. Richard Rudgley, *The Lost Civilizations of the Stone Age* (New York: Simon & Schuster, 2000), 48–57.

3. Neil Postman, *Amusing Ourselves to Death* (New York: Penguin, 1987), 44–49.

4. James Watson and Anne Hill, *A Dictionary of Communication and Media Studies* (New York: St. Martin's Press, 1997).

5. Joseph Gibbs, *Gorbachev's Glasnost: The Soviet Media in the First Phase of Perestroika* (College Station: Texas A&M University Press, 1999).

6. Postman, *Amusing Ourselves to Death*, 88.

7. Walter Lippmann, *Liberty and the News* (Boston: Little, Brown, 1919/1995).

8. Steven E. Finkel, "Reexamining the 'Minimal Effects' Model in Recent Presidential Campaigns," *Journal of Politics* 55 (1993): 1–21.

9. Quoted in Jeremy D. Mayer, *American Media Politics in Transition* (New York: McGraw-Hill, 2008), 38.

10. Phillip E. Converse, "The Nature of Belief Systems in Mass Publics," in *Ideology and Discontent*, ed. D. E. Apter (London: Free Press, 1964), 206–61.

11. Jim A. Kuypers, *Press Bias and Politics: How the Media Frame Controversial Issues* (Westport, CT: Praeger, 2002).

12. Edward S. Herman and Noam Chomsky, *Manufacturing Consent: The Political Economy of the Mass Media* (New York: Pantheon, 1988).

13. Michael Parenti, *Inventing Reality: The Politics of News Media*, 2nd ed. (New York: Wadsworth, 1993).

14. Tom Patterson, *Out of Order* (New York: Knopf, 1993).

15. Larry J. Sabato, *Feeding Frenzy: Attack Journalism and American Politics* (New York: Free Press, 1991).

1

The Presidency and the News Media

Jeffrey Crouch and John Anthony Maltese

PRESIDENTIAL NEWS

"The press," Walter Lippmann wrote in his 1922 classic *Public Opinion*, "is like the beam of a searchlight that moves restlessly about, bringing one episode and then another out of darkness into vision."[1] More than eight decades later, the modern press has more "spotlights" than ever at its disposal, as more reporters search for stories to fill the never-ending demand of the twenty-four-hour news cycle.

The president of the United States is the focal point of most political media coverage coming out of Washington, D.C. In observing the coverage of our modern chief executives, one could easily come to the wrong conclusion that the United States has something analogous to a presidential system of government. Three key factors have contributed to the high demand for presidential content: the evolution of the executive branch's responsibilities, explosive technological growth, and modern presidents' tendency to "go public" to raise support for their initiatives. In other words, modern presidents have a role in more newsworthy areas of policy than ever before; they occupy a political environment populated by "old media" (television networks and newspapers) and—increasingly—"new media" (cable television channels, Internet Web sites and blogs) all competing to fill time and space with presidential material. Over time presidents and their staffs have become increasingly adept at using the mass media to try to promote their agendas.

Presidential Leadership Is No Longer a "Solo Performance"

The fact that the presidency has assumed more responsibility for governing over the years is the first key reason it receives so much attention from the press and the public today. Indeed, since the Budget and Accounting Act of 1921, which created the Bureau of the Budget (now called the Office of Management and Budget) to serve the executive branch, presidents are expected to propose legislation and usher it through Congress. The growth of the modern bureaucratic state since the presidency of Franklin D. Roosevelt has made communication between the executive branch, the other branches of government, and the American public a vital priority. As a result of this changed relationship, the high demand for stories about the president has pushed the executive to respond by increasing the size and scope of his White House press operation. As Lester Seligman wrote in the 1950s, the growth of staff "altered the behavior of the president in *all significant aspects.*" Presidential leadership, he added, was no longer "a solo performance, but part of a continuing line of executive action."[2]

The president's every move is covered by a small group of reporters called the White House press corps. Their stories are picked up by the wire services and find their way to newspapers and network and cable television news shows. These reporters in particular demand more information from the president than in the past because there is an increased interest in updated information on the president to be viewed via these mass media outlets.

Although the core of the relationship between the president and the White House press has always been the same—they need each other to fulfill their obligations to the public[3]—it is more vital than ever for presidents to effectively communicate their messages to the public because of the influential role of mass opinion. This long-standing symbiotic relationship between the president and the White House press corps has faced various challenges, as will be discussed here.

More, Faster Media

A second key difference between media demands on past and modern presidents is how quickly and easily the public can access information. As the new media have grown more popular, the influence of newspapers and network news programs has waned. A Pew Research poll shows that regular readership of newspapers has dropped from 58 percent to 42 percent in ten years, and the evening news audience has dropped from 60 percent to 34 percent.[4] Both have given way to a twenty-four-hour news cycle featuring cable television channels such as CNN and Fox News, and Internet Web pages and blogs such as Drudge Report and Daily Kos. More recently, Apple's iPod and iPhone, teamed with the iTunes online library, have made podcasts of books, speeches, and even television programs and movies affordable, widely available, and portable. Overall, the number and speed of mass media outlets is greater now than ever before.

"Going Public"

The third—and perhaps most important—factor driving the hunger for presidential news is modern presidents' tendency to "go public" and use precious White House resources (budgets, staff, and time) to engage the mass media and persuade the public to pressure Congress to support the president's legislative proposals. By doing so, these presidents have raised expectations among observers that presidential initiatives will be proposed and explained to the public, rather than just to Congress.

This change in the president-public relationship was a long time coming. Most pre-twentieth-century presidents were content to limit their political appeals for support to Congress. Many presidents and even the public considered "popular" appeals for support to be undignified.[5]

Roughly a century ago, during the presidency of Theodore Roosevelt, this view started to erode. During his stint as chief executive, Roosevelt used his "swings around the circle" to rally public support.[6] Aside from Woodrow Wilson, other early to mid-twentieth-century presidents were less comfortable and less skilled than Roosevelt at using the "public presidency," until Roosevelt's cousin Franklin became president in 1932. During the Great Depression and World War II, Franklin D. Roosevelt used his "fireside chat" radio addresses to speak directly to the American public, inform citizens of the government's plans, and assuage their concerns.

Since the time of Franklin D. Roosevelt, most presidents have tried to turn the press's "searchlight" to their advantage. For example, modern presidents are more apt than their early predecessors to travel, using speeches and public appearances to raise popular support for policy proposals.[7] However, basking in the glow of television cameras also requires the president to face a penetrating examination by the public and the press, which also can have its downside, as not all presidents are effective communicators.

The mass media today are in many ways more intense and probing than they were just thirty-five years ago, due largely to the Vietnam War and the Watergate scandal. The highly contentious modern media environment is still influenced by these decades-old stories that continue to color press–White House interactions.[8] One study analyzing the years from 1976 to 1992 found that "bad news" about presidential candidates outweighed "good news" in three of the most recent four elections, suggesting that "[i]f Vietnam and Watergate marked a time when the press turned *against* the politicians, the recent period represents a time when the press has turned *on* them."[9]

The relationship between reporters, their readers, and the presidents they cover has certainly transformed, and not always for the better. Presidents Lyndon B. Johnson and Richard M. Nixon complained—with some justification— that the tone of news coverage of the presidency had become highly critical, a view fervently expressed by all of their successors as well. In the 1970s the television newsmagazine *60 Minutes* showed executives that television news programs could make a profit, and TV journalism has never looked back.[10] In the past, reporters had largely considered themselves to be a part of a "working-class" profession and thus advocates for people such as themselves. Author James Fallows argues that after the uncovering of political scandals that made certain reporters famous, there arose a culture of "celebrity journalism" in which America's best-known journalists were no longer advocates of the "little guy" but instead themselves became a part of the elite who could push people around.[11] At some point, certain elite journalists, such as Walter Cronkite, Dan Rather, and Tom Brokaw, became wealthy celebrities in their own right. And after two young reporters for the *Washington Post* achieved enormous fame for uncovering the Watergate scandal, journalism schools were flush with aspiring reporters enamored with muckraking and hoping for celebrity themselves by bringing down the big shots in public life.

Fallows argues that by the 1990s, many top reporters had joined the class of "pushers."[12] Along with their fatter wallets, the elite journalists' attitudes changed as well. Gone were the days of the "friendly conspiracy," when White House reporters willingly participated in a cover-up to prevent the public from learning that Franklin D. Roosevelt was wheelchair bound.[13] The newer breed of journalist is characterized by "attitude and snarl" and descends into "feeding frenzies" because she is afraid of being "the reporter who missed the next Watergate."[14]

Technology has made the life of a journalist easier in some ways and more difficult in others. In 1973's *The Boys on the Bus*, a journalist marveled at the luxury of one presidential campaign's press suite, boasting "twelve typewriters, eight [land-line] phones, [and] a Xerox Telecopier."[15] Today, journalists may carry high-tech gadgets such as BlackBerries in addition to their trusty cellular telephones, pagers, and laptop computers. As the pace of news has accelerated, journalists have adapted by providing more content, updated news, and—perhaps most taxing of all—twenty-four-hour vigilance for any notable changes in the political environment. A faster pace means more pressure for reporters to get a story right quickly—and get it out as soon as possible.

White House reporters in particular are more harried than they have ever been. At the same time, the job of the White House communications officials who respond to their queries is a lot more difficult as well, as their waking hours are increasingly spent in "nonstop response" mode, trying to put the best spin possible on the news as it occurs.[16]

Thus, "going public" has become the norm in the modern media age, and a president's decision to do so has ripple effects on the press and the public. Although a fairly strong argument can be made that "going public" has only a limited impact on changing citizens' minds, that possibility has not stopped recent presidents from conducting "permanent campaigns" for public support.[17] One scholar contends that President George W. Bush's guiding philosophy is "governing by campaigning."[18] This is no surprise: Unless a president is out in front, attempting to define the issues and events in favorable terms, he risks allowing the press and the public to define the issues for him.

As demonstrated by our latest two presidents—spanning sixteen years, once Bush's second term ends in January 2009—the political landscape looks very different than it did back in Lippmann's era. The "searchlight" of Lippmann's day shines more intensely than ever as the number of outlets from the press, the public, and presidents has exploded. As this chapter will explore, presidents Bill Clinton and George W. Bush have governed in challenging times. Each man faced an aggressive media demanding new content throughout his presidency, and each man's capacity for reaching the public was altered by technological innovations. Technological breakthroughs are continuing to change how presidents run for office and govern, as well as how the mass media and the public evaluate their leadership.

THE CLINTON ADMINISTRATION

As the first "baby boomer" president, Bill Clinton grabbed the reins of the presidency with a strong appreciation for the power of the mass media, particularly new media such as cable television, fax machines, and the Internet. Coming out of a contentious campaign season where allegations of extramarital affairs and shady business deals were an almost regular occurrence, the Clinton communications team was in "damage control" mode from the start.[19] For example, White House staffers used fax machines to speed their own "spin" on stories to reporters as part of their "rapid response" to deflect allegations within the same news cycle.[20]

Despite their campaign-ready savvy, however, the Clinton administration's early days were characterized more by their hubris and how green they seemed compared to the staff of the outgoing president, George H. W. Bush. Instead of well-dressed, seasoned professionals, the new White House staff was younger and sometimes less respectful in dress and manner.[21] More importantly, the brash young Clinton team initially tried to circumvent the old media (for example, NBC, CBS and ABC) by using the new media to avoid the filter of the press and beam their messages directly to the American people. Notably, Clinton attempted to transmit his message to certain public constituencies via town hall forums and *Larry King Live*, MTV, and *The Arsenio Hall Show*, among others—an approach called *narrowcasting*.[22] By targeting a specific media outlet via narrowcasting, Clinton could transmit an unfiltered message around the gatekeepers of the old media and communicate directly with a particular constituency.

At the same time, the Clintonites irked the White House press corps by banning reporters from the offices of communications director George Stephanopoulos and press secretary Dee Dee Myers.[23] "Even in the worst moments of Watergate, we were always able to get to the press office," lamented veteran reporter Helen Thomas, "[b]ut all of a sudden, where we've always tread freely, we are the intruders."[24]

Not surprisingly, a week later, the *Washington Post* noted the press's "sour tone" in Clinton administration coverage. "We're very unhappy, frustrated and discouraged," reported *Baltimore Sun* reporter and White House Correspondents' Association president Karen Hosler.[25] "You're trying to get information from people you don't know, who won't return your phone calls, who won't even answer their phones."[26] The press's frustration carried over through Clinton's first one hundred days in office and was visible in television news stories on the administration. What is more, the administration's decision to change a three-decade-long practice by permitting television broadcasts of Stephanopoulos's daily briefings directly brought the contentious relationship to viewers nationwide.[27]

Instead of emphasizing Clinton's personality and intentions for his presidency, as the president had hoped, the mass media preferred to run more sensational stories on Clinton's famous junk food habit, his failed pledge to allow gays to openly serve in the military, and his unsuccessful nominations of Zoë Baird for attorney general and Lani Guinier for an assistant attorney general post.[28] One *Washington Post* writer suggested that Clinton had, in part, been victimized by a burgeoning entertainment and news industry and a "talk show culture that renders instant, thumbs-up or thumbs-down verdicts on virtually everything."[29]

Still, Clinton had a goodwill reservoir he could return to because, according to former *USA Today* White House correspondent Richard Benedetto, whether they would admit it or not, "[t]he White House press corps basically agreed with Clinton's domestic policies, which helped to dampen their criticism."[30]

Clinton's early presidential days were characterized by responding to events and spending little time trying to push the direction of the news,[31] but he rode the press's goodwill long enough to adapt and save his presidency. Turning to former GOP White House communications guru David Gergen in the spring of 1993, the administration's relationship with the press rebounded for a time, thanks to wise moves such as reopening the door to the White House press offices and holding private dinners with media elites.[32]

The administration was able to gauge its progress via evening news broadcasts and newspapers as well as polling data.[33] Eventually, Clinton successfully redirected his administration's communications focus. The Clinton team developed particular expertise at changing the subject. As close aide John Podesta pointed out, "The thing that amazes me is how much we can turn on a dime. It's actually something I always attribute to learning from [David] Gergen . . . that you can stop, assess that you're going in a bad direction, turn on a dime, and go someplace else rather than just keep going down."[34]

The Clinton team needed all of its savvy and skill to survive the blockbuster story from January 1998 that the president had carried on an affair with White House intern Monica Lewinsky. *Newsweek* reporter Michael Isikoff had the Lewinsky story and was forced by his editors to withhold it.[35] Most major media outlets at the time followed an unwritten rule that they would not use their Web sites to break a story.[36] Instead, the story was broken by Drudge Report, and the Internet came to shape the way the media covered the scandal. What is more, the story was picked up and carried by conservative talk radio shows, which had flourished following the repeal of the Fairness Doctrine in 1987.[37]

Despite the media frenzy, Clinton's public approval ratings remained high. He survived impeachment thanks in part to the public's dissatisfaction with the inquiry, his own high job performance ratings, and a strong economy.[38] Instead of a referendum on Clinton's private behavior, he urged the American public to focus on the fact that despite the impeachment chaos, he was still doing a good job as president. In the end, that was enough to preserve his presidency—and probably his legacy as well.

THE BUSH ADMINISTRATION

The beginning of the George W. Bush presidency promised to be different from the first weeks of the Clinton era. "The days of the 'war room' and the permanent campaign are over," vowed Vice President Dick Cheney approximately a month into the administration's first term.[39] Nonetheless, Cheney and other Bush administration higher-ups assumed office with a clear view about how they were going to manage the press.

Then-congressman Cheney (R-WY) had explained in 1989 that it is essential for the White House to manage the news: "That means that about half the time the White House press corps is going to be pissed off," he admitted, "and that's all right. You're not there to please them. You're there to run an effective presidency. And to do that, you have to be disciplined in what you convey to the country." In other words, the president, not the press, decides what is newsworthy. "You don't let the press set the agenda," Cheney insisted. "They like to decide what's important and what isn't important. But if you let them do that, they're going to trash your presidency."[40]

To effect this approach of White House managed news control, the Bush administration was joined by a skilled communications team. Longtime Bush confidante Karen Hughes managed all four communications-related offices at the start of the Bush presidency: the Press Office, the Communications Office, the Media Affairs Office, and Speechwriting.[41] While another longtime Bush ally, Karl Rove, focused on political matters, Hughes brought in the broader perspective and tried to coordinate how best to communicate the president's policies to the public.[42] The two most visible offices in the Bush administration's communication apparatus are the Press Office and the Communications Office.

White House Press Office

First created by Franklin D. Roosevelt in 1933, the Press Office's overall role is to meet reporters' daily information needs. The Bush Press Office—as in other administrations—is more concerned with "the day ahead," as former press secretary Ari Fleischer explained: "The Press Office is much more operational, much more implementation" than the overall communications effort.[43]

Located downstairs in the West Wing of the White House, the Press Office's most visible part is the Briefing Room, where the press secretary meets with reporters at regular intervals (usually two daily briefings). An informal morning briefing (called the *gaggle*) takes place off camera, but the afternoon briefing is now televised on C-SPAN, with transcripts and audio available at the White House Web site (http://www.whitehouse.gov/news/briefings/). Junior Press Office staffers occupy space next to the Briefing Room, and Fleischer, Bush's first press secretary, had an office located just down the hall from the Oval Office.[44]

The Bush White House recently acknowledged that its Briefing Room was woefully inadequate for the twenty-first century and beyond. Built on top of the White House swimming pool, the old room was "a cramped junkyard of jumbled cables, ladders, equipment, busted seats, ancient desks, falling ceiling tiles and rodents"—in other words, according to White House Correspondents' Association president Steve Scully, "a pit."[45] Eleven months and $8 million later, the White House press corps was welcomed back to a brand-new high-tech environment.[46] The newly redone area featured state-of-the-art air-conditioning, lighting, and video technology and left the swimming pool—which was built for President Franklin D. Roosevelt's use—intact.[47]

White House Communications Office

According to the White House Web site, the Communications Office "oversees message and communications development and planning, and works with the Advance office on planning and production of presidential events."[48] It was created in 1969 by President Richard Nixon in an early manifestation of "going public." Nixon created the Communications Office to be an institutional response to the need to coordinate the flow of news from the entire executive branch and to communicate more directly with the American people through town meetings, local media outlets, and other forms of direct appeal. Nixon hoped to use the Communications Office to avoid any foot dragging or criticism of his policies from executive branch career bureaucrats, many of whom were Democrats.

The Communications Office, housed upstairs in the West Wing at Bush's request, is more proactively concerned with building public support for particular policy initiatives than the Press Office, and more concerned with long-range communications planning and the coordination of the line of the day among a wide range of presidential surrogates both in and out of the executive branch.

Other White House Communications Staff

Media Affairs Office

The Media Affairs Office handles regional, local, and specialty presses, as well as the White House Web site.[49] The goal of this office is to create an "echo" effect by contacting ethnic media (Hispanic, African American, etc.) and local newspapers following a presidential event to see how well the president's message was received by these constituencies.[50] According to long-time Bush aide Dan Bartlett, "the most common piece of advice we received from every administration, both Democrat and Republican, was don't ignore, and, in fact, give more priority to local media than to national media."[51] Indeed, polling data suggest that the public trusts local media more than the national media.[52]

Speechwriting

As other presidents, Bush has to prepare as president to speak frequently to a number of constituencies. However, the burden on Bush to speak can be overwhelming: immediately before and after 9/11 (between 2001 and 2002), the president gave about 425 public remarks—similar to the number of such speeches made by President Dwight D. Eisenhower in his *eight* years as president. What is more, Bush faces enormous pressure to speak in an environment where his words can be recorded, edited, and rebroadcast nearly seamlessly.[53]

Additional Offices

Other White House communications staff units include the News Analysis Office (which dissects how the media are covering the White House), the Office of Foreign Affairs (which serves as a liaison with foreign media), and the Office of Media Liaison.

THE BUSH ADMINISTRATION AND 9/11

After the terrorist attacks in New York and near Washington, D.C., the president's communications skills took on added significance as his popularity soared. The war on terror "changed everything," according to Richard Benedetto. "It consumed the administration."[54] The already-high stakes were now even higher. In response to the new overseas challenges presented by the war on terror, the White House added two new communications offices to reach foreign markets: the Coalition Information Centers (CIC) and the Office of Global Communications.

Coalition Information Centers

Unlike many of his predecessors, Bush was faced with a crisis at home and abroad following the attacks. Encouraging American support for attacks in Afghanistan was difficult enough, but Bush had to also counter—within the same news cycle, if possible—anti-American propaganda perpetuated by the Taliban.[55] Indeed, the twenty-four-hour news cycle is not strictly an American phenomenon. Journalists worldwide are adapting to covering a war even while half of the world is asleep: "This is the first war that has a never-ending news cycle," explained CIC director James Wilkinson. "It may be 3 o'clock in the morning in the United States, but somewhere in the world, a journalist is on deadline. A 24-hour news cycle required the coalition to set up a 24-hour operation to communicate the facts."[56]

Office of Global Communications

Established as part of the White House in 2002, the Office of Global Communications was intended to, in the words of its head, Tucker Eskew, "coordinate among agencies to try to take the president's . . . framework for communications, and integrate it in to what we're already doing and . . . provide support for and elevate good ideas, good programs so that they can become part of the president's . . . legislative and governmental agenda."[57]

Bush and the Press

Opinions on the president's relationship with the press—particularly since 9/11—are quite polarized. This was not always the case. For a time, Bush's public standing, along with the type of coverage he received, improved dramatically. Not surprisingly, the key event was the terrorist attacks.

A Gallup Poll conducted September 7–10, 2001, showed Bush's approval ratings at a new low: 51 percent. Not until the galvanizing events of 9/11 did Bush's stature soar to 90 percent.[58] The popularity spike enjoyed by the president came largely from Democrats and independents.[59] Democrats went from a dismal 28 percent approval rating for Bush at the beginning of September to an almost unbelievable 81 percent just a couple of weeks later, according to a Pew Research poll.[60] One study found that network news and local newspaper coverage of the president went from about two to one negative before 9/11 to almost two to one positive coverage afterward.[61]

As the war on terror has gone on and the Iraq operation appears to be at a stalemate, Bush has become more and more unpopular. According to a Gallup Poll conducted December 14–16, 2007, Bush's approval rating is 32 percent, with 77 percent of Republicans supporting him, but only 23 percent of independents and 6 percent of Democrats.[62] As circumstances have changed, competing interpretations of how Bush has been covered by the press have emerged on both sides of the political aisle.

Liberal observers argue that the press has essentially given in to the White House, telling the American public only what the president wants it to know.[63] According to this perspective, the press uncritically accepts the White House's characterization, or *frame*, of events overseas, which is essentially that the United States is at war with terrorism and may need to protect itself by preemptively attacking other nations that may harbor terrorists, including Iraq, Iran, and North Korea, the so-called Axis of Evil.[64]

One study argued that Bush's public statements from summer and fall 2002 through the 2002 midterm elections slyly shifted emphasis from the attacks and protecting America from terrorists to taking out Saddam Hussein's government in Iraq; the news media then followed the president's lead.[65] Polls taken thereafter show that large numbers of Americans believed a clear link between Iraq and the terrorists existed, despite any hard evidence for that conclusion.[66] Another study suggested that how the public understood what were indeed proven facts about the war in Iraq depended heavily upon the sources from which they received national news. When queried about the accuracy of three common misperceptions about the war—that weapons of mass destruction had been located, that Iraq was connected to al-Qaeda, and that worldwide public opinion supported the war—the National Public Radio/Public Broadcasting Service audience held the most accurate understandings; the Fox News audience, the least accurate.[67]

When attempting to ascertain the truth, the liberal argument goes, it is difficult to obtain information from a president who is inaccessible. Indeed, security concerns have the pleasant side effect of limiting the amount of time the president spends in front of reporters. As *Newsweek*'s Howard Fineman observed, "The trend line is to fewer press conferences, smaller press pools, fewer opportunities for the reporters to eyeball the president."[68] With fewer opportunities to make a mistake, the president has arguably been able to get away with more than he should.

On the other hand, conservatives contend that the president has been treated unfairly by a press that is overly critical and unsympathetic to the president's precarious position. They point to CBS News's Dan Rather and his decision to air what was later found to be an inaccurate story challenging Bush's Air National Guard record.[69] Because the large media outlets set the "agenda," or what topics are discussed and put forth to the public as newsworthy, conservatives suggest that the public is receiving an inaccurate version of political realities in Iraq and elsewhere. Considering the fragmented state of the media and the number of outlets available on both sides of the ideological aisle, the debate seems unlikely to abate any time soon.

DIFFERENCES BETWEEN THE CLINTON
AND BUSH ADMINISTRATIONS

Although presidents Clinton and Bush had relatively similar communications setups, each man's personal style and the situations he encountered as president influenced his White House's response to those circumstances. In some cases, the president's approach worked well. In other cases, he had to try to control the damage while also righting the ship.

The main difference between the Bush and Clinton approaches to communications is that the Bush team early on focused more on creating a message and sticking to it, rather than responding to questions about the news as it occurred.[70] The emphasis in the Clinton administration was to be flexible and respond to the news cycle; the Bush administration—at least at first—focused on the future. The Bush team came around by 2006 and became more reactive as events began to drive the administration into a defensive posture.[71] For a time, though, as White House communications scholar Martha Joynt Kumar points out, "[t]he communications operation of George W. Bush was strong where the Clinton one was weak and weak where Clinton excelled."[72]

The Bush team viewed control of the policy agenda as vital to the president's success.[73] Learning from Clinton's mistakes, Bush not only presided over a very disciplined staff, but followed Ronald Reagan's example by planning a simple, clear-cut legislative agenda for his first one hundred days in office. He focused on a short list of priorities that included education reform, faith-based initiatives, tax cuts, and military preparedness, and centered his communications agenda on those priorities.[74]

The Bush communications team even stuck to its message when the news cycle was heading in a different direction: According to former communications director Dan Bartlett, "[w]e'll pass up opportunities if something presents itself in the headlines that day or if television broadcast hits with some news. We're not as eager to jump on something and ride that wave, so to speak, if it's not fulfilling or consistent with our strategic communications goal for that week . . . or whatever it may be."[75]

This approach proved costly for the Bush administration on several occasions. The Bush team took a beating from the press by refusing to swiftly engage corporate scandal, particularly when Enron and WorldCom went bankrupt.[76] It took the Bush administration months to identify and acknowledge that corporate fraud was a presidential priority.[77]

Perhaps more costly was the Bush administration's response to Hurricane Katrina. Bush absorbed harsh criticism for what the public perceived to be a slow response to the disaster unfolding in Louisiana, Alabama, and Mississippi. Rather than return to Washington, D.C., Bush chose to run the federal government's response to the hurricane from his home in Crawford, Texas, as he was on vacation at the time.

In the meantime, horrifying pictures of the devastation were making the rounds on television and the Internet. ABC's Ted Koppel, stumped by Federal Emergency Management Agency director Michael Brown's reaction to the situation, queried Brown: "Don't you guys watch television?"[78] The federal government's sluggish response, paired with Bush's perplexing and highly publicized compliment to Brown—"Brownie, you are doing a heck of a job"—led many to conclude that the president was out of touch and had not adjusted adequately to changing circumstances that cried out for a quick, focused federal government response.[79] As with other issues, the public's reaction to how well Bush handled the Katrina disaster split along party lines, with about two-thirds of Republicans approving of Bush's actions and about two-thirds of Democrats disapproving.[80]

By 2006 Dan Bartlett acknowledged that the Bush team needed to do a better job responding to news: "[I]t can't be either/or. It has to be hybrid."[81] Not only did the Bush team want to dictate the terms of the agenda, it wanted the media to focus on the president. In contrast to the approach of his immediate predecessor, who urged cabinet secretaries and others to speak on behalf of the White House, Bush made himself the focus of media announcements.[82] This is no surprise because, as Bartlett admitted, the White House's goal was to shift attention to the president and away from the presidency. It wanted "more reporters covering the person and not the institution," because "one of [the president's] strengths is his personality."[83]

Bush has used his staff strategically to direct one focused message to the rest of the country. In the hierarchical Bush staff arrangement, only top-level aides such as Karen Hughes and Karl Rove were privy to sensitive information.[84] As a result, leaks were a much rarer occurrence than in the "famously loose" Clinton administration, where information was less restricted and even lower-ranking officials had tantalizing bits for journalists.[85]

What is more, the Bush administration took great pains to exert control over the White House's image, influencing the messages released by cabinet public affairs officers by appointing loyal officials and dictating communication messages for the whole executive branch.[86] Bush targeted Texans or "loyalists" for staffers rather than "hired hands" who may have career aspirations outside the executive branch.[87] The hope behind releasing a consistent message from the executive branch was to fight the tendency of department spokespeople to emphasize the department secretary's priorities over those of the White House.[88]

Key Technological Changes between Administrations

Managing the press has become more complex. During the Clinton years, White House staff had to deal with new cable news networks CNN, Fox News, and MSNBC, along with the Internet.[89] The Lewinsky scandal presented a particularly tough challenge, as it was an inexpensive and simple way to fill air time, and the cable networks ran nearly nonstop "talking head" analysis even when there was no news to report.[90] The daily presence of CNN posed a unique motivation to respond quickly and accurately to the news, according to former Clinton press secretary Mike McCurry: "[H]ere would be Wolf Blitzer . . . based on God knows who he had talked to, beginning to shape the story that you were still trying to think through."[91]

Although the Clinton administration developed the first White House Web site in 1994,[92] the Bush administration has from the start had to learn to work around five major news networks and an Internet that continues to grow by leaps and bounds.[93] The news cycle's speed increased in Bush's second term, with more information outlets, more information available, and more demand for White House information from journalists.[94]

The Bush administration has served in a period of mass media transition, as both the White House and reporters have become comfortable relying on technology to do their jobs. For example, the e-mail revolution has allowed press releases and other documents from the White House Press Office that used to require printing to be quickly and easily dispersed to interested parties.[95]

Technology has made it easier for the president to reach the public from a variety of locations. Fiber-optic cables installed in the Briefing Room and the East Room by the end of the Clinton years expanded to allow Bush to address the nation from several locations in the White House and the surrounding complex in a short period of time.[96] One of the more memorable moments of the Bush presidency was the president's landing on the USS *Abraham Lincoln* before he announced of the end of major combat in Iraq while standing in front of a "Mission Accomplished" banner. This striking bit of political stagecraft was only possible because of modern technology: The live broadcast of the president's jet landing on the aircraft carrier resulted from advances in satellite and video technology, as well as better editing software.[97]

TECHNOLOGY AND RECENT CAMPAIGNS

The 2004 election marked the point at which the Internet became a main source of political information.[98] Arguably the most important figure in the development of campaign technology in 2004 didn't even win his party's nomination: former Vermont governor Howard Dean. The Dean campaign used the Internet both to raise huge amounts of money (in the third quarter of 2003, Dean for America raised a record-breaking $15 million from mostly small online contributions) and, via the social networking Web site meetup.com, to organize thousands of supporters.[99] Unfortunately for Dean, this online support did not translate into votes, and he will perhaps always be remembered more for the infamous "Dean Scream," a much-replayed clip of Dean addressing supporters following his Iowa caucus loss that has become a cable TV news and YouTube staple.

On both sides of the political aisle, 527 groups (named after the provision in the tax code that allows their existence) affected the election by coordinating attacks on the opposition and raising millions of dollars. The Swift Boat Veterans for Truth, a group of Vietnam veterans who questioned the veracity of Democratic presidential nominee John Kerry's claims about his overseas service, used the Internet to contact supporters and pass on television clips attacking Kerry.[100] Another emerging force, MoveOn.org, produced pro-Kerry spots and helped raise millions of dollars for the Democratic effort.[101] In the end, Bush raised $82 million and Kerry raised $14 million in online contributions alone, a staggering sum for a medium that, for all intents and purposes, was still in its infancy.[102]

No one can deny the impact of blogs on the 2004 election. The growing audience for blogs was a regular source of media stories throughout the 2004 election, as blogs took credit for fact-checking claims from both candidates and those made in stories published by TV networks and newspapers.[103] Conservative blogs such as Power Line took on Dan Rather and CBS over Bush's military record, while liberal blogs such as Daily Kos and the Huffington Post took on Bush's use of information (or lack thereof) in the lead up to the Iraq war.[104] Perhaps fittingly, Drudge Report declared at 1:00 A.M. on November 3 (Election Day was November 2) that George W. Bush had earned reelection.[105] Several months after Election Day, bloggers' march for mainstream legitimacy saw another victory when Garrett Graff, editor of FishbowlDC, became the first blogger ever given a daily White House pass to write a blog after the White House apparently caved to pressure from traditional media outlets such as CNN and *USA Today.*[106]

Although not a presidential election year, technology continued to play a role in the 2006 congressional election outcomes. The public learned that Rep. Mark Foley (R-FL) had sent explicit instant messages to underage male congressional pages, a fact that was apparently known to Republican leadership for months. Foley resigned. Sen. George Allen (R-VA) lost his reelection bid after his on-camera blunder of calling a supporter of his challenger, Jim Webb, "macaca," later discovered to be a racial slur in some cultures.

Campaign 2008 and Beyond

At this writing in early 2008, the trends identified above continue. Republican and Democratic presidential candidates have embraced new media as ways to reach the public and raise money. Social networking sites such as Facebook and MySpace are valuable recruiting tools for campaigns. The wildly popular file-sharing Web site YouTube (recently purchased by Google) has sponsored presidential YouTube debates for both major parties in which the major party presidential candidates answered questions posed via video clips submitted by everyday people. This is a major coup: More than 100 million videos are seen by users on YouTube each day.[107]

Some of the 2008 candidates are receiving attention for campaigning innovations that they have no control over themselves. Sen. Barack Obama (D-IL) seems to be developing a reputation as the "hip" Democratic candidate, as evidenced by the popular YouTube clip featuring "Obama Girl"—model Amber Lee Ettinger—lip-synching the song "I Got a Crush . . . on Obama" in a variety of provocative outfits. The clip received more than 2 million hits, or viewings, in its first three weeks.[108] Obama has also earned the first-ever presidential endorsement from one of the most powerful celebrities in the world: Oprah Winfrey.[109]

Meanwhile, Republican candidate Rep. Ron Paul (R-TX) raised oodles of cash from his online operation. In a record-breaking display of Internet fundraising prowess, Paul supporters—acting independently of the candidate himself—raised $4 million in one day.[110] Howard Dean's former director of online organizing, Zephyr Teachout, characterizing the influence of decentralized, unpaid supporters on the Paul campaign, saw the phenomenon as "[t]he buggy is pulling the horse."[111] Matt Lewis, operations director for the conservative news Web site Townhall.com, perhaps summarized the stakes best: "Technology will happen, and the question is whether it will happen for you or to you."[112]

CONCLUSION

"Reporting used to be easy," Richard Benedetto observes. "You went places other people don't go and came back and told them what you saw and heard. Today, you still go places other people don't go, but you have to come back and tell them what you didn't see and didn't hear, or what you should have seen and should have heard."[113]

The world has changed for presidents, the press, and the public. For better or worse, as Martha Joynt Kumar notes, "Our situation is defined by an abundance of information but a lack of understanding of what it means."[114] Journalists, bloggers, presidents—pretty much everyone with a computer and an interest in the news—all have a stake in attempting to define what the news is, and what it means. In our modern media environment, characterized by a "cacophony of voices,"[115] it is more difficult than ever to sort out what is and is not news.

This situation is complicated by the fact that the lines between entertainment and news continue to blur. One major cultural touchstone for "fake news," or political satire presented as reporting, is *NBC's Saturday Night* in 1975 (later renamed *Saturday Night Live*). This show, which initially featured the faux news of Chevy Chase's "Weekend Update," still features the popular segment (albeit hosted by younger performers) some thirty-plus years later. At the same time, the audience for pseudo-news on cable television is substantial, evidenced by the phenomenal popularity of two Comedy Central shows: Jon Stewart's *The Daily Show* and Stephen Colbert's *The Colbert Report*, which both feature wicked political satire and often feature important news figures as guests (who no doubt see the shows as an opportunity both to appear hip *and* hawk their latest books). Since Stewart took over as host in 1999 and Colbert, a former *Daily Show* correspondent, received his own show in 2005, these programs have earned high ratings, particularly among younger viewers.

Today, the "searchlight" of the press shines brighter than ever, but the stories it unearths are more subject to interpretation by more people than ever. For better or for worse, the relationship between the president and the press will continue to be a struggle to define reality. As Colbert might say, the "truthiness" of a story occurring in our current media environment is truly in the eye of the beholder.

DISCUSSION QUESTIONS

1. Compare and contrast the media tactics of the Clinton and Bush White Houses. Do you think greater centralization of messaging was, overall, a good strategy for Bush?
2. In the chapter, Vice President Dick Cheney says, "You don't let the press set the agenda. . . . They like to decide what's important and what isn't important. But if you let them do that, they're going to trash your presidency." Do you agree with Cheney that the White House must aggressively tell its story, regardless of what the media wants to focus on?
3. Do you think presidents must have "permanent campaigns" to maintain popular support while in office? Is there any danger that the public will eventually stop listening if the White House is on the news every day?
4. According to the chapter, some people think that the press corps is easier on presidents when they agree with the president's agenda and politics. Others have suggested that sometimes journalists come down harder on presidents they agree with to actively prevent accusations of bias. Which side seems likely to be true to you?
5. What moments of media management by a recent president were you most impressed with? And do you recall moments when you felt that the White House had blundered in its efforts to manage the media?

SUGGESTIONS FOR FURTHER READING

Howard Kurtz. *Spin Cycle: How the White House and the Media Manipulate the News.* New York: Free Press, 1998.

John Anthony Maltese. *Spin Control: The White House Office of Communications and the Management of Presidential News.* Chapel Hill: University of North Carolina Press, 1994.

Jeremy D. Mayer. "The Presidency and Image Management: Discipline in Pursuit of Illusion." *Presidential Studies Quarterly* 34 (2004).

Alexandra Pelosi. *Sneaking into the Flying Circus: How the Media Turn Our Presidential Campaigns into Freak Shows.* New York: Free Press, 2005.

Jon Western. *Selling Intervention and War: The Presidency, the Media, and the American Public.* Baltimore: Johns Hopkins University Press, 2005.

NOTES

1. Walter Lippmann, *Public Opinion* (New York: Free Press, 1997), 229.

2. Lester Seligman, "Developments in the Presidency and the Conception of Political Leadership," *American Sociological Review* 20 (1955): 707.

3. Michael Baruch Grossman and Martha Joynt Kumar, *Portraying the President* (Baltimore: Johns Hopkins University Press, 1981), 14.

4. Dana Milbank, "My Bias for Mainstream News," *Washington Post*, March 20, 2005.

5. See generally, Jeffrey Tulis, *The Rhetorical Presidency* (Princeton, NJ: Princeton University Press, 1988).

6. Ibid.

7. Samuel Kernell, *Going Public*, 4th ed. (Washington, DC: CQ Press, 2007), 128.

8. Kenneth Walsh, *Feeding the Beast* (New York: Random House, 1996), 12.

9. Thomas Patterson, *Out of Order* (New York: Vintage, 1994), 20–21.

10. James Fallows, *Breaking the News* (New York: Vintage, 1997), 55.

11. Ibid., 76.

12. Ibid.

13. Timothy Crouse, *The Boys on the Bus* (New York: Random House, 2003), 198.

14. Fallows, *Breaking the News*, 132, 178. For more on "feeding frenzies," see Larry Sabato, *Feeding Frenzy* (Baltimore: Lanahan, 2000).

15. Crouse, *The Boys on the Bus*, 6.

16. Fallows, *Breaking the News*, 185.

17. George Edwards, *On Deaf Ears* (New Haven, CT: Yale University Press, 2003), ix.

18. George Edwards, *Governing by Campaigning* (New York: Pearson Longman, 2007), ix.

19. Martha Joynt Kumar, *Managing the President's Message* (Baltimore: Johns Hopkins University Press, 2007), 71.

20. See John Anthony Maltese, *Spin Control*, 2nd ed., rev. (Chapel Hill: University of North Carolina Press, 1994), 227–30.

21. John Anthony Maltese, "The New Media and the Lure of the Clinton Scandal," in *Contemporary Readings in American Government*, ed. Mark J. Rozell and John Kenneth White (Upper Saddle River, NJ: Prentice Hall, 2002), 205.

22. Ibid., 202.

23. Richard Berke, "Outdoing Bush, President Keeps the Press at Bay," *The New York Times*, January 24, 1993.

24. Ibid.

25. Howard Kurtz, "Coverage Quickly Turns Sour as Media Highlight Troubles," *Washington Post*, January 31, 1993.

26. Ibid.

27. Ibid.

28. Johanna Neuman, "At White House, Press Distress," *USA Today*, January 3, 1994.

29. Kurtz, "Coverage Quickly Turns Sour."

30. Richard Benedetto, interview with Jeffrey Crouch, Washington, DC, October 10, 2007.

31. Kumar, *Managing the President's Messsage*, 34.

32. Johanna Neuman, "At White House, Press Distress," *USA Today*, January 3, 1994.

33. Kumar, *Managing the President's Message*, 57–58.

34. Ibid., 64.

35. Maltese, "The New Media and the Lure of the Clinton Scandal," 199.

36. David Noack, "Clinton Sex Story Forces Print Media Changes," *Editor & Publisher*, January 31, 1998, 62.

37. Maltese, "The New Media and the Lure of the Clinton Scandal," 203.

38. See Molly Andolina and Clyde Wilcox, "Public Opinion: The Paradoxes of Clinton's Popularity," in *The Clinton Scandal*, ed. Mark Rozell and Clyde Wilcox (Washington, DC: Georgetown University Press, 2000), 171–94.

39. Mimi Hall, "New White House, New 'War Room' for Strategizing; 'This Is as Political an Administration as We've Ever Had,' Say Presidential Observers," *USA Today*, July 5, 2001.

40. Dick Cheney, interview with John Anthony Maltese, in Maltese, *Spin Control*, 2.

41. Martha Joynt Kumar, "Recruiting and Organizing the White House Staff," *PS: Political Science and Politics* 35 (March 2002): 40.

42. Martha Joynt Kumar, "Communications Operations in the White House of President George W. Bush: Making News on His Terms," *Presidential Studies Quarterly* 33 (June 2003): 373.

43. Ibid., 378.

44. President George W. Bush has employed four press secretaries: Ari Fleischer, Scott McClellan, Tony Snow, and—most recently—Dana Perino, the second woman to serve as a presidential press secretary (the Clinton administration's Dee Dee Myers was the first).

45. Peter Baker, "Media Pull Out of One Combat Zone; White House to Be Free of Embedded Press During Rebuilding," *Washington Post*, August 3, 2006.

46. Jon Ward, "White House Welcomes Back Press," *Washington Times*, July 12, 2007.

47. Helen Thomas, "New Press Room, Same Old Answers," *Virginian-Pilot*, July 30, 2007.

48. Office of the Press Secretary, "Bartlett Named White House Communications Director," October 2, 2001, http://www.whitehouse.gov/news/releases/2001/10/200 11002-9.html (accessed October 20, 2007).

49. Kumar, "Communications Operations in the White House of President George W. Bush," 380.

50. Ibid.

51. Kumar, *Managing the President's Message*, 98.

52. Ibid., 99.

53. Kumar, "Communications Operations in the White House of President George W. Bush," 381.

54. Benedetto interview.

55. Kumar, "Communications Operations in the White House of President George W. Bush," 381.

56. Johanna Neuman, "Response to Terror: Public Diplomacy Is Shaped in President's Ornate War Room," *Los Angeles Times*, December 22, 2001.

57. Kumar, "Communications Operations in the White House of President George W. Bush," 382.

58. Overnight, Bush's Gallup approval rating skyrocketed to 90 percent and stayed over 80 percent into 2002. For up-to-date poll numbers, see http://www.gallup.com.

59. Michael Dimock, "Bush and Public Opinion," in *Considering the Bush Presidency*, ed. Gary Gregg and Mark Rozell (New York: Oxford University Press, 2004), 79.

60. Ibid.

61. Stephen Farnsworth and S. Robert Lichter, "Reporting on Two Presidencies: News Coverage of George W. Bush's First Year in Office," *Congress & the Presidency* 32 (Autumn 2005): 98.

62. Gallup, "Presidential Job Approval in Depth," http://www.gallup.com/poll/1723/Presidential-Job-Approval-Depth.aspx#2 and http://www.gallup.com/poll/1723/Presidential-Job-Approval-Depth.aspx#3 (accessed January 23, 2008).

63. See Eric Boehlert, *Lapdogs* (New York: Free Press, 2006).

64. David Frum, *The Right Man* (New York: Random House, 2003), 224–45.

65. Sue Lockett John et al., "Going Public, Crisis After Crisis: The Bush Administration and the Press from September 11 to Saddam," *Rhetoric & Public Affairs* 10 (2007): 211.

66. Ibid., 212.

67. Steven Kull et al., "Misperceptions, the Media, and the Iraq War," *Political Science Quarterly* 118 (Winter 2003/2004): 583.

68. Lori Robertson, "In Control," *American Journalism Review* 27 (February/March 2005): 29.

69. Howard Kurtz and Dana Milbank, "A Setback for a Network, and the Mainstream Media," *Washington Post*, January 11, 2005.

70. Ryan Lizza, "The White House Doesn't Need the Press," *The New York Times*, December 9, 2001.

71. Peter Baker, "A Modern History of White House Spin," *Washington Post*, August 13, 2007.

72. Kumar, *Managing the President's Message*, 71.

73. Ibid., 9.

74. Mark Halperin and Elizabeth Wilner, "Bush 100 Days Marked by 5 Issues," April 30, 2001, http://www.abcnews.com/US/story?id=93417&page=1.

75. Kumar, *Managing the President's Message*, 82.

76. Ibid., 104–105.

77. Kumar, "Communications Operations in the White House of President George W. Bush," 392.

78. Frank Durham, "Exposed by Katrina: The Gulf between the President and the Press," *Critical Studies in Media Communication* 23 (March 2006): 82.

79. Kumar, *Managing the President's Message*, 295–97.

80. Gary Jacobson, *A Divider, Not a Uniter* (New York: Pearson Longman, 2007), 240–41.

81. Kumar, *Managing the President's Message*, 105.

82. Ibid., 80–81.

83. Ibid., 77.

84. Ryan Lizza, "The White House Doesn't Need the Press," *The New York Times*, December 9, 2001.

85. Ibid.

86. Jeremy Mayer, "The Presidency and Image Management: Discipline in Pursuit of Illusion," *Presidential Studies Quarterly* 34 (September 2004): 624.

87. Robertson, "In Control," 29.

88. Kumar, "Communications Operations in the White House of President George W. Bush," 384.

89. Kumar, *Managing the President's Message*, 47.

90. Maltese, "The New Media and the Lure of the Clinton Scandal," 204.

91. Kumar, *Managing the President's Message*, 48.

92. See William J. Clinton Presidential Library, Archive Search, http://www.clintonlibrary.gov/archivesearch.html (accessed October 6, 2007). For a screenshot of the first White House Web site, see http://clinton1.nara.gov/ (accessed October 6, 2007).

93. Kumar, *Managing the President's Message*, 3.

94. Ibid., 92

95. Kumar, "Communications Operations in the White House of President George W. Bush," 379.

96. Kumar, *Managing the President's Message*, 102.

97. Ibid., 103.

98. Andrew Paul Williams, "The Main Frame: Assessing the Role of the Internet in the 2004 U.S. Presidential Contest," in *The 2004 Presidential Campaign*, ed. Robert Denton Jr. (Lanham, MD: Rowman & Littlefield, 2005), 242.

99. Danielle Wiese and Bruce Gronbeck, "Campaign 2004 Developments in Cyberpolitics," in *The 2004 Presidential Campaign*, ed. Robert Denton Jr. (Lanham, MD: Rowman & Littlefield, 2005), 217.

100. Ibid., 222.

101. Ibid.; Williams, "The Main Frame," 245.

102. Williams, "The Main Frame," 247.

103. Leslie Walker, "Bloggers Gain Attention in 2004 Election," *Washington Post*, November 4, 2004.

104. Ibid.; Wiese and Gronbeck, "Campaign 2004 Developments in Cyberpolitics," 224.

105. Walker, "Bloggers Gain Attention in 2004 Election."

106. Katharine Seelye, "White House Approves Pass for Blogger," *The New York Times*, March 7, 2005.

107. Katharine Seelye, "New Presidential Debate Site? Obviously, YouTube," *The New York Times*, June 13, 2007.

108. Associated Press, "Web Video New '08 Political Battlefield," *The New York Times*, July 5, 2007.

109. Martha Moore, "Oprah Becomes Test of What an Endorsement Means," *USA Today*, October 21, 2007.

110. Katharine Seelye and Leslie Wayne, "The Web Takes Ron Paul for a Ride," *The New York Times*, November 11, 2007.

111. Ibid.

112. Seelye, "New Presidential Debate Site? Obviously, YouTube."

113. Benedetto interview.

114. Kumar, *Managing the President's Message*, 2.

115. Benedetto interview.

2

Congress and the News Media

Mark J. Rozell and Richard J. Semiatin

Political life for most Americans is a mediated experience. People learn about our national institutions and leaders through the news media. As Maxwell McCombs and Donald Shaw report, people "learn how much importance to attach to an issue or topic from the emphasis placed on it by the mass media."[1] Unless that subject is repeatedly covered, the depth of recall by citizens about the nuances of an issue is low. The famed media critic Marshall McLuhan stated, "[A] small pellet or pattern in a noisy, redundant barrage of repetition will gradually assert itself."[2] While McLuhan's adage was given to advertising, the same inferences could be made to news coverage, because what does the public learn from the media about Congress? Usually very little, or at least very little that isn't unfavorable to the institution, such as scandal. The extensive coverage given to Sen. Larry Craig's (R-ID) guilty plea for disorderly conduct in a Minneapolis airport bathroom in 2007 demonstrates the media's infatuation with salacious stories, often to the neglect of more substantive issues.

Numerous studies on media coverage of Congress arrive at the same conclusion: Congress receives very little respect from the national media. The news either ignores much of what goes on in Congress or presents the institution in the most unflattering light possible.

National opinion polls reflect generally negative perceptions of Congress and its members. Congress rarely ranks ahead of presidents in national polls, even when presidents are unpopular. Although individual members of Congress may fare well in polls of their own constituents, members of Congress as a group almost always fare poorly in national opinion. A Gallup poll from October 2007 found that only 23 percent of respondents approved of the job Congress was doing.[3] Years earlier a national poll asked respondents to rank the honesty and ethical standards of people by their professions. U.S. senators ranked 18 percent favorable, just two percentage points better than lawyers and TV talk show hosts and substantially lower than funeral directors and reporters.[4] Congressional institutional ratings over time tend to be consistently low, except for times of national emergency, crisis, or when party control of the institution changes (the "honeymoon" period).

Members of Congress bear some responsibility for the negative image of the institution. Members are very astute at protecting their own political interests by attacking the institution in which they serve. Is it at all surprising that the public often holds Congress in low esteem when the members themselves bad-mouth the institution? Scholars have long noted the phenomenon that people make differential judgments between their own member of Congress, on the one hand, and members of Congress as a group, on the other. Also, candidates for Congress use negative advertising appeals to exaggerate claims of impropriety on the part of their opponents. Imagine the esteem in which we would hold the airline industry if carriers frequently ran ads accusing each other of losing baggage, missing arrival times, and engaging in unsafe practices that endanger the public: "Unreliable. Unsafe. You just can't trust Eagle Airlines." A public exposed to a constant barrage of such campaign appeals cannot easily be blamed for harboring negative views of their elected leaders.

There are other reasons the public generally harbors such a negative view of Congress. One is that people expect conflicting things from the institution and its members. For example, citizens perceive Congress as both too beholden to interest groups and out of touch with the public it serves. People demand expensive government programs, better-quality delivery of public services, and lower taxes. They want Congress to be responsive, to articulate various constituents' views, yet they implore members to put an end to partisan squabbling. Constituents demand an end to pork barrel spending—except when it benefits them.

An ABC News poll found that despite widespread complaints about such congressional perks as travel budgets and franked mail, 93 percent responded that their own member should try to keep constituents informed through district visits or newsletters. And despite complaints about special interests and congressional pork, 73 percent said that their own member should try to direct more federal projects to their district.[5]

Another problem is that the public doesn't know very much about Congress and its activities. In mid-1995, only half of the public could identify Newt Gingrich (R-GA) as the Speaker of the House, even though he had received enormous coverage, yet two-thirds of the public could identify Lance Ito, the judge presiding over the double-murder trial of former football player O. J. Simpson.

Only four in ten were familiar with the Republican Party's "Contract with America" and only one-half knew that Congress had passed the landmark North American Free Trade Agreement (NAFTA).[6] It is not surprising that people harbor inaccurate perceptions of an institution about which they know very little.

Some data suggest that those segments of the public that have the most knowledge of the Congress are often the most hostile to the institution. For years, pollsters had found that an educated segment of the population provided a foundation of support for Congress and representative government, even when most of the public was skeptical. Yet a study by Herb Asher and Mike Barr shows that even though the less informed citizens remain dubious of Congress, as people learn more about the institution they like it even less.[7]

The purpose of this chapter is to examine how the traditional news media (television, radio, newspapers, and periodicals) have covered Congress in the past. Then we show how C-SPAN coverage revolutionized news media coverage of Congress in the 1980s. From there, our research demonstrates that declining ratings and circulation of traditional news have affected how the press covers Congress. We then discuss the emerging and powerful role of new media (primarily on the Internet). New media coverage has transformed the reporting about Congress and its members. The resulting effect of increasing scrutiny has led to a blurring of how members operate on Capitol Hill ("Hill style") and back in the district ("home style").

TRADITIONAL NEWS MEDIA COVERAGE OF CONGRESS

If Congress is held in such low esteem, there is no doubt that much of this condition can be attributed to highly negative press coverage. To be sure, Congress has always been a favorite target for critics and comedians. Stereotypes of legislators who use public office for private gain and subvert the national interest have been a press staple since the earliest Congresses. Indeed, skepticism about the motives and activities of the nation's leaders has long been considered a necessary, and even beneficial, element of representative government. Yet some perspective is in order. In 2001–2002, the revelation that a missing person had previously been having an affair with Rep. Gary Condit (D-CA) resulted in an avalanche of news coverage that made Condit the most recognizable face in Congress. That some law enforcement officials openly criticized Condit for not being helpful to their investigation—leading some to wonder whether the congressman knew more than he was telling—certainly justified strong journalistic interest in the story. But ultimately the intensity of the media coverage of this story pushed out of the news many items of importance taking place in Congress.

What do many of the studies of media coverage of Congress specifically reveal? Primarily that members of Congress are either incompetent or corrupt—or both—and that the legislative process does not work. For example, Charles Tidmarch and John Pitney analyzed all items on Congress in ten news dailies during one month in 1978 and found that journalists focused on "conflict, malfeasance and breach of public trust."[8] "On the whole," they concluded, the press "has little good to report about Congress and its membership." Such coverage has tended to "harden the image of Congress as a defective institution."[9]

A major study of the impact of newspaper coverage on public confidence in institutions, also focusing on the late 1970s, found that coverage of Congress was much more unfavorable than that of either the presidency or the Supreme Court.[10] Michael Robinson and Kevin Appel's analysis of network news coverage of Congress during a five-week period in 1976 found that all news stories that presented a point of view about the institution were critical of it.[11] Even the first post-Watergate Congress failed to receive a single favorable assessment.[12]

Robert Gilbert concluded that congressional coverage during the spring of 1989 emphasized scandal and further contributed to the legislature's weak reputation,[13] and Norman Ornstein's study of network news reporting on Congress in 1989 concluded that two-thirds of the coverage "concerned . . . three episodes of turmoil and scandal that had little to do with the constitutionally mandated duties of Congress."[14] Studies conducted in the 1990s also confirmed that press reporting of Congress was generally negative.[15]

Press coverage of Congress over the years has moved from healthy skepticism to outright cynicism. When Congress enacted a 25 percent pay increase for its members in 1946, for example, both *The New York Times* and the *Washington Post* commented that the pay increase was needed to attract top-quality people to public service and that political leaders must be paid a salary commensurate with the responsibilities of public service. The few criticisms of the raise emphasized either the principle of public service as its own reward or the need for an even larger pay increase. The press did not lead a drumbeat of criticism of Congress for enacting a pay increase. More recently, however, the story has been far different. To believe modern congressional coverage, the nation's legislators are egregiously overpaid, indulged, and indifferent to the problems of constituents who lack six-figure incomes and fantastic job perquisites. The press portrait of Congress members is one of self-interested, self-indulgent politicians who exploit the legislative process for personal gain.[16]

Many studies have speculated about the reasons for the intense interest in scandal, rivalry, and conflict. A partial explanation is the emergence of a more aggressive, scandal-conscious news media after Watergate. Thomas Dye and Harmon Zeigler point to "a post-Watergate code of ethics" in which journalists seek out scandal and delve into the personal lives of public figures and other areas once considered off limits to reporters.[17] Ornstein also notes that a new generation of investigative reporters, inspired by Watergate sleuths Bob Woodward and Carl Bernstein, "accentuated and refocused the media coverage of Congress" toward "scandal and sloth."[18]

Journalists themselves confirm this tendency. A *Times-Mirror* survey found that two-thirds of journalists downplay good news and spend "too much time on the failures of public officials." Many journalists fear being perceived by their colleagues as "in the tank" with politicians, writes *U.S. News*'s Gloria Borger. Consequently, "for the press, good news is not news."[19] According to Ellen Hume, formerly of the *Wall Street Journal*, "[j]ournalists usually err on the side of negativity."[20]

Furthermore, journalists know that conflict and scandal interest the public. Competition within the print media—which more recently has seen declining revenues—has driven many journalists toward increased scandal coverage to satisfy what they perceive as the public's appetite for such a focus. Regrettably, the elite press exhibits some of the same tawdry characteristics of the tabloids. As Thomas Mann and Norman Ornstein lament, "the prestige news outlets have adopted the sensationalist approach of their less reputable counterparts. Coverage of the House bank scandal, for example, was as overdone in the *Washington Post* as it was on radio talk shows."[21]

At one point in the 1990s, some members of Congress decided to strike back. Disgusted at constant media digging into their financial affairs, the Senate passed a nonbinding resolution requiring reporters covering Capitol Hill to file financial disclosures. Senators accused the correspondents of hypocrisy because many who reported on conflicts of interest in Congress had themselves accepted honoraria for speeches before lobbying and corporate groups.[22] The senators knew this resolution had no potential for impact, other than to send a message to the press of a growing discontent with journalistic hypocrisy. They were not alone in this feeling, as many journalists themselves began to wonder whether the practice of reporters accepting honoraria was hurting the profession's credibility with the public.[23]

Scandal, rivalry, and conflict may also be emphasized because the legislative process is tedious—"the very driest form of human endeavor," as former Senator Alan Simpson (R-WY) once said.[24] Consequently, reporters avoid writing process and policy stories except when they are related to interbranch conflicts, rivalries among colorful personalities on Capitol Hill, or scandals. William Safire explained that editors instruct reporters to avoid "MEGOs": stories that make "my eyes glaze over."[25] Stephen Hess examined one hundred Congress stories in *The New York Times* in 1991; only five were process-oriented stories.[26]

David Broder admits that personal scandals are exciting and interesting, whereas stories about institutional reform put reporters to sleep.[27] A reporter will have an easier time selling his editor a story of petty scandal than a good many "stories of larger consequence." Junket stories sell to editors "because they fit [editors'] stereotypes of graft and sin on Capitol Hill."[28]

Both Broder and William Raspberry have written that the public holds Congress in such low esteem, in part, because of the journalistic trend of emphasizing conflict and controversy over substance. They cited the example of a vitally important job-training bill in late 1995 that garnered little news coverage. The legislation attracted so little attention because it lacked serious opposition and there was therefore no conflict to report.[29]

The press thus has difficulty conveying the complexities of the legislative process. The magnitude of coverage devoted to such important events as legislative reorganization efforts and ethics reform almost never matches the number of stories devoted to a scandal involving a single member of Congress. To the extent that the press does cover procedural issues, it seems to do so only when they are related to scandals and can be explained in terms of—and as reactions to—interbranch, partisan, or personal rivalries.

According to S. Robert Lichter and Daniel Amundson, this tendency—well documented in studies of the print media—is evident in television coverage of Congress as well. They examined comprehensively the three major networks' coverage of Congress during a period from the 1970s to the 1990s and found that the coverage increasingly has focused on scandal, with decreasing emphasis on process and policy. "The news," they write, "has also increasingly emphasized conflict, both within Congress and between the institution and other participants in political affairs. . . . [T]he tone of coverage was already derogatory a generation ago and has become worse."[30]

The negative tone and narrow focus of coverage are particularly important because, as Herb Asher comments, "everything that people learn about Congress is mediated."[31] And there seems to be a link between the nature of congressional coverage and poor public understanding of the legislative process. Charles O. Jones looked at media coverage of a busy week on Capitol Hill and found that even though the legislature had undertaken some important activities, "the American people learned hardly a smidgen about congressional action that directly affected them."[32] "Turning specifically to the committees, one does not have to wonder why the public knows so little of this ceaseless activity on Capitol Hill. The answer is that very little attention is paid to it in the press."[33]

Dye and Zeigler describe coverage of Congress as "almost without exception demeaning. As a result, people regard the *institution* of Congress with cynicism and mistrust." Furthermore, "the public knows very little about Congress in its abstract, institutional form."[34] Mary Russell also found a lack of public knowledge of Congress due to sensational news and the failure of the press to cover procedures, rules, and long-range activity.[35]

In addition to being less exciting than petty scandal, institutional stories are more complicated for reporters and editors to understand and to write about in single news stories and columns. Besides, the presidency is the focus of Washington journalism. Journalists often cover lawmaking from the vantage of how the legislature is responding to presidential initiatives. The press perceives Congress as generally incapable of leadership. Thus under normal circumstances, Congress works best under the guiding hand of a strong president attuned to the national interest and willing to move the government in an activist, progressive direction. Members of Congress, according to much of the media coverage, are primarily concerned with parochial issues.

One explanation is the difficulty of identifying a focal point in Congress. The presidency, in contrast, is easily personalized: The focus is the president himself. Congress lacks a single voice. It presents a cacophony of perspectives, often in conflict. As Richard Davis writes: "Its bicameral structure and the partisan divisions in both houses ensure that at least four leaders will compete for the role of congressional spokesperson, and the profusion of congressional committees and subcommittees . . . adds to the confusion."[36] Robert Denton and Gary Woodward add that whereas the presidency can, if presented effectively, appear unified, "the Congress, by contrast, is more a place of arguments, political negotiation, and compromise."[37]

Congressional coverage also suffers because of intense media interest in the horse race of presidential campaigns. In June 1995, nearly eight months before the first presidential primary of 1996, Howard Kurtz found that the media's interest in the campaign was high, whereas their interest in the governing process remained low, despite the fact that there was little of real substance at that time to report about the emerging campaigns. Borger candidly admitted, "We don't have anything very interesting to write about these days. The other choice is covering the budget, and nobody wants to write about that."[38]

The press's image of what Congress should be is clearly incompatible with the traditional role of the legislative branch. There is a strong press preference for a reform-oriented, progressive, policy-activist Congress that works effectively with an activist, strong president. During a congressional studies conference at the American Enterprise Institute, a number of journalists confirmed this finding. One argued that Congress deserves praise "when Congress acts," especially when the institution displays "heroism" and policy innovation. Several colleagues agreed.[39]

Yet the Constitution's framers designed Congress to frustrate the popular will as necessary, to *not* act in an efficient, innovative fashion. Consequently, the drumbeat of press criticism, interrupted occasionally by favorable coverage during unusual circumstances, helps explain the disjunction between the legislature's intended constitutional role and journalistic expectations. No wonder Congress is held in such low public esteem: The press criticizes the institution for behaving as the Constitution's framers intended it to and then focuses on petty scandal and members' peccadilloes to the exclusion of examining process and policy.

Nonetheless, not all the blame for Congress's poor reputation belongs to the media. Congress needs to educate the press and the public about its activities—what it does and why it does what it does. Otherwise, journalists and the public will continue to harbor expectations—routine efficiency, activist policymaking, large-scale internal reform, strong leadership during crises and when the president is under siege—that the institution generally is not designed to live up to.

Congress indeed does a poor job of protecting its own image. In Richard Fenno's classic argument, members "run *for* Congress by running *against* Congress."[40] In their districts they reinforce unfavorable opinions of the institution so that they can distance themselves from it and, by implication, assume the virtues that it supposedly lacks. Even electorally safe incumbents do not educate constituents about the strengths of their institution; instead, they attack it as a way of protecting themselves politically.[41] Robinson and Appel note that members of the legislature "complain about Congress and praise themselves as individuals."[42] And James McCartney of Knight-Ridder comments, "Congress does a lousy job in telling a reporter what goes on. The problem with Congress is that it has no organization and is just babble. It needs to present its information better, like the White House."[43]

Individual members can also orient their own behavior in a way that better protects the institutional reputation. Electorally safe members have the leeway to educate constituents properly about Congress and take some responsibility for its actions.[44] Members could also do a better job of lowering constituents' expectations of legislative performance and avoid perpetuating conflicts that generate short-term publicity and political gain at the expense of Congress's image.

Finally, responsibility for presenting a balanced and realistic representation of Congress lies with the journalists. In 1975 the former senator J. William Fulbright (D-AR) wrote that "the national press would do well to reconsider its priorities. It has excelled in exposing . . . the high crimes and peccadilloes of persons in high places. But it has fallen short—far short—in its higher responsibility of public education."[45]

It is difficult to imagine that congressional coverage will ever deemphasize controversy, scandal, and intrigue, and focus on process and policy. But reporters and editors can voluntarily do a better job of educating the public about Congress and representative government. Whether they are motivated by concern over the impact of fueling public cynicism toward the institution or by professional pride in factual and fair-minded reporting, journalists could truly serve the public by covering the legislative branch in a manner that befits the most representative institution of our government.

THE C-SPAN EFFECT

The Cable-Satellite Public Affairs Network (C-SPAN) has an important, though not clearly recognized or understood, influence on Congress. Created in 1977, the network is funded by the cable industry as a public service and provides direct and unedited coverage of congressional proceedings, as well as interview programs with journalists and scholars who follow Congress, live viewer call-in programs, and interviews with book authors. C-SPAN began coverage of House proceedings in 1979 and Senate proceedings in 1986.

The audience for C-SPAN is not large, and the Nielsen rating system does not measure its audience size. Nonetheless, the people who watch C-SPAN tend to be highly politically interested and very inclined toward participation in representative government. An academic study shows that the typical C-SPAN viewer is well educated, has a good income, and is knowledgeable about government.[46] Perhaps more significant is the fact that some of the most active C-SPAN viewers are members of Congress and their staff, executive branch officials, and political party leaders and activists. An event covered by C-SPAN may not have a large national audience, but it is seen by a substantial number of members of the so-called political class in Washington. C-SPAN has thus become a means by which political actors in Washington keep a watchful eye on government. Examples may include White House staff observing how one of their colleagues is performing as a witness at a congressional hearing, without having to leave the office to do so or having to rely on secondhand accounts; lobbyists interested in a bill watching a House or Senate debate unfold; or merely interested citizens who may become inspired by what they see happening in Congress to make contact with their representatives.

Putting Congress on television full-time was a controversial proposition at first. Created as a deliberative body, Congress sometimes benefits from the opportunity to debate outside the public limelight. It was easier to make the case for direct television coverage of the House than the Senate. The House's intended constitutional role is to be "closer to the people" than the Senate and thus more attuned to the constant shifts of public opinion. The constitutional framers created the House—with its short terms and direct election from relatively small constituencies—as an entity for reflecting the opinions of the people. By contrast, the constitutional framers created the Senate—with long terms and, initially, indirect election—as a check against the potential excesses of the House. Thus the Senate was to be more insulated than the House from public opinion, and, it was thought, more capable reasoned deliberation. It is no surprise, then, that the Senate resisted for some time being put on display by C-SPAN. Ultimately, however, senators saw the benefits from such television exposure to their own public profiles.

Some members of Congress worried that televised coverage would harm the quality of debate in the legislative branch. In particular, some representatives expressed concern that certain colleagues would grandstand before the cameras rather than engage in genuine deliberation. Others feared that the presence of television would unnecessarily lengthen debates in Congress because many members would be eager for the opportunity for coverage. Yet the evidence suggests that there is probably no more grandstanding than before C-SPAN and that debates in Congress have not become longer. The exception is that more members than ever use the period for special orders to deliver speeches.[47] Indeed, some have credited the rise of such figures as former Speaker of the House Newt Gingrich to the strategic use of special orders speeches to raise their public profiles.

The major benefit attributed to C-SPAN is that it has provided a different means by which citizens can keep in touch with their government. It provides the opportunity for citizens to view Congress in action, uninterrupted, rather than having to rely on the scattershot coverage of the legislative process offered by the leading news media.

CONGRESS AND THE DECLINE OF
TRADITIONAL MEDIA COVERAGE

Press coverage of Congress is undergoing a major change that reflects news coverage as a whole—decentralized and entrepreneurial. The traditional hierarchy that drove political and congressional coverage until the emergence of new media (Internet Web sites and blogs, for example) has diminished. Print stories that appeared in the morning's *Washington Post*, *The New York Times*, and *Wall Street Journal* or the wire services drove evening news coverage on television. The major networks had correspondents in both chambers of Congress reporting stories as they appeared. Today, the networks have one correspondent who covers Capitol Hill, and when Congress is out of session that reporter is often assigned to other tasks. News divisions are now supposed to be revenue makers for the networks, as opposed to fifty years ago, when news was not expected to generate profit. That means cutbacks in coverage of traditional political news and more coverage of consumer, health, and personal news. Such consolidation of news coverage leads to more superficial reporting. In television, this means coverage of major issues on Capitol Hill tends to focus on the outcomes of debates and votes in Congress and not on the process.

Media became more decentralized during the 1980s, with the emergence of twenty-four-hour cable news networks such as CNN, and later MSNBC and Fox News. Competition led to a major decline in news ratings overall. Cable news added another dimension to broadcast television, radio, and newspapers. The demand to fill twenty-four hours per day with news coverage drove the press to cover more sensational stories to generate viewers.

More recently, the explosion of new technology and changes in legal regulations have led to a further decline in newspaper circulation and television news ratings. The *Washington Post* reported in 2005 that newspaper circulation continued a twenty-year decline, including a 1.9 percent decline from September 2004 to March 2005. Interestingly, from the newspaper perspective this had more to do with the change in telemarketing laws—the Do Not Call List—than with competition.[48] Furthermore, the Project for Excellence in Journalism shows a 50 percent decline in network news ratings from 1980 to 2006. Moreover, the median age of persons watching those networks is over sixty years of age.[49] If viewers under the age of sixty are moving away from network news, they are likely using the Internet as a news and entertainment source.

Today, traditional media such as television are often out of step with what the public considers important news in Congress. The Pew Research Center reports that only 2 percent of news coverage in late September 2007 was devoted to President George W. Bush's veto of the State Children's Health Insurance Program (SCHIP), which both houses of Congress had passed overwhelmingly. Meanwhile, 12 percent of the public was paying close attention to the issue.[50] By placing an increasing proportion of its news on consumer and personality-driven reportage, television news may be underestimating how hard news resonates with voters.

CONGRESS AND NEW MEDIA COVERAGE

The growth of new media has transformed American culture, politics, and institutions. The Internet has increased the instantaneous nature of reporting, or what has become known as "breaking news." As Jeremy Mayer demonstrates, the proliferation of Web sites that report "news" without the traditional filter of sourcing information has contributed to a reporting environment where the difference between rumor and fact is often blurred.[51] And technology has only increased the responsiveness by Congress. Compared to the president, Congress has always been slower to respond because of its collective decision-making apparatus. Often the response is piecemeal or, even worse, individualistic. While the norm of policy entrepreneurship was touted as a virtue by David Price a generation ago, the political entrepreneurship of getting re-elected is more preeminent than ever as members seek to inoculate themselves against political attack in a hyper-responsive news environment.[52]

The hyper-responsive news environment, where reporting is decentralized, decreases civility and creates a disincentive for members to adhere to institutional norms. Partisan blogs, from the liberal Huffington Post to the conservative RedState, drive an agenda designed to influence policy rather than to report fact. The viral explosion of rumor over the Internet only exacerbates partisan tensions and contributes to conflict rather than cooperation.

The decline of civility in Congress is well documented in the literature and is not a new phenomenon. Civility among members declined as partisanship grew, in part, from the prevalence of divided party government for the past forty years. Norms of reciprocity and collegiality frayed as Democrats controlled both houses of Congress, nearly uninterrupted, until 1994. In 1994 the Republican revolution, led by Gingrich, toppled the Democratic majority and supplanted it with an aggressive new GOP majority. While Democrats recently wrested control of Congress back in the 2006 elections, they have acted as partisan as the Republicans before them did.

This lack of civility is reinforced by new media that strive to advocate rather than report. Editorials often supplant news as sources of information. In a sense, the new media are a reflection back to the times when partisan newspapers served as instruments for the nascent political parties communicating their messages to voters. In the election of 1800 between Democratic-Republican Thomas Jefferson and Federalist president John Adams, such partisanship was on display. The Federalist newspaper the *New England Palladium* stated, "Should the infidel Jefferson be elected to the Presidency, the seal of death is that moment set on our holy religion, our churches will be prostrated, and some infamous prostitute, under the title of goddess of reason, will preside in the sanctuaries now devoted to the worship of the most High."[53]

Similar invective appears today on well-established partisan Web sites that editorialize on Congress. Miles Mogulescu, a columnist for the Huffington Post, posted the following in a 2006 piece regarding privacy concerns and the Patriot Act: "The Republican Congress, with the votes of all too many Democrats, has emasculated the Constitution and given the President dictatorial powers which have been denied even to English Kings since the 12th Century."[54] The parallels are not only striking, but they underscore that the role of new media is much like the oldest media that covered politics and institutions in the United States—full of partisan rancor and unsubstantiated rumors.

Expanding the venues for news and news interaction by visitors has become commonplace. Blogging, videos, and discussion groups have become the means by which Web sites attract more visitors, thus obtaining more advertising revenue. This is news generated by non-newspeople. The *Washington Post*, one of the trendsetting news media organizations, features many of these citizen interactive forums for major news stories. For example, Congress honored the Dalai Lama by giving him the honorary Congressional Gold Medal, Congress's top honor, on October 17, 2007. The *Washington Post* did not run a story on its homepage, but rather presented a video slideshow and attached blog. Essentially, a newspaper was reporting news by slideshow and comment, with no traditional news reporting.[55]

INSTITUTIONAL EFFECTS

How do such changes affect Congress as an institution? Coverage of Congress is not 24/7 anymore; it is now 1440/7—that is, minute-by-minute coverage, every day. Today, members of Congress cannot escape the lens of reporting. Every statement a member makes can be parsed, captured by a blogger, and appear on the Web instantly. Thus, the *politicization* of Congress is magnified instantaneously, while the time for policy reflection is diminished. Members must not only take a position, but they must be able to respond more quickly than ever. Members' explanations of votes can now appear instantly on their Web sites, www.house.gov and www.senate.gov. Once an explanation is provided, members move on to the next issue. Thus, the nuances of understanding policies have become increasingly replaced by the branding of responses to controversial votes. The Web site is the ultimate in Mayhewian advertising for members of Congress. While the phenomenon is not new, the speed and minimalist approach to explaining issues has been exacerbated by the 1440/7 news cycle.

Fragmentation of the media has decreased incentives for collegiality and disintegrated the structure of norms that characterized an era of good feelings in Congress from the 1940s through the 1960s. Fragmentation has increased the value of personality and decreased the value of institutional responsibility, particularly in the House, where collegiality, which began to wane in the 1970s, has crumbled today. In the House, where majoritarian rule prevails, there is little incentive for the majority party to cooperate. Furthermore, members are less apt to engage in risk-taking policy initiatives when they are continually watched by bloggers, Internet reporters, and trackers (individuals who follow candidates around with digital video cameras and "track" every public statement a member makes while campaigning back in the district or state).

Agenda setting and *position taking* have now become even more responsive given the pressures felt by members of Congress from the Internet. As a deliberative institution with 535 members, Congress has always lagged behind the president because of its size. But Congress's 2005 resolution to overturn the state of Florida's decision to take comatose patient Terri Schiavo off a respirator was an extraordinary example of responsiveness. Mentions of Schiavo's name on blogs rose from ten a day in December 2004 to more than four thousand per day by March 22, 2005.[56] While the attempt was ultimately blocked by the courts, the swiftness of the debate coming to the forefront of Congress was unusual—and that pressure came through new media grassroots, primarily the Internet. Many of these blogs not only serve as a persuasive source but are also used as an information/news source by readers.

BlogPulse, which is a service of Nielsen BuzzMetrics, shows that there are more than 61 million blogs, with 745,000 blog posts appearing per day.[57] Many of those blog posts purport to be carrying or reporting real news. However, there is no ombudsman or news organization capable to monitor the veracity of "facts" that are reported as news on the Internet. Thus, in a highly emotional and hyper-responsive news environment, a gut issue such as terminating Terri Schiavo's life demonstrates that agenda setting and position taking are responsive to hourly (traditional media) and now minute-by-minute (Internet) pressures. This has led to an increasingly frenetic pace on Capitol Hill, with members under greater pressure than ever. The problem is that such pressures exacerbate tensions between members (especially those from different parties), reduce collegiality, fray nerves, and reduce the time for reflection. If that occurs, then what are the implications for serious policymaking?

NEW MEDIA BLURS HOME AND HILL STYLE OF MEMBERS

Sen. Birch Bayh (D-IN) was a leading liberal member of the Judiciary Committee who, thirty-five years ago, led the opposition to Nixon Supreme Court nominees Clement Haynesworth and Harold Carswell. Yet at home, Bayh often dressed in fatigues, taking his shotgun and going hunting on weekends. Bayh could market himself differently at home and in Congress and still win reelection—twice—in a Republican state. That would be much harder today given that members' words, actions, and appearances appear almost instantaneously on the Internet. This model of campaigning, which served members well—particularly those from districts or states where such individuals were marginally elected—is virtually impossible today given the intensity of media exposure. In the past, as Fenno reported, members worried about hometown news coverage and occasional national or regional coverage in rare instances.[58] Today, activists who support and oppose members are often self-anointed "reporters" who can "gin up" the political base in favor of or in opposition to a member, depending on the story.

Members thus seek to inoculate themselves from attack by opponents by being more cautious in rhetoric and action. Sen. George Allen's (R-VA) use of the word *macaca* (a South Asian racial slur) to describe the ethnicity of a tracker from Democratic opponent Jim Webb's campaign contributed to his defeat. The video was uploaded to YouTube, then it was picked up by the national press as an important news story. Years ago, there would have been no tracker, and the event—which took place in a small state park in southwestern Virginia—would have gone unnoticed. Whether the member is in Washington, D.C., at home, or even traveling, he or she is in an environment in which almost any activity can be observed and reported.[59]

The blurring of home and Hill styles shows how communications have become an increasingly important feature of a Congress member's life. Whether it is the role of the press secretary on Capitol Hill or Web site manager in the Washington office or for the campaign, members are increasingly aware how they choose their words even when speaking to small audiences, fearing the repercussions of a misstep being reported. That news may emanate from traditional press coverage (television, radio, or newspaper) or it may be reported from new media sources (Web sites, blogs, video, and mass e-mails). Paul S. Herrnson articulated a dozen years ago how eager members were to attract free (or earned media) from the press.[60] Today, members might regret what they are trying to "earn" because they are dealing with an unknown quantity outside of the traditional media.

More importantly, the lines between campaigning and governing are blurred as well. Price explains that those consequences demonstrate the dysfunctionality of the policymaking process, since campaigning never truly ends anymore.[61] The focus of media on personality-driven coverage diminishes the attention on the substance of issues. As traditional media compete with new media for viewers, press attention gloms onto the scandalous, sensationalist, and meretricious behaviors of members rather than on policy. Advocacy and position taking become more important than policymaking.

CONGRESS AND THE FUTURE OF PRESS COVERAGE

Technological developments in the future will enable citizens to access information more conveniently than in the past. iPhones represent the first iteration of handheld integrated multimedia devices that play videos, access the Web, and work as computers. Future technology will help increase the demand for immediate information. On the positive side, citizens can remain in touch with news at the push of a button. This means the volume of information available will continue to expand, and, as Samuel Kernell implies, the volume of information can help citizens sort through choices.[62] However, the volume of information can also lead to distortion as a result of information overload, and the distinction between fact and rumor may become more obscured.

Members will likely engage in communication strategies that either directly or indirectly (through earned media) focuses attention on constituents as customers. Messages tailored home to constituents are more likely to focus on citizen interaction with the member as a way to pry the citizen from traditional or new media. By remaining in constant communication with citizens, technology has the ability to enable a member to capture a constituent's attention about local or national issues in a much more intimate way. Nevertheless, the Internet remains an environment where the user seeks out information, and requires the user to be proactive compared to television, which is a more passive information source. Certainly, the Internet today, much like cable television in the past, is a niche information source. Visitors online are often the politically interested (or faithful), who have a heightened awareness about politics and policy. As we have implied, citizens will continue to become both producers and consumers of news. The task for members, both through traditional communications techniques and new communications techniques, is to cut through the cacophony of information to reach constituents. E-mail can provide such an opportunity. Citizens can sign up for e-mail from members, providing an unfiltered source for members to communicate with their constituents. One can find this on the homepages of many members. However, e-mail is just one small piece of a member's entire communications effort. For example, Rep. Lois Capps (D-CA) not only allows citizens to sign up for e-mail updates, but keeps her own blog featuring daily subject matter that is sometimes local ("A Victory for Protecting Our Coasts") and sometimes national ("Another Sad Milestone for the President's Failed Policy in Iraq").[63] However, few members are keeping blogs, and a random review of thirty House member Web sites found that none carried links citizens could use to post comments about the member's blog. That is a rational act by members, since opposing groups could bombard the Web site with negative messages.

Finally, messages are increasingly focused and concise because the attention span of citizens is diminishing. The task for members is to drive more citizens to the congressional Web sites, where Congress members can control their message.

Whereas increasing congressional partisanship was a separate phenomenon from the advent of new media, nevertheless, the presence of new media will make that divide harder to overcome in the future. The ability of Democrats and Republicans to build coalitions and trust will remain difficult, as long as third-party forces such as bloggers, which are becoming more prominent, have their own agenda. The good news for members of Congress is that there is no evidence—now, or even for the near future—that the advent of new media will correlate with diminishing reelection rates. Yet members are always concerned about reelection (particularly for House members serving two-year terms of office). Given that members are sometimes oversensitive to their own political welfare, that decision to encourage citizens to go to congressional Web sites may in fact be a smart one. But at least in the short term, if members remain cautious and watch their political step, the explosion of new media will have less effect in the House where individuals have less overall name recognition. For senators, however, the explosion and competition for information can put their careers front and center in the news. The effects are thus particular to each body, and not to the institution as a whole, when examining the impact on individual members. However, reportage of Congress as a whole certainly does weaken the institution and affects its ability to make coherent and lasting policies.

DISCUSSION QUESTIONS

1. How have the new media changed the nature of congressional coverage?
2. What are the most important implications of the relentlessly negative congressional media coverage?
3. What are the leading causes of the critical news coverage and commentary about Congress?
4. Why does Congress have such difficulty competing with the president for media and public attention?
5. What, if anything, can Congress do to combat its prevailing negative image?

SUGGESTIONS FOR FURTHER READING

R. Douglas Arnold. *Congress, the Press, and Political Accountability*. Princeton, NJ: Princeton University Press, 2006.
Stephen Hess. *Live! From Capitol Hill*. Washington, DC: Brookings, 1991.

Thomas Mann and Norman Ornstein, eds. *Congress, the Press, and the Public*. Washington, DC: Brookings/American Enterprise Institute, 1994.

Jan Pons Vermeer, ed. *Campaigns in the News: Mass Media and Congressional Elections*. Westport, CT: Greenwood, 1987.

C. Danielle Vinson. *Local Media Coverage of Congress and Its Members*. Cresskill, NH: Hampton, 2002.

NOTES

1. Maxwell E. McCombs and Donald L. Shaw, "The Agenda-Setting Function of the Press," in *Media Power in Politics*, ed. Doris A. Graber (Washington, DC: Congressional Quarterly, 1984), 65.

2. Marshall McLuhan, *Understanding Media: The Extensions of Man* (Cambridge, MA: MIT Press, 1964), chap. 23.

3. Gallup Poll, October 4–7, 2007, as reported on http://www.pollingreport.com (accessed October 12, 2007).

4. Survey conducted by the Gallup Organization, July 19–21, 1993. Cited in Karlyn Bowman and Everett Ladd, "Public Opinion toward Congress: A Historical Look," in *Congress, the Press, and the Public*, ed. Thomas Mann and Norman Ornstein (Washington, DC: Brookings/American Enterprise Institute, 1994), 50.

5. Richard Morin, "You Think Congress Is Out of Touch?" *Washington Post*, October 16, 1994, C1, 4.

6. Howard Kurtz, "Tuning Out Traditional News," *Washington Post*, May 15, 1995, A1, 6.

7. Herb Asher and Mike Barr, "Popular Support for Congress and Its Members," in *Congress, the Press, and the Public*, ed. Thomas Mann and Norman Ornstein (Washington: Brookings/American Enterprise Institute, 1994), 19.

8. Charles M. Tidmarch and John J. Pitney Jr., "Covering Congress," *Polity* 17 (Spring 1985): 482.

9. Ibid., 481.

10. Arthur Miller, Edie Goldenberg, and Lutz Erbring, "Type-Set Politics: Impact of Newspapers of Public Confidence," *American Political Science Review* 73 (March 1979): 70.

11. Michael J. Robinson and Kevin R. Appel, "Network News Coverage of Congress," *Political Science Quarterly* 94 (Fall 1979): 412.

12. Ibid., 417.

13. Robert E. Gilbert, "President versus Congress: The Struggle for Public Attention," *Congress & the Presidency* 16 (Autumn 1989): 99.

14. Norman Ornstein, "What TV News Doesn't Report About Congress—and Should," *TV Guide*, October 21, 1989, 11.

15. See Mark J. Rozell, *In Contempt of Congress: Postwar Press Coverage on Capitol Hill* (Westport, CT: Praeger, 1996).

16. See ibid., chap. 2 and 5.

17. Thomas R. Dye and Harmon Zeigler, *American Politics in the Media Age*, 2nd ed. (Monterey, CA: Brooks/Cole, 1986), 212.

18. Norman J. Ornstein, "The Open Congress Meets the President," in *Both Ends of the Avenue: The Presidency, the Executive Branch, and Congress in the 1980s*, ed. Anthony King (Washington, DC: American Enterprise Institute, 1983) 201.

19. Gloria Borger, "Cynicism and Tanknophobia," *U.S. News & World Report*, June 5, 1995, 34.

20. Quoted in Stephen Hess, "The Decline and Fall of Congressional News," in *Congress, the Press, and the Public*, ed. Thomas Mann and Norman Ornstein (Washington, DC: Brookings/American Enterprise Institute, 1994), 149.

21. Thomas Mann and Norman Ornstein, "Introduction," in *Congress, the Press, and the Public*, ed. Thomas Mann and Norman Ornstein (Washington, DC: Brookings/American Enterprise Institute, 1994), 8.

22. Howard Kurtz, "Senate Eyes Reporters' Honoraria," *Washington Post*, July 21, 1995, C1, 4.

23. On this point see James Fallows, *Breaking the News: How the Media Undermine American Democracy* (New York: Vintage Press, 1996).

24. Quoted in Gregg Schneiders, "The 90-Second Handicap: Why TV Coverage of Legislation Falls Short," *Washington Journalism Review* (June 1985): 44.

25. William Safire, "The MEGO News Era," *Washington Star*, September 6, 1973, A15.

26. Hess, "The Decline and Fall of Congressional News," 150.

27. David Broder, *Behind the Front Page: A Candid Look at How the News Is Made* (New York: Simon & Schuster, 1987), 216.

28. Ibid., 227.

29. William Raspberry, "Blow-By-Blow Coverage," *Washington Post*, October 30, 1995, A17.

30. S. Robert Lichter and Daniel R. Amundson, "Less News Is Worse News: Television News Coverage of Congress, 1972–1992," in *Congress, the Press, and the Public*, ed. Thomas Mann and Norman Ornstein (Washington, DC: Brookings/American Enterprise Institute, 1994), 139.

31. Herb Asher, panel discussion comment.

32. Charles O. Jones, *The United States Congress: People, Place, and Policy* (Homewood, IL: Dorsey Press, 1982), 48.

33. Ibid., 46.

34. Dye and Zeigler, *American Politics in the Media Age*, 211–12.

35. Mary Russell, "The Press and the Committee System," in *Media Power in Politics*, ed. Doris A. Graber (Washington, DC: Congressional Quarterly, 1984), 228.

36. Richard Davis, *The Press and American Politics: The New Mediator* (New York; Longman, 1992), 161.

37. Robert E. Denton Jr. and Gary C. Woodward, *Political Communication in America*, 2nd ed. (New York: Praeger, 1990), 284.

38. Howard Kurtz, "Hot Tips on the Horse-Race to Nowhere," *Washington Post*, June 25, 1995, C1, 2.

39. "Congress, the Press and the Public," conference co-sponsored by the Brookings Institution and the American Enterprise Institute, Washington, DC, May 1993.

40. Richard F. Fenno Jr., *Home Style: House Members in Their Districts* (Boston: Little, Brown, 1978), 168.

41. Ibid., 246–47.

42. Robinson and Appel, "Network News Coverage of Congress," 416.

43. Quoted in Richard Davis, *The Press and American Politics: The New Mediator* (New York: Longman, 1992), 170.

44. Fenno, *Home Style*, 246.

45. Quoted in Broder, *Behind the Front Page*, 213.

46. Stephen Frantzich and John Sullivan, *The C-SPAN Revolution* (Norman: University of Oklahoma Press, 1996), 232.

47. Ibid., 262–64.

48. Annys Shin, "Newspaper Circulation Continues to Decline," *Washington Post*, May 3, 2005, E3. According to the article, 50–55 percent of the decline was due to the registry. Newspapers have traditionally relied more on telemarketing to generate new subscribers than any other medium.

49. "The State of the News Media, 2007," Project for Excellence in Journalism, http://stateofthenewsmedia.com/2007/ (accessed October 12, 2007).

50. "The Top Story Index," Pew Research Center for the People and the Press, September 30–October 5, 2007, http://www.pewresearch.org (accessed October 14, 2007).

51. Jeremy Mayer, *American Media Politics in Transition* (New York: McGraw-Hill, 2007).

52. David E. Price, *The Congressional Experience* (Boulder, CO: Westview, 2004), chap. 6.

53. See Charles O. Lerche Jr., "Jefferson and the Election of 1800: A Case Study in the Political Smear," *William and Mary Quarterly* 5, no. 4 (October 1948): 467–91.

54. Miles Mogulescu, "Bush and Republican Congress Erase 800 Years of Human Rights," Huffington Post, September 30, 2006, http://www.huffingtonpost.com (accessed October 14, 2007).

55. "Dalai Lama Receives Congressional Gold Medal," *Washington Post*, October 18, 2007, http://www.washingtonpost.com (accessed October 18, 2007).

56. Such information is kept by Technorati, which tracks the numbers of blogs, activities, and common subject matter on a daily basis. Technorati monitors approximately 109 million blogs per day. See http://www.technorati.com.

57. See the homepage of http://www.blogpulse.com. Nielsen BuzzMetrics is a division of the Nielsen ratings company.

58. Richard F. Fenno, *Home Style: House Members in Their Districts*, 3rd ed. (New York: Longman, 2002).

59. See Mayer, *American Media Politics in Transition*, for more discussion on the role of watchfulness by new media.

60. Paul S. Herrnson, *Congressional Elections* (Washington, DC: CQ Press, 1995), 191–94.

61. Price, *The Congressional Experience*.

62. Samuel L. Popkin, *The Reasoning Voter: Communication and Persuasion in Presidential Campaigns* (Chicago: University of Chicago Press, 1991).

63. See Congresswoman Lois Capps, "Lois's Blog," http://www.house.gov/capps/media/blog.shtml (accessed October 19, 2007).

INTERVIEW: THE HONORABLE
STEPHANIE HERSETH SANDLIN (D-SD)

Stephanie Herseth Sandlin is South Dakota's at-large member of Congress. She is a leader of the Blue Dog Coalition, a group of moderate Democrats committed to fiscal discipline and strong national security. She serves on three committees— Agriculture, Veterans' Affairs, and Natural Resources—and chairs the Veterans' Affairs Subcommittee on Economic Opportunity.

Herseth Sandlin was born in South Dakota to a political family, with a grandfather who served as governor and a grandmother who was the first female secretary of state. Her father was also a successful state politician.

After an unsuccessful run in 2002, Herseth Sandlin won her seat in Congress in a special election in 2004, and was reelected to a full term that fall. In 2006 Herseth Sandlin was reelected, receiving more than 230,000 votes—the second highest vote total in the nation among House members. She married former Congressman Max Sandlin of Texas that same year.

This interview was conducted in her Washington offices in December 2007.

How have you been treated by the press?
Overall, very fairly. There are many reasons for that. But by and large it has to do with the small congressional delegation whereby its easy for reporters back home when something develops . . . to simply email three press secretaries to say, "What's Stephanie's take; what are the senators' takes?"

So we get into stories because they are very proactive but we've also been very proactive of trying to take what I'm doing on my committees and what the House is working on separate from the Senate, and we know our reporters well—especially in the print media—and so we sometimes go to one or two that we think would be particularly interested, provide them with some background on a particular issue that we think is important to a certain region of the state, and talk about how this is making its way through committee or what I did at the committee level once it got to the House. So we have a good give and take, and I make myself very accessible; that was rule number one from 2002, when you start out as someone who is in a very crowded field and reporters are . . . narrowing their coverage over time. And folks on the radio say, "Just stop in any time"—take them up on that offer! And if someone wants to talk to you as a candidate you can't put your spokesperson on the line, you as the candidate have to get on the line.

. . . I think I have been treated as fair as I could have expected both in 2002, when I was running against a sitting governor, and he got the endorsements from the editorial boards, but what they had to say about me I thought was fairly positive and fair. And since that time, separate from getting the endorsements, which I didn't always get in the special election, I feel that they have been fair, and that is in part because we make time in a nonelection year, once and sometimes twice a year when we are in town to stop in and sit down with their entire editorial board and take whatever questions they want to ask.

Difference between print and broadcast media?
Yes . . . the print media, there are reporters who have particular interests in certain areas . . . so you get a better shot at getting more of your substance and more of your work into the story. . . . The print media in our two largest cities just go into more substance and take more time and that is somewhat by design on how we built that relationship. They trust that we'll get back to them if they need more information, and we'll get them information from the Congressional Research Service; we'll actually do some of the leg work for them. They can't do it all, whereas the TV folks don't tend to ask for that, because there's no way that they're going to get longer than a two-minute story.

Biggest mistakes in dealing with the media?
You have to be very careful in how you talk about the war. And this has started out since my 2002 race before we even went to Iraq, and my opponent, the governor, would parse statements that I would make, so I have become just conditioned to be very careful in how I talk about my position, my votes—anything related to the war. And I think that . . . I don't know that I have made a big mistake, but I have at times phrased something in a way that I catch myself and I will try to take an opportunity to rephrase it.

Ever talk off the record to reporters?
Once or twice.

Difference in quality between state and national reporters?
Our state press corps does a very good job of covering those issues that the delegation's been very involved in. We are a small delegation and a pretty active delegation, so that's why of course you have all the coverage on the energy bill or the farm bill or veterans' issues or tribal issues, you know, get some attention . . . but a lot of it is just direct with the tribes. . . . The state media, obviously does a much better job, the two major newspapers in particular, of covering the conditions on the reservations. The national media does a terrible job in my opinion of covering native American news, that's why you have certain outlets or NPR's *Native News*. . . . I don't think the national media has done a very good job at all of letting people know that certain tribes in this country don't have casinos located next to urban areas making as much money as they're making and we have people living in third-world conditions. And a lot of the gang violence that's reported is always in urban areas. We have serious gang violence going on in the most rural parts of South Dakota. We have a teenage suicide epidemic going on in two of our reservations and three or four before that. We'll maybe get some national coverage out of *The New York Times*, that's all.

Ever gotten angry at a journalist for an unfair or inaccurate story?
First was in South Dakota during my 2002 race. Again, front page above the fold, a story that was so off-base, and I don't know quite who drove it, although I think my opposing campaign may have had something to do with it, based on information that the National Republican Congressional [Committee] got out here. I just don't see how that story ever could have made front page had it not been fuel being added to the fire. And it was on the money that I was going to raise when I came to Washington from tribes, from wealthy casino tribes. Well, the National Indian Gaming Association had a breakfast event for me—and some of the tribes I represent, eight of the nine of them, have a gaming operation, it's just that they're not lucrative; they may generate some economic development money, they may provide jobs to some on the reservation, but it's not an operation that generates these huge per capita payments to everyone in the tribe. So I come out here to do a number of other things, in terms of trying to raise resources, introduce myself to people, and we go to this breakfast, we had some commitments, maybe four or five people that actually came to the breakfast brought a contribution—I would say the most we raised at that breakfast was six or eight thousand dollars—and it made front page above the fold, basically trying to suggest that I was going to be bought out by Indian gambling interests.

All you can do is call the paper and the reporter to try and set the record straight from your perspective, share information that we think is relevant, explain how we think they got it wrong, but also use it as an opportunity to get information from them—where did you get this information? Obviously not so much sources, but where did you think to suggest that I might raise six figures, and to try and understand the decision-making process of the people making the editorial decisions about what made this front-page news. . . . You know, when we provide information in our financial reports, should we break it down so that they can see readily what that amount is compared to other amounts that we're raising? Some people say, don't make it easy for them; well in my case, I sort of feel like if you don't make it easy . . . then you're running the risk that they're going to get it wrong, whether there's a bias or whether they are getting their information from another source that's inaccurate. You just do your best to be firm, to explain. Obviously they are going to respect that if you think they got it wrong and you lay out the case for them, they are going to have more respect for you, even if they disagree, than if you just roll over and take it and you don't make a peep.

Any other examples?
Within a week after I was elected in the special election . . . the gossip columnist for *Roll Call* [a newspaper focusing on Congress published in Washington, D.C.—ed.] contacts my office asking about a personal relationship with another member of Congress, and our decision, since we thought it was fairly well known anyway, was to acknowledge it rather than have *Roll Call* follow us. . . . And so the gossip columnist assured my press secretary that it was going to be a story in

good taste—and what we got was *Roll Call* printing where I lived, which was a security issue, putting in facts that clearly came from National Republican Party operatives to suggest that this person and I were living together when we weren't, and it was just awful. And here I was, a new member of Congress, the youngest woman in Congress, we're straightforward in providing information and then we get slammed with something that could potentially cause a political problem, based on things that weren't true, and then the security risk. They ended up apologizing for the fact that they printed where I was living. But that has affected my relationship with *Roll Call* ever since.

Can you tell us about the 2006 Wikipedia incident?
I remember I was in Pierre, South Dakota, and I was getting on the road that morning to go to Pine Ridge, to the powwow on the reservation . . . and I got a call from my then chief of staff saying, "I need to talk to you about something that is the strangest, most egregious thing I've come across . . . since I've been working in politics." . . . And when I first heard it, it was of course ridiculous . . . that I was pregnant by my chief of staff, and I think that the reason it had come to our attention was because it wasn't just posted on Wikipedia that I was pregnant by my chief of staff, it was the fact that my opponent's campaign manager took the post in Wikipedia and actually sent it around to what I call the legitimate press corps and put it out there and said something along the lines of "Well, this is far different from the homewrecker of 2004," or some sort of allegation that I had broken up a marriage, and asked for verification. So [he] took a Wikipedia entry that was false, added his own allegation, which was false, a whisper campaign . . . and he had circulated that. . . . This goes too far; what in the world is a campaign manager doing circulating this? And I'm of course upset because it's not just on the blogs—the blogs can be awful, but it's the blogs—. . . but once the inquiries came for us to respond to this and all of a sudden these allegations are being put into print, and knowing that people sometimes don't read that carefully, and knowing that we were going to have go back and explain things that were all on the up and up so to speak just was really . . . sickening. . . . Because then we had to explain to reporters, I didn't even meet Max Sandlin, that's obviously who they were referring to, being a "homewrecker" with a Congressman, that I didn't even meet until a year and a half after he was divorced. So then we had to explain that what you're accusing me of could also legally be defined as sexual harassment, in terms of being pregnant by my chief of staff, who, by the way, is married. . . . So I knew that once that got into one story, let alone the two or three stories, it ended up in the two major newspapers that it was going to cause confusion. . . . Now it is out there, now it is in print, now it's not just in the blogosphere. And I would have people that I knew, an older woman in Brookings who came up to me in August . . . [asking,] "Is it true . . . why would you have to get pregnant now?" And so if you have questions from constituents like that on the one allegation, then of course you know there are people out there that just dismiss the facts, think that I somehow

got involved when he was married, that I broke up the marriage . . . so that's how damaging it can be. You cannot measure the damage. That damage could be done to me even six years from now, because there are people out there who didn't read the stories carefully, that could think that I was pregnant, that I was involved with my chief of staff, so that's the danger, because you not only have what people can pick up on the blogosphere, which is simply just a different venue of sharing the rumor and sharing the whisper campaign, but as soon as that stuff gets in to a print medium that's a legitimate source that people read and think that "if it made it into the paper . . . "

Did you expect this type of stuff when you entered politics?
I anticipated rumors always. I grew up in a political family, so I know that there are always rumor campaigns. Sometimes they may have an element of truth, other times they don't, and it can be anything from your finances to where you own land, to . . . more personal stuff about relationships you're in. So I anticipated because I was a single woman . . . certain whisper campaigns questioning my sexual orientation, although the first whisper campaign that went around was that I was married, but I left my husband in D.C. to come home to run for Congress—I'd never been married before. . . . But generally whisper campaigns are just that; they don't reach your average voters, it goes through the political circles . . . it's not available to everybody. And so I never expected that an official spokesperson for someone's campaign would spread the kind of lies about my personal life, the most personal of one's personal life, and that that would then get translated because we had to respond to it, to generating two or three or more stories in the legitimate print media of the state, and that would it then lead to even supporters asking me about whether or not I was pregnant.

Advice for young people thinking about running for office?
That you just have to know there are going to be certain things outside of your control, you have to feel comfortable in your own skin, the good and the bad that you've done, and that at some point something could come to light and . . . the truth will not necessarily reach everybody you hope that it would reach, and that's just a part of campaigns. But whisper campaigns, that's been around forever, it's the fact that we have this other medium, and then we have certain types drawn into politics, political operatives, who would be either so malicious or so sloppy that they would actually try to infuse that into a broader more widely read audience. . . . I think a young person simply has to adjust and I think the blogosphere now being around for a couple years. . . . We're all adapting, and I think one of the ways in which young people have to adapt is that it is just easier for misinformation to be shared with many more people, and yet if you let that discourage you that would be a shame, because most young people who are drawn to [politics] want to serve. You know, we all make poor choices, but by and large we make good choices and when someone puts out misinformation

you have to address it aggressively; you have to put out sometimes maybe more information than you would like . . . you just have to not let it get to you too much, but as you can tell from my reaction it was so over the line, and that's why when I talk about it, [it] gets me going, but it is not something that I think about; I really haven't thought much about it . . . since the election . . . because we used it not only to make sure that people knew the truth . . . but to destroy the credibility of my opponent's campaign. And so you always have to turn what's coming at you as an attack out of nowhere—when you get an attack out of left field . . . what we chose to do, and what worked effectively, was we responded aggressively, even though it would have to be put into print and it was more information than perhaps I wanted to share about my personal life, but it was the truth and it knocked both allegations . . . and it destroyed the credibility of that campaign . . . and they never really recuperated.

Structure of your press organization on your staff?
I have had the benefit of having one person, Russ Levsen, who has been with me since my 2002 campaign serve as my communications director, press secretary, different titles . . . until just about a month and a half ago, and that's when Betsy Hart joined me. I had the benefit of someone who just got to know me so well, knew my voice. It always helps when someone knows the state . . . and when you have a pretty small press corps of kind of people who are really covering the delegation attentively, and so you can develop those relationships. . . . It just helps and that's what Russ had and that's what Betsy will have. But it again then working very closely with your legislative team as well the state staff to know what's going on, how we might want to take advantage of an opportunity with something that developed in the state, to let the reporter know of something going in committee or in Congress that they might not know otherwise that's related to a development back home or with the legislative team, working with them to get their ideas on how we can agitate for a story based on something we're doing that we don't think is getting attention back home. . . . It's been primarily a one-person position . . . but then she's got the rest of the staff to get ideas from, to get the policy expertise from, and then of course the longer she's with our office and around me, adapting the statements and the press releases to how she knows I've talked about the issue, or coming to me and saying it would be really helpful to go do an interview with this radio reporter or we're going to make a call to Mary Claire Jalonick with the AP [Associated Press], just to find ways, not just with a press release, or a joint release with the senators. . . . Every office does their press shop a little differently. Some have press secretaries back in the district, and I think that could be helpful too, except I think our press corps there and if we have something going on in one of our district offices, we can help share information, but it is what's happening out here that we're responsible for communicating to our press corps.

3

Press Coverage of the United States Supreme Court

Vincent James Strickler and Richard Davis

At the time of America's founding, many people assumed that the judiciary would be the weakest of the three branches of the new national government. With "no influence over either the sword or the purse," Alexander Hamilton could argue that courts would assert "neither *force* nor *will*, but only merely judgment"[1] Yet in the exercise of mere "judgment" rest the roots of great power. The Constitution rules the land, and the Court dictates the meaning of that document—if it can persuade the nation to accept its rulings. In truth, "the only power that the Court can assert is the power of public opinion"[2]—and the Court knows this. In the case of *Planned Parenthood of Southeastern Pennsylvania v. Casey*, Justices Sandra Day O'Connor, Anthony Kennedy, and David Souter frankly acknowledged the fountain of their authority: "The Court's power lies . . . in its legitimacy, a product of substance and perception that shows itself in the people's acceptance of the Judiciary as fit to determine what the Nation's law means and to declare what it demands."[3]

Larry Berkson has identified two constituencies to which the Court must appeal to legitimize its authority: legal professionals and, more importantly, segments of the general public.[4] The Court has proved quite successful at building and maintaining its popular authority. The public consistently gives the Court a higher approval rating than the other branches of government,[5] and that support has remained remarkably even over time.[6] It did not dip significantly even in the aftermath of the Court's controversial decision ending the 2000 presidential election.[7] Such solid support is no accident, but has been carefully cultivated through the Supreme Court's efforts to develop an image of authority and expertise, stability and unanimity—and independence.

The justices of the United States Supreme Court serve as the high priests of a "secular church."[8] They sit at the cloistered pinnacle of a hierarchical legal priesthood, reciting ritualized Latin phrases, dressing in black robes, presiding from a raised altar while laboring in a Greek temple. Like the pre-Reformation church, they claim sole authority to interpret America's sacred texts—the Constitution and Bill of Rights. While politicians generally seek to relate to the common man, Supreme Court justices are expected to have received an elite education in legal seminaries and to have developed uncommon expertise,[9] that they might "possess a special competence" for their duties.[10] We are implicitly led to believe that constitutional salvation must come through their institutional wisdom and power.

To avoid challenges to the institution's perceived authority, the Court strives to never discredit its own past wisdom, for "[t]he legitimacy of the Court would fade with the frequency of its vacillation."[11] Even when the Court does change its mind, it usually does so by small degrees, imperceptible to casual observers and obfuscated by claims of continuing fidelity. The Court then justifies its subterfuge by appealing to an "undoubted public interest in 'stability and orderly development of the law.'"[12] When the Supreme Court's authority has been directly challenged, the justices have closed ranks and issued unanimous opinions, such as in *Cooper v. Aaron* (when state governments resisted orders issued by the courts) and in *United States v. Nixon* (when the president threatened to ignore any court ruling).[13] Even in resolving the 2000 presidential election controversy, the Court desperately attempted to maintain the illusion of unanimity by issuing unsigned *per curiam* decisions in the divisive cases of *Bush v. Palm Beach County Canvassing Board* and *Bush v. Gore*.[14]

Particularly in politically charged situations, the Court must maintain the perception of distance from, and immunity to, the political process: "The Court's authority . . . ultimately rests on sustained public confidence in its moral sanction. Such feeling must be nourished by the Court's complete detachment, in fact and in appearance, from political entanglements."[15] Life tenure and the nonelective, nonpartisan nature of federal judicial service help establish a presumption of unallied independence, which increases the Court's legitimacy. But these presumptions must be consciously preserved. As an example, during the 2006 State of the Union address,

> [w]hen [President] Bush said "We love our freedom, and we will fight to keep it," [Justice] Thomas looked at [Justice] Roberts, who looked at [Justice] Breyer, who gave an approving shrug; [they] stood and gave unanimous applause. . . . It seemed from their frequent conferences that the justices had agreed on some ground rules: Any mention of [the war in] Iraq or hot domestic disputes were off limits; broad appeals to patriotism were deemed applause-worthy.[16]

To maintain its positive image—and thus its power—the Court must engage the public, to sense what is required to enhance confidence and to deliver appropriate messages that reinforce its preferred image. But the Court lacks the mechanisms available to other political actors—polls, newsletters, town meetings—to carry on such interactive communication. The Court needs assistance to accomplish these purposes; it needs the press.

The potential value of the media to the Court is magnified by the dearth of knowledge about the Court possessed by the public. News content is dictated by journalistic values—such as proximity, simplicity, and conflict—rather than legal importance.[17] As a result, the other branches of government receive far more attention, with one study showing that the president receives ten times as many minutes of coverage as the Court on evening news programs.[18] What coverage the Court does receive is often superficial and inaccurate.[19] Only rarely will a decision penetrate public awareness—even when it is highly relevant. A survey conducted more than a decade after the Court struck down school prayer found only 17 percent of teachers were aware of it.[20] "Citizens, as individuals, evince little or no knowledge of or concern for the Court; to the extent that they express sensible opinions, they base judgments on the vaguest and crudest of ideological frameworks."[21]

Yet despite such mass ignorance, the potential for enlightenment lies with the media. Public awareness of even an obscure policy area increases when the Court renders a decision on that topic[22] if the case is given even limited media attention.[23] If the Court could better mobilize the media to carry its preferred messages, it clearly could have a greater impact on public knowledge and, perhaps, on popular attitudes and public policy. And it is essential for the Court's power that the media cooperate in conveying images of the Court as an authoritative and independent force in American politics. But do they cooperate?

COVERING THE COURT

Working the Supreme Court beat is a prestigious but possibly unappealing assignment, generally devoid of interviews, investigations, or scoops.[24] "[A]t the appellate level, ninety-eight percent of it is all out in front and public. There is not . . . a highly sourced story. There [is] not a lot of scooping. There [is] not a lot of stuff that anybody could get that other people didn't know. . . . [I]t's purely an interpretive function that you play as a reporter."[25] Such reporting requires particular expertise. Some of the reporters who cover the Court have law degrees, which better prepare them to understand the workings of the Court, the opinions of the justices, and the commentary of legal experts.[26]

Those without such training may find their assignment "daunting" as they effectively have to go "to law school the way Abe Lincoln did."[27] But some "editors do not want to assign reporters [to the Supreme Court beat] whose knowledge of fine points of the law might make their stories too technical and dull."[28]

Ability is also developed through experience, with tenures on the Court beat typically lasting a half decade or more.[29] A few reporters, such as Nina Totenberg of National Public Radio, Tony Mauro of *USA Today*, and Linda Greenhouse of *The New York Times*, have become experts who give speeches and grant interviews regarding the Court. Coverage of the Court is often dominated by these elite journalists. For example, in one term nearly 90 percent of the press stories filed about the Court came from just six reporters representing five news sources.[30]

At the beginning of each Supreme Court term reporters "[sift] through the Supreme Court docket in search of whiz-bang fact situations" on which to focus their attention.[31] In 1998 term, with 145 cases taken up by the Court, the typical large newspaper covered only fifteen and the broadcast news networks covered only ten on average. Even *The New York Times* covered only forty-seven.[32] Attention given to a case or issue by the media is an important signal to the public concerning its importance—and only few cases are deemed worthy by the press.[33]

Newspaper stories regarding the Court go into significantly more depth than television news, better presenting information about such things as vote breakdown, case facts, and history of the legal issue, while averaging nearly twice as many sentences per story.[34] Television coverage imposes severe boundaries on story presentation. Former ABC News correspondent Tim O'Brien explains, "One of my stories, if it runs a minute-forty . . . that might be one column in a newspaper. Barely a column. . . . We can't be as comprehensive as you can in a newspaper simply because we do not have the time."[35] Television news, however, according to one study, was three times as likely as newspapers to discuss the political implications of Court decisions.[36] And broadcast journalists are more likely to frame cases as human dramas: "[W]hat television is able to do is put a human face on the decisions when they are allowed to. They go out and put the people who were involved on camera."[37] Wire services are different still, with their reporters rushing to file skeletal stories within minutes of a decision.[38] These wire reports often set the story frame for other reporters to follow.

Only on very rare occasions is a case covered before it is argued before the Court, with 98 percent of stories being filed thereafter.[39] Though filled with conflict, oral arguments receive limited coverage because they are usually built around dry technicalities. One reporter laments, "Sometimes I come out of an oral argument with hardly a quotable quote."[40] When a final decision is announced, printed opinions are immediately distributed to reporters.[41] Understanding and interpretation of these decisions is facilitated by preparatory study, such as reading case briefs—which is how the bulk of a Court reporter's time is spent. Frank Aukofer of the *Milwaukee Journal* explains:

> Most of the stuff that you need is right there at the Court—you have read the briefs, the amicus briefs. There isn't much need to go out and interview anybody. Sometimes to personalize it, to make a better story out of it, I will go out and talk to the people involved or talk to their lawyers. On a big case, when you have 20–30 amicus briefs, you pretty much get the gist of what's going on from the documentation at the Court. It's a nice, comfortable way to operate as a reporter because it's all there right in front of you.[42]

With such preparation, reporters can often predict the outcome of cases.[43] But digesting an opinion can still be difficult. Justices "write these horrendously long law review articles for decisions. . . . The plain fact is that Supreme Court decisions today look like the periodic tables in chemistry."[44] To make these complicated opinions understandable for a lay audience, a Court reporter must act as "a kind of translator."[45] Acting collegially, reporters "frequently . . . put our heads together and kind of ask each other, 'What do you think it means?'"[46] One part-time Court reporter explains that "once in a while you get a complex decision with no clear majority. Then I would talk it over with some of my colleagues who would have covered the case more closely."[47]

Often, journalists will also look to outside sources, such as interested groups, for help with interpretation. Some groups maintain easily accessible offices near the Court building, others hold briefings in the area, and some even mill about the Supreme Court plaza after a decision, looking for a chance to present their spin: "[P]eople are falling all over themselves to offer you information, offering stories, offering access to major players."[48] Following his oral argument on behalf of Al Gore in *Bush v. Palm Beach County Canvassing Board*, attorney Lawrence Tribe "proved media-savvy, storming the microphones [on the plaza] after the hearing so that he, not [Bush's attorney Ted] Olson, got on the tube [first]."[49] Elite reporters avoid the plaza and let groups call them.[50]

Court reporters frequently use legal experts, such as law professors, as sources.[51] Sometimes sources end up just being the "people you can get through to."[52] ABC News reporter Jan Crawford Greenburg observes, "You're pretty reliant on who you happen to call. And that means also, I think, that sometimes you see reporters who are pretty susceptible to spin."[53] Unfortunately, which sources get the most play may be a function of who gives the best quotes. "I try to get a key quote to illuminate the issue—a quote that is funny, or sexy, or unusual, or in a slightly off beat way illuminates the case," one reporter admits.[54] Stories can end up being more about reactions to decisions than about the decisions themselves.[55]

Editors can also greatly impact the content of stories,[56] as they rely on wire service reports to judge the work of their own reporters.[57] A nonelite reporter may be severely challenged if his version of events differs from that on the wire. Editors also will attempt to manage the technical content of a story to make it more readable—though possibly less accurate. Reporters can find editorial interference frustrating:

> *[A]ny* words I used to describe the Court's reasoning were rejected as beyond the understanding of the average Joe. Analogies were usually substituted from sports or warfare. . . . I would say, "But that's not what he said," and they would say, "[W]ell that's what he really meant." And I would say, "No, that's not what he meant, and that's not correct." And then it came down to, "Do you want to get on the air tonight or don't you want to get on the air tonight?"[58]

With limited—and, it seems, shrinking—media attention paid to the Court,[59] what coverage does "get on the air" is dictated by news values that favor drama, conflict, and proximity to the lives of viewers.[60] According to one reporter, "Get the ratings and you're forgiven all else. The sin there is not being inaccurate. The sin is being boring."[61] These standards are not easily met by the Court, for, as one former CBS reporter concludes, its "proceedings are so dull that it is a public service to keep them off the tube."[62] The Court's agenda can be partially blamed. Society-changing cases from a couple decades ago—regarding school desegregation, obscenity, abortion, and the like—were dripping with newsworthiness. David von Drehle of *Time* magazine argues that the cases that now find their way to the Court have simply become less likely to attract public notice:

> As the dust rises and the opinions, concurrences and dissents pile up, the court turns its attention to ever smaller cases related to ever narrower points of law. . . . [T]he Court's ideology is playing a dwindling role in the lives of Americans. The familiar hot-button controversies—abortion, affirmative action, the death penalty, police powers and so on—have been around so long, sifted and resifted so many times, that they now arrive at the court in highly specific cases affecting few, if any, real people. . . . What once was salient is now mostly symbolic.[63]

News values create an inaccurate picture of the Court. Social policy issues are focused on "to the exclusion of other types of cases."[64] First Amendment and civil rights cases are overexposed compared to their percentage of the docket, while cases involving judicial power, federalism, and the economy are underreported.[65] And even for those cases that are covered, the coverage is woefully superficial. A study of media coverage of the high-profile cases of *Webster v. Reproductive Health Services* and *Regents of the University of California v. Bakke* found that most stories failed to explain the claims being made or the factual scenarios underpinning them.[66] The authors concluded that news coverage of these cases was "relatively ahistorical and acontextual."[67]

The Court as an institution and its justices were rarely mentioned in stories about *Bakke* and *Webster*.[68] A broader analysis of the content of news stories about the Court found that fewer than one-third mentioned a justice by name.[69] Interest groups were mentioned more often than the authors of the Court's opinions.[70] And descriptions of case votes (indicating how many justices did or did not endorse the majority outcome in a particular case), which were mentioned in fewer than half of the stories concerning particular cases in 1989, had almost entirely disappeared by 1994.[71]

The worst omissions and inaccuracies take place in the coverage of certiorari petitions, which request that the Court hear a case. In one term, less than 1 percent of denials of certiorari were reported, and the few that were covered dealt only with hot-button social issues.[72] But even in this small pool, errors were common. Almost half were mistakenly reported as decisions on the merits.[73] Toni House, the late public information officer for the Court, once said that the worst thing reporters do is misrepresent certiorari denials, making them sound like decisions.[74]

In sum, reporting about the Court is meager, superficial, often inaccurate, and almost entirely focused on the Court's work product. Overwhelmingly, coverage is focused on cases on the current docket.[75] And even then, what is usually missing is discussion of what prompted the decisions, the effects of the decisions, and the role of the individual justices in the creation of the decisions. The exceptions to docket-centered coverage are resignations and confirmations of justices.[76]

COVERING COURT VACANCIES

Driven by journalism's hunger for drama and conflict,[77] media interest in Supreme Court vacancies sometimes begins even before a vacancy exists.[78] During presidential campaigns, the press attempts to gauge what impact candidates will have on the Court if elected, speculating about which justices may retire in the ensuing four years, who their replacements might be, and what impact those changes may have on public policy.[79] As justices experience illnesses or weaken with age, speculation about impending retirement or death may become frenzied.

When Chief Justice William Rehnquist was stricken with thyroid cancer, the media seemed willing to broadcast every unsubstantiated rumor:

> [Rehnquist] was first said to have informed the White House that he would an-nounce his retirement on Monday. The rescheduling from Monday until Tues-day of a meeting between the president and the Senate leadership was taken as proof of the chief justice's intention; in fact, the change was made to accommo-date the schedule of Senator Bill Frist. . . . Then reports had the retirement be-ing announced on Friday afternoon, after President Bush returned from Scot-land.[80]

"[A]lmost comical[ly], . . . Robert D. Novak declared on CNN that the chief justice's retirement would be announced at 4:50 that afternoon"—but he was wrong.[81]

When directly asked about his retirement plans by a shouting news pro-ducer, Rehnquist replied, "That's for me to know and you to find out."[82] Fi-nally, after Rehnquist returned home from a brief hospitalization to battle a fever, the media's macabre watch was mercifully ended:

> Rehnquist, ending months of increasingly frenzied speculation about his retire-ment plans, declared on Thursday night that he would continue to serve "as long as my health permits." . . . Photographers were camped out in front of the house as they had been for weeks, recording his daily trip to and from his chambers at the court and awaiting word of a retirement that was expected in many quarters to be imminent. The prospect that the scene on his lawn, with its overtones of a ghoulish death watch, would continue all summer was evidently what drove the famously tight-lipped chief justice to issue his statement.[83]

Journalists are not the only ones who carefully chart possible retirement sce-narios. Pressure groups do more than just observe and report: They also prepare for battle. Since the failed nomination of Robert Bork—which may have cost anti-Bork groups as much as $15 million (mostly for paid advertisements)—interests groups have believed that nominees they do not find acceptable can be defeated through well-financed, well-coordinated campaigns.[84] Now groups stand ready with e-mail lists hundreds of thousand addresses long, "war rooms" filled with phone lines and computers, and millions of dollars pledged to buy television spots promoting or opposing nominees.[85] These groups, organized in "megacoalitions, linked by a constant flow of e-mail, thrash out talking points and strategy over conference calls that may include up to 70 participants."[86]

Within moments of the announcement of a Court vacancy (well before a nominee is chosen), preemptive battle plans are initiated through mass e-mails and even television commercials designed to frame the debate before it begins.[87] *The New York Times* reported that "[a]t the abortion rights group

NARAL Pro-Choice America, organizers were sending e-mail alerts to 800,000 activists within 15 minutes after the announcement of Justice Sandra Day O'Connor's resignation. 'Don't let Bush take away your choice!' they declared."[88] Just a half hour later, "the conservative group Progress for America Inc. launched a preemptive e-mail ad against 'smear attacks' on President Bush's judicial nominees that reached 8.7 million Americans."[89]

Presidents may also make use of the media in the weeks leading up to a nomination by leaking the names of possible nominees to reporters. These "trial balloons" are released to both help sift potential choices (as reactions are gauged) and send signals to constituents and allies that their favored candidates are under consideration for the position.[90] But such ploys can backfire. Publicizing a short list allows interest groups and the media to help shape the process.[91] Media investigations may uncover disconcerting facts,[92] groups may organize opposition campaigns,[93] and the president may be forced to embarrassingly withdraw individuals from consideration due to the appearance of outside pressures—even if a damaged potential nominee was never under serious consideration.[94]

Interest groups and the media may act symbiotically to influence nominations. Media outlets, hungry for information and opinion about an ongoing story, often turn to pressure group press releases, spokespersons, and op-eds.[95] Some groups—such as NARAL, the NAACP, and NOW—have dominated this role in recent decades by providing opposition to primarily Republican nominees.[96] The press may also turn to unnamed "inside" sources and end up building whole story lines around misinformation (such as when *The New York Times* reported that David Souter was under consideration by the Reagan administration—which simply was not true).[97] The process can become controversial and drawn out, littered with discarded prospective nominees and making an administration appear inept.[98] As a result, presidents generally try to keep the selection process as quiet, secretive, and quick as possible.[99]

A dramatic example of the power of interested groups using the media—both old and new—to influence the nomination process can be seen in the case of Harriet Miers, who withdrew less than a month after being chosen.[100] George W. Bush announced the Miers nomination at 8:00 A.M. on September 29, 2005. At 9:00 A.M. conservative radio talk show host Laura Ingraham was on the air criticizing the choice. Bill Kristol, editor of the *Weekly Standard*, was on Fox News moments later doing the same. At 10:17 A.M., former Bush speech writer and influential blogger David Frum posted an essay attacking the nomination.[101] The swift outpouring of opposition from the right kept "Republican senators from immediately jumping behind Miers."[102] It was difficult for the administration and its allies to fight back: "[A]nytime we put out something positive about her it gets shot to pieces by . . . the blogs."[103] According to blogger Jonah Goldberg, "We played a part in changing the climate simply because of the megaphone we have."[104] For some, the anti-Miers zealotry was reminiscent of the left's attacks on Bork eighteen years before.[105]

Battles to sink the nominations of John Roberts and Samuel Alito were also recently fought in the media—both free and paid—but without success.[106] In the case of Alito, detailed debates raged in newspapers, on radio and television, and in the blogosphere over the significance of a memo he wrote when seeking a job in the Reagan administration,[107] the nature of his argument in a case concerning the strip search of a twelve-year old girl,[108] the accuracy of a Knight-Ridder news agency study of the ideological bent of his past judicial opinions,[109] and the importance of his impact on the "balance" of the Court.[110]

The biggest media events in the nomination process are Senate hearings regarding the nominee. They have grown in importance in the eyes of the media since the failed nomination of Bork because of their potential for drama as the president's nominee, the Senate, and interested groups collide.[111] The champion for fulfilling press values was the second round of Senate hearings considering the nomination of Clarence Thomas, which were saturated with sex, race, and politics. The drama began when a confidential FBI report of Anita Hill's accusations of sexual harassment—which the Senate Judiciary Committee had considered too unsubstantiated to be worthy of public discussion—was illegally leaked to the press.[112] The three major broadcast networks devoted sixty-six hours to the hastily called hearings, which an estimated 30 million viewers watched the first night.[113] Surveys found, amazingly, that nearly 90 percent of Americans watched at least part of the second round of hearings.[114]

Even less controversial nominations now receive extensive, high-profile media coverage—at least during the first day of hearings.[115] Unlike Bork, who seemed ill prepared for the media's scrutiny—sporting an unattractive beard, fidgeting in the witness chair, and providing "lengthy, byzantine answers"—nominees are now intensely coached for the event.[116] As an example, Ruth Bader Ginsburg's "murder boards" were conducted in two stages, with her first being briefed on various areas of law to "help bring it to the front of my mind" and then participating in mock hearings in which she was berated with questions for hours.[117] The purpose of such practice, according to Justice Stephen Breyer, is to be able "to say things in words that will in fact be comprehensible to the people who are watching you."[118] Such care must be taken because ill-worded sound bites cut from a nominee's testimony can be damaging.[119]

Otherwise uneventful hearings may even produce unexpectedly newsworthy events that can dramatically impact the proceedings. The two most noteworthy moments during the confirmation hearings for Alito occurred when his wife was driven to tears by the pointed questions directed at her husband and when Sen. Joe Biden used almost all of his allotted time to pontificate rather than asks questions.[120] Some Democrats felt "the pictures of a weeping Mrs. Alito . . . being broadcast across the nation" made it impossible for them to continue pressing the nominee, thus unfairly clearing the path for his confirmation.[121] At the same time, lengthy lectures by members of the Judiciary Committee make the proceedings appear more about senators taking advantage of the cameras for self-promotion than about conducting a responsible investigation into the nominee's qualifications.[122] In response to the way the Alito hearings unfolded—with little of substance discussed or reported—Biden called for the abandonment of the hearing process, because the "system's kind of broken."[123]

JUSTICES AND JOURNALISTS

The relationship between the justices of the United States Supreme Court and the media that covers them is not entirely one way. Rather than just passively tolerating being observed while they endure hearings and confirmations, listen to oral arguments, and hand down decisions, the Court quietly interacts with the media to a surprising degree. Justices realize the importance of the press as the conduit through which their efforts are made known to the public. As Chief Justice Earl Warren frankly admitted, "Since the public cannot be expected to read the opinions themselves, it must depend on newspapers, periodicals, radio, and television for its information."[124] To monitor the media's efforts, the justices may pay close attention to news stories about their decisions, to make sure, as Justice Harold H. Burton reported to Warren in 1956 that an "opinion is being understood and taken as it was intended to be taken."[125]

Justices may praise journalists they think do their job well[126] while privately chastising those who do not—such as when Chief Justice Warren Burger called a correspondent to his chambers to dispute a story aired on the *CBS Evening News*.[127] Justice William O. Douglas was particularly ready to complain about the press. He believed that someone should "give them a seminar on judicial procedure," called them "depraved," and concluded that they attempted to use their editorials as "a club . . . against the Court."[128] Justice Abe Fortas held a "hatred of the press" and called reporters "dirty" and "crooked."[129]

In addition to seeing the press as an imperfect conveyer of information from the Court to the public, at least some justices recognize that information flows the other way too. Justice William Brennan emphatically claimed that public opinion had no impact on the Court's work,[130] but Rehnquist believed this was impossible, and perhaps unwise:

> Judges, so long as they are relatively normal human beings can no more escape being influenced by public opinion in the long run than can people working at other jobs. And if a judge on coming to the bench were to decide to hermetically seal himself off from all manifestations of public opinion, he would accomplish very little; he would not be influenced by current public opinion, but instead by the state of public opinion at the time that he came onto the bench.[131]

One justice even anonymously admitted that "people just demand that the Supreme Court resolve an issue whether we really ought to or not. That does affect us sometimes."[132]

There are additional reasons to believe that the Court is in fact impacted by public opinion. Social science studies have found that the Court marginally adjusts its decision outcomes to better match the public's changing policy preferences.[133] But the Court also appears unwilling to move too far out ahead of public opinion.[134] A possible explanation is that "institutionally minded justices will want to avoid public defeat and the accompanying weakening of the Court's implicit authority. . . . [T]his implies paying some attention to what the public wants from government."[135]

Some observers argue that the justices may also be influenced by journalists' opinions and use their decision-making power to "curry favor with the press."[136] According to Judge Lawrence Silberman, "[i]t seems that the primary objective of *The [New York] Times*'s legal reporters is to put activist heat on recently appointed Supreme Court justices."[137] This theoretical process has become known among conservative critics as the "Greenhouse effect," in reference to Linda Greenhouse of *The New York Times*.[138] Greenhouse has taken public positions on important judicial issues—even marching in an abortion rights rally at the same time that the Court was considering several abortion cases—while she covers those issues for the nation's paper of record.[139] The influence of people like Greenhouse is frequently cited as an explanation for the "evolving" opinions of justices such as Anthony Kennedy.[140] But the "Greenhouse effect" remains unproven and fiercely disputed.[141]

Though the Court may defer to popular sentiment in some cases while following elite opinion in others, it must not appear to be doing so in either case. Appearing to be affected by external influences would cast doubt on the Court's independence and weaken it as an institution. Thus, even as they respond to constituent desires in order to maintain popularity (or, at least, respect) and power, they must paradoxically cultivate an image of aloofness, denying that they even care what people think of them. This tension causes the justices to try to formally separate themselves from the media, at least as flesh and blood individuals.

When David Souter joined the Court, he attended a reception in the press room, described by Tony Mauro of *USA Today*: "At the very end of it, Souter turned to us and said, 'Well, thank you for this. I enjoyed it. Let's do it again when I retire.' We realized as he walked away, [that] you just don't see them much. Once they get life tenure, they tend to get inaccessible—until they're old and they want to adjust their obituaries."[142] Justice Antonin Scalia, who loves giving provocative speeches to select groups but desperately does not want his efforts featured in the press, tries to walk a tightrope between accessibility and aloofness:

> When he's giving a speech, he doesn't want to be televised. He doesn't want anyone from the press to cover it. When he's making a speech somewhere if he sees a television camera, he'll go off stage and say "I'm not going back on until that camera is gone." The explanation he gives is that he doesn't think Supreme Court justices should be public figures, out on the hustings making arguments. He can't resist doing it; he just doesn't want the image of what he's doing widely disseminated. . . . [T]here is a certain tension between his urge to assert himself and his desire not to be perceived as asserting himself in certain ways.[143]

As Anthony Kennedy has explained, the justices wish to be "judged ultimately by what we write"—meaning the opinions they author for the cases decided by the Court—not by anything else they say or do.[144] The distance between the justices and the press is great enough that one Court reporter lamented that "this is more like covering Buckingham Palace or the Vatican than an institution in American government."[145]

MANAGING THE MEDIA

Emphasizing their written opinions is just one way in which the Court attempts to control its relationship with outsiders—and particularly with the press. The justices also engage in selective personal interactions with journalists while trying to shut off other avenues of information.

The Court has been actively managing its interaction with the press at least since 1935, when the Public Information Office was opened to assist journalists covering the Court.[146] By 1947 a full-time public information officer had been appointed. Unlike similar offices maintained by the other branches of the national government, the Court's public information officer does not promote policy; he or she does little more than distribute the official documents of the Court to the public and the press. A former public information officer at the Court proudly explained: "My job is peculiar in Washington because this office doesn't spin, it doesn't flap, it doesn't interpret."[147]

Yet through its official documents, the Court actually says a great deal to the press: "While the Supreme Court is the most insular of the nation's public institutions, justices like to say they are already the most open. Every piece of paper that comes to the court—petitions, briefs, decisions—is a public document."[148] Taken together, "[n]o other institution explains itself at such length, such frightening length."[149] Reporters covering the Court are expected to digest the contents of thousands of pages of certiorari petitions, Court orders, briefs, and opinions in any single term. Richard Carelli, who covered the Court for the Associated Press, said he spent half of his time just reading the certiorari petitions.[150] Journalists on the Supreme Court beat have little time or opportunity to look beyond the printed materials published by the Court.

But the ideal of the Court's speaking only through its opinions should not be misinterpreted as a desire to not interact with the larger political world. Justices do wish to have a larger influence, but on their own carefully controlled terms, which will not detract from the ritualized images of the Court. The most pointed examples of such managed communication are the concurrences and dissents published by the justices. These nonmajority opinions, which carry no authoritative weight within the judicial system, often seem designed to appeal to constituencies beyond the Court rather than to fellow justices. Such writings may be intended to influence and mobilize elite opinion to assist with internal disputes.

Obviously, the justices believe concurrences and dissents serve some value, whatever it may be, because the number of such opinions has increased significantly over time. Up until the 1950s about the same number of concurrences and dissents as majority opinions were filed each term. Since then the number of concurrences and dissents has grown to more than double the number of majority opinions.[151] It seems that "individual opinions are more highly prized than the opinions of the Court."[152]

Beyond their written work, justices also interact with reporters in more personal settings, such as private interviews (often conducted off-the-record). Some of the reporters on the Supreme Court beat sit down and talk with the justices on a regular basis.[153] In such a setting, a justice may effectively direct the press, but without being seen doing so. Helping maintain the Court's image of aloofness is the price a reporter inherently pays for these more intimate interactions. Justices may take advantage of such sessions to work on their personal images. Justices Harry Blackmun and William Rehnquist are known to have granted interviews to counteract mistaken impressions of their personalities.[154] Other justices, like William Brennan and Byron White, denied requests for interviews as a way to punish the press for what they perceived as unfair coverage.[155]

While the members of the Supreme Court feed the press selected information through their written work and personal interviews, they also try to cut off other sources. Clerks working at the Court are infamously warned about the "twenty-second rule"—which declares that they will be fired within twenty seconds if they talk to a reporter.[156] Leaks are so rare that reporters covering the Court do not expect them and generally do not attempt to cultivate them. When leaks do happen, the justices often have the power to discredit the source (even if it is unknown) by simply altering their plans. According to Tim O'Brien, the Court can "make you look foolish if you say decision on such and such day. . . . The Court doesn't like it when someone announces their decision before they do."[157] Because the Court eventually does make its decisions public, it is unwise for a journalist to report leaked information and incur the Court's displeasure. It is best to just wait for the written opinions.

The importance the Court places on the content of its press coverage can be seen in steps it has taken to ensure the accuracy of that coverage. When a journalist told Chief Justice Burger that he had misreported a decision, the practice of attaching clarifying headnotes to each decision was initiated.[158] When reporters expressed concern about never knowing when case decisions would be announced, the Court began scheduling certain days for handing down decisions (though still not announcing which decision will come on which day).[159] Such changes were designed to make it easier for the press to report all the Court's decisions swiftly and correctly. Thus they serve the needs of the Court more than the needs of the media.

Other changes suggested by the press, which do not help the Court do its job or build its image, are routinely rejected. The most obvious example is the placement of cameras in the Supreme Court chamber to broadcast oral arguments. Justice Souter famously once said, "I can tell you the day you see a camera come into our courtroom it's going to roll over my dead body."[160] Though he expresses it less dramatically, Justice Breyer agrees with Souter that cameras should be kept out because their presence would erode "public's trust" in the Court.[161] And there is reason to believe that live television coverage of the Court could impact its image. When Justice Ginsburg fell asleep on the bench during an important redistricting case, the *Washington Post* noted that "[i]t's lucky for Justice Ginsburg that the Supreme Court has so far refused to allow television cameras in the courtroom, for her visit to the land of nod would have found its way onto late-night shows."[162] Thomas opposes cameras; Kennedy, Scalia, and Ginsburg would tolerate them; and Roberts and Alito appear open to the idea.[163] But cameras nonetheless remain banned.

The call for cameras in the Court became most intense during the Florida recount cases in 2000. Television networks petitioned for live access to the historic oral arguments, and newspapers editorials criticized the Court's continued backwardness on the issue.[164] Just a short time before, senators Arlen Specter and Joseph Biden had proposed legislation to force the Court to accept camera coverage.[165] Yet despite such pressures, the Court did not admit cameras, instead choosing to distribute audiotapes of the arguments immediately following their conclusion: "Quickly releasing an audiotape was, by the court's 18th-century standards, revolutionary."[166]

Now, transcripts and recordings of oral arguments are readily available online.[167] Such unprecedented openness has produced some surprising new topics for media coverage. In a front-page story in *The New York Times*, it was reported that based on the number of times he causes laughter during oral arguments (as counted in the Court's transcripts), Justice Scalia is the funniest justice. Justice Ginsburg is the least funny.[168] Yet despite the availability of such "insightful" information about the Court from its transcripts and audio recordings, Specter continues to push for cameras in the country's highest courtroom. In a *Washington Post* editorial, the senator wrote,

> While we have come to accept the maxim that the Constitution is what the Supreme Court says it is, it is in the public interest for the public to at least know what the court is doing. By analogy to Justice Louis Brandeis's famous dictum that, "Sunlight is . . . the best disinfectant," television's klieg lights in the Supreme Court would be the public's best informant.[169]

It would seem that the Court's careful management of its image remains under threat.

COURTING CONTROVERSY

The media have generally shown little interest in churning up controversy or criticism regarding the Supreme Court and its justices beyond its official battles waged over nominees and fought in case opinions. The primary reason may just be opportunity. Journalists on the Supreme Court beat usually do not follow justices around outside the Court's formal functions looking for news—unlike White House reporters, who unflaggingly tail the president, waiting for him to misspeak or stumble. But reporters may also be protective of the Court's image. One journalist explains the media's attitude this way:

We have all of us—the public, the court, and the media—signed off on an invi-
olate, unspoken bargain that allows us to think of Supreme Court justices as
bona fide humans only up to the date of their swearing-in. We then pack them
into a vast marble box, where their moods, biases, politics, and friendships become secret. . . . The core assumption of the unspoken bargain . . . is that if we
knew the justices wrote notes, screened pornography, lobbied for votes, read
limericks, and sometime burped after a visit to Taco Bell, the court's stockpile
of public trust would be eroded. We might come to view them as political, ideological, interested stakeholders, rather than as divine interpreters of oracle
truths.[170]

Yet despite the general deference shown by the press to the actions of
Supreme Court justices, their behavior outside the courtroom does occasionally grab the news media's interest. Justice Antonin Scalia is easily the most
attractive lightning rod for media scrutiny—usually bringing the attention
upon himself by "speaking frequently off-the-cuff."[171] As an example, in a
question-and-answer session after a speech in Switzerland, Scalia commented
on the detainment of suspected terrorists, a topic that was closely related to a
case pending before the Court. Criticism about Scalia's comments quickly
followed, and a public effort was made to pressure the outspoken justice to
recuse himself from the case. Scalia refused, initiating another round of publicity.[172]

This was not an isolated incident. In recent years, Scalia has become newsworthy because of his comments about, and eventual recusal from, another
then-current case involving the pledge of allegiance;[173] his presence in a
duck-hunting party that also included Dick Cheney just weeks after the Court
had agreed to hear a case involving the vice president;[174] his honorary position as grand marshal of New York's Columbus Day parade that sparked
protests;[175] and an apology he gave to two reporters after a federal marshal
protecting him demanded the journalists erase tapes of a Scalia speech because of the justice's prohibition of recordings of his public appearances.[176]

Though he is the most common target, Scalia is not entirely alone among
Supreme Court justices in garnering press notice away from the Supreme
Court building. In the past, Justice William O. Douglas publicly attacked oil
companies;[177] Justices William Brennan and John Paul Stevens indirectly debated Attorney General Edwin Meese concerning original intent and judicial
activism;[178] Justice Stevens publicly endorsed the nomination of Robert Bork
to the Supreme Court;[179] while Justice Thurgood Marshall publicly questioned the credentials of David Souter, telling Sam Donaldson of ABC News
that he "never heard of him";[180] and Justice Clarence Thomas spoke out
against conservatives being intimidated to speak their views.[181]

More recently, in arguing in favor of allowing cameras to televise Supreme Court oral arguments, Specter noted that "Chief Justice Roberts and Justice Stevens were on . . . on ABC TV. Justice Ruth Bader Ginsburg was on CBS with Mike Wallace. Justice Breyer was on 'Fox News Sunday.' Justice Scalia and Justice Breyer had an extensive debate last December, which is available for viewing on the Web—and in television archives."[182] Even the normally media shy Justice Clarence Thomas engaged in a wide-ranging media tour to promote the publication of his autobiography.[183] The more public profile being assumed by the justices stands in sharp contrast to their traditionally faceless role, which has left most Americans (57 percent in a 2006 poll) unable to name a single member of the nation's highest court.[184] Though increasingly common, these public appearances tend to be quiet, inside-page events—but not always: "[T]o an unusual degree, justices have . . . been making headlines off the bench" in recent years.[185]

Several justices have sparked news stories with their entry into two public debates regarding legal issues that concern the Court. One is the role of the judiciary in American governance. Justices Ginsburg and O'Connor gave widely reported speeches defending the independence of the judiciary in the wake of criticisms of judicial power and even threats against some justices' lives.[186] Ginsburg also called a proposal put forward by some congressional Republicans to set up an inspector general to monitor the ethical behavior of judges "a scary idea" and claimed that "the judiciary is under assault in a way that I haven't seen before."[187]

The other issue that has drawn recent attention is whether justices should consider the rulings of foreign courts in their decision-making process. Justices Scalia, Breyer, Kennedy, and Ginsburg have sparred publicly over that issue in speeches and public forums.[188] The press's handling of the topic, which Kennedy feels often misinterprets the Court's reasoning, has left the justice exasperated and critical of the media. When asked what could be done to improve press coverage of the issue, Kenendy caustically remarked, "One thing you can do is suggest to editorial writers that they read [our] opinions before they write their editorials."[189]

These scattershot forays by the justices into public debates, and thus into the public eye, can feel a bit odd, if not downright unseemly. Dahlia Lithwick has pointed out the problem of judicial communication:

> Because the Supreme Court justices want to be a part of the national conversation—especially where it pertains to Supreme Court justices—they often launch these little speech bombs into the ether. Since there is no Supreme Court blog, no cable television show about them, they are left with the most roundabout modes of communicating: O'Connor talks to [Texas senator John] Cornyn through the students at Georgetown, with an assist from NPR's Nina Totenberg.

Scalia talks to his fellow justices through the students at the University of Freiburg in Switzerland. And Kennedy talks to editorialists through international lawyers. It's the same way parents fight in front of their children.[190]

But perhaps what has changed is not the civility or sanity of the justices themselves. They have similarly vented their frustrations and concerns in the past, but with the visibility that now comes from the nomination process, as viewed through a pervasive modern media, the justices are public figures whether they like it or not: "[T]he combination of the Internet, bloggers and bored law students means that everything a justice now says . . . is public."[191] Maybe the members of the Supreme Court—where even cameras are still not allowed—are still adjusting to this newfound celebrity.

Yet there is calculation in their new openness. Justices *know* the press will cover their speeches. They know their public comments will be newsworthy and be communicated to policy makers, the public, and even their fellow justices. Possibly they feel that going public will help them in their internal struggles with colleagues on the bench. If so, then justices are pursuing a form of "outside lobbying."[192]

But such strategies may impose a severe cost, as the long-nurtured reputation of the Court—the ultimate source of its power—becomes tarnished in the process. The more the justices speak out, the more politicized and the less neutral and trustworthy they appear. How justices will balance their celebrity status with the need to retain public confidence in and deference for the Court is yet to be determined.

DISCUSSION QUESTIONS

1. Do you think the Supreme Court should allow television cameras into its hearings? What are the pros and cons?
2. Do you think the media should be more or less aggressive in covering the Supreme Court on a personal level? Should we know more about the justices as people, as we do about presidents?
3. Do you think Americans would respect the Supreme Court less if they knew more about it, or would their appreciation grow as they learned more?
4. Can you think of any Supreme Court decisions this year? How do you think they were handled by the media?
5. To the extent that you follow the Supreme Court in the media, do you get an overall positive or negative impression of it? How does this compare with the other two branches of our national government?

6. Should reporters who cover the Supreme Court attempt to find out more about the behind-the-scenes tensions and deliberations? Why should we have to wait years and sometimes decades to find out how justices felt about key decisions, when papers are released, retired justices give interviews, former clerks finally go public?

SUGGESTIONS FOR FURTHER READING

Keith Bybee, ed. *Bench Press: The Collision of Courts, Politics, and the Media.* Stanford, CA: Stanford University Press, 2007.

Richard Davis. *Decisions and Images: The Supreme Court and the Press.* Englewood Cliffs, NJ: Prentice Hall, 1994.

Edward Lazarus. *Closed Chambers: The Rise, Fall, and Future of the Modern Supreme Court.* New York: Penguin, 2005.

Eliot Slotnic and Jennifer A. Segal. *Television News and the Supreme Court: All the News That's Fit to Air?* New York: Cambridge University Press, 1998.

NOTES

1. Alexander Hamilton, James Madison, and John Jay, *The Federalist Papers* (New York, NY: Mentor, 1961), 465.

2. Philip B. Kurland, "'The Cult of the Robe' and the Jaworski Case," *Washington Post*, June 23, 1974, C2.

3. *Planned Parenthood of Southeastern Pennsylvania v. Casey*, 505 U.S. 833, 865 (1992).

4. Larry Berkson, *The Supreme Court and Its Publics* (New York: Lexington Books, 1978).

5. Jeffery J. Mondak and Shannon Ishiyama Smithey, "The Dynamics of Public Support for the Supreme Court," *Journal of Politics* 59 (November 1997): 1119; Thomas R. Marshall, *Public Opinion and the Supreme Court* (Boston: Unwin Hyman, 1989).

6. Roger Handberg, "Public Opinion and the United States Supreme Court, 1935–1981," *International Social Science Review* 59 (1984): 3–13; Joseph Tanenhaus and Walter Murphy, "Patterns of Public Support for the Supreme Court: A Panel Study," *Journal of Politics* 43 (February 1981): 24–39; Marshall, *Public Opinion and the Supreme Court*.

7. See Herbert M. Kritzer, "The Impact of *Bush v. Gore* on Public Perceptions and Knowledge of the Supreme Court," in *Judicial Politics: Readings from Judicature*, 3rd ed., ed. Elliot Slotnick (Washington, DC: CQ Press, 2005), 500–506; and Stephen P. Nicholson and Robert M. Howard, "Framing Support for the Supreme Court in the Aftermath of 'Bush v. Gore,'" *Journal of Politics* 65 (August 2003): 676.

8. John B. Attanasio, "Everyman's Constitutional Law: A Theory of the Power of Judicial Review," *Georgetown Law Journal* 72 (August 1984): 1665.

9. John R. Schmidhauser, *Judges and Justices: The Federal Appellate Judiciary* (Boston: Little, Brown, 1979).

10. John Brigham, *The Cult of the Court* (Philadelphia: Temple University Press, 1987), 7.

11. *Planned Parenthood of Southeastern Pennsylvania v. Casey*, 505 U.S. 833, 866 (1992).

12. *Johnson v. Transportation Agency, Santa Clara County*, 480 U.S. 616, 644 (1987).

13. *Cooper v. Aaron*, 358 U.S. 1 (1958); *United States v. Nixon*, 418 U.S. 683 (1974).

14. *Bush v. Palm Beach County Canvassing Board*, 121 S. Ct. 471 (2000); *Bush v. Gore*, 121 S. Ct. 525 (2000).

15. *Baker v. Carr* 369 U.S. 186, 267 (1962) (Frankfurter, J., and Harlan, J., dissenting).

16. Dana Milbank, "New Justice's First Challenge: Clap On or Clap Off?" *Washington Post*, February 1, 2006, A2.

17. Richard Davis, *Decisions and Images: The Supreme Court and the Press* (Englewood Cliffs, NJ: Prentice Hall, 1994); Jerome O'Callaghan and James O. Dukes, "Media Coverage of the Supreme Court's Caseload," *Journalism Quarterly* 69 (Spring 1992): 195–203.

18. Doris A. Graber, *Mass Media & American Politics*, 7th ed. (Washington, DC: CQ Press, 2006), 251–53. See also Charles H. Franklin and Liane C. Kosaki, "Media, Knowledge, and Public Evaluations of the Supreme Court," in *Contemplating Courts*, ed. Lee Epstein (Washington, DC: CQ Press, 1995), 357; Dorothy A. Bowles and Rebekah V. Bromley, "Newsmagazine Coverage of the Supreme Court During the Reagan Administration," *Journalism Quarterly* 69 (Winter 1992): 948–59; Richard Davis, "Lifting the Shroud: News Media Portrayal of the U.S. Supreme Court," *Communications and the Law* 9 (October 1987): 43–58; Michael Solimine, "Newsmagazine Coverage of the Supreme Court," *Journalism Quarterly* 57 (Winter 1980): 661–63.

19. David Ericson, "Newspaper Coverage of the Supreme Court," *Journalism Quarterly* 54 (Autumn 1977): 605–607; Ethan Katsh, "The Supreme Court Beat: How Television Covers the U.S. Supreme Court," *Judicature* 67 (June–July 1983): 6–12; Chester A. Newland, "Press Coverage of the United States Supreme Court," *Western Political Quarterly* 17 (1964): 15–36; Elliot E. Slotnick and Jennifer A. Segal, *Television News and the Supreme Court: All the News That's Fit to Air?* (New York: Cambridge University Press, 1998), 105.

20. Lawrence Baum, *The Supreme Court*, 3rd ed. (Washington, DC: CQ Press, 1989), 206.

21. Gregory Caldiera, "Neither the Purse Nor the Sword: Dynamics of Public Confidence in the U.S. Supreme Court," *American Political Science Review* 80 (December 1986): 1223.

22. Charles H. Franklin, Liane C. Kosaki, and Herbert Kritzer, "The Salience of United States Supreme Court Decisions," paper presented at the annual meeting of the American Political Science Association, Washington DC, September 2–5, 1993.

23. Franklin and Kosaki, "Media, Knowledge, and Public Evaluations of the Supreme Court."

24. Stephen Hess, *The Washington Reporters* (Washington, DC: Brookings, 1981), 18–19, 58–59.

25. Roberto Suro, in Symposium, "The Prime Time Election, from Courtroom to Newsroom: The Media and the Legal Resolution of the 2000 Presidential Election," *Cardozo Studies in Law and Literature* 13 (Spring 2001): 18.

26. Davis, *Decisions and Images*, 67.

27. Charles Bierbauer, in Symposium, "The Prime Time Election, from Courtroom to Newsroom," 9.

28. Graber, *Mass Media & American Politics*, 290.

29. Davis, *Decisions and Images*, 66.

30. Rorie L. Spill and Zoe M. Oxley, "Philosopher Kings or Political Actors? How the Media Portray the Supreme Court," in *Judicial Politics: Readings from Judicature*, 3rd ed., ed. Elliot Slotnick (Washington, DC: CQ Press, 2005), 465.

31. Fred Graham, *Happy Talk: Confessions of a TV Newsman* (New York: Norton, 1990), 237.

32. Spill and Oxley, "Philosopher Kings or Political Actors?" 465, 470 n24; see also Franklin and Kosaki, "Media Knowledge, and Public Evaluations of the Supreme Court," 352.

33. Franklin and Kosaki, "Media Knowledge, and Public Evaluations of the Supreme Court," 366. See also generally Shanto Iyengar and Donald Kinder, *News That Matters: Television and American Opinion* (Chicago: University of Chicago Press, 1987).

34. Spill and Oxley, "Philosopher Kings or Political Actors?" 465–66.

35. Slotnick and Segal, *Television News and the Supreme Court*, 48.

36. Spill and Oxley, "Philosopher Kings or Political Actors?" 466.

37. Toni House, former Public Information Officer for the Court, quoted in Slotnick and Segal, *Television News and the Supreme Court*, 47.

38. David Shaw, *Press Watch* (New York: Macmillan, 1984), 125.

39. Spill and Oxley, "Philosopher Kings or Political Actors?" 470 n25.

40. Davis, *Decisions and Images*, 76.

41. Elder Witt, *Guide to the Supreme Court* (Washington, DC: CQ Press, 1990), 713.

42. Davis, *Decisions and Images*, 73.

43. Slotnick and Segal, *Television News and the Supreme Court*, 80.

44. Carl Stern, quoted in ibid., 54.

45. Linda Greenhouse, quoted in ibid., 29.

46. Carl Stern, quoted in ibid., 42.

47. Davis, *Decisions and Images*, 65.

48. Ibid., 87.

49. Howard Kurtz, "TV's Court Watchers Put an Ear to the Closed Door," *Washington Post*, December 2, 2000, C1.

50. Davis, *Decisions and Images*, 87.

51. Ibid., 86.

52. Ibid.

53. Jan Crawford Greenburg, in Symposium, "The Prime Time Election, from Courtroom to Newsroom," 7.

54. Davis, *Decisions and Images*, 90.

55. Newland, "Press Coverage of the United States Supreme Court," 15–36.

56. Davis, *Decisions and Images*, 94.

57. Slotnick and Segal, *Television News and the Supreme Court*, 44.

58. Carl Stern, quoted in ibid., 67, 73.

59. Davis, *Decisions and Images*, 95; Graber, *Mass Media & American Politics*, 287–89.

60. Stephanie Larson, "How *The New York Times* Covered Discrimination Cases," *Journalism Quarterly* 62 (Winter 1985): 894–96.

61. James Fallows, *Breaking the News: How the Media Undermine American Democracy* (New York: Pantheon, 1996), 278.

62. Graham, *Happy Talk*, 102.

63. David von Drehle, "The Incredible Shrinking Court," *Time*, October 11, 2007, http://www.time.com/time/magazine/article/0,9171,1670489,00.html (accessed October 13, 2007).

64. Davis, *Decisions and Images*, 52–53.

65. Spill and Oxley, "Philosopher Kings or Political Actors?" 467; Davis, *Decisions and Images*, 136; Slotnick and Segal, *Television News and the Supreme Court*, 226–28; and generally O'Callaghan and Dukes, "Media Coverage of the Supreme Court's Caseload."

66. Slotnick and Segal, *Television News and the Supreme Court*, 105.

67. Ibid., 104–105.

68. Ibid., 154.

69. Davis, *Decisions and Images*, 134.

70. Slotnick and Segal, *Television News and the Supreme Court*, 183–84.

71. Ibid., 185.

72. Ibid., 201.

73. Ibid., 197, 199.

74. Ibid., 190.

75. Ibid., 167.

76. Ibid., 167–68.

77. Richard Davis, *Electing Justice: Fixing the Supreme Court Nomination Process* (New York: Oxford University Press, 2005), 97; *The Press and American Politics: The New Mediator*, 3rd ed. (Upper Saddle River, NJ: Prentice Hall, 2001), 143–46.

78. See, as examples, Angie Cannon, "The Supremes' Future: The Next President Will Make Dramatic Changes on the High Court," *U.S. News & World Report*, May 15, 2000, 18; Charles Lane and Amy Goldstein, "At High Court, a Retirement Watch: Rehnquist O'Connor Top List of Possibilities as Speculation on Replacement Grows," *Washington Post*, June 17, 2001, A4; Bob Egelko, "GOP Win Puts Focus on Supreme Court," *San Francisco Chronicle*, November 7, 2002, A20; and David G. Savage, "Bush Ally Is Top Contender for Nomination for Supreme Court," *Los Angeles Times*, December 30, 2002, 1.

79. Davis, *Electing Justice*, 117. As examples, see Stephen Henderson, "Court Unlikely to Make a Hard Right: Even if Bush Calls in 'Chits' to Get Conservative Justices, His Appointments Would Not Necessarily Radically Alter the Law," *Philadelphia Inquirer*, November 7, 2004, A22; Maggie Mulvihill, "Campaign 2000: Opportunity to Reshape High Court Concerns Voters," *Boston Herald*, November 7, 2000, 7; and Stewart

M. Powell and Mark Helm, "Court's Future Rides on Vote," *Albany Times Union*, June 18, 2000, A1.

80. Lawrence K. Altman and Linda Greenhouse, "Suspense Builds and Rumors Fly as Rehnquist Remains Silent on His Health and Plans," *The New York Times*, July 9, 2005, A9.

81. Linda Greenhouse, "Despite Rumors, Rehnquist Has No Plans to Retire Now," *The New York Times*, July 15, 2005, A5.

82. Greenhouse, "Despite Rumors, Rehnquist Has No Plans to Retire Now"; Jan Crawford Greenburg, *Supreme Conflict: The Inside Story of the Struggle for Control of the United States Supreme Court* (New York: Penguin, 2007), 202.

83. Greenhouse, "Despite Rumors, Rehnquist Has No Plans to Retire Now."

84. Suzanne Garment, "The War against Robert Bork," *Commentary* (January 1988): 19; George L. Watson and John A. Stookey, *Shaping America: The Politics of Supreme Court Appointments* (New York: HarperCollins, 1995), 112–17.

85. Janet Hook, "If High Court Vacancy Opens, Activists Are Poised for Battle; With Past Judicial Fights in Mind, Interest Groups Have New Tactics Ready If Rehnquist Retires Soon," *Los Angeles Times*, June 20, 2005, A1; Robin Toner, "After a Brief Shock, Advocates Quickly Mobilize," *The New York Times*, July 2, 2005, A1; Lois Romano and Juliet Eilperin, "Republicans Were Masters in the Race to Paint Alito: Democrats' Portrayal Failed to Sway the Public," *Washington Post*, February 2, 2006, A1.

86. Gail Russell Chaddock, "Court Nominees Will Trigger Rapid Response," *Christian Science Monitor*, July 7, 2007, 2.

87. Richard Lacayo et al., "The Tipping Point," *Time*, July 11, 2005, 22.

88. Toner, "After a Brief Shock, Advocates Quickly Mobilize."

89. Chaddock, "Court Nominees Will Trigger Rapid Response."

90. Davis, *Electing Justice*, 116; John W. Dean, *The Rehnquist Choice: The Untold Story of the Nixon Appointment That Redefined the Supreme Court* (New York: Touchstone, 2001), 179.

91. Davis, *Electing Justice*, 91.

92. Ibid., 117, 131; Dean, *The Rehnquist Choice*, 158, 187.

93. Davis, *Electing Justice*, 112, 116; as an example, see Thomas L. Friedman, "Latest Version of Supreme Court List: Babbitt in Lead, 2 Judges Close Behind," *The New York Times*, June 8, 1993, A20.

94. Davis, *Electing Justice*, 92.

95. Ibid., 93, 146.

96. Ibid., 146–147.

97. Greenburg, *Supreme Conflict*, 99, citing Linda Greenhouse, "A New Contender Is Seen for Court," *The New York Times*, October 29, 1990, A22.

98. Davis, *Electing Justice*, 142–43.

99. Dean, *The Rehnquist Choice*, 23, 158; Edward C. Burks, "Arizona Judge, a Woman, Is High Court Contender," *The New York Times*, July 2, 1981, A17.

100. The Miers nomination was the first in which the blogosphere played a critical role for mobilizing elite opinion. As examples of important judicially oriented blogs and Web sites, see ConfirmThem (http://www.confirmthem.com/); Alliance for Justice (http://www.afj.org/); Bench Memos, *National Review* Online (http://bench

.nationalreview.com/); American Constititution Society (http://www.acsblog.org/); Federalist Society (http://www.fed-soc.org/); Scotusblog (http://www.scotusblog .com/wp/); How Appealing (http://howappealing.law.com/); The Volokh Conspiracy (http://volokh.com/); Balkinization (http://balkin.blogspot.com/); Oyez (http://www .oyez.org/); FindLaw (http://lp.findlaw.com/); and the Supreme Court's own site (http://www.supremecourtus.gov/).

101. Howard Kurtz, "Conservative Pundits Packed a Real Punch," *Washington Post*, October 28, 2005, C1. See also Harold Meyerson, "The Right's Dissed Intellectuals," *Washington Post*, October 5, 2005, A23.

102. Kurtz, "Conservative Pundits Packed a Real Punch."

103. Sheryl Gay Stolberg, "Bush Works to Reassure G.O.P. Over Nominee for Supreme Court," *The New York Times*, October 9, 2005, A1.

104. Kurtz, "Conservative Pundits Packed a Real Punch."

105. Hugh Hewitt, "Why the Right Was Wrong," *The New York Times*, October 28, 2005, A21.

106. Toner, "After a Brief Shock."

107. David D. Kirkpatrick, "In Alito, G.O.P. Reaps Harvest Planted in '82," *The New York Times*, January 30, 2006, A1; E. J. Dionne Jr., "Dodging Debate on Alito" *Washington Post*, December 6, 2005, A29; Editorial, "Ignore the Man Behind That Memo," *The New York Times*, November 16, 2005, A22; Charles Babington, "Alito Distances Himself from 1985 Memos: Senator Says Nominee Drew a Line Between Expressed Views and Potential Rulings," *Washington Post*, December 3, 2005, A1; Edward Whelan, "Spin Paper: The *Washington Post* Acts as a Mouthpiece of the Left's Attack on Alito," *National Review Online*, December 3, 2005, http://www.nationalreview .com/whelan/whelan200512031434.asp (accessed November 1, 2007).

108. David Reinhard, "Alito Nomination: Sleazy Ad 'Borks' Judge's Position on Legality of Warrants," *Portland Oregonian*, December 20, 2005, F5; Sheryl Gay Solberg, "Internet Ads Back Nominee on Search Case," *The New York Times*, December 14, 2005, A31.

109. Stephen Henderson and Howard Mintz, "Alito Opinions Reveal Pattern of Conservatism: A Review of Dozens of Cases Shows a Pattern So Consistent It Appears That Results Are Important to Him and That He Would Be a More Reliably Conservative Justice than O'Connor Has Been," *Philadelphia Inquirer*, December 4, 2005, A6; Amy Goldstein and Sarah Cohen, "Alito, In and Out of the Mainstream: Nominee's Record Defies Stereotyping," *Washington Post*, January 1, 2006, A1.

110. Toner, "After a Brief Shock"; David Boaz, "Ginsburg in the Balance: It Didn't Matter Then—It Shouldn't Now," *Reason Online*, January 19, 2006, http://www .reason.com/news/show/33017.html (accessed November 1, 2007); David D. Kirkpatrick, "Alito Sworn In as Justice After Senate Gives Approval," *The New York Times*, February 1, 2006, A21; Nina Totenberg, *All Things Considered*, NPR, January 24, 2006.

111. Davis, *Electing Justice: Fixing the Supreme Court Nomination Process*, 96–98.

112. Guy Gugliotta, "Senate Tries To Make Best Of Bad Day: Rules Are Trampled, Feathers Are Ruffled," *Washington Post*, October 9, 1991, A6.

113. Davis, *Electing Justice*, 96, citing "Thomas Takes TV's Center Stage," *Broadcasting*, October 21, 1991, 24.

114. Davis, *Electing Justice*, 96, 124, citing CBS/*The New York Times* Survey, October 13, 1991, and Elizabeth Kolbert, "The Thomas Nomination: Most in National Survey Say Judge Is the More Believable," *The New York Times*, October 15, 1991, A1.

115. Davis, *Electing Justice*, 99–100.

116. Ibid., 127–98. See also Marcia Coyle, "Alito's 'Murder Board' a Mix of the Legal Elite," *National Law Journal*, January 30, 2006, http://www.law.com/jsp/article.jsp?id=1138356400498 (accessed November 1, 2007).

117. Davis, *Electing Justice*, 120, quoting interview with Ginsburg by Davis.

118. Ibid., 167, quoting interview with Breyer by Davis.

119. Ibid., 101–102.

120. Dana Milbank, "Bipartisan Agreement: Roberts Was Just Terrific," *Washington Post*, January 10, 2006, A7.

121. Adam Nagourney, Richard W. Stevenson, and Neil A. Lewis, "Glum Democrats Can't See Halting Bush on Courts," *The New York Times*, January 15, 2006, A1; see also Michael McAuliff, "Dems' Alito Defeato: Path Looks Clear After Wife's Tears," *New York Daily News*, January 13, 2006, 8.

122. Davis, *Electing Justice*, 90, 120; Elisabeth Bumiller, "But Enough about You, Judge; Let's Hear What I Have to Say," *The New York Times*, January 11, 2006, A1; Nagourney et al., "Glum Democrats Can't See Halting Bush on Courts."

123. Joe Biden, "Senator Joe Biden Discusses Supreme Court Nominee Samuel Alito," *Today*, NBC, January 12, 2006; Steve Goldstein, "Get Rid of Hearings, Biden Suggests: Nominations Should Go Right to the Full Senate, He Said after Using Up His Questioning Time," *Philadelphia Inquirer*, January 13, 2006, A16; Martha Brant, "Is It Over Yet? The Alito Hearings Have Produced Little of Substance. No Wonder Critics Are Questioning the System," *Newsweek*, January 12, 2006, http://www.newsweek.com/id/47291 (accessed November 1, 2007). See also Dana Milbank, "A Day of Q's and A's—and a Few Z's," *Washington Post*, January 11, 2006, A12; and E. J. Dionne Jr., "A Hearing about Nothing," *Washington Post*, January 13, 2006, A21.

124. Earl Warren, letter to Louis H. Pollack, June 23, 1966, Earl Warren Papers, Box 617. Library of Congress, Washington, DC.

125. Harold H. Burton, memorandum, April 15, 1956, Earl Warren Papers, Box 349. Library of Congress, Washington, DC.

126. Davis, *Decisions and Images*, 112. As an example, see Earl Warren, letter to Edward P. Morgan, June 25, 1966, Earl Warren Papers, Box 617. Library of Congress, Washington, DC; referring to *Miranda v. State of Arizona* 384 U.S. 436 (1966).

127. Graham, *Happy Talk*, 103.

128. Melvin I. Urofsky, ed., *The Douglas Letters: Selections from the Private Papers of Justice William O. Douglas* (Baltimore: Adler & Adler, 1987), 66–67; William O. Douglas, *The Court Years 1939–1975* (New York: Random House, 1980), 197, 206.

129. Bruce A. Murphy, *Fortas* (New York: William Morrow, 1988), 229–30.

130. Baum, *The Supreme Court*, 129.

131. R. W. Apple Jr., "Justices Are People," *The New York Times*, April 10, 1989, A1.

132. H. W. Perry Jr., *Deciding to Decide: Agenda Setting in the United States Supreme Court* (Cambridge, MA: Harvard University Press, 1991), 259–60.

133. Roy B. Flemming and B. Dan Wood, "The Public and the Supreme Court: Individual Justice Responsiveness to American Policy Moods," *American Journal of Political Science* 41 (April 1997): 468–98.

134. David G. Barnum, "The Supreme Court and Public Opinion: Judicial Decision-making in the Post New Deal Period," *Journal of Politics* 46 (1985): 652–66. See also Marshall, *Public Opinion and the Supreme Court*; Richard Funston, "The Supreme Court and Critical Elections," *American Political Science Review* 69 (September 1975): 795–811. For an opposing view, see Jonathon Casper, "The Supreme Court and National Policy Making," *American Political Science Review* 70 (March 1976): 50–63.

135. James A. Stimson, Michael B. MacKuen, and Robert S. Erikson, "Dynamic Representation," *American Political Science Review* 89 (September 1995): 555.

136. Tony Mauro, "Federal Judge Attacks Press for Influencing Judiciary," *Connecticut Law Tribune*, June 22, 1992, 14. It has even been argued that the Court "maintains its legitimacy so long as its . . . opinions coincide with the views of a broad national consensus of elite opinion"—such as the opinions of journalists. Lawrence Silberman, quoted in Robert Novak, "The Dysfunctional Supreme Court," *Chicago Sun-Times*, June 30, 2003, 37.

137. Martin Tolchin, "Press Is Condemned by a Federal Judge for Court Coverage," *The New York Times*, June 15, 1992, A13.

138. Thomas Sowell, "The Greenhouse Effect," *Albany Times Union*, March 8, 1994, A10.

139. David Folkenflik, "Critics Question Reporter's Airing of Personal Views," National Public Radio, September 27, 2006, http://www.npr.org/templates/story/story.php?storyId=6146693 (accessed November 1, 2007).

140. Greenburg, *Supreme Conflict*, 161. See also Stuart Taylor Jr., "Veering Left: The Art of Judicial Evolution," *National Journal* 35 (July 5, 2003): 2154.

141. Dahlia Lithwick, "The Souter Factor," Slate, August 3, 2005, http://www.slate.com/id/2123935/ (accessed November 1, 2007).

142. Davis, *Decisions and Images*, 113.

143. Stuart Taylor, quoted in ibid., 111.

144. Robert Barnes, "A Renewed Call to Televise High Court," *Washington Post*, February 12, 2007, A15.

145. Steve Nevas, NBC News, "This Honoarble Court: Inside the Marble Temple," PBS, May 1988.

146. Lewis Wood, "Press Needs Met by Supreme Court," *The New York Times*, January 5, 1936, 7.

147. "Cameras in the Courtroom," C-SPAN, March 14, 1996.

148. Robert Barnes, "A Renewed Call to Televise High Court," *Washington Post*, February 12, 2007, A15.

149. Quoted in Mitchell Tropin, "What Exactly is the Court Saying?" *Barrister Magazine* 68 (Spring 1984): 14.

150. Rorie Sherman, "The Media and the Law," *National Law Journal*, June 6, 1988, 33.

151. David M. O'Brien, *Storm Center*, 4th ed. (New York: Norton, 1996), 318–19.

152. Ibid., 267.

153. Davis, *Decisions and Images*, 120.

154. Ibid., 106.

155. Ibid., 106–107.

156. Bob Woodward and Scott Armstrong, *The Brethren* (New York: Simon & Schuster, 1979), 417.

157. Davis, *Decisions and Images*, 124.

158. Slotnick and Segal, *Television News and the Supreme Court*, 84.

159. See Mark H. Woolsey, Fred Graham, and James E. Clayton, letter to Earl Warren, October 6, 1965, Earl Warren Papers, Box 666, Library of Congress, Washington, DC; and Earl Warren, memorandum for the clerk, November 16, 1966, Earl Warren Papers, Box 666, Library of Congress, Washington, DC.

160. Quoted in Laurie Asseo, "And Now, the Supreme Court Live?" *San Diego Union-Tribune*, November 26, 2000, G6.

161. Quoted in "TV and the Supreme Court; The Issue: High Court Denies Coverage of Arguments Friday; Our View: Its Objections Treat Americans Like Children," *Denver Rocky Mountain News*, November 28, 2000, A34

162. Dana Milbank, "The Justices Look at Some Shapely . . . Congressional Districts," *Washington Post*, March 2, 2006, A2.

163. Robert Barnes, "A Renewed Call to Televise High Court," *Washington Post*, February 12, 2007, A15; Gina Holland, "Supreme Court Justices Conflicted on Benefits of Courtroom Cameras," Law.com, November 11, 2005, http://www.law.com/jsp/article.jsp?id=1131640496602 (accessed November 1, 2007).

164. See, for examples, "TV and the Supreme Court; The Issue: High Court Denies Coverage of Arguments Friday"; "Court Misses Opportunity," *Milwaukee Journal Sentinel*, November 28, 2000, A14; and "Opening the Hearing to Cameras," *San Francisco Chronicle*, November 29, 2000, A26.

165. Charles Lane, "Full Court Press; Oral Arguments: Few Concessions Online," *Washington Post*, November 6, 2000, A33.

166. Kurtz, "TV's Court Watchers Put an Ear to the Closed Door."

167. Barnes, "A Renewed Call to Televise High Court"; see Oyez (http://www.oyez.org/) and Supreme Court (http://www.supremecourtus.gov/).

168. Adam Liptak, "So, Guy Walks Up to the Bar, and Scalia Says. . . ," *The New York Times*, December 31, 2005, A1.

169. Arlen Specter, "Hidden Justice(s)," *Washington Post*, April 25, 2006, A23.

170. Dahlia Lithwick, "Justice Burps: Shock and Awe Over the Blackmun Papers," Slate, March 5, 2004, http://www.slate.com/id/2096719/ (accessed November 1, 2007).

171. Charles Lane, "Once Again, Scalia's the Talk of the Town: Justice Renders Frank Out-of-Court Opinions on 2000 Presidential Election, 'Sicilian' Gesture," *Washington Post*, April 15, 2006, A2.

172. "Charles Lane, "Scalia' Refusal Sought in Key Detainee Case," *Washington Post*, March 28, 2006, A6; and "The Over-the-Top Justice," *The New York Times*, April 2, 2006, D11.

173. Linda Greenhouse, "Supreme Court to Consider Case on 'Under God' in Pledge to Flag," *The New York Times*, October 15, 2003, A1.

174. Richard Willing, "In Memo, Scalia Stands Ground on Cheney Case," *USA Today*, March 19, 2005, A14; "Scalia Defends Involvement in Cheney Case," *Washington Post*, April 13, 2005, A6.

175. Ashley Harrell and Pete Bowles, "Proud to be Italian!" *Newsday*, October 11, 2005, A14.

176. Adam Liptak, "Scalia Apologizes for Seizure of Recordings," *The New York Times*, April 13, 2006, A13.

177. Davis, *Decisions and Images*, 54.

178. Stuart A. Taylor Jr., "Meese v. Brennan," *New York Times Magazine,* January 6 and 13, 1986, 17–21.

179. Stuart A. Taylor Jr., "Justice Stevens, in Unusual Move, Praises Bork as a Nominee to Court," *The New York Times*, August 1, 1987, A1.

180. *World News Tonight with Peter Jennings*, ABC News, July 26, 1990. See also "Marshall Says He Never Heard of Bush's Nominee," *The New York Times*, July 27, 1990, A12.

181. Neil A. Lewis, "Justice Thomas Raises Issue of Cultural Intimidation," *The New York Times*, February 14, 2001, A28.

182. Robert Barnes, "A Renewed Call to Televise High Court," *Washington Post*, February 12, 2007, A15.

183. As examples, see "The Justice Nobody Knows," *60 Minutes*, CBS News, September 30, 2007; "A Justice's Candid Opinions," *Newsweek*, October 14, 2007, http://www.newsweek.com/id/43358 (accessed November 1, 2007); and "Clarence Thomas: A Silent Justice Speaks Out," *ABC News*, September 30, 2007, http://abcnews.go.com/TheLaw/story?id=3668863 (accessed November 1, 2007).

184. "Most Americans Can't Name Any Supreme Court Justices, Says Findlaw.Com Survey," FindLaw, January 10, 2006, http://company.findlaw.com/pr/2006/011006.supremes.html (accessed November 1, 2007).

185. Tony Mauro, "Justices Fight Back: U.S. Supreme Court Jurists, Expected to Stay Mum in Public, Have Been Piping Up about a Range of Issues Not on the Docket. Despite Tsk Tsks From Some Corners, This Is Actually a Good Thing," *USA Today*, June 20, 2006, 13A.

186. Adam Liptak, "Public Comments by Justices Veer Toward the Political," *The New York Times*, March 19, 2006, 22; Tony Mauro, "O'Connor Fires Back on Judicial Independence," *Legal Times*, Law.com, November 28, 2005, http://www.law.com/jsp/article.jsp?id=1132740311603 (accessed November 1, 2007); Charles Lane, "Ginsburg Faults GOP Critics, Cites a Threat From 'Fringe,'" *Washington Post*, March 17, 2006, A3.

187. Gina Holland, "Justice Ginsburg Concerned by Congressional Plan for Court Watchdog," Associated Press, Law.com, May 4, 2006, http://www.law.com/jsp/article.jsp?id=1146647126259 (accessed November 1, 2007).

188. Charles Lane, "The High Court Looks Abroad; As Congress Backs Bush Foreign Policy, Justices Voice Qualms," *Washington Post*, November 12, 2005, A5; Anne E. Kornblut, "Justice Ginsburg Backs Value of Foreign Law," *The New York Times*, April 2, 2005, A10; and Joan Biskupic, "High Court Justices Hold Rare Public Debate," *USA Today*, January 14, 2005, A3.

189. Charles Lane, "Kennedy's Assault on Editorial Writers," *Washington Post*, April 3, 2006, A17.

190. Dahlia Lithwick, "Courting Attention," *Washington Post*, April 9, 2006, B2 (paragraph break omitted).

191. Dahlia Lithwick, "Courting Attention."

192. See Ken Kollman, *Outside Lobbying: Public Opinion and Interest Group Strategies* (Princeton, NJ: Princeton University Press, 1998).

ASSIGNMENT: GENERATIONAL CHANGE
IN MEDIA CONSUMPTION

Are you different in your media consumption than your parents? What about your grandparents?

Study after study confirms that young people are reading newspapers less and using the Internet more in their search for information about politics. How about your family? Do they follow this trend or are they distinctly different?

For this assignment, you will have to interview at least three members of your family from different generations. If there is no one living in your direct family from a particular generation, perhaps a great-uncle or aunt will be able to substitute. You will first have to construct a very simple survey about media consumption. Some questions you will probably want to ask are

- What is your main source of news about politics?
  Newspapers   Magazines   Radio   Television   Internet
- If you want, you can get more specific, ask about which magazines and types of television programs.

Other questions might involve measuring access and exposure, rather than preference; for instance, your grandmother may not have the Internet or cable television. You should also ask the older generations if their media habits have changed. Did your mother, for example, read the newspaper a lot during young adult years, but now she watches television?

You may also want to ask some basic questions about which party each individual supports, and whether he or she is conservative or liberal.

Based on the answers, write a three-page paper comparing and contrasting how the different generations in your family consume the media. Based on the results found in your family, where do you think media consumption in America is going? (If you are not an American citizen, go ahead and answer the question for your country.)

If you have the time and your professor agrees, you can profile two families, perhaps that of a classmate or friend. In addition to generational change, we would expect that there would be cross-generational influence from parents to children. If your father grew up in a house where newspapers were read every day and your friend's father did not, your father would be more likely to read newspapers—and so would you. Following politics in the media can be thought of as a hobby, like hunting or bowling, that we learn to enjoy from our parents. In communication studies, the media theory of uses and gratifications is very popular. This way of thinking about the media looks at the precise functions media consumption serves for any given consumer. For one family, following politics closely may be a way for family members to feel closer to each other—while in another, following politics closely is not the norm.

4

The Gatekeeping Power of the Media as Illustrated in Its Coverage of Civil Rights and Liberties

Nina Therese Kasniunas

The headline read, "Bush Lets U.S. Spy on Callers without Courts."[1] On December 16, 2005, the *The New York Times* broke the story that the Bush administration had authorized the National Security Agency (NSA) to use wiretaps without a court order. The article revealed the president had signed an executive order in 2002 that enabled the agency to monitor international telephone calls and e-mails sent to Americans. Uncovering the domestic surveillance program of the NSA, this story was the first of many that would dominate the news agenda concerning civil liberties for the year to come.

Suddenly, on September 19, 2007, there appeared a barrage of stories talking about a racial incident that had occurred in the small town of Jena, Louisiana. Almost overnight, out of nowhere, there was suddenly a buzz anywhere you went and it was about the "Jena Six." The horrific story is about six young African American high school students who found themselves charged with attempted murder and conspiracy, all stemming from an incident that had taken place one year earlier. But the buzz did not appear out of nowhere; it came about with the national media outlets finally turning their attention to this story. If you listened closely to the drone, you inevitably heard concerns like, "Why was I not aware this was occurring?"

These are two very different stories with one thing in common: They highlight the gatekeeping power of the media. The media's most insidious power is the ability to control what gets reported and whose voice is heard in that story. As this chapter will reveal, one group gets media access disproportionately more than other interests. Repeated reliance on this group as a source of information on civil liberties over time creates a bias in which only its point of view is known. In the other case, the story reveals the problems with gatekeeping when the media fails to report what is considered to be important news. In both instances the gatekeeping power contributes to a bias within the media that itself factors into societal distrust of the media.

BACKGROUND

The collection of writings in this book grapples with the power of media in the political realm. In the original version of this book, the chapter on civil liberties and the media focused on how the media portrays Supreme Court cases dealing with civil liberties and civil rights.[2] Fully intent on updating that chapter for this second edition, I believed I would be choosing the same tack as the original author. However, a cursory examination of the news coverage of civil liberties reflected the changed political environment since 9/11. Since that day, the media have given very little treatment to Supreme Court cases dealing with civil liberties, because terrorism and the Bush administration's attempts to fight the war on terror were dominating the political agenda.

This is not to say all media stories on civil liberties related to the post-9/11 environment, because this is not the case. The media still covered Supreme Court cases and other issues pertaining to civil liberties, but clearly there was a sea change regarding which stories were making it onto print or into the airwaves. As interesting as this trend is, it was not all too surprising. Life has changed significantly since September 11, 2001, and anyone remotely paying attention to American government acknowledges the salience of the terror issues and others relating to homeland security.

What is striking is another pattern that was discerned in examining media stories about civil liberties—that is, the extensive access given to the American Civil Liberties Union (ACLU) to report on civil liberties issues. The predominance of the ACLU in stories dealing with civil liberties points to their privileged status within the media. This raises issues of the gatekeeping power of the media and biases that develop by relying on the same sources over time.[3] Media power and media politics is the focus of this volume, and the preceding speaks directly to this question.

While delving into the issues of the power of gatekeeping, another story played out in the media relating to the series of racial incidents and injustices occurring in Jena, Louisiana. Here, the national media neglected to report an important story with grave consequences until it could no longer be ignored—almost one year later. This time the subject matter was civil rights. The media coverage of civil liberties—and now civil rights—leads to the same significant power of the media and thus serves as the focus of this article.

MEDIA DISTRUST

Central to the broader power of the media is its ability to select which stories to air or print. The media are a resource used by individuals to gain information about political occurrences and events at home and abroad. In a type of agent-client relationship, the American public hires the media to monitor news events and to report on the stories most relevant to their lives and livelihood. Implicit in this relationship is a trust that the media are fulfilling their end of the bargain in an objective, impartial manner. Journalists and news reporters are expected to be professional, educated, and competent. They are to embody the ideas of fair and balanced reporting and not allow their personal viewpoints or ideologies enter into the mix. Every day, when an individual purchases and reads a newspaper, this trust is acknowledged. This occurs every evening, too, when viewers tune into the network news.

At the same time, there is a cynicism lodged toward the media. While loyal newspaper subscribers and network news viewers trust the reliability of the reports and consume that news on a daily basis, others choose not to do so, in part because they do not trust the media. Whereas 47 percent of Americans trust the media to report the news fully, fairly, and accurately, 52 percent do not.[4] The lack of trust in the media, in a certain sense, appears to reflect a trend in which Americans distrust most institutions: government, big business, and organized interests. Even if the misgivings about the media are part of a larger cultural norm of cynicism, it is affecting media consumption. A survey conducted in 2006 reveals that only 57 percent of Americans watch the network news on television and only 40 percent read a newspaper. This is down from 72 percent and 49 percent, respectively, in 1994.[5] The lack of confidence in the media is affecting consumption, which is why it merits more consideration.

THREE TYPES OF MEDIA BIAS

There are many allegations of media bias that are perhaps the root of this distrust. In 1981 S. Robert Lichter, Stanley Rothman, and Linda S. Lichter published *The Media Elite*,[6] which revealed the results of a survey conducted on the political beliefs and attitudes of journalists employed at the major media outlets. Lending credibility to allegations of media bias, they found journalists were disproportionately liberal and supportive of the Democratic Party when compared to the American public. This groundbreaking book paved the way for many similar studies that followed, finding time and again the Democratic leanings of those covering and reporting the news.[7]

Extending the research beyond partisan identification, political scientists Tim Groseclose and Jeffrey Milyo created a measure of media bias by applying Americans for Democratic Action (ADA) scores of liberality to twenty major media outlets.[8] They found a strong liberal bias within the media, with *CBS Evening News*, *The New York Times*, and the *Los Angeles Times* ranking in the top five most liberal outlets. While the preceding studies on media bias most likely have a narrow readership that excludes most of the American public, this evidence tracks well with public opinion. Rasmussen Report polling indicates that only 25 percent believe the major news networks (ABC, CBS, NBC) report without bias, only 14 percent believe CNN does not have a liberal bias, and only 15 percent say Fox News does not have a conservative bias.[9] Criticisms of a liberal media abound.

Another school of thought argues that the bias in the media today is not slanted toward any political ideology but rather toward the interests of the corporations who own the media. Fairness and Accuracy in Reporting, self-described as a media watchdog group, is a lead proponent of this view. They recognize that the source of the true profits to be made is not the news audience but rather the commercial interests that purchase advertising time; the media therefore caters to those commercial interests. It is those commercial interests that would prefer the delivery of a certain type of news, news that "puts audiences in a passive, non-critical state of mind—making them easier to sell things to."[10] The content of the news, then, is not as critical, and reporters are especially careful not to tread on corporate interests and do not take on difficult or disturbing issues. While both types of bias exist within the media, it is a third type of bias that serves as the focal point of this article.

The third type of bias results from a process in which the media, through their power of gatekeeping, come to rely on a handful of sources. This bias is suggested by Doris Graber in her book *Mass Media and American Politics*.[11] Reporters rely on a select number of sources: government officials or nongovernmental organizational staff. These sources become news feeders who serve to create an efficient system of reporting where, running under tight deadlines, reporters can turn to these individuals and report their stories. Over time a dependency is established and only those interests are reported by the media, creating the third type of bias. This bias emanates from the significant source of media power: the power of gatekeeping.

THE GATEKEEPING POWER OF THE MEDIA

An essential part in reporting accurately, objectively, and in a fair and balanced manner is the news source. Especially for American democracy, it is critically important for the media to rely on a wide variety of sources that represent the full range of interests in society. Just as our government is to stand for the plural interests in society, so too should the media that reports on political affairs. A free and fair media is necessary for any democracy to survive, let alone flourish. Because it is such a critical component, early studies on the media examined the sources used by the media to report the news.

Much of the news stems from official proceedings, press conferences, and press releases. However, examining the news over a twenty-year period, Leon Sigal found that American and foreign government officials accounted for more than 75 percent of those.[12] There is clearly a lack of diversity when one type of source accounts for an overwhelming majority of the news. Sigal's study dates back to the 1950s and 1960s, and because there have been significant changes in the media since then, this issue was reexamined.

The most significant change has been the consolidation of media ownership to a little more than a handful of corporations. Anticipating that this could potentially have the effect of creating larger staffs with more resources within media outlets, a group of scholars wanted to learn whether the greater concentration of media ownership might in fact lead to greater source diversity. Of course these scholars also recognized that the opposite effect—even less source diversity since the same corporations owned all of the media outlets—could also occur. Examining the news in 1979 and 1980, they found the average number of sources for stories written by *The New York Times* and *Washington Post* staff was 7.6.[13] Of the sources, more than half were governmental entities. By the late 1970s, however, 25 percent of the sources were nongovernmental organizations. Even with the marginal shift, the authors conclude that the media rely on routine reporting whereby the same sources of information are used time and again.

Routine reporting that continually uses the same informants creates a point of view that is not reflective of the diversity of American interests. This bias is perhaps more detrimental than political or corporate biases because a news consumer who is cognizant of political or commercial bias can see beyond that and still get the reported news. Bias resulting from source dependence creates a barrier that cannot be overcome. If certain news sources are not recognized, certain types of news stories are never reported and thus no one is aware that they ever even occurred. The only way to overcome this is to unearth the news for oneself or to turn to alternative media sources such as Internet Web sites or blogs.

The power of gatekeeping and the resultant bias is explored here through the media coverage of civil liberties and rights. Civil liberties are those rights given to the American people through the Bill of Rights: rights that may not be impinged upon by the government. Distinct from civil liberties are civil rights—rights given to us to guarantee protection from discrimination based upon characteristics such as race, gender, age, or disability. Media coverage of civil liberties and rights in recent times tells two separate stories of media gatekeeping, both of which serve to warn against the potential harm of the gatekeeping power.

MEDIA COVERAGE OF CIVIL LIBERTIES

As early as ten years ago, most media coverage of civil liberties centered on Supreme Court cases. This is not surprising, given that when there is a dispute between the rights of an individual and governmental action, the adjudicator is the courts. Further, the Supreme Court is a governmental entity that routinely uses press conferences and releases to announce its decisions to the public through reliable news media. *The New York Times*, considered to be a keystone media outlet, has a staff writer who specializes in the Supreme Court and not only reports on the Court's activities but also helps to interpret what the rulings mean.

But American life changed with the 9/11 attacks. Following the tragic events of that day, President George W. Bush took what he considered the necessary steps to ensure the United States' protection against future terrorist attacks. Among the actions taken were passing the Patriot Act, fighting the war on terror, and increasing the power of the security agencies. Whether one agrees with these actions or not, certainly they had a collective impact on media coverage of civil liberties.

To investigate the media coverage of civil liberties, two media outlets were examined by the author over two periods of time. A search was done of all stories printed or aired on ABC News or in *The New York Times* for both 1999 and 2006 in which "civil liberties" was the keyword. *The New York Times* was selected because it is considered a news standard; that is, the stories the *Times* reports are a guidepost for other media outlets. ABC News was selected to serve as a network comparison to the print media. It should also be recognized that network news programs operate under significant time constraints and therefore must be much more selective about the news they choose to report. The time frames chosen enable a comparison of both a period before 9/11 and a year in the period after. But the years chosen also provide a contrast between a Democratic president and a Republican president. The stories (or transcripts) were read to identify the subject of the story being reported as well as the sources relied upon.[14]

The subject of civil liberties stories varied. In 1999 ABC News reported forty-six stories about civil liberties. Of those stories, only two related to terror or domestic surveillance. *The New York Times* in 1999 reported nearly double that number of civil liberties stories (ninety-nine), with five relating to terror or domestic surveillance. None of the stories on ABC News discussed Supreme Court cases, whereas seven in *The New York Times* did. This figure seems low, as the Supreme Court handed down decisions for fourteen cases involving civil liberties in 1999. Curious about the paucity of reporting on these cases, the situation was more thoroughly examined.

First Amendment rights are generally thought of as those freedoms that are fundamental to our understanding of civil liberties.[15] They are the freedoms that are considered essential for a democracy to exist. When most people talk about civil liberties, it is these First Amendment rights they are referencing. This is the case even though all of the amendments contained in the Bill of Rights pertain to civil liberties, including the Fifth through Eighth Amendments that deal with the rights of the accused, and the Fourth Amendment guarantees of privacy that also protect those accused of crime. Knowing this, it is likely that only those cases dealing with First Amendment rights were detected in this study since "civil liberties" was the keyword used in the search. This means that—just like the general public—journalists use the term to reference mostly First Amendment rights. This is not out of line with the data, as only three of the fourteen Supreme Court cases dealt specifically with First Amendment rights.

The subject matter of stories about civil liberties reported by the media does shift in the aftermath of 9/11. The number of stories reported by ABC News is 27. Of those, 13 stories deal with the Bush administration's use of wiretaps, and 6 more relate to terrorism. For *The New York Times*, the number of civil liberties stories is double that in 1999: fully 187 stories. Fifty stories are about wiretaps, 14 are about detainees, 5 are about the Patriot Act, 23 are about terrorism, and another 11 relate to immigration issues stemming from 9/11. *The New York Times* reported on only 4 stories about civil liberties cases decided by the Supreme Court, and ABC News reported on none.

Not much coverage is given to civil liberties cases decided by the Supreme Court. In 2006, twenty-three cases were decided that concerned liberties guaranteed by the Bill of Rights. In this instance, the previous explanation for the sparse reporting of cases also seems to apply. This time around, the Supreme Court heard and decided six cases dealing with First Amendment rights, fifteen dealing with the rights of the accused, and two dealing with abortion.

The subject matter of civil liberties stories certainly shifted, with more reporting of stories about post-9/11 concerns of surveillance, security, detainees, terrorism, and immigration. But this is just one aspect of the study. The more important concern normatively is the sourcing of these stories: Which voices are amplified by the media, to the exclusion of others?

Media reporting of civil liberties does not rely on governmental sources. To the contrary, the media rely overwhelmingly on one source: the American Civil Liberties Union (ACLU). In 1999, 67 percent of the civil liberties stories aired by ABC News stemmed from the ACLU. Similarly, the ACLU served as the source for 89 percent of those reported in *The New York Times*. The ACLU is clearly the source for nearly all news about civil liberties. The reliance on this interest group dropped slightly for *The New York Times* in 2006, to 68 percent. ABC News, in a dramatic shift, used the ACLU as the source in only 22 percent of the stories. This significant decrease is likely due to the fact that ABC News aired many presidential press conferences in which Bush used the term "civil liberties," and these appear in a search of ABC News transcripts.

Even though there is such a dependence on the American Civil Liberties Union, each story is balanced out with an account from a source with an opposing point of view. For example, a story aired in 1999 on ABC News about a policy of a school district requiring choir and band members to submit to drug testing. While the ACLU was leading the charge against the policy as a violation of civil liberties, the story was balanced by also including the point of view of the Tecumseh School Board, which initiated the policy. Viewing just one of these stories in isolation from the other, there seemingly is no bias present and as a result would not be problematic. However, reading story after story about civil liberties, one is continually confronted with the ACLU and its protective stance on individual freedoms. Even when the reporters do as they should—provide an objective account allowing both sides involved in the story to offer their piece—the problem is that the cumulative effect is one in which civil liberties reporting is slanted toward the position of the ACLU.

This clearly illustrates the debilitating effects of relying on a small number of resources. The media hold the power to decide which stories get aired, and, more importantly, whose voices will be heard in those stories. Whereas in the 1950s and 1960s government was predominantly the media's news source, this had changed somewhat by the 1980s. While government sources still accounted for 75 percent of the stories, increasingly the media was turning to nongovernmental organizations. Although this appears to be a positive change, it should be recognized that there is still a tendency to selectively rely upon a small number of groups, even if those groups are not a part of the government. Skeptics gleefully point to this as evidence that this is just another manifestation of the liberality of the media. This might be the case, but it just may be that the ACLU has a monopoly on information relating to civil liberties cases and stories within the nongovernmental sphere. While some groups, such as People for the American Way, are also concerned with the protection of civil liberties, the American Civil Liberties Union is the bedrock organization in this issue area. The reach of the ACLU is broad, and many Americans are familiar with it regardless of their feelings toward it. The ACLU has been able to cultivate its position within the American governmental system by expending significant resources so that it is perceived to be all things relating to civil liberties. It has the resources to hold press conferences and issue press briefings as stories arise. It has money to spend hiring lobbyists who have helped engender an issue niche on civil liberties. It has built similar relationships with the media, so when deadlines loom and stories are needed, press releases put out daily by the ACLU are a good and expedient source of information. This occurs to the detriment of other voices that are not recognized and to the detriment of the American public, which is, by and large, getting only one point of view.

MEDIA COVERAGE OF CIVIL RIGHTS

On college and university campuses across America and echoing in the streets of cities everywhere in the fall of 2006 was the painful story of Mychal Bell and five other young men sitting in jail on charges of attempted murder for beating a white student, leaving him with a concussion. The fight followed a series of events beginning the day a black student asked if he could sit under a tree in the schoolyard that was, by custom, reserved for white students only. The next day—September 1, 2006—three large nooses hung from the tree.

Retelling the story from this point is tricky at best. This is because there are many accounts of what occurred, none of which can rule out other accounts, and amid all these accounts is the absence of an "official" account. This is to say, the national media giants that serve as the standard for smaller media outlets throughout the country were absent. There was no coverage by *The New York Times*, the AP Wire, the *Washington Post*, or any of the news networks. The accounts, given after the fact, do not give a complete detailing of the story to fully understand what occurred. After the fact, *The New York Times* simply reported, "Three nooses quickly appeared on the tree a day after the black student sat under it, and not long afterward, the authorities said a white student had been beaten by six black schoolmates. The white student was treated at a local hospital and released; the black students were charged, not with assault, but with attempted murder."[16] This story appeared in print on September 19, 2007. The first story relating to the Jena incident in *The New York Times* was printed only four days earlier, on September 15, 2007—one full year after the nooses were found hanging from the tree.

From other accounts, not deemed as reputable as *The New York Times*, the story is missing many important details. According to what many deem to be a most unreliable source, the Internet Web site Wikipedia, that next event in this series of incidents was the school's decision to expel the students responsible for hanging the nooses, only to have that decision overruled by the school board—backed by the superintendent. Instead, the students served a variety of punishments, including attending an alternative school for a little over a week, serving detentions, and conducting community service.

According to Wikipedia, after the incident involving the hanging nooses, black students attempted to meet with the school administration to air their concerns, but they were met with indifference. Another series of events then occurred: fights, including those with a gun, and a mysterious arson case involving the school. This all led up to the fight—or assault—on December 4, 2006, in which Justin Barker, a white student, was attacked from behind in his school hallway. Barker was knocked out with a concussion and six black students, including Mychal Bell, were consequently charged with attempted murder and conspiracy. The charges were eventually scaled back to aggravated battery, but Bell, the first of the six to sit trial, was convicted on June 28. Bell's attorney appealed the conviction, charging his client was improperly tried in adult court. The appeals court threw out the charge, along with the conspiracy charge that had previously been cleared. Bell was cleared of all charges on September 14, 2007—yet he remained in jail, because prosecutors wanted to deliberate on whether to try him in a juvenile court and, if so, what crimes he should be charged with.

At this point, the national media were paying attention—not because the news had just hit their radar screens, but because a coalition of civil rights groups that planned to march on Jena, Louisiana, refused to let the media sit silent about what they perceived to be a grave injustice. On Thursday, September 20, 2007, ten thousand civil rights activists descended on Jena to march in protest. This time the national media took notice and covered the story. And since that march, the media have continued to report stories related to the Jena incidents. The question is: Why did it take so long?

Media ownership is highly concentrated in the hands of a few large corporations. This raises the concern of media gatekeeping power: This small number of owners have a stranglehold on what news is reported. Still, within this environment individual news outlets purportedly have not lost editorial control; they have not lost the ability to determine which stories make it to print (or air) and which do not. Many of the smaller media outlets, whose staff consist of journalists and reporters whose credentials pale in comparison to some of the larger outlets, look to the larger news entities for guidance on which stories to carry. *The New York Times* is, by and large, at the top of this list and serves as the media standard. Even larger media outlets, like the network news, look to see what stories are being reported by the *Times* and then follow suit. This serves to exponentially enhance the gatekeeping power of *The New York Times*, which is why it is so problematic when the *Times* does not acknowledge an important story such as the one about the Jena Six.

The New York Times waited until September 15, 2007, to report on the Jena incident. The AP Wire, a feeder of news stories for many other news outlets, first reported on the story of the noose in September 2006 and similarly reported on the convictions in June 2007, which is commendable in comparison to other media. But it also failed to consistently devote attention to the circumstances until mid-September 2007, when the civil rights groups decided to take the matter into their own hands. Searching the media accounts of the Jena Six using LexisNexis reveals that one media outlet took the lead in reporting these events: the *Chicago Tribune*. The *Chicago Tribune* first began reporting the story on May 20, 2007, and continued to consistently cover the story. The reporter of the initial story, Howard Witt, received press releases from a grassroots group called Friends of Justice. This group that had organized specifically to advocate on behalf of the accused young black men[17] and had sent out a number of press releases. Witt was the only national reporter to write the story.

Although the question of why it took the national media so long to finally report the story cannot be laid to rest, another question can: What happens

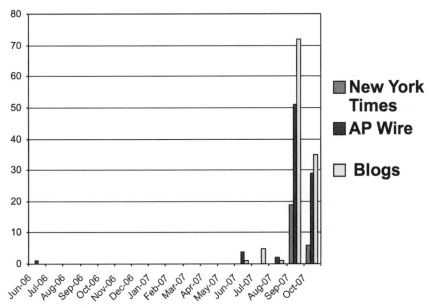

Figure 4.1. Timing of the Media Coverage of the Jena Six.
Source: Author.

when the media, in using its gatekeeping power, fail to report what the public would consider important stories? The answer is: The public turn to alternative media. The story about Jena was communicated widely through the Internet. Student groups, mobilizing on behalf of the Jena Six since 2006, found an audience that continued to disseminate the story on hundreds of blogs and Web sites and through video postings on YouTube. Notice that figure 4.1 includes a tracking of the story as being reported blogs. Each entry is a separate blog that has the word *Jena* in the title.[18] YouTube postings are not included in the chart; that would be incredibly difficult, as 1,376 entries appear with the keyword *Jena 6* and 3,640 entries appear with simply *Jena*.

CONCLUSION

A free and fair media that reports objectively is critical to the functioning of a democracy. Especially in the United States, a nation with a wide range of interests, the media must reflect those interests. Just as it is essential that minority interests are protected by government, their viewpoints must not be ignored by the media. Reporting on the news must be balanced, and all of the significant news must be accounted for.

These two responsibilities of the media have the potential to be corroded because of the media's inordinate power. Because media ownership is so highly concentrated, there is not much competition to ensure that all viewpoints are represented and that all significant news is reported. In essence, this responsibility and the influence the media have over these decisions are considered the power of gatekeeping.

The examination of news coverage of civil rights and liberties presented here suggests the gatekeeping power of the media is a concern. The coverage of civil liberties is highly dependent on one news source: the American Civil Liberties Union. Routine reliance on the ACLU over time has created a bias in reporting of the news in which the ACLU's view is dominant in this issue area. That it took the national media over a year to finally report on the Jena Six incidents showcases the other peril of media gatekeeping. Lack of competition among the media and its power of gatekeeping are problematic and likely have contributed greatly to American distrust of this institution. On a positive note, as the civil rights story of Jena illustrates, the public will find a way to overcome the failures of the media. Americans are increasingly turning to alternative media sources on the Internet, such as blogs and Web sites such as YouTube. Still, most Americans continue to rely on traditional media outlets and therefore we must continue to monitor how it uses its gatekeeping power.

DISCUSSION QUESTIONS

1. Do you agree with the author that the American Civil Liberties Union gets too much media attention? What is your opinion of the ACLU, and how has the media influenced that opinion?
2. Did you first learn about the Jena Six incident from this chapter, or was it a matter you were already familiar with? Do you think the media gave it enough attention or too much?
3. Is there an important civil liberty that you feel is undercovered by the media? For example, many conservatives believe that the media are liberal, and that, in particular, they are pro–gun control. Do you believe that the media does a good job of portraying the anti–gun control position?
4. Can you think of another interest group that dominates media coverage of an issue area the way the ACLU dominates civil rights and liberties?
5. If you were working for a conservative group that opposed the ACLU's issue stances, what steps could you take to get coverage from the mainstream media equal to the coverage given to the ACLU?

SUGGESTIONS FOR FURTHER READING

Robert M. Entman and Andrew Rojecki. *The Black Image in the White Mind: Media and Race in America*. Chicago: University of Chicago Press, 2001.

George E. Marcus, John L. Sullivan, Elizabeth Theiss-Morse, and Sandra Wood. *With Malice toward Some: How People Make Civil Liberties Judgments*. New York: Cambridge University Press, 1995.

Herbert McClosky and Alida Brill. *Dimensions of Tolerance: What Americans Believe about Civil Liberties*. New York: Russell Sage, 1983.

Thomas E. Nelson, Rosalee A. Clawson, and Zoe M. Oxley. "Media Framing of a Civil Liberties Conflict and Its Effect on Tolerance." *American Political Science Review* 91, no. 3 (September 1997): 567–83.

NOTES

1. This article appeared in the December 16, 2005, edition of *The New York Times* and was written by James Risen and Eric Lichtblau.

2. That original chapter was "The Media and Civil Rights and Liberties," authored by Barbara A. Perry.

3. Doris A. Graber. *Mass Media and American Politics*. Washington, DC: CQ Press, 2005.

4. This is according to a Gallup Poll question that asked, "In general, how much trust and confidence do you have in the mass media—such as newspapers, TV and radio—

when it comes to reporting the news fully, accurately and fairly: a great deal, a fair amount, not very much, or none at all?" The question was part of a survey conducted from September 14–16, 2007; N = 1,010 adults nationwide.

5. This information comes from a report by the Pew Research Center for the People and the Press titled "Online Papers Modestly Boost Newspaper Readership: Maturing Internet News Audience Broader than Deep." It can be accessed from the center's Web site, http://people-press.org/reports/display.php3?ReportID=282.

6. S. Robert Lichter, Stanley Rothman, and Linda S. Lichter, *The Media Elite* (Bethesda, MD: Adler & Adler, 1986).

7. The Media Research Center maintains a Web site located at http://www.media research.org that details many of the other studies on the political leanings of the media.

8. Tim Groseclose and Jeffrey Milyo, "A Measure of Media Bias," *Quarterly Journal of Econmics* (November 2005): 1191.

9. These results are reported in a Rasmussen Report titled "Americans See Liberal Media Bias on TV News," published on July 13, 2007. It can be accessed from http://www.rasmussenreports.com/public_content/politics/current_events/general_current_events/media/americans_see_liberal_media_bias_on_tv_news.

10. "Issue Area: Advertiser Influence," Fairness and Accuracy in Reporting, http://www.fair.org/index.php?page=7&issue_area_id=60.

11. Doris Graber, *Mass Media and American Politics* (Washington, DC: CQ Press, 1980).

12. Leon V. Sigal, *Reporters and Officials: The Organization and Politics of Newsmaking* (Lexington, MA: Heath, 1973).

13. Jane Delano Brown et al., "Invisible Power: Newspaper News Sources and the Limits of Diversity," *Journalism Quarterly* 64 (1987): 49.

14. LexisNexis was used to do a news search using the search term *civil liberties*. Then the stories were read to indicate what the story was about and who was being cited as the source for the story.

15. It is believed that this notion is derived from Justice Felix Frankfurter's doctrine of partial incorporation of the Bill of Rights.

16. Richard G. Jones, "In Louisiana a Tree, a Fight and a Question of Justice," *The New York Times*, September 19, 2007.

17. "Jena Six," Wikipedia, http://en.wikipedia.org/wiki/jena_6.

18. LexisNexis Academic now has the search option of tracking blogs. It includes thirty blogs, many of which are not even the types of blogs that were heavily used by students in spreading the word about the Jena Six.

INTERVIEW: JANET TERRY,
LOCAL NEWS WRITER/PRODUCER

Janet Terry is a segment producer, booker, and writer for Channel 9 News (CBS) in Washington, D.C.

Why journalism?

I started out as a French teacher outside of Boston, Massachusetts. And around Watergate I got totally inspired and decided—number one—teaching was not for me, and—number two—journalism was my passion. I took a master's degree and undergraduate at the same time at American University in foreign languages and journalism combined and then I got my first job actually working for my husband, who owned a news service on Capitol Hill, covering for about forty different television stations. And I became a reporter covering the Hill, covering the White House, getting paid next to nothing but it was a great experience.

I was a reporter there for a couple years and I also worked at WETA as a producer and researcher for a now-defunct show about the Hill called *The Lawmakers*. Then my husband knew the meteorologist at Channel 9 at the time, Gordon Barnes—we were at his house one day and happened to ask if there were any jobs at Channel 9 and he said yes, there was a writer's job—and I got the job. It was a weekend job at first; I loved it. We had our own little news team on the weekends, no managers around. And it was terrific, and eventually it became a full-time job. I was a writer; that was my official job title for years. I'm still a writer today, but also a segment producer and booker.

How much politics on your show?

This is Washington, so obviously it is in the blood. Politics is huge for us. We're a local television station but we're also national since many members of Congress watch us, the president watches us, sometimes. We've actually heard that, since we've had administration people on. And we do know that congresspeople watch because people who work there have told us that the television is on Channel 9 during our newscast. We have many members of Congress on our 9:00 A.M. broadcast as guests so they've told us that too.

Biggest interviews?

We've had Sen. Kay Bailey Hutchinson was one guest, we had Marilyn Quayle on when Dan Quayle was vice president, senators, congressmen, Eleanor Holmes Norton. It's an hour show so we think we have room for everything but we do focus on hard news.

Liberal bias in the media?

I've seen the exact opposite. I've been hearing that for so many years. I've been at Channel 9 for about twenty-five years. . . . Eight or nine years ago someone said that, and I said, I can't believe that I'm surrounded by conservatives. The person sitting opposite me, who is now a producer at a different TV station, was beyond conservative, to the right of the right; the writer sitting next to me was a huge gun advocate and now works for a conservative Internet site. Basically, I was surrounded by people from the right, and I kept hearing all this about the left, and I'm like, "Not here!"

As a journalist you try to be objective. Everybody has views; you try to come out somewhere in the middle. For me, the way I do that is that I sometimes lean over to the other side. In fact one time I was accused of being conservative and I thought I must be doing my job because I knew what my own bias was but bent over to the other side to make sure that we were including the other side. We've had guests accuse myself, accuse the anchors of tilting one way or the other. . . but we've had even from some candidates' offices in Virginia . . . some accusations that we had been much tougher on their candidate than the other . . . and we knew that wasn't the case. . . . [W]e knew our own bias and who we might favor and . . . it was a serious accusation and it was completely unfair. . . . [S]omebody hung up on us, they were so angry that we had quote/unquote "asked much tougher questions of their candidate."

As a journalist I bend over backward to make sure the other side is included. It's one of my first rules as a journalist is to make sure that we always get the other side or at least make an effort to get that. From time to time we do get accusations like that, but I always say, "I made every call to every person imaginable to try and get that person." I have to say in D.C. we do have a harder time getting . . . Republican congresspeople to come to our studio . . . the Democrats freely will come to our station . . . but the Republicans always seem to have another engagement.

Infotainment and celebrity news in broadcast journalism?
I think in some cases that's true and I think it's horrible. I'm a journalist, I'll always be a journalist and no matter what anyone tells me to do, if it is something different from that, I will not accept that. I've had this discussion, actually, with some of my fellow journalists. People are also saying the line is being blurred between news and sales, even giving examples of *The New York Times* and the Web site. And they might be changing but I have to say, I am not ready to change. My newscast is going to always be a broadcast that features journalists and we will never go that route.

We've had occasions where the sales department tries to tell you what to do and who you should have on your broadcast. And that's a really difficult issue. But the answer is you cannot let that happen. Every few years they try to encroach and want you to do certain topics or get certain guests.

We actually did have an incident a few years ago when I had been doing a big Washington metropolitan area program called Lighten Up Washington. The idea was to try and end childhood obesity and try to help adults and try to get everyone to band together and it was a big success. We had a big weigh-in at the MCI Center, we had all kinds of doctors helping us out, and then when the program ended, our sales department thought, *Wow, this is something we can take advantage of*, and it was very upsetting to me personally and actually it became news and it was something that the station realized should not be happening, and we did end that part of the program. It's something I won't let happen.

What makes up a typical program?
It's an hour program; we emphasize hard news. So it's always "What is the news of the day?" For instance, today we knew that the peace talks were starting in Annapolis; they start tomorrow. So our first guest was there to talk about both the Middle East peace talks and Pakistan and all the changes that have been happening and the big news of the weekend. . . . [S]ometimes we would get a phone interview if it is breaking news. For instance, the Sean Taylor [murder], the Redskins story. That actually happened right after the broadcast but had it happened during the broadcast I would have been on the phone with Miami police or maybe a Miami television station or radio station or the Redskins and my goal would have been to get that news right then and there and try to get a phone interview right away. . . .

   On Wednesdays . . . we always do a health segment and we try to be timely with every guest that we have so I think we're going to do flu shots, or there was a new autism study so we're going to do one of those this Wednesday. . . . On Thursdays we're doing debates now. I know there was a story about a Texas man, he went and shot some robbers . . . that will be the topic for our debate on Thursday. We often do politics; politics is a big part of it.

Where do story ideas come from?
Sometimes reporters pitch ideas to me; sometimes they pitch guests to me. Sometimes if I see something in the news, as in the Texas shooting, I immediately think I need to get someone on that; who can I get to debate that topic on Thursday, so I'm looking all over. . . . I start my day about 4 in the morning by reading *The New York Times*, as much as I can . . . the *LA Times*, the *Washington Post*, the *Baltimore Sun*, anything newsworthy I can get my hands on at 4 in the morning. . . . [T]hat's definitely one way that we get our news, but it's not the only way that we get our news. We try to do enterprise journalism . . . you might get a tip from somebody. Since I've been in the business for so long, I do have some people who call me . . . I try to rely on some people I've known. I have a certain D.C. activist, who is everywhere, I rely on him to call me and give me ideas . . . but of course I make the phone calls to confirm to make sure that it really happens.

Is it important to beat the competition and get a story first?
This is a question that is being debated in my own station. It always used to be really important to be first. I still think it's important to show that you have the

edge, but if you're first and you're not right I think it's a bad thing—I think it's a terrible thing. You need to be first and also correct.

How important are ratings?
For my particular program, not important, believe it or not. But it's an exception to the rule. The ratings are very important to most broadcasts. Our broadcast, part of the reason for being is to get topnotch guests on our show and we think that we have the D.C. police chief, the Mayor is a regular guest, various congresspeople, governors, these are regular guests, tomorrow I'll have the comptroller of Maryland, Peter Franchot, he's a regular guest. So the credibility is what's most important and also to make news on our broadcast. The ratings for us, on our 9-o'clock broadcast are secondary. For the rest of our station, they're very important.

Biggest mistake in journalism?
The *Exxon Valdez* oil spill. . . . I was a writer at the time and I remember our 4-o'clock broadcast was on the air and we kept seeing little snippets coming over, breaking news from Associated Press, about this big spill that kept getting bigger and bigger, and so we kept telling a certain producer that this sounds like a story, this sounds like a story, and he kept saying, no, no . . . it was very disappointing. We didn't cover it.

Proudest moment?
There was an IBM shooting. Somebody opened fire in Bethesda; the guy took hostages too. The reason I'm really most proud was I got a witness, somebody in the office, somebody who was being held hostage, on the air.

For me, my biggest success is breaking news, jumping on it, trying to get an eyewitness immediately . . . somehow making so many calls that we do find that person. We've had our anchor on, shooting in the background, in Colombia, South America, and we were able to get a phone interview with someone while the shooting was going on.

Ethical qualms in covering tragedies?
Absolutely. Any reporter is asked to go, if someone's lost a loved one, you're asked to go to their door and get their reaction. And it's a really difficult thing. . . . Sometimes a person who's grieving wants to talk. So I think there's a way to do it to see if that person does want to share their thoughts but then you need to also know that if they don't then you have to just leave it alone and not do it.

Advice for young people thinking about a career in broadcast journalism?
Number one, don't shoot for being anchor, you want to be a serious reporter, you want to have credibility, you want to get out in the field, you want to learn how to write and . . . to write well, you also want to learn how to report and report well. You want to be a serious journalist.

Do looks play a role in broadcast news?
Looks do play a role, but I think in Washington I think we're not nearly as focused on that. We actually have anchors who've been around for years, we got
one anchor who's sixty-plus, a woman, which is really unusual in any market
these days. And we've got other anchors who are fifty-five-plus . . . they still
actually look good so yeah it is important but the key thing is your credibility.
In a town like Washington where politics is king, people are looking more for
who do they believe, who can they trust, who has the credibility.

Who are your journalism heroes?
Definitely Edward R. Murrow, Walter Cronkite . . . Ed Bliss, who was Walter
Cronkite chief's newswriter for years, who to me wrote the Bible on broadcast
writing. . . . *Writing For Broadcast News.*

5

Bureaucracy and the Media

Jan Vermeer

Really, what do you and I, as average citizens, know about the federal bureaucracy? The word itself brings shudders to our spines. Bureaucracies, we all seem to know, are rigid, inscrutable, daunting institutions housed in large building with offices and agencies hidden away inside. The people who work there, we automatically think, are uncaring, concerned only with paperwork and job security, unwilling to take risks or do anything differently than before. Hidebound, rule-bound, and devoted to self-preservation: Isn't that the federal bureaucracy?

As is the case with all stereotypes, we have all heard secondhand or third-hand stories of people who just couldn't get bureaucrats to do what's right, to handle their concerns expeditiously and fairly—in short, to care about the people they are supposed to be serving. How many times did your friend's grandmother have to go see the local Social Security Administration office to get her Medicare Part D started? Which potential intern in Washington, D.C., couldn't get a security clearance in time because the paperwork got lost somewhere?

And if we haven't heard those stories, we've seen media coverage of similar incidents: The local retailer who was denied a Small Business Administration loan because the paperwork was simply too cumbersome and it didn't get filled out correctly. The student loan that the local college couldn't process because the bureaucracy[1] hasn't issued the regulations for the upcoming academic year yet—and here it is, late August.

Now, we all know we shouldn't generalize from exceptions, but if all we see and read in the media are incidents of this sort, and those reports seem to be supported by similar stories our friends, relatives, and acquaintances tell, how can we not conclude that bureaucracy is unresponsive, difficult to work with, and set in its ways—just as our preconceptions lead us to think?

Yet that picture of federal agencies and administrations is incomplete. We all know that the mail gets delivered pretty much every day, even on snowy days in the upper Midwest; hot, muggy days in the South; and rainy, miserable days in the Northwest. We all know that the income tax withheld from our paychecks is properly accounted for and kept track of by the Internal Revenue Service (much as we might prefer less money sent their way). We all know the Centers for Disease Control track the outbreaks of infectious illnesses so that they can alert physicians, hospitals, and the general public about them. We all know the National Weather Service issues frequent weather forecasts. But these things go virtually unnoticed—they become part of our subconscious view of the world. We notice them only when they don't work as we expect—when there is no mail delivery because it is Columbus Day, for instance, and we forgot. And so these patterns of effective day-to-day functioning do not interfere with our stereotypical image of the bureaucracy.

The negative images of government agencies do not automatically extend to the transactions we have with them. Charles Goodsell reports that most citizens evaluate the bureaucracies they deal with rather favorably.[2] Not only do people think they were treated well and properly, but generally they were also satisfied with they way employees handled their complaints when problems did arise. In most of their individual day-to-day dealings with bureaucracy, people think well of government agencies. As Brian Cook puts it, "[W]hen government bureaucrats serv[e] people's wants and needs, as is usually the case in close, specific, client-oriented encounters, public administration wins positive public judgments."[3]

Let's face it, though. Most of us have simply too little personal contact with federal agencies to hold an informed opinion of them. There is little the Department of Commerce does, for instance, that affects me directly in a way that I am aware of, and I venture to say that you are similarly unaffected. Most of what the Department of Veterans Affairs does falls into that category, too, despite the fact that I happen to be a veteran. The Department of Labor? The Interstate Commerce Commission? The Federal Services Administration? The Maritime Administration? I can't recall the last time I dealt with any of these (or many other) agencies, and you probably haven't had contact with them either.

Our contact with the federal bureaucracy is generally limited and unnoticed. Much of what we think we know about how those agencies operate comes from our political socialization, where we form basic attitudes and beliefs about government. Ronald Reagan was fond of saying, "Government is not the solution to our problem; government is the problem."[4] The sentiment fits with most Americans' feelings about government and its agencies, and that sentiment is probably more the product of political socialization than it is actual experience with the bureaucracy itself.

MEDIA COVERAGE OF THE BUREAUCRACY

What we know about the executive branch and its work, beyond those preconceptions and stereotypes, tends to come from media coverage. And to understand the media's coverage of the bureaucracy, we need to remind ourselves about some basic elements of how the media function and report news. Rather than repeat what you already know, I want to highlight some elements of the media's procedures and choices that have an exceptional influence on our perceptions of federal agencies and their work. The media both reflect and distort the reality they report, and we have to keep in mind how that happens if we want to understand what the media have to say about bureaucracies.

Newsworthiness

The media report developments reporters and editors think of as newsworthy. Doris Graber and others have examined news choices and deduced from them the criteria journalists use in making the choices that face them daily.[5] After all, newspaper space is limited and the time allotted for a news broadcast is even tighter. The growth of the Internet in making news available to an audience does not suffer as much from these limits, but it is still constrained by another limited resource: the time of reporters themselves. As a result, the media simply cannot report everything that occurs on a given day. News reporting results from a series of selections, and some kinds of events are more likely to wind up in the paper, on the Web, or on a telecast.

If we want to understand media coverage of the bureaucracy, we must recognize, first, that exceptional developments, not typical ones, are much more likely to be covered. You've heard about this principle: "Dog bites man" is not news; "Man bites dog" is. So a federal agency doing what it is supposed to do, quietly, effectively, and routinely, attracts little news coverage. But let it make a mistake, let it miss a pressing need, let it make a noticeable blunder, and the media may show up with their notebooks, their cameras, and their microphones. The Environmental Protection Agency may screen for thirty pollutants in a local river, but if one of its tests gives incorrect results leading to severe illnesses downstream, and you can bet the media will show up searching for who is to blame.

The second kind of occurrence most likely to be reported as news is the kind that involves conflict. Tobacco companies versus the Surgeon General, the Environmental Protection Agency (EPA) versus polluting industries, any regulatory agency versus businesses trying to avoid the costs involved in what they call "needless" or "excessive" regulation—those are the kinds of issues that will reach the news columns. When the Interstate Commerce Commission works behind the scenes to reach accommodations with railroads about the latest proposed change in regulations, the news media pay scant attention. Other events of the day attract larger audiences—presidential pronouncements or congressional debates, for instance. But when actions by the bureaucracy bring conflict to the fore, the media are more likely to be there, probing and questioning.

Conflict by itself is not enough, though. It has to be conflict with wide enough interest to attract public attention from lots of people. And bureaucracies tend to deal with narrow, limited issues. Yes, they deal with broad, important policies, but governmental agencies generally focus their attention on a limited segment of those policies at any one time. And most conflict that arises out of those confined concerns attracts little attention from most media. So it is conflict about major issues that affect—often dramatically—a large portion of the population, or impinge on a concern that the public already cares about, that gets the coverage. The rest simply does not.

The Federal Emergency Management Administration serves as a good example here. It has been widely castigated for its seemingly halfhearted and ineffective response to Hurricane Katrina in 2005. It was the whipping boy for everyone disappointed by the national government's response to the human suffering caused by the storm. And the media kept the agency's responses—and nonresponses—in the public eye. But a decade earlier, FEMA operated effectively in helping the Midwest cope with spring floods. Ironically, overflowing rivers disrupted water supplies for drinking and cooking. FEMA quietly handled the situation as efficiently as one could hope—and it got little attention in the process.[6] Which actions are more typical of FEMA's work? The people of Southern California, who at this writing are dealing with massive dislocations caused by wildfires, hope that FEMA's record in New Orleans with Katrina is the exception and that its performance in the Midwest flooding is more the standard.

But the media produce a product they want to sell. That means they have to serve their market. As a result, news outlets tend to report events with a local connection: Proximity is an important news value. Actions by a governmental agency may affect one locality more than another, and the media in the affected place may report the action, while media in the rest of the nation ignore it. When bureaucratic decisions affect the nation as a whole, few media may bother to report it absent the local tie-in. There is no reason for the *Saginaw News* in Michigan to run a story about a personnel change at the upper levels of the Department of Commerce unless the new or old occupant of the position in question is from Michigan. For the *Washington Post*, however, the federal bureaucracy is local news, and so the *Post* reports news from governmental agencies regularly.

Agency Needs

Newsworthiness is only half the story about media attention to the federal bureaucracy. The other half deals not with media choices and patterns but with agency needs and operations. It deals with how the various offices approach the media. Stephen Hess made the point clearly years ago when he said, "[I]nstitutional differences among government agencies . . . help determine their media strategies. Some agencies, such as those responsible for consumer protection, need attention; others may consider publicity counterproductive."[7] If agencies want to avoid media coverage, it isn't that hard to do. If they seek it, they usually have to work at it. In either case, the practices and needs of the bureaucracy go a long way toward explaining the nature and extent of their news coverage. From the media's perspective, some agencies are hard to cover and some are easy to cover.

What are some of the things bureaucrats can do to make their agencies and their work "easy to cover"? Issuing press releases is one technique. Press releases are written as news stories, ready to run verbatim, although most are summarized in a long story, are rewritten extensively, or serve as a springboard for a reporter's own story—if the release is used at all. Holding press conferences is another technique. You'd better have something to announce at the press conference, or few if any reporters will attend it—or future press conferences. Scheduling interviews with key agency personnel and individual reporters may generate news coverage, too. Here, again, media will want access to a person in a significant role who has something to say.

Who handles these chores and other matters of press relations, such as fielding inquiries for information? Virtually every major agency in Washington employs a public information officer (PIO) charged with these duties. The more an office wants media attention, the more helpful this officer will be. The more the agency relies on media coverage, the more extensive the public information operation will be. PIOs tend to be straightforward in their approach to their tasks. David Paletz puts it this way: PIOs "more often respond to rather than manipulate the press."[8] One such response involves explaining the relatively technical issues an agency may work with in terms that generalist newspersons can report accurately to their audience. The more technical the issues an agency works with, the more helpful the PIO can be.

What leads an agency to seek news coverage? Some basic issues need to be kept in mind. First, if a program requires public cooperation to succeed, the agency must try to stimulate news coverage for its activity. People need to know what they should do before there is any hope of widespread compliance with the policy. When the prescription drug program Medicare Part D was introduced, the Department of Health and Human Services had to get information out to lots of people. Luckily for the agency, this new program was politically important, so the media had an incentive to write and talk about it. But if, for example, there's an increased danger of people eating contaminated raw spinach, the Department of Agriculture has to reach consumers as well as spinach growers and packers and supermarkets.

The easiest way to do this is through the media. Many newspapers, for instance, regularly publish lists of "recalls" of various items, many of which have come about because of some agency's action. In 2007 many toys manufactured in China were recalled. Getting them off the store shelves was relatively easy, but contacting people who may have bought the toys was harder. The agency couldn't simply send each purchaser a letter about the danger, because no one knows exactly who bought the items. Media coverage in such an instance is essential—and even then many people will still not know.

Second, sometimes the agency needs to cultivate public support for its work. Do we really need the Centers for Disease Control? By keeping its work in the public eye, the agency minimizes opposition. Take NASA as a case in point: After the Columbia space shuttle did not return safely from its 2003 trip, the agency was subject to extensive criticism of its procedures. Some people wondered whether the agency had been given too much money and had not used it wisely, or whether the nation even needed NASA. The agency responded over the next several years by making a lot of information available about what it had done and what good had come out of its efforts. NASA worked hard to try to reestablish its standing in the public's eyes.

Other agencies would just as soon be ignored. A classic example would be the National Security Agency (NSA), which needs no publicity. When it comes down to it, that organization spends its time spying (actually, decoding messages sent by foreign governments). The less known about its work, the better it can do its job. The more technical the work of an office, the less it needs—or wants—the attention of the popular press, the media most of us pay attention to.

The overall picture of news coverage of the federal bureaucracy is varied; some agencies can be seen in sharp focus, others in vague outline, and others simply missing from the portrait. To generalize about the media and the executive branch is to overemphasize some bureaus and underemphasize others. But taking media choices and agency needs and efforts into account, we see a more accurate image.

SOURCES OF NEWS COVERAGE OF THE BUREAUCRACY

News that is publicized in newspapers, on the Internet, or on television does not magically appear. Some of it, of course, is due to the efforts of individual journalists, many of whom have been assigned a beat that requires them to report the news occurring there. Big, important agencies, such as the Department of Defense, have permanent reporters assigned to it, but other agencies may be covered by several different reporters. But the news they report is frequently brought to their attention rather than ferreted out by their determined efforts. So the "magic" is how material worth reporting comes to the attention of these journalists.

Clearly, the agencies themselves are frequently the source of news for the media, as we have discussed. The prevalence of PIOs, the plethora of news releases, and even the relatively frequent press conferences officials hold all reflect an organization's need to generate news coverage. A good indication of the extent to which a unit in the federal bureaucracy works to achieve news coverage is the size of their public information efforts. For instance, the *U.S. Government Manual* (a publication that catalogs all the agencies of the national government) provides guidance for journalists:

News Media Inquiries: Specific information about the U.S. Fish and Wildlife Service and its activities is available from the Office of Media Services (phone, 202–208–5634) or the public affairs officer in each of the Service's regional offices.[9]

The availability of Internet access to agency Web sites may make it easier for reporters to cover developments in the bureaucracy.[10] To the extent that agencies update the information on their Web sites, make press releases and ideas about policy changes available there, and respond to e-mail queries from reporters promptly, journalists may be able to report more about the bureaucracy with less effort and in less time than before. Further, reporters can refer readers and viewers to the agencies' Web sites for more information. And on the media's own Web sites, it is a simple matter to provide direct links to documents and other information about agency Web sites.

Other sources for news about the bureaucracy are more varied. Consider interest groups and their activities. Not only are they active in publicizing agency proposals and decisions for their members, they also serve to call public attention to developments for which they can claim some credit or about which they think the public needs to be warned. In the former case, interest groups frequently publish periodicals and newsletters that give them a chance to let their members know what is happening. Some are quite specific in their content; others are more general. For instance, the American Association of Retired Persons (AARP) publishes *Modern Maturity* to let its members know what the national government is doing in regards to issues affecting senior citizens. The American Automobile Association (AAA) issues *Home and Away* in some regions of the nation, and part of that publication is devoted to talking about highway and gasoline policies, including their implementation by relevant national agencies.

Interest groups also consider stimulating news coverage for their concerns in the mass media. Although their efforts in focusing public attention on Congress or on the presidency are best known, they also send out press releases, hold news conferences, or prepare "white papers" that report the results of research on matters the bureaucracy deals with. When a governmental agency publishes a proposed regulation in the *Federal Register*, affected groups sometimes generate whatever news coverage they can to make their voices heard. What newspapers and news broadcasts say about the bureaucracy and its actions is often the result of interest group activity.

News reporting has its effects, too. Daniel Carpenter, for instance, found that print coverage of a disease reduces the time the Food and Drug Administration (FDA) takes to approve a new drug to deal with it (although he did not find such an effect for broadcast news coverage).[11] He suggests that print news mention of a disease has this effect because "FDA personnel are likely concerned not only with what the general public is consuming, but also with what *politicians* and *political elites* are paying attention to."[12] By extension, we could expect that greater media attention to a problem or situation makes it more likely that the bureaucracy will respond—and perhaps respond quickly.

Sometimes news coverage of the bureaucracy comes about from the activities of congressional committees overseeing the agencies. Rarely is this kind of publicity favorable. Something is amiss, in the view of a member of Congress, and if he or she sits on the right committee, a hearing to look into the matter may be scheduled. Especially if the hearing is confrontational and if the matter in question has a wide applicability, reporters on the Hill are likely to cover it. If the issue is controversial enough, the hearing may result in television news coverage as well. In either case, the picture drawn of the bureaucracy is not likely to be a pretty one.

When state and local officials become concerned with a decision or an action by a federal agency, they frequently try to use the media to call public attention to the matter. The effectiveness in terms of changing the bureaucratic decision is likely to be small—that would be more apt to be successful in going through established channels, such as personal contact with the decision makers, getting members of the state's congressional delegation to make calls, and using the lobbying organizations that virtually all states and most large cities belong to. But attracting local media attention to federal policy has an another benefit for state or local officials: It places the official in the public eye battling an uncaring bureaucracy on behalf of the good people the official has been elected to serve. If illegal immigration, for instance, can be depicted as a problem for a locality, when a mayor criticizes the Border Patrol for its inability to stem the flow and the federal bureaucracy as a whole for leaving cities to pay for the services that may be required, the mayor looks good—regardless of the actual contribution the immigrants make to the community.

At other times, agency action—or inaction—may result in coverage. In October 2007 Dr. Walter Friedel sued Home Depot because the store sold him a product that caused him to suffer severe lung damage. It turned out that the Consumer Product Safety Commission (CPSC) had had issued a recall on the sealant Friedel used in a bathroom remodeling project. Sealant sold after the recall was supposed to be safe. According to the CNN news story on the lawsuit, the manufacturer said it "had fixed the problem after the recall. The CPSC allowed [the sealant] back on the market with a new formula."[13] The senior director of *Consumer Reports* said the commission "failed to get an unsafe product off the market." Why? It is "a woefully underfunded, understaffed safety agency."[14] Without the lawsuit, the work of the CPSC would simply not have come to media attention.

SOME EXAMPLES

The media, then, tend to cover the bureaucracy when they perceive conflict, especially when the conflict potentially affects or interests large numbers of people, and when the means of covering it are readily accessible. That explains the news we read and see, but what explains the tone or frame[15] the media adopt in presenting the story? Here media choices tend to reinforce the preconceptions most people hold about bureaucracies in the first place.

Bureaucratic inflexibility in the face of local circumstances is one common criticism, sometimes implicit (in the sense that such inflexibility is more likely than bureaucratic accommodation to result in a news story) and sometimes explicit, especially in newspaper editorials. Especially for media serving local markets, the appropriateness of an agency directive for that locality becomes an important touchstone. For an agency to adapt a policy to every area, for instance, may require more information than it has. So testing for certain pollutants in drinking water makes sense for many locations but is inappropriate in areas where those pollutants rarely occur. Agency personnel, however, may have no way of knowing enough about each of the circumstances in which their regulations are going to be applied to make exceptions, or they may not have the authority to exempt some localities from general requirements.[16] As a consequence, bureaucracies wind up requiring people, businesses, and local governments to take sometimes onerous actions that will have no effect on the problem the program is designed to alleviate. In those circumstances, the media will pounce.

A second common criticism is simply that bureaucratic procedures are so cumbersome that the agency loses sight of the purpose of the policy in question. It seems, to many journalists, that an agency's main goal is to perpetuate itself, primarily by requiring others to respond to its demands before it will act. We call this "red tape," and reporters simply find it hard to believe that an agency does not simply act when the problem is clear: Following standard operating procedures often looks like bureaucrats hiding behind paperwork to avoid action and responsibility.

So what does that look like in the media? As part of a larger study, I examined all the editorials in ten daily newspapers from medium-sized cities across the nation.[17] They ranged from the *Fresno (California) Bee*, which included a lot of editorials about national political affairs, to the *Lansing (Michigan) State Journal*, whose editors rarely addressed those matters. The editors devoted considerable attention to the workings of the federal bureaucracy. As expected, their commentary centered on dissatisfaction with agency decisions or agency actions. Actions by familiar agencies—the Environmental Protection Agency, the Immigration and Naturalization Service, the Forest Service, the Department of Agriculture, and the Department of Defense— bore the brunt of most editorial criticism. Unfamiliar ones, such as the departments of Commerce, Labor, and Transportation, were virtually invisible in these editorials. When agency actions affected local concerns, editors responded. When agency actions offended editorial sensibilities, editors took up their pens. Successes occasionally—but rarely—stimulated editorial commentary. In general, editorial attention was reserved for the bureaucracy's mistakes and missteps, thereby reinforcing the public's image of problems and ineptitude that has plagued governmental agencies for decades.

Local Concerns and Bureaucratic Action

Few concerns are more local in nature than the condition of an area's land and water. The Environmental Protection Agency, charged with maintaining the quality of the environment, ran into some editorial roadblocks in 1994 when its regulations (or proposed regulations) collided head-on with local conditions. The EPA proposed limits for radon in drinking water of around 200 picocuries per liter. In New Mexico, where naturally occurring radon concentrations reach over 2,000 picocuries per liter, meeting the EPA's standards "could cost New Mexico communities hundreds of millions of dollars." Calling it a "ridiculously stringent standard," the *Albuquerque Journal* editors called for "a dose of common sense and proportion" that "the federal government too often lacks."[18] The *Lincoln Journal* similarly objected to an EPA water-monitoring requirement "for hundreds of substances that may or may not be present and may or may not be harmful," suggesting that it be postponed "until [communities] found a foolish Swiss banker or a buried treasure big enough to pay for it."[19]

Land use policy was criticized in a similar manner. The *Albuquerque Journal* published five editorials in five weeks about Interior Department policies in managing federal grasslands, concerned about what effect proposed increases in grazing fees would have on ranchers in New Mexico: "It would be unconscionable for the Democrats in Santa Fe and their fellow Democrat from Arizona [Interior Secretary Bruce Babbitt] by way of Washington to collaborate in rewriting the grazing rules without hearing from and considering . . . the needs of the people who have lived here for generations."[20]

One could readily write an editorial on almost any subject a government office works with from the perspective of local newspapers: "Although the agency has lofty goals in mind that we all appreciate and value, it suffers from major difficulties in reaching the right decision. The right decision for this area means taking into account what makes us different. The agency has not done so, and as a consequence, it will cause more problems than it will solve. If it would rid itself of its bureaucratic blinders, it would recognize that the proper decision is the one we are suggesting here."[21] Whether it is the impact on North Carolina tobacco farmers of the Food and Drug Administration's declaration that nicotine is addictive[22] or the difficulties Nebraska farmers would have if their new pickup trucks had less power in order to meet Department of Transportation fuel economy standards,[23] the argument is the same: The bureaucracy has failed adequately to understand and therefore to address the real problems people face.

National Issues

When the issues in question do not affect any one locality more than another, a different set of criticisms seem to emerge from the media's pens. For the most part, the criticism contrasted agency decisions with basic values. The *Providence Journal* disagreed with the Food and Drug Administration's refusal to require labeling of milk from cows treated with a synthetic growth hormone that increases milk production. Labeling would let people themselves "decide which risks they find acceptable"; otherwise "the government wrongly deprives citizens of this important choice."[24] The *Lincoln Journal* and the *Albany Times Union* sided with the Providence paper. Lincoln editors insisted that if consumers "want the information, they should get the information . . . . Their government should not stand in their way."[25] Albany editors bluntly asked, "[W]hy should consumers trust the government . . . on this matter? It's not as if the government has not counseled us falsely in the past on health matters."[26]

These examples illustrate the extent to which editors view the results of bureaucratic decision making skeptically. Not only does it reach results too frequently inconsistent with basic principles of this society, it is slow and cumbersome. The Federal Aviation Administration's work is a case in point, according to the *Fresno Bee*: "A cumbersome risk benefit analysis process has delayed implementation of safety reforms that have long been regarded as cost effective."[27] In hyperbolic fashion, the *Albuquerque Journal* described the EPA's Superfund caustically: "as fast and effective in restoring the nation's worst toxic waste sites as Superman cleaning up an illegal kryptonite dump."[28]

One would think a slow process would enable agencies to reach results consistent with shared values. According to the editors, that does not happen. When the Commission on Immigration Reform proposed that national identity cards be issued to all legal residents as a way of combating illegal immigration and its accompanying problem—the hiring of undocumented aliens—several newspapers jumped on the idea. Providence readers learned that the proposal "has the potential for the invasion of privacy . . . Big Brother and all that."[29] The *Albany Times Union* compared it to "an internal identity card of the kinds that had become so infamous in Europe at one time."[30]

Surprisingly, relatively few editorials lambasted federal agencies for stereotypical bureaucratic bungling. Several, however, fit the pattern. Lexington, KY editors gave a "thumbs down" to the EPA for granting $500,000 to Utah for "rounding up cattle and fitting them with a device that will measure the amount of methane released when a cow belches."[31] Editors in Raleigh, North Carolina, described the building of a new facility for the National Reconnaissance Office as a "marble-clad $304 million megaboondoggle." Calling it "a child of Cold War . . . secrecy-paranoia," the paper decried the use of federal funds for "exterior marble from Italy and Norway [and] a racquetball court as well as aerobics and locker rooms."[32] When the Internal Revenue Service printed half a million income tax forms in Spanish and only 718 had been used and submitted by May, the *Providence Journal* gave "the IRS credit for at least trying," but it called the targeting of non-English-speaking populations "dubious." People showed "those well-intentioned IRS officials what an ordinary taxpayer could have told them in a minute: In a country where 327 languages are spoken, it makes sense to concentrate on English."[33]

CONCLUSION

We could multiply examples that would reinforce the same conclusions: The media depict the bureaucracy as cumbersome, rule-bound, and out of touch with the real needs of the people. The occasions that result in media coverage are most often those instances where things have gone wrong. The consistent efficient administration of government operations attracts little media attention—it is simply not news. Individual bureaucrats are rarely named in the media, strengthening the perception that governmental officials are faceless, anonymous functionaries, interchangeable and almost robotic in their application of the bureaucracy's rules and regulations.

Not much is likely to change this situation. Agencies that need media attention have few resources to attract it. Agencies that prefer working without the spotlight of media shining on them can expect to continue to work out of the public eye. But with the growth of the Internet as a means for citizens to gather information, people can get information about the resources an agency has available or the services it may provide without relying on journalists to report a news story. One possible upshot is that media may spend even less time on routine agency activities and therefore more time on agency missteps.

DISCUSSION QUESTIONS

1. Do you agree with the author that the media tends to focus on bureaucratic mistakes and scandals rather than bureaucratic successes? Do you also agree that the bureaucracy is in fact better than we are told by the media?
2. Which federal agencies and bureaucracies do you see most often in the media you consume? Are they actually the most important bureaucracies? What makes a bureaucracy worthy of press coverage to you?
3. Find a news story on the web about a bureaucracy. Can you tell from the story what caused the media to cover it initially? Was it a press release or press conference by the bureaucracy? An investigation by the media? What does this tell you about the way the media covers agencies?
4. Which federal bureaucracy do you most frequently interact with? (some ideas: the U.S. Postal Service, student loans, Medicaid, the IRS) How

would you characterize your experience—positive, negative, neutral, mixed? Do you think the depiction of that agency in the media is accurate? Is there any depiction at all?

5. Suppose you were brought in by a specific federal bureaucracy to advise them on how to improve their image in the national media. What sort of steps could they take to convince reporters of their competence and integrity?

SUGGESTIONS FOR FURTHER READING

A. Lee Fritschler and Catherine E. Rudder. *Smoking and Politics: Bureaucracy Centered Policymaking*, 6th ed. Upper Saddle River, NJ: Prentice Hall, 2006.

Charles T. Goodsell. *The Case for Bureaucracy: A Public Administration Polemic*. Chatham, NJ: Chatham House, 1994.

Stephen Hess. *The Government-Press Connection*. Washington, DC: Brookings, 1984.

Kenneth J. Meier and John Bohte. *Politics and the Bureaucracy*. New York: Wadsworth, 2006.

NOTES

1. When I refer to the *bureaucracy* here, I mean all the agencies in the executive branch of the national government below the level of the executive office of the president. The term therefore refers to the cabinet departments and the independent agencies in the rest of the executive branch.

2. Charles T. Goodsell, *The Case for Bureaucracy: A Public Administration Polemic*, 3rd ed. (Chatham, NJ: Chatham House, 1994), esp. chap. 2.

3. Brian J. Cook, *Bureaucracy and Self-Government: Reconsidering the Role of Public Administration in American Politics* (Baltimore, MD: Johns Hopkins University Press, 1996), 3.

4. Ronald Reagan, Inaugural Address, Washington, DC, January 20, 1981.

5. Doris A. Graber, *Mass Media and American Politics*, 7th ed. (Washington, DC: CQ Press, 2006), 99–102.

6. Daniel Franklin, "The FEMA Phoenix," *Washington Monthly* (July/August 1995): 38.

7. Stephen Hess, *The Government/Press Connection* (Washington, DC: Brookings, 1984), 101.

8. David Paletz, *The Media in American Politics: Contents and Consequences* (New York: Longman, 1999), 265.

9. *U.S. Government Manual* (Washington, DC: Government Printing Office).

10. For a discussion of the implications of new technologies on the bureaucracy, see Andrew Chadwick, *Internet Politics: States, Citizens, and New Communication Technologies* (New York: Oxford University Press, 2006), chap. 8.

11. Daniel P. Carpenter, "Groups, the Media, Agency Waiting Costs, and FDA Drug Approval," *American Journal of Political Science* 46 (July 2002): 490–505.

12. Ibid., 501 (emphasis in original).

13. Randi Kaye, "Doctor Says Grout Sealer Caused 'Chemical Pneumonia,'" CNN.com, October 30, 2007, http://www.cnn.com/2007/US/10/30/safety.commission/index.html (accessed October 30, 2007).

14. Ibid.

15. For a general discussion of framing, see Shanto Iyengar and Jennifer A. Mc-Grady, *Media Politics: A Citizen's Guide* (New York: Norton, 2007), 219–23. For a discussion of framing as applied to the movement to limit nuclear armaments, see Robert M. Entman and Andrew Rojecki, "Freezing Out the Public: Elite and Media Framing of the U.S. Anti-Nuclear Movement," *Political Communication* 10 (April–June 1993): 155–73.

16. For an examination of a policy that allows bureaucrats to use their discretion to reflect state differences, see Lael R. Keiser and Joel Soss, "With Good Cause: Bureaucratic Discretion and the Politics of Child Support Enforcement," *American Journal of Political Science* 42, no. 4 (October 1998), 1133–56.

17. Jan P. Vermeer, *The View from the States: National Politics in Local Newspaper Editorials* (Lanham, MD: Rowman and Littlefield, 2002).

18. "Don't Impose Stringent Radon Limits for Water," *Albuquerque (NM) Journal*, July 31, 1994, B2.

19. "Drinking Water: Testy about Testing," *Lincoln (NE) Journal*, October 16, 1994, 12B.

20. "Hear All the Voices, " *Albuquerque (NM) Journal*, January 23, 1994, B2.

21. "Pickups: A Power Trip," *Lincoln (NE) Journal*, 13 September 1994, 8.

22. "Tobacco Woes Are Real," *Raleigh (NC) News & Observer*, August 4, 1994.

23. "Pickups: A Power Trip," *Lincoln (NE) Journal*, September 13, 1994, 8.

24. "This Milk Needs Labeling," *Providence (RI) Journal*, February 6, 1994, D10.

25. "Milk Hormone: Consumers Entitled to Labeling," *Lincoln (NE) Journal*, February 17, 1994, 16.

26. "Tell Us What's in Our Milk," *Albany (NY) Times Union*, February 28, 1994, A-6.

27. "How Safe Is Air Travel?" *Fresno (CA) Bee*, December 22, 1994, B8.

28. "Superfund Super-Snafu," *Albuquerque (NM) Journal*, February 7, 1994, A6.

29. "A National I.D. Card," *Providence (RI) Journal*, August 5, 1994, A12.

30. "We Don't Need National ID," *Albany (NY) Times Union*, November 17, 1994, A-12.

31. "Ups and Downs: Beaver Hits Middle Age; Methane Matters," *Lexington (KY) Herald-Leader*, June 4, 1994, A12.

32. "Here's What They Hate," *Raleigh (NC) News & Observer*, November 14, 1994.

33. "IRS's Bilingual Flop," *Providence (RI) Journal*, September 9, 1994, A12.

ASSIGNMENT: MEDIA EXPOSURE SURVEY

One of the ways political scientists and communications scholars have studied the effect of media is through surveys that ask respondents about their media consumption. Important questions can be answered using this technique. Do readers and viewers perceive bias in the media? Do liberals tend to favor particular media outlets? Do readers of conservative newspapers become more conservative over time? In what ways are those who get their news from the Internet different from other media consumers?

To be statistically valid surveys applicable of the entire nation, these surveys have to be completed by six hundred to one thousand people selected through a randomization procedure. But you can get suggestive results from a very small survey of a target population, such as college students at one university, or even residents of a particular dormitory.

For this assignment, compose a short survey about media usage. Take a look at any of the questions raised in the chapters of this book and imagine ways to ask about them. Here are some examples, but feel free to write your own questions based on your readings in the book and what interests you about media exposure:

ON MEDIA CONSUMPTION

- Which of the following is your major source of news (pick one)?
  Internet   Newspapers   Television news   Magazines   Other (don't know)
- How often do you visit political Web sites or blogs, such as Daily Kos, andrewsullivan.com, FreeRepublic.com, or others?
  Daily   Weekly   From time to time   Never (don't know)
- How closely do you follow national politics?
  Very closely   Somewhat closely   Not that closely   Not at all (don't know)

All of these questions are "closed" in that they have only set options for your respondents. You can also have some open-ended questions:

- Which specific media outlet do you get most of your political news from? _____

- Which political blog, if any, is your favorite? _____

ON BIAS

- Do you have a preference between media outlets that have a political viewpoint and those that do not?
  A. I prefer liberal outlets.
  B. I prefer conservative outlets.

C. I prefer media outlets that try to be objective.
D. I don't have a preference.
E. Don't know.

Which of the following best characterizes your views about bias in the mainstream media such as national newspapers and network news broadcasts?

A. The mainstream media are very liberal.
B. The mainstream media are somewhat liberal.
C. The mainstream media are fairly neutral.
D. The mainstream media are somewhat conservative.
E. The mainstream media are very conservative.
F. Don't know.

DEMOGRAPHICS

It is essential that your survey include some basic demographic information. You can use this to make simple comparisons to the substantive questions about media consumption and bias. Some suggestions: sex, race, religion, ideology, partisan identity, age, or college major. To keep your survey short, you should focus on the demographic questions that will be of interest to you and relate to your topic.

DISTRIBUTING YOUR SURVEY

Most likely, you will use what is called a "convenience" method, as compared to a random sample method, for distributing your survey. This limits the generalizability of your findings. A survey of all the people in a freshman political science class is not necessarily representative even of the student body of your university, because it is likely to be composed of students who are more interested in politics than the average student. Talk to your professor about what would be a good number of surveys to distribute. Sometimes as few as ten can tell you something, but it should be possible to get twenty-five to fifty. On some campuses, a much higher number is feasible, particularly if you are working with other students on a shared project.

ANALYSIS

Once you have collected the completed surveys, you can analyze your data. Professional researchers use advanced statistical techniques, such as regression analysis, to look at surveys. For your project, it should be sufficient to look at simple percentages. If you want to be more sophisticated, you can do subgroup analysis. Suppose that 50 percent of your survey gets its news from the Internet, but only 20 percent of the women in your group do. You will have discovered a very large gender gap in media consumption. You can speculate on why that is the case in your conclusion.

CAUTIONS

Remember that even in professional media surveys, there are limits to what a survey on media use can tell us. People will not always remember accurately what media they use. They may not perceive bias accurately. People are also usually unwilling to admit that bias of any kind affects them. This is why good media studies use multiple methods—surveys, experiments, and content analysis. Still, conducting a survey can be an interesting exercise, and it is a good way to understand the job of media researchers.

6

A Little Knowledge Is a Dangerous Thing

What We Know about the Role of the Media in State Politics

Tari Renner and G. Patrick Lynch

No one would have predicted it in the 1950s, but at the beginning of the twenty-first century, scholarly attention within political science has once again focused on the American states. State governments once again have power over significant public policies. Governors, even those who aren't former professional bodybuilders or actors, are receiving the national spotlight and helping to shape the national agenda on issues such as education and health-care reform. State legislatures are continuing to gain greater stature and resources. It's now common and perfectly acceptable to hear politicians such as President George W. Bush answer questions about public policy by saying, "Let the states decide for themselves."

The current renaissance of interest in state politics has given political scientists an opportunity to explore topics that have heretofore been studied extensively at the national level. For example, scholars have now been able to study the possibility of economic retrospective voting in state elections,[1] fiscal policy differences between Democrats and Republicans in state budgets,[2] and models of Supreme Court decision making in the states.[3]

Despite these recent increases in both state political power and scholarly research on the states, there is one conspicuous gap in our knowledge about state politics. While there has been a virtual mountain of literature written about the impact of both the news media and paid political advertising on national politics, scholars have largely overlooked the role of the media in the states. This oversight exists despite ample evidence that state campaigns are getting much more expensive and media oriented.[4] There may be a good reason for this oversight. The structure of the news media works against quality news coverage of state politics. Many large and medium-sized media markets, for example, cross state lines, and the majority of states have more than one media market within their boundaries. Consequently, the coverage of state politics is not naturally a top priority for most journalists. The exceptions include the few media markets covering the metropolitan areas of state capitals such as Sacramento, California, or Madison, Wisconsin.

There are three broad goals in this chapter: first, to outline what we know about both news coverage of state politics and paid advertising during state political campaigns; second, to discuss some of the difficulties state politicians face in getting fair and adequate coverage of their activities reported to voters; and finally, to examine some future trends that should give governors, state legislators, and other state officials more extensive media attention in the twenty-first century.

WHAT DO WE KNOW ABOUT
THE NEWS MEDIA AND STATE POLITICS?

There has been relatively little research on how the news media influence state politics. Most work in this area has documented how little coverage the press gives to state politics. In the 1970s William Gormley showed that state governments suffered "from a serious visibility problem."[5] He found that newspapers devoted less than 18 percent of their stories to reporting about state and local news to politics. Television was even worse, with less than 14 percent of all state and local news stories on television addressing politics and or government—a policy he called "benign neglect."[6] Other observers, such as Tom Littlewood, did not dispel the notion of an inadequately reported state political system.[7]

This trend in news coverage continued through the end of the twentieth century. Graber referred to news coverage of state politics as "Swiss cheese journalism," arguing that "Swiss cheese has more substance than holes while the reverse is true for the press" in their coverage of state government.[8] Why does state politics get so little attention from the media? Graber attributes the holes in state media coverage to market failure—state political news appeals to only a small portion of the news media's readership or audience—and to shallow media expertise.

In examining the perceived impact of the news media on the daily politics and policymaking of American states, scholars have relied on surveys of state politicians for their impressions of the importance of the press in the politics of their states. While political scientists may be ignoring the role of the press in state politics, politicians—who have long viewed newspapers and the wire services as important players in state politics—certainly are not.[9] Surprisingly, state politicians—particularly politicians from rural districts—have tremendous respect for the importance of the wire services. However, even politicians from urban and suburban districts believe that wire service reporters are typically more experienced and write better stories then their counterparts in television, radio, and newspapers. In this way, the role of the media is different in state politics then it is on the national level.

However, national trends in media coverage are beginning to be felt in state politics. For example, television has begun to make its presence felt in state politics. Between 1995 and 1998, the number of politicians in surveys who rated the political importance of television as "high" had more than tripled.[10] In fact, more than 85 percent of respondents in 1998 rated the political importance of television as either "high" or "medium," placing it just behind the print media in terms of political impact.[11] Respondents were quite critical of the quality of the coverage provided by television news, but they acknowledged that state political television news reached more people with more powerful images than those presented in the print media.

There has been increasing scholarship examining the impact of the media on state campaigns. Gubernatorial races are heavily influenced by paid advertising. Campaign expenditures have increased dramatically over the past thirty years, and those increases are largely the result of larger media budgets.[12] Gubernatorial campaigns now spend millions of dollars, and much of that money goes to television and radio ads and media consultants. In fact, this trend toward paid communication and mass marketing has trickled down to state legislative races. Robert Hogan's[13] work shows that, while voter contact is still very important in state house races, campaign ads are becoming a more important part of state legislative campaign budgets, particularly in larger, more populated states. This trend toward increasing reliance on media-based campaigns and professional consultants in state legislative elections has been fueled by the rise of so-called leadership PACs. These political action committees (PACs) are formed by the top party leaders in state houses and state senates who seek to gain or retain their positions as speaker of the house or state senate president. These leaders form PACs to raise large sums of money to funnel into the few marginal districts that will determine which party has a majority in the legislative body. State leadership PACs often take over the races in the targeted districts by sending in professional "hired guns" to craft the message and communication and manage the campaign operations through Election Day.

Recent survey research of state politicians clearly reflects the dramatic trend toward more media-centered campaigns. In 1998, 97 percent of state politicians surveyed agreed that politicians in statewide campaigns used broadcast television advertising. In addition, more than half of those surveyed said that legislative candidates were using cable television ads in their campaigns. Cable television allows legislative candidates relatively inexpensive and efficient ways to reach voters in their districts.[14]

The recent heightened interest in campaigns and the growing consensus that state politics is becoming more similar to national politics may prompt more research on the media in the future. However, there is virtually no scholarship examining what role the news media play in state politics and government. Graber and Gormley point out a fundamental problem: The news media provide very little coverage to state politics and government. Why is this so? This systematic neglect is explained by the factors affecting news selection. The media likes to focus on conflicts, major crises and disasters, major figures, and Washington politics.[15] Daily coverage of state politics fits none of these categories. Therefore, unless a governor is caught in scandal, state politics won't likely receive national or substantial local coverage. This is particularly true for television, which needs visual images to produce stories. The details of education and social welfare policy debates aren't as visual as earthquakes and presidential press conferences.

WHAT IS NEWS?

Reporters do not arbitrarily select the news. Members of the news media generally form a consensus on the "major" international, national, and local stories of the day. There is a substantial amount of overlap among the various local and national nightly news programs. But how does this consensus on the news form? Why do reporters follow some stories, but not others? What criteria do editors and producers use in choosing the news?

Most reporters have "standard operating procedures" that dictate what they cover, and most editors have similar procedures to help them determine what will become news. Who are the news "gatekeepers" and what do they look for in stories to make them "newsworthy"?

GATEKEEPERS

Every half-hour CNN Headline News promises to take you "Around the World in 30 Minutes." It is doubtful that any television newscast or newspaper could provide complete "around the world" coverage in thirty hours, let alone thirty minutes. News organizations must make decisions about which stories to run from the massive amount of potential news available to them everyday. Part of the potential news comes from unplanned events, but a substantial part of the news is also planned and structured. For example, many private and public organizations hire public relations firms that solicit news coverage by inviting reporters to events. Technology has also made getting information much easier. Therefore, editors and producers have a lot of news to choose from.

Different media face different decisions in choosing their news. For example, structuring a television newscast is fundamentally different than laying out the front page of a newspaper. After commercials, a television newscast has roughly twenty to twenty-two minutes to broadcast news, weather, and sports. In some markets, sports and weather comprise more than 30 percent of the typical newscast.[16] This places a premium on brevity and simplicity. Robert McNeil, former coanchor of the widely respected *McNeil/Lehrer NewsHour* on PBS (now known as the *Jim Lehrer NewsHour*), noted that even the emphasis in broadcast journalism is "to keep everything brief, not to strain the attention of anyone but instead to provide constant stimulation through variety, novelty, action, and movement."[17] In contrast, newspapers can present many more stories, but most readers notice and read only prominently placed stories. The process of making the "news" involves the gathering of information by reporters, the sorting of that information by publishers and producers, and the packaging and presentation of that news in the newspapers we read and newscasts we watch.

Because of their control over the information that makes it onto television newscasts and into newspapers, reporters, editors, and producers can be thought of as "gatekeepers."[18] In short, they hold back a flood of information—*potential news*—and allow a small trickle of it—*news*—to be seen and read by their viewers and readers. Unfortunately, *most* of the traditional standards used by gatekeepers impede coverage of state politics.

Since networks and large newspapers must make money, they put a premium on stories that appeal to readers and viewers. Scholarly work on the content of most news stories has found, not surprisingly, that the news focuses on conflicts, major crises and disasters, major figures, and Washington politics.[19] These biases steer the news media *away* from providing thorough coverage of state government and politics. As states gain more political power from the federal government, this may create significant problems. Here are some of the criteria gatekeepers use to help decide what news to let through the floodgates. As you will see, none of these standards helps promote good coverage of state politics.

VIEWER INTEREST

Readers or viewers must first believe news stories are interesting, important, or relevant to their lives. To this end, journalists often "personalize" stories to make them seem real to the audience. Gary Woodward calls this the "search for expressive 'moments' with emotional intensity."[20] For example, a story about welfare might combine a review of welfare policy and a profile of a welfare family struggling to make ends meet. This gives the story a human face for the audience, who can now link welfare with names and faces.

On the surface this practice would seem to benefit coverage of state government and politics, because state governments handle the administration of most social welfare policies. Therefore, personalizing should increase awareness of the role that state government plays in people's lives. Unfortunately the practice of personalizing often has the opposite effect. The news media are trying to make ratings or sell newspapers, and editors and reporters must present news that's easily digestible to their audiences. Therefore, the human side of the story, which appeals to mass audiences, is often emphasized at the expense of detailed coverage about the policy, which is viewed as dry and dull.

This is especially problematic for television news because of the limited time available for each story. If a personalized story about welfare reform in Wisconsin receives two minutes on a nightly newscast—a fairly long block of time—typically one-half of that coverage will focus on a personalized family. This leaves one minute to summarize welfare reform. Personalizing stories often report on important state political issues on the news, but it can also leave readers misinformed about the details of these state government policies.

THE "NONTECHNICAL BIAS" IN THE NEWS

State politics can be more technical and appear less exciting than national politics. For example, foreign affairs, which plays an important role in national politics, is much sexier than state budgets to journalists. However journalists not only view state politics as less interesting, they are also generally not trained in the nuances of state politics and government. For example, state political news covers a wide range of public policies. Knowledge about education, economic development, social welfare, and road construction are not acquired overnight. It takes experience and savvy to report well on state government. This is especially true when journalists cover stories that are more technical in nature.

Because many journalists lack the background to cover state politics and government, they often have to rely on information from politicians and policy makers when they are writing and producing state political stories. In these instances, politicians and policy makers are making the news. It is the politicians who are dictating the spin of the story because they provide the "facts" necessary for journalists. In 1984 both state and local government officials in

Washington State were pushing hard for Seattle to become the home base for a U.S. Navy task force. To bolster support for the plan, then-governor John Spellman released a study on the economic impact of the proposed base construction. Based on that study, the *Seattle Times* reported that if the task force were based in Seattle, ten thousand jobs would be created in the metropolitan area. However, the *Times* failed to note one detail of the study: Nine thousand of those jobs would be filled by military personal rather than locally unemployed citizens. The reporter lacked the background in economic development to sift through the numbers and accurately present the news.[21]

CRISIS REPORTING

"Crisis" stories are regularly reported on by the news media. As Doris Graber notes, stories involving natural or man-made disasters, violence, or conflicts are much more likely to receive news coverage.[22] Numerous studies of the content of broadcast and print news have consistently found that coverage of violent crimes dominates the news. Of course this is not a new development. The newspapers of the penny press in the mid-1800s began covering crime and scandal stories to increase their readership. More recently, in his study of the most prominent stories on the nightly local news in Indianapolis, Dan Berkowitz found that accidents/disasters and crime were two of the top three topics aired. Political stories were third, but, as we shall see below, in large cities most political stories do not involve state politics.[23]

How does this emphasis on crime and violence impact coverage of state government? Coverage of violent crimes usually involves local law enforcement officials and focuses on local aspects of the crime squeezing out coverage of state politics. International conflicts and wars are the business of the national government. Some disaster coverage may discuss state government officials. How well state government responds to natural disasters—such as hurricanes, floods, and earthquakes—is often measured in the press. This coverage still doesn't provide the public with news of the regular, normal business of state government.

MUCKRAKING/INVESTIGATIVE JOURNALISM

Unlike our previous criteria, muckraking can put state political news in the limelight, but it does not always paint an attractive picture of state government to the public. Muckraking journalism is antagonistic, investigative reporting of political events and figures. The term *muckraking* was first coined by President Theodore Roosevelt, who used it to describe the aggressive, scandal-seeking style of newspaper reporting that was common during the late nineteenth and early twentieth centuries. The best recent example of muckraking would be the Watergate scandal during the Nixon administration.

However, muckraking is not limited to coverage of national politics. State reporters have aggressively pursued investigative stories about state political leaders since the advent of machine politics in the late nineteenth century. The often cozy but corrupt relationship between machine politicians and state legislators received a lot of attention from newspaper reporters anxious to sell papers in highly competitive major-city markets. Muckraking has many appeals for reporters and editors. Scandals get headlines and sell newspapers, but "dry" reports about policies typically do not. Since most journalists have "nontechnical" backgrounds, it is easier for them to write investigative pieces than technical ones.

However, reporters themselves often rightly see this kind of coverage as part of their civic responsibility. And such stories can lead to coverage of state politics. *Chicago Tribune* columnist Eric Zorn, who helped free two men wrongfully prosecuted by the Illinois attorney general, argued that by "holding their feet to the fire"[24] the news media keep politicians on their toes and help to prevent abuses by government officials.

In 1983, ten-year-old Jeanine Nicarico was brutally murdered during a break-in at her family home in DuPage County near Chicago, Illinois. Then DuPage County state's attorney James Ryan prosecuted Rolando Cruz and Alejandro Hernandez for the crimes, despite serious questions about the quality and validity of the evidence and testimony against them. Both men were convicted for the crime and sentenced to die in the Illinois gas chamber.

Then, in 1985, Brian Dugan, a man with a history of sex offenses, confessed to raping and killing Nicarico. Prosecutors—including Ryan—held fast to their contention that Cruz and Hernandez were involved in the crime. At the time of the trial, the *Chicago Sun Times* ran a series of articles questioning the conviction of the two men, but the story soon faded from public view.

Enter *Chicago Tribune* columnist Eric Zorn. In 1994 Zorn began researching the Cruz case. He was unconvinced that Cruz and Hernandez had anything to do with Nicarico's abduction and killing. He began researching the details of the case and writing articles critical of State's Attorney Ryan's handling of the case. At one point Zorn even challenged Ryan to a public radio debate over the facts of the case. Partially as a result of Zorn's digging, both Cruz and Hernandez were granted new trials. During Cruz's trial the judge granted the defense's motion that the charges be dropped, and Hernandez was subsequently freed. The pressure from a writer for the *Chicago Tribune*, which had traditionally been a Republican newspaper, on Ryan, a Republican politician, also led to the appointment of a special prosecutor to examine Ryan's actions during the prosecution of Cruz and Hernandez.

The special prosecutor filed charges against Ryan and several others involved with Cruz's initial conviction. After a trial, which spawned intense national media coverage, the police officers and prosecutors involved in the Cruz case were acquitted by a DuPage County jury in the spring of 1999. However, this scandal continued to haunt Jim Ryan as his political career progressed, and was one reason why he lost the 2002 Illinois gubernatorial election.

"GOTCHA" JOURNALISM

However, overzealous or potentially misleading investigative reporting can be counterproductive. Our surveys found that many state politicians believe journalists are primarily interested in pursuing what one state government official called *"gotcha" journalism*. In contrast to investigative journalism, "gotcha" journalism is when the news media try to catch politicians in embarrassing or compromising positions taken largely out of context. "Gotcha" journalism usually has very little to do with government policies or practices, focusing instead on the lives of politicians outside of the statehouse or governor's mansion.

Consider the case of the annual meeting of the National Conference of State Legislatures (NCSL), which is designed to promote the exchange of new ideas among state representatives and senators from all over the United States. Numerous lectures and seminars give legislators the opportunity to learn about new trends in other states and improve the quality of their work. But in recent years the conference has served as an opportunity for journalists to try to catch legislators in compromising situations—playing golf, lounging by the pool, drinking at bars, or yachting all afternoon—presumably at taxpayer expense. The situation has become so bad that may state legislators refuse to go to these conferences, even if they pay for them with personal funds, because of concerns about adverse press coverage. For example, many didn't attend a subsequent meeting, in San Juan, Puerto Rico, because they didn't want to receive the negative press.[25]

Obviously, abuses of taxpayer dollars should be covered by the press. However, many of these stories ignore important facts and take legislators' actions out of context. In recent years, television stations and newspapers have sent reporters, often undercover with false press credentials, to do nothing more than follow legislators *outside* of the business sessions. In one instance, Seattle's KING-TV sent a camera crew with the sole purpose of photographing people at the hotel pool where the conference was being held. The crew never reported on the vast majority of participants who were diligently working.[26] Such reporting often leaves out important details and can be very misleading. In the case of the NCSL, many state legislators do not make enough money to afford the trip—the average annual pay of a state legislator was $18,500 in 1994—and must pay for it with personal funds.[27] Obviously there are instances when some legislators turn the convention into a junket rather than an opportunity to work, but the media tend to ignore the constructive aspects of the event.

The distinction between investigative reporting and "gotcha" journalism is often blurred and unclear. This is apparent from the dramatic political decline of Illinois governor Rod Blagojevich in 2007. The governor's fall from grace was not the result of a single scandal or problem, but rather a series of actions, missteps, and bad press in the year following his reelection. This example also illustrates a central point that, despite many of the problems discussed above, the media matter in state politics.

In the November election of 2006, Democrat Rod Blagojevich was elected to a second term by a comfortable 368,000 vote margin (more than 10 percentage points) over a three-term state treasurer. Less than a year later, in October 2007, an Illinois Wesleyan University statewide poll found that only 23 percent of Illinois voters approved of the governor's job performance. Blagojevich's disapprovals outnumbered his approvals in every demographic group and category of political orientation (Democrats, Republicans, independents, liberals, moderates, conservatives, blacks, whites, and Hispanics).[28] How could an incumbent governor experience such a steep decline in public support in the absence of a single dramatic event?

Blagojevich hit a wall at the beginning of his second term with the surprise introduction of a business tax increase. This proposal angered people on both sides of the aisle and was soundly defeated by the state legislature. The governor came off as clueless and delusional when he was widely quoted after the vote as saying it was a "good day." The situation deteriorated after Blagojevich consistently and publicly bickered with the Democratic leadership and the Republican minority in the legislature throughout the year over how to solve the state's budgetary crisis. The situation resulted in numerous special sessions, a political stalemate, and no long-term financial solutions. The press articles and editorials throughout this process consistently criticized the governor's performance and lack of responsible leadership.

To make matters worse for the governor, numerous stories appeared like the following by Kurt Erickson of the *Bloomington Pantagraph*:

Plane Frequently Used by Governor Getting a Makeover

One of the airplanes used by Gov. Rod Blagojevich is in line for a $133,900 makeover.

Included in the taxpayer-funded upgrades to the state-owned Beechcraft King Air 350 are new leather seat covers, new carpeting and new leather interior sidewalls with blue and maroon accent stripes.

The contract also calls for a new sheepskin cover for the pilot's seat and various other cosmetic interior and exterior upgrades.

State lawmakers, who watched last week as Blagojevich slashed money for projects and programs in their home districts, questioned the expense.

"Meals on Wheels could feed a lot of people for what it would cost to paint that airplane," said state Rep. John Bradley, D-Marion, whose district lost about $650,000 in funding for social service programs because of Blagojevich's cuts.[29]

Articles such as this one—a combination of investigative reporting and "gotcha" journalism—helped increase the impression among voters that the incumbent was out of touch and incapable of providing the political leadership necessary to resolve the state's fiscal dilemmas. A governor who was re-elected comfortably in 2006 had record-low job approval ratings—and no political capital—by the next fall.

POOR POLL COVERAGE

The news media also do a fairly poor job when it comes to reporting on polls. Instead of reporting the results of the polls and how different types of respondents feel about problems, issues, candidates, and government, the news media only broadly report the results of polls. A recent analysis by the Mason Dixon Polling Organization criticized news organizations that treat polls like football scores. It provided several examples in which news organizations misled readers by not interpreting or understanding polls correctly. For example, undecided voters tend to break toward incumbents in elections, yet news organizations regularly ignore this fact—even if there are a large number of undecided voters and the incumbent holds a lead. As Mason Dixon notes, "[I]n a situation where an incumbent leads 48%–36% a week before an election, it is not uncommon for the challenger to eventually win 51%–49%. Still, the headline or lead story will scream "Governor Jones leads by 12 points in re-election bid."[30]

HOW THE ECONOMICS OF NEWS
IMPACTS STATE POLITICAL COVERAGE

For every source of news in the United States, with the exception of the Corporation for Public Broadcasting, journalism is a business, and businesses must make profits. To understand how the news media work, we must consider how market forces influence news selection. The drive for ratings decreases state political coverage in two ways. First, as we have already discussed, state news is not "sexy" or crisis oriented unless it is personalized or involves "gotcha" stories. Second, as we shall see below, state political news does not have a natural audience.

However, market forces play another role in determining how the news media cover state politics and government. In the past thirty years there has been an amazing change in the ownership patterns of media outlets. Far fewer companies now own newspapers, wire services, and television and radio stations than in the past. Twenty-three companies now control the vast majority of the more than twenty-five thousand print and broadcast outlets in the United States. In short, a few big corporations have come to dominate the media industry. Within a single state, one or two firms may dominate many of the news outlets and thus have effective control over much of the political information available to the public.

Despite the growth of Fox and other cable alternatives, there are still three dominant networks (firms) in the television industry—ABC, CBS, and NBC. There are now fourteen dominant chains (firms) in the newspaper industry. And the demise of the UPI wire service has left AP as the predominant wire outlet in the United States. Furthermore, some of these media corporations own both electronic and print outlets. The growth of Web-based news services may eventually provide individuals a wider variety of news sources, but currently a person's "corporate" news choices are extremely limited.

What are the ramifications of this change on state political news? Let's consider North Carolina. The *Charlotte Observer* is part of the Knight-Ridder newspaper chain, which also publishes the *Miami Herald* and the *Philadelphia Inquirer*. The *Wilmington Star* is owned by the New York Times Company. The state's "paper of record," the *Raleigh News and Observer* was recently bought out by the McClatchy newspaper chain, located in Northern California. Corporate ownership of all three of the state's major newspapers is now located outside of North Carolina. Decisions crucial to those papers—and their coverage of state political news—are now made by individuals without a single tie to the state and almost certainly little knowledge about North Carolina. Obviously editors still retain a lot of authority over what is published in each paper, but "absentee" ownership detracts from the quality of state and local coverage.

Some observers—most notably, Ben Bagdikian—have bemoaned this concentration of media ownership, arguing that corporate interests have begun to influence decisions made about news coverage. While Bagdikian agrees that the days of blatant bias within the media have largely passed, he argues that a subtler type of bias has crept into news coverage: supporting the views of the corporate ownership. As more newspapers and television stations are owned by fewer companies, the local flavor and traditions in news reporting may vanish. Others have argued that the trend toward fewer media companies has created more homogeneous local newspapers and television newscasts. If these concerns are valid, they further limit the quality of state political news.

For national news outlets, business considerations strongly discourage coverage of state politics. News about a particular state typically has limited national appeal. Therefore, state news is unlikely to generate higher ratings for national news broadcasts or increase circulation for national newspapers. For local or even regional news outlets, coverage of state politics is also an expensive proposition with limited financial rewards. It is expensive to maintain a news bureau—or even just one full-time reporter—in the state capital. Instead, many newspapers and television stations report on their own metropolitan areas rather than about state politics.

There are alternative ways for news organizations to cover the state capital. Television stations send remote crews to do live interviews and broadcasts from the state legislature. Camera crews are normally sent to react to breaking news. These types of stories help to fill the gap in state news, but they don't substitute for an experienced, knowledgeable full-time reporter. Full-time reporters have more experience and insight into state politics and break stories themselves.

A second, cheaper alternative is to use either wire services or news services that write stories and then sell them to newspapers and television newscasts. News services keep full-time reporters in state and foreign capitals (and Washington, D.C.) to write stories that are printed in smaller papers throughout the United States. For example, Cox News Service, which is a part of the Cox Newspapers (owners of fifteen newspapers, including the *Atlanta Journal-Constitution*) and Cox Communications (which owns Cox Cable, Cox Digital TV, and Cox Digital Telephone), provides coverage to other papers for a fee. News services allow smaller papers to get state news more cheaply, but, as you can see, these news services are hardly independent—which again raises the question of how absentee owners influence news selection.

METROPOLITAN NEWS

As the demographics of the country have changed, newspapers and television news have also changed. In the last half century, millions of Americans left major cities for the suburbs, and businesses followed. Now, most large U.S. cities have sprawling suburban areas. Newspapers and television news have metropolitan audiences that encompass cities and suburbs, rather than just large cities. In a metropolitan area, readers may not share the same interests; what is important news in the suburbs may be relatively insignificant in central cities, and vice versa.

Newspapers and television stations must maintain their circulation and viewer base while balancing the interests of different audiences. They also must attract advertisers to survive. Advertisers want to reach both urban and suburban audiences. Suburban audiences are particularly important to advertisers because suburban areas now account for a large percentage of the nation's retail sales. However, most major newspapers are based in cities and have substantial economic interests in central city areas.

The news media have tried to deal with these changes in their audiences in three ways. First, journalists still use the central city area as a unifying symbol for the metropolitan area. Despite the explosive growth in suburban populations and declines in urban populations, newspapers still allocate significant space to reporting on city news, because even individuals in suburbs are more likely to identify with the central city than with another suburban area.[31] The news media focus on other "unifying" news: Professional sports are of interest to people living in both the city and suburbs, and sports coverage in newspapers and television broadcasts is growing.

Second, newspapers and television news have paid greater attention to suburban news. Newspapers now engage in *zoning*. Zoning is the practice of printing separate content in the same edition for readers in different parts of the metropolitan area. The change is usually in the advertising, editorial, and news content of the local sections of the paper. Zoning not only lets newspapers reach a broader audience, but it also allows them to compete with suburban newspapers. Most major regional newspapers, such as the *Atlanta Journal-Constitution*, the *Hartford Courant*, and the *Los Angeles Times*, zone their paper every day.[32]

Third, newspapers have added sections that contain nontraditional news. If you were to compare the newspapers of the early twentieth century with those of today, you would find that today's newspapers have many more sections that report on entertainment, art, automobiles, health issues, home repair and decor, and food "news." Newspapers have done this to compete with the diversity of news programming available on television. However, this practice takes resources away from state political news.

While each of these strategies helps the news media gain a broader metropolitan audience, news on state politics and government has been squeezed out by this growing coverage of suburban and nontraditional news. This has led to what Phyliss Kaniss calls "city myopia."[33] Print, television, and radio reporters are far more likely to know city politics, and therefore pursue and write stories that address metropolitan politics. As suburbs continue to grow, suburban news will become more prevalent. Reporters aren't going to travel to the state capital when there are plenty of city/metropolitan news stories right outside their front doors. Also, events in major cities produce the kind of crime and violence stories that help to fulfill the standard I mentioned earlier. Furthermore, most news organizations maintain their offices in central cities. If the state capital is a major media market, that may partially offset the "city myopia," but even in those situations it's likely that state political news will play second fiddle to metropolitan news.

Most urban radio stations also ignore state politics. Radio news receives its highest ratings during "drive time," when commuters are heading to and from work. In order to appeal to the broadest audience possible, radio news coverage focuses on city issues. Regional "news-talk" shows with a political flavor (hoping to tap into the popularity of Rush Limbaugh, among others) deal predominantly with national political issues. When they do address state political issues, radio talk shows don't necessarily provide the most objective coverage available.

THE TWO-NEWSPAPER TOWN

In the early twentieth century, competition among newspapers in large cities was cutthroat. The movie *The Front Page* depicts life in a big-city newspaper office during the 1930s. In the film, competition for stories among the numerous papers in town is so intense that at one point the movie's main character, a seasoned newspaper reporter, actually hides an accused murderer in his office in exchange for an exclusive interview.

In recent years the number of papers in direct competition in the same cities has declined dramatically. Having more news outlets is generally considered to be a good thing; the more choices individuals have for news, the more likely they are to be well informed. Also, competing papers trying to fight for readers will cover news more aggressively and fully than a single newspaper. Federal Communications Commission (FCC) regulations try to promote as much competition as possible in individual media markets, but there are loopholes to these rules, in particular as they relate cross-ownership—ownership of both a radio station and newspaper in the same market, for example. According to Bagdikian, 98 percent of all American cities now have just one daily newspaper. Most of the remaining 2 percent are large cities with extensive metropolitan areas.[34] As noted earlier, newspapers in major cities have refocused their coverage on metropolitan news and deemphasized state news. Since the number of newspapers is also declining, less state news is getting through to readers in cities, suburbs, and small towns alike.

PROSPECTS FOR THE FUTURE

There are some glimmers of change on the horizon. In some recent elections, the news media in several states tried to provide voters with more in-depth information about the candidates. Fearing that issues had been lost among all the attack ads and charges, some news outlets have made an effort to cover how candidates stand on the issues. For example, many major newspapers have begun the practice—already common in federal races—of sending questionnaires to candidates for state executive and legislative offices. The papers then print and report on the candidates' answers prior to the election. Rather then simply endorsing a given candidate, these newspapers try to give their readers tangible information about the candidates' policy positions. Another constructive role increasingly played by the print and electronic media is the sponsorship of public debates between candidates.

Politicians are becoming more sensitive to the press and learning how to work with reporters to improve coverage. All governors, some state agencies, and a growing number of legislatures have established press offices to work with—and even cater to—the news media and its needs. This means that each governor has a press secretary or communications director. Many governors and state legislative leaders use weekly television or radio shows to maintain their public profiles and promote their preferred policies.

State legislators have come to realize the need for news media liaisons who work for either a party caucus or the party leadership. This means legislators try to slant the views of reporters by providing information favorable to what the legislators want. If legislators can influence the news media with press releases and prewritten stories, they can attempt to ensure that stories have a more positive tone in presenting the perspective they feel is most important.

The rise of the Internet has also created many new nontraditional outlets for political news, commentary, and activism. There has been an explosion of new political Web sites and blogs in recent years, many of them exclusively focused upon state politics. As with those at the federal level, however, there is a tremendous variation in the quality, reliability, professionalism, and ideological biases of state blogs and Web sites. Some sites, such as Capitol Fax, run by journalist Rich Miller and covering Illinois state politics, are nonpartisan and well respected, while others represent distinct ideological causes.

CONCLUSION

For a variety of reasons, the American news media are ill equipped to adequately cover state politics and policy. The news media have inherent biases toward either local/metropolitan coverage or national political news. The policies state governments follow require more experience and technical expertise than the typical state political reporter may possess. Furthermore, when the media do turn their attention to state politics, it's often to unearth scandal or pursue "gotcha" journalism—not to provide constructive coverage of state politics. Many of these problems are not likely to improve in the near future. Vertical ownership in the media business may further decrease state political news. As suburbs continue to grow, newspapers may have to zone their papers and further dilute coverage of topics like state government.

Consequently, it is important to ask questions such as these: If voters can't get useful political information about statewide candidates, how will they make responsible choices in elections or hold officials accountable after elections? How can politicians try to rally public support for political issues without media coverage? These are significant challenges for the new generation of state politicians.

It is clear, however, that despite many of the impediments to effective and systematic coverage of state politics, that the media matter and voters' attitudes are affected by the information reported. The political decline of Illinois governor Rod Blagojevich in 2007 is a dramatic illustration of the impact of media coverage. The recent rise of many alternative forms of political communication on the Internet is likely to increase citizens' knowledge of state political affairs, albeit in an imperfect and uneven fashion. Despite increased visibility, Graber's description of state media coverage as "Swiss cheese journalism" is likely to be as accurate in the foreseeable future as it was a generation ago.

DISCUSSION QUESTIONS

1. Do you find it easier to follow state politics or national politics in the media you consume? Are the authors right when they claim that the media do a poor job of covering state politics, in your experience?

2. Do you live in a media market that contains mostly citizens from one state? Does it also contain the state capital? Why might the answers to these questions affect how much news you get about state politics?

3. Do you think state politics deserves more coverage than it receives? Or should the media continue to focus on national politics? After all, the average citizen has only so much time for politics. Are state political issues important enough to merit more coverage?

4. If it is true that state politics gets less coverage than national politics and/or less coverage than it deserves, what are the implications for the potential for scandal and abuse to go unreported? If the press isn't covering much about state politics, does this mean that the press's watchdog function is not being performed? Or is the press always ready to jump in and cover a good scandal?

5. What are the three biggest issues in your state, in terms of things that are decided at the state level? How do your state media do in covering these three issues?
6. If you had to find out about a current state political issue, would you go to television news, a political blog focusing on state matters, or a newspaper (online or otherwise)? Which media do you think do the best job of covering state politics?

SUGGESTIONS FOR FURTHER READING

Phyllis Kaniss. *Making Local News*. Chicago: University of Chicago Press, 1991.
David B. Magleby, David M. O'Brien, Paul C. Light, Jack W. Peltason, and Tom E. Cronin. *State and Local Politics: Government by the People*. 13th ed. Upper Saddle River, NJ: Prentice Hall, 2007.
Tom Rosenstiel, Marion Just, Todd Belt, Atiba Pertilla, Walter Dean, and Dante Chinni. *We Interrupt This Newscast: How to Improve Local News and Win Ratings, Too*. New York: Cambridge University Press, 2007.
Rachel Smolkin. "Star Power: Arnold Schwarzenegger's Celebrity Status Attracted Massive Media Attention to California's Recall Election."*American Journalism Review*, December 1, 2003.

NOTES

1. Lonna Rae Atkeson and Randall W. Partin, "Economic and Referendum Voting: A Comparison of Gubernatorial and Senatorial Elections," *American Political Science Review* 89 (1995): 99–107.

2. Robert C. Lowry, James E. Alt, and Karen E. Ferree, "Fiscal Policy Outcomes and Electoral Accountability in American States," *American Political Science Review* 92 (1998): 759–74.

3. Gregory N. Flemming, David B. Holian, and Susan Gluck Mezey, "An Integrated Model of Privacy Decision Making in State Supreme Courts," *American Politics Quarterly* 26 (1998): 35–58.

4. See, for example, Thad Beyle. "Governors: The Middlemen and Women in Our Political System," in *Politics of the American States*, ed. Virginia Gray and Herbert Jacob (Washington, DC: Congressional Quarterly Press, 1996).

5. William Gormley, "Coverage of State Government in the Mass Media," *State Government* 52 (1979): 46–51.

6. Ibid., 46.

7. Tom Littlewood, "What's Wrong with Statehouse Coverage?" *Columbia Journalism Review* 10 (1972): 39–45.

8. Doris Graber, "Swiss cheese journalism." *State Government News* 36 (1993): 19.

9. Thad Beyle and G. Patrick Lynch, "Measuring State Officials' Views of the Media," *Comparative State Politics* 14, no. 3 (June 1993): 32–41.

10. G. Patrick Lynch, "The Media and State Politics: The View from Political Elites," presented at the annual meeting of the Southern Political Science Association, Savannah, GA, November 1999.

11. Ibid.

12. Beyle, "Governors."

13. Robert E. Hogan, "Voter Contact Techniques in State Legislative Campaigns: The Prevalence of Mass Media Advertising," *Legislative Studies Quarterly* 4 (1997): 551–71.

14. Lynch, "The Media and State Politics," 16.

15. Herbert Gans, *Deciding What's News* (New York: Vintage, 1969); W. Lance Bennett, *The Politics of Illusion*, 2nd ed. (New York: Longman, 1988).

16. Stephen Hess, *Live from Capitol Hill!* (Washington, DC: Brookings, 1991), 49.

17. Gary C. Woodward, *Perspectives on American Political Media* (Boston: Allyn and Bacon, 1997), 44–45.

18. There is an ocean of research on this topic. For a good review from the field of journalism see Dan Berkowitz, "Refining the Gatekeeping Metaphor for Local Television News," *Journal of Broadcasting and Electronic Media* 34 (1990): 55–68.

19. The literature here is vast. The classics include Gans, *Deciding What's News*, and Bennett, *The Politics of Illusion*.

20. Woodward, *Perspectives on American Political Media*, 78.

21. Phyllis Kaniss, *Making Local News* (Chicago: University of Chicago Press, 1991), 92.

22. Doris Graber, *Mass Media and American Politics* (Washington, DC: Congressional Quarterly Press, 1993), 118.

23. Berkowitz, "Refining the Gatekeeping Metaphor," 60.

24. Eric Zorn, phone interview with author, July 1995.

25. Alan Rosenthal, "Ethics: Political Protocol," *State Government News* 39, no. 3 (1996): 35.

26. Peter Brown, "Gotcha Journalism: Journalists Efforts to Expose Politicians," *State Legislatures* 20, no. 5 (May 1994): 22.

27. Ibid.

28. Illinois statewide survey conducted through the Survey Research Center of Illinois Wesleyan University, October 15–18, 2007. The systematic geographically stratified sample size was 390 for a +/- 5 percent confidence interval.

29. Story by Kurt Erickson appeared in the *Bloomington Pantagraph,* August 31, 2007.

30. Mason-Dixon Polling Organization, "Understanding 'Undecided' Voters," http://www.mason-dixon.com/mason_line.htm (accessed July 7, 1999).

31. Kaniss, *Making Local News*, 64–70.

32. Ibid., 60.

33. Ibid., 74.

34. Ben H. Bagdikian, *The Media Monopoly* (Boston: Beacon Press, 1983), 8–9.

INTERVIEW: BRENNA HOLMES,
ONLINE POLITICAL ACTIVIST/CONSULTANT

Brenna Holmes is a project manager for 720 Strategies, an award-winning grassroots advocacy and political persuasion firm, specializing in integrated communications campaigns—online, on video, and in print. Headquartered in Washington, D.C., 720 Strategies specializes in making the Internet work in new and innovative ways for its clients.

Holmes holds two master's degrees from Syracuse University, in public relations at the S. I. Newhouse School of Public Communications and in public administration at the Maxwell School.

First involvement with online campaigns?
I first got involved through an organization called Free the Grapes! I was working in the tourism industry in Napa, teaching wine and food pairing at a luxury inn, and one of the wineries that came to pour told me and the guests about the direct-shipping issue and how we could make a difference by e-mailing our elected officials. I did, and joined the organization and began organizing e-mail campaigns through the inn's guests.

I was a pretty early adopter with the Internet; I was all over AOL chat rooms back when you had to pay by the hour. In the 2000 election I volunteered with a Rock the Vote local Northern California chapter and helped organize voter registration drives at the Napa Valley College campus through forum posts and it was amazing. If all the students that signed up online had actually voted that year, we'd be in a very different place now.

Any concerns about the Internet's effects on politics?
I feel that the Internet is the last bastion of free speech, and while I personally would prefer that all postings/comments, etc., had to be attributed, it's simply impossible and so I'd rather deal with the fringe elements that are enticed by anonymity than censor the speech. Electronic/Internet voting is the only thing that worries me about politics on the Internet, but we are a ways away from that.

Typical day at your job?
What I love about my job is [that] it's almost never typical, but there are a few norms. Every morning we gather at 9:30 for a staff "fire" meeting. This is supposed to focus solely on the emergency things we need from others, but almost always runs amok with hilarious tangents. When we finish the meeting, it's in to check and reply to emails and depending on the phases of my projects I will check in with our designers, create a new project timeline and get it internally vetted by my project team, have a conference call or two with clients, and quite possibly do some design work myself. I'm typically able to leave the office by 6:00 P.M. though I don't take a full lunch break and usually just eat at my desk while working.

Difference between corporate advocacy and political advocacy online?
While there are similarities—it's all advocacy—I believe the main difference stems from intentions. Politics isn't about making that next dollar; it's about gaining the trust, support, and commitment of the next voter. The same tools will be used (if the corporate advertisers are savvy) and it's not just banners and paid placements, it's about building a network, a community and having active dialogues with one's audience(s).

Where is the Internet going?
It will only increase in its impact; the number of people on the Internet is increasing and so are the ways that they use it. More and more sites are increasing their "stickiness" and finding ways to further engage users.

Do you think that some young people are going to be in trouble when they decide to run for office in a few years because of personal things they have put on their MySpace or Facebook pages?
It is very likely. Though my hope is that the personal nature of these sites will force Americans to take politicians down from the absurd pedestals they've been placed on recently.

Worst mistake a political campaign can make with the Internet?
I think there are two and, oddly enough, they are almost the flip sides of each other. First, not being willing to lose some message control, and second allowing (and thus silently endorsing) yellow journalism.

Advice for young people interested in online politics?
Do it. Volunteer, blog, and read everything you can on the subject. If you're able, go to the seminars that Facebook and the like hold; they are exceedingly useful and give you a chance to meet others in the field. You will be considered the experts in the workforce in this field, so do everything you can to prepare yourself for this title.

7

Political Parties and the Media

C. Danielle Vinson

In the fall of 2007, President George W. Bush and the Democratic-led Congress were in a standoff over legislation to reauthorize and expand the State Children's Health Insurance Program (SCHIP). Bush had vetoed the legislation, and congressional Democrats mobilized to override the veto and, in the words of Speaker Nancy Pelosi (D-CA), "galvanize the support of the American people behind this legislation."[1] The public relations effort included press conferences featuring Democratic leaders and some Republicans who supported the legislation as well as a family who had benefited from SCHIP. One of the children from that family also participated in the Democratic response to the president's weekly radio address. The Democratic Congressional Campaign Committee (DCCC) sent out press releases to the districts of vulnerable Republicans who voted against the bill to make sure local media were aware of the vote, and followed up with paid ads to pressure Republicans to override the veto. Although Congress failed to overturn the president's veto, the public relations efforts are noteworthy as a typical example of the central role that media and communications play in the political parties today.

It was not so long ago that scholars and pundits declared the political parties in decline, if not yet dead, and pointed to the media as a major contributor to their demise. Increasing numbers of split-ticket voters and people who identify themselves as political independents, a tendency toward divided government, and some political candidates' reluctance to attach themselves too closely to a party label suggested that parties were less relevant to the political system than they once had been. Contributing at least in part to this apparent decline in party power were the media, because of their growing role as an intermediary between public officials and citizens.

At their high point, parties connected citizens to candidates and government officials. Parties helped to recruit candidates, and party leaders often controlled nominations. Voters' strong attachments to a party frequently determined how they voted. In the 1970s, as voters gained more of a voice in the nominating process through primaries, candidates were forced to appeal directly to the public rather than rely on the party. The media became an important tool for communicating with voters.

Simultaneously, reporters found covering candidates rather than parties more to their liking because it suited the evolving journalistic formats that emphasized entertainment as much as information. Candidate-centered coverage allowed the media to focus on real people rather than abstract labels or faceless parties, personalities rather than intangible ideas and dry issue positions. The combination of primaries and media coverage helped to create more candidate-centered campaigns. And presumably, candidates who won election with little help from the party felt less tied to the party platform once they were in office. Furthermore, they continued to rely on the media and campaign tactics to enact their policies rather than working through the parties in government. Thus, the media arguably contributed to the decline of the parties.

Today, parties have reclaimed a more central role in American politics as scholars and pundits debate increasing partisan and ideological polarization inside government. As the Democratic Party's public relations campaign around the SCHIP vote illustrates, political parties have found new ways to play an important role in the political system, and the media are a centerpiece of their strategy. Parties have evolved into communications organizations that often act as a mouthpiece and communication strategist for politicians both in campaigns and in government. This chapter looks at how the media have enabled parties to secure their place and influence within the political system. We begin by looking at the parties' role in campaigns and then turn our attention to the party in government. Finally, we will examine how trends in media coverage of politics have helped to reinvigorate the parties.

CAMPAIGN COMMUNICATION

In the 1990s parties expanded their role in campaigns beyond fund-raising to participating actively in shaping campaign communications. Much of the parties' communication was paid for by soft money contributions (unlimited donations from individuals and corporations) and came in the form of issue advocacy through a variety of media—mailings as well as advertising on television and radio. Parties discovered they could get around limits on express advocacy for a candidate by simply avoiding words like "vote for" or "defeat." Thus, in 1996 the Republican National Committee (RNC) created ads that talked about the life of Republican presidential candidate Bob Dole, noting that he valued discipline and hard work, but they did not actually tell people to vote for him. The RNC also aired ads attacking President Bill Clinton's record. The RNC's $3 million ad campaign helped to keep Dole's campaign going through the summer after he had reached his preconvention spending limits.[2]

In 2002 Congress passed the Bipartisan Campaign Reform Act (BCRA), which banned soft money contributions to the parties. Many feared this would diminish the parties' role in elections. Congressional elections in 2004 and 2006 suggest the concerns were unfounded. Collecting only hard money, the parties and their congressional campaign committees raised nearly as much as they had before the BCRA—and in some cases more.[3] Much of this money went to independent expenditures, primarily independent advertising on television and radio, which explicitly advocated the election or defeat of specific candidates in competitive congressional races. Both Senate and House party campaign committees spent more on these ads in 2004 and 2006 than they had before the campaign finance reform, though these were targeted toward the closest races.[4] In one study of twelve competitive House and Senate races in 2006, researchers found that parties outspent their candidates on radio and television ads in nine of the campaigns.[5] The BCRA may have changed the kind of ads parties can run during elections, but they have not curtailed party ads.

These independent party ads have been almost exclusively negative. The Democratic Congressional Campaign Committee ran ads in races across the country in 2006 linking Republican incumbents with corruption in the Republican Party and tying them to the Bush administration's unpopular policy in the Iraq war.[6] Recognizing the unfavorable national climate facing Republicans in 2006, the National Republican Congressional Committee (NRCC) went on the air early to try to define Democratic challengers in negative ways.[7]

Often the parties' ads complement the candidates' campaigns, and, in some cases, almost appear to be coordinated. The race for New Mexico's First Congressional District in 2006 illustrates this.[8] The DCCC ads tried to connect incumbent Republican Heather Wilson to Republicans' problems with special interest influence, the war in Iraq, and George W. Bush. One ad showed a highway billboard sign with a picture of Bush and Wilson together and the tagline, "They just keep driving in the same lane"; other ads criticized Wilson's contributions from interest groups.[9] The themes highlighted in the DCCC ads supported and reinforced the Democratic candidate's positive ads, which explained how she was different from Bush and why special interest groups would not like her. The result was a consistent message repeatedly delivered to voters through a variety of media channels in both positive and negative tones.

In some circumstances, the party and its candidate may take on distinct but complementary roles through their ads and interaction with the media. Candidates may emphasize their own qualifications and records while party leaders attack the opponent. For example, in Michigan's Eighth Congressional District race in 2000, both parties paid for attack ads against the opposing party's candidate; at the same time, the candidates themselves tried to remain more cordial. Thus, while the Republican Party attacked Democratic candidate Diane Byrum for voting to borrow money from a state trust fund for veterans and wondered if she could be trusted to protect the Social Security trust fund if she were in Congress, the Republican candidate appeared in an ad in which he claimed that he "believe[d] in bringing people together, not tearing down others."[10] By employing this strategy, parties may help their candidates distance themselves from the possible backlash of going negative.

But even as many candidates have welcomed advertising by the parties, it has not been without problems. In a few cases, the party's message has unintentionally undermined its own candidate. In the 1998 South Carolina Senate race, the state Republican Party's hard-hitting ads against the Democratic incumbent turned out to be a major headache for the Republican candidate, Bob Inglis, who had pledged to run a civil campaign. After one of the ads was played during a debate between the two candidates, Inglis agreed with his opponent that the ad was ridiculous in its claims and presentation, and he spent much time denouncing the ads to reporters, who used the party's efforts as an opportunity to question Inglis's sincerity about his commitment to a courteous campaign.[11] And in the 2006 House race in Minnesota's Sixth District, a negative NRCC ad accusing the Democratic candidate, Patty Wetterling, of favoring a variety of taxes prompted Wetterling to respond with her own negative ad attacking the Republican candidate for supporting a national sales tax.[12]

It is obvious from campaign fund-raising and spending reports over the last decade that parties have reasserted themselves in elections even as election coverage by the media has remained candidate centered. But much of the parties' resurgence has come from their willingness to use the media—particularly for advertising—sometimes without much emphasis on the party label itself.[13] The results are most apparent in congressional elections, where the airwaves are often swamped by political ads paid for not only by candidates but also by parties. The involvement of the parties has made some races more competitive than they might otherwise have been. In the Montana Senate race in 2006, incumbent Republican Conrad Burns raised $2.5 million more than his Democratic challenger, Jon Tester, but more than $3 million in independent ads from the Democratic Senate Campaign Committee and the Montana Democratic Party supported Tester and negated Burns's fund-raising advantage, enabling Tester to eke out a victory with 49.2 percent of the vote.[14]

Under the right conditions, the ad campaigns made possible by the resources of the national parties and their party campaign committees in Congress can nationalize congressional campaigns. Both parties have experimented with a common theme or agenda in congressional elections. In 1994, House Republican candidates signed the Contract with America in an orchestrated media event on the Capitol steps, and the contract was published in *TV Guide*. Even though fewer than 20 percent of voters were familiar with the contract prior to the election,[15] GOP candidates highlighted some of the issues in their own campaigns, and the contract ultimately became the agenda for the new Republican majority in 1995. In 1998, Republicans spent $10 million on a national ad campaign entitled Operation Breakout that reminded voters of Clinton's scandal with Monica Lewinsky.[16] However, the ads appeared to backfire, as Republicans lost seats. In 2006, Democrats rallied around several themes that started with attacks against the corruption, cronyism, and failures of Republicans and the Bush administration and concluded with the Democrats' promise of a "New Direction for America."[17] Although the effort was not as formally coordinated as the 1994 Contract with America, it helped propel the Democrats to a majority.

While the national themes in 1994 and 2006 appeared to benefit the respective parties, the failure of the Republicans' 1998 Operation Breakout campaign reveals the limits of this communication strategy. A national ad campaign seems to work best when the party can put a face on the opposing party *and* link it to issues or policy problems the public is concerned about. In 1994 the face was Clinton and the public concern was big government and higher taxes and deficit spending. In 2006 the Democrats could point to Bush and lobbyist Jack Abramoff as the face of a Republican Party that was corrupt and pursuing a failing policy in Iraq. Operation Breakout in 1998 ran into the problem that Clinton was not as universally disliked as Republicans had expected, and, possibly more importantly, a large part of the public was opposed to impeachment—or at least tired of hearing about it. Either way, it made for a weak issue around which to try to rally support.

In some years when there is no individual to represent either party and no single issue arousing public concern, both parties have retreated from a national campaign with common themes. In 2000, both national party organizations focused most of their attention on a handful of battleground states and tailored the ads for the state. For example, in Iowa the DNC ran an issue ad against Bush that mentioned Texas's falling SAT scores, saying that Iowa (second in the nation in SAT scores) "doesn't need a Texas plan for its schools."[18] In Florida the Democrats talked about toxic chemicals dumped into Texas waterways and then asked Floridians to "imagine Bush's record in Florida's Everglades."[19] For their part, in the congressional campaigns, Republicans not only stuck to local issues, they even paid for some ads that praised Republican members of Congress for voting against their party on some issues.[20]

GOVERNING

In government, the parties have become very visible communicators, increasingly adept at using the media to focus on their agendas and frame policy debate. This strategic use of the media can be seen in the efforts of congressional party leaders to coordinate the communication of their membership in an attempt to capture media coverage and in the national parties' availability to national media and experimentation with their own party-produced media. We will look in some detail at each of these developments.

While party leaders have traditionally been among the most covered members of Congress in the national media, they have in recent years shown a greater willingness to go public through the media to accomplish the party's goals. Beginning in 1981, party leaders in Congress have become more visible in the media, with a majority of their media appearances related to legislation in Congress.[21] This is in stark contrast to earlier eras in Congress, where legislation was worked out behind closed doors. Today's party leaders are expected to promote not only the party agenda but also its image publicly.[22]

As they have increasingly gone public, party leaders have not merely tried to carry out their own personal agendas. Rather, they often seem to shape their messages around issues "owned" by the party—that is, issues about which there is consensus within the party.[23] Doing this has allowed them to gain more credibility and power as spokespersons in Congress. News coverage of coordinated efforts to go public—that is, a group in Congress or an individual speaking on behalf of a group attempting to gain media attention— reflects the growing power of party leaders to speak for their members. News coverage of Congress from 1977 through the early 1980s reveals that even though party leaders were active in seeking and gaining media attention for the legislative agenda, committee chairs and ranking minority members speaking for their cohorts on their committee, and sometimes for their party, seemed most successful in communicating through the press. But over time party leaders have made up a growing proportion of the efforts by members of Congress to go public, and today, on major issues, they are usually more prominent than committee chairs.[24]

Using the media to promote the party's agenda, party leaders not only improve their own credibility and visibility as spokespersons for their parties, but they make it more likely that other members of the party will work with them to publicize the message.[25] To this end, we have seen both parties in both houses of Congress pay more attention to involving their members in coordinated communication. From calling press conferences on the Capitol steps with many members of the party participating to lining up special orders speeches on a common theme to orchestrating deliberate obstructionist tactics, party members in Congress have found ways to cooperate with each other to attract media coverage to help accomplish their goals.

But the party caucuses, particularly in the House, have tried to extend their influence even further by institutionalizing their communications apparatus. In the House, the Democratic Policy Committee, under the auspices of the Democratic leader, defines the caucus's message and attempts to disseminate it.[26] For the House Republicans this falls under the duties of the chairman of the Republican Conference, with considerable input from the other Republican leaders. In the Senate these responsibilities largely fall on the party leaders, though the policy committees and particularly the Republican conference chairman have begun to play more of a communications role. In addition to keeping members informed about the party's message, these leaders and groups provide party members with talking points and themes to emphasize on trips back to their districts or states on weekends or during congressional recesses.[27] For example, as members headed back home for the Memorial Day recess in 2001, Senate Republican leaders suggested a "Gas Price Busters Tour" in which members would "travel to gas stations around their states, highlight the skyrocketing price of gasoline and make the pitch for the [Bush] administration's energy plan"; the leadership provided talking points, a sample press release, and a sample op-ed on the issue.[28]

One result of these coordinated communications efforts by parties is increasingly partisan messages from Congress. One study of coverage finds that partisan messages are particularly unified when they focus on "negative commentary about the opposition party" and when the parties have the "least control over government," either because they are in the minority or there is divided government.[29] News coverage of how congressional members have reacted to presidents from 1977 to 2001 shows that during the first half of that time period, members of the president's own party were only slightly less likely than members of the opposition party to oppose the president. After 1994, however, the president's party was nearly 78 percent more likely to

support than oppose the president, and the opposition party has rarely supported him publicly since 1994.[30]

As party leaders in Congress and their rank-and-file members have found
new ways to utilize the media to accomplish their policy goals, the national
party organizations have not been idle. They too have become more active in
communicating their parties' messages publicly, and the media have been a
centerpiece of this strategy.

In 1993, when Haley Barbour became chairman of the RNC, he made it clear
that his job was not just to raise money, but to be a spokesperson for the party
and its agenda. Evidence of the enhanced communications role of the chairman
can be seen in *The New York Times* coverage of party chairs. Barbour averaged
nearly thirty-one mentions a year in the *Times* during his four years at the helm
of the RNC, more than three times the average yearly coverage of his four predecessors. Barbour also became a frequent guest on news talk shows and even
hosted his own satellite television show. Recent party chairmen, including Ed
Gillespie and Ken Mehlman, have maintained the public profile.

While Barbour took the lead in making the Republican Party aware of the
importance of a communications strategy, the Democrats have also recognized the potential of the party chair to be a chief spokesperson of the party.
During most of the 1990s, the Democrats divided the party chairman's responsibilities between two people—one would manage the day-to-day operations of the party and fund-raising, and the other would be the chief
spokesperson. Usually a behind-the-scenes party activist such as Don Fowler,
who served from 1995–1997, was given the first position, while a media-
savvy elected official such as Sen. Christopher Dodd (1995–1997) or Col-
orado governor Roy Romer (1997–1999) took on the more visible job of
party general chairman to deal with the media. More recently, the Democrats
restored both roles under one title, choosing leaders like Terry McAuliffe and
Howard Dean, who appear equally comfortable with fundraising and media
relations to fill the position.

In addition to incorporating media relations into the job of party chairman,
the party organizations have taken advantage of the fairly recent concept of
governing as a permanent campaign,[31] producing issue ads to influence congressional and public debate and to generate public support or opposition to
particular policy proposals, as the Democrats' public campaign on SCHIP illustrates. While congressional Democrats were most visible on the issue, the
DCCC ran ads, the Democratic National Committee provided information
about the veto on its Web site, and the DNC chair was one of the party's public spokespersons on the issue.

The parties and their related organizations have also experimented with
new media, including satellite television and the Internet, to communicate

their message and to coordinate their members. During Barbour's tenure as chairman, the Republican National Committee had a weekly television program called *The Rising Tide*. In appearance, it followed the format of a combination news/talk show, with reports on current events in Washington, D.C., and a segment hosted by the party chair that included commentary. The stories were done from a Republican perspective, relying primarily on Republicans sources. The reports on the program and additional stories put together by the show's staff were made available via satellite to local television stations around the country.

More recently, the parties have paid more attention to the Internet as a way to communicate their message to the public and to party members. Both the RNC and the DNC have Web sites that include links to the party platforms, information about issues in the news, contact information for national and state party organizations, and a way to register to receive e-mail updates from the parties. Recognizing that the Internet is an important medium for young people, the Young Republicans and the Young Democrats, extensions of the national parties, have their own Web sites with information about local chapters of these organizations and other party resources.[32] While the party organization Web sites are designed primarily to connect the public to the party, the congressional party Web sites try to alert the media to the parties' positions and equip congressional members to carry the party's message to the public and to the media. Both party conferences in both houses of Congress have Web sites that include the respective party's agenda with synopses of the issues, and they often highlight a current issue in Congress. They also are a repository for selected video of party members' press conferences, leadership press releases, and news stories favorable to the party's position on current issues. The House Republican Conference Web site includes resources for its own members to help them deal with the press, including information on key issues (some localized for different states) and talking points.

PARTIES IN THE NEWS MEDIA

To this point, this chapter has focused on how parties have used the media to reassert themselves in the political system. But this is not just a story of the parties figuring out the media. The way the news media cover politics, particularly in this age of twenty-four-hour news channels and televised political punditry, has helped to reinvigorate the parties and contributed to the perception of partisan polarization. Often when we think of parties and the media, the discussion devolves into whether there is a partisan bias in the press. Although there may never be agreement or conclusive evidence that the political preferences of reporters, editors, publishers, and owners create a consistent political bias in political coverage, there is a clear trend (bias?) across all news media from CNN (derisively labeled the "Clinton News Network" by conservatives for its alleged liberal leanings) to Fox News ("fair and balanced"—but in a conservative sort of way?): All of them "exalt controversy."[33]

Since the 1970s, journalists have engaged in a brand of reporting that has alternately been called adversarial, critical, or attack journalism. Rather than simply reporting what political elites say and do, journalists have questioned public officials and their motives, looked for opportunities to catch them in wrongdoing, and highlighted conflicts among them. According to Thomas Patterson,[34] journalists have been careful to avoid appearing partisan by having the criticisms and attacks on politicians come from their political adversaries. And this is where the parties have benefited. Democrats are the natural adversaries of Republicans: "The media look to the two political parties as the 'teams' that are competing in the game of national politics . . . [and present] every situation as Republicans versus the Democrats. . . . Thus, from the public's point of view, the parties still play a meaningful role in structuring policy debates."[35]

In addition to the media's penchant for conflict, they have added more interpretation to their reporting and programming.[36] Newspapers now include "news analysis" stories, and network and cable television stations now have panels of experts and pundits discussing the top stories on their newscasts and political talk shows. Often these formats pair supporters of each party to discuss (or yell about) current issues. Party chairs frequently appear opposite each other, as do media-friendly members of Congress from opposing parties. Presumably, the presence of a representative from each party ensures balance. Although this tends to oversimplify issues and may ignore intraparty divisions and bipartisanship, it does enhance the perception that the parties are central in policy debates. Indeed, one study has shown that in media coverage, parties are portrayed as active participants in the political process, not merely reactors to events.[37]

Finally, the media coverage of parties has helped the parties extend their influence beyond what their resources would allow, particularly in campaigns. Media coverage of political advertising during campaigns has increased in the last two decades.[38] Therefore, when party organizations launch an ad campaign, whether it is issue advocacy to prop up their candidates during an election or to influence policy debate, they can target the ads to a few major media markets, confident that the news media will cover the ads and broaden the reach to the rest of the country. In the 2000 presidential campaign, both parties paid for advertising in a handful of battleground states, but thanks to ad watches meant to evaluate the ads, people all over the country saw the ads replayed on news shows or described in detail in their local newspapers, thus extending the parties' reach.

Though it gives them more visibility and a way to disseminate their message, news coverage of the parties may not be all good news for the parties. Because the parties have become the de facto representatives of political conflict for journalists, they may be blamed for what the public perceives is wrong with the system. Terms such as *partisan bickering* and *gridlock* are often what people associate with the parties. Thus, while the parties have used the media to reassert themselves in the political system and while media coverage has made the parties more visible in public debate, the image the public has of the parties may not necessarily be favorable.

Furthermore, media coverage of minor parties is virtually nonexistent. Coverage of the parties in *The New York Times* reveals this marginalization. It is not uncommon for the Democratic and Republican parties each to be mentioned prominently (in the headline or first paragraph) in more than four hundred stories a year in the *Times*. In contrast, between 1995 and 2000 the Reform Party drew prominent attention in more than one hundred stories in only three years—only once in a nonelection year during Reform Party governor Jesse Ventura's first year in office. The Green Party received this extensive coverage only in 2000 when well-known government watchdog Ralph Nader ran as the party's nominee for president. In the other years, these parties gained prominent notice in fewer than thirty stories, and the Libertarian Party was never mentioned prominently in more than twelve stories during a year. Unless a third party has a high-profile candidate or elected official who can command media attention on his own—such as Ross Perot, who had money to buy his own advertising and make himself a credible candidate, or Ventura, a former wrestler, and Nader, who was already well known—the party is unlikely to gain notice and be taken seriously by the media as a player in policy debate.

CONCLUSION

Not long ago, there were whispers that the parties were in danger of becoming irrelevant in American politics in part because the media had become a more important intermediary. However, we have seen in this chapter that the parties have redefined their place in the political system by taking advantage of opportunities made possible through the media. Advertising has been an effective tool for parties to aid their candidates during political campaigns and to frame policy debates beyond the context of elections. Better media relations and coordinated communication among party members both within Congress and in the national party organizations have allowed the parties to capitalize on the media's willingness to discuss policy in the context of party conflict.

But even as the parties have used the media to reassert their political importance, several questions about the relationship between American parties and the media exist. There is a growing body of research on increasing polarization in American government. It seems intuitive the media might have some impact on this trend, but we know little about how the public relations efforts of the parties and the way the media cover them affect the perception of polarization or contribute to its continuation. There is much we do not know about the effects of party communications on the public or political officials. Do issue ads influence debate, and does coordinated communication of the party message in Congress affect public opinion or policy outcomes? There is also little research on how the media cover parties—not in the sense of political bias that favors one party over another, but in the sense of what the public learns about parties from the media and what perceptions coverage creates about the parties and their role in the political system. Answers to these questions await further scholarly research that should bring us a better understanding of how political parties influence political communication, political processes, and policy outcomes in the end.

DISCUSSION QUESTIONS

1. How have the media enabled parties to reassert themselves as important participants in the political system?
2. How can party advertisements in campaigns benefit a party's candidates? How might party ads create problems for candidates? Without coordinating with their candidates, what can parties do to ensure their ads help rather than hurt their own candidates?
3. In congressional and presidential campaigns, what are the advantages and disadvantages of party ads focusing on national issues or themes rather than local concerns?
4. What challenges do parties and their leaders face in communicating through the media? How have party leaders in Congress attempted to overcome these challenges?
5. How have parties used new media such as the Internet? How might these new tools be effective ways to enhance the role of the parties in the political system?
6. How do the media cover political parties? What do we learn about parties from the media and what kind of perceptions about parties might coverage create?

SUGGESTIONS FOR FURTHER READING

Douglas B. Harris. "The Rise of the Public Speakership." *Political Science Quarterly* 113 (Summer 1998): 193–213.
Daniel Lipinski. "The Outside Game: Communication as a Party Strategy in Congress." In *Communication and U.S. Elections: New Agendas*, ed. Roderick Hart and Daron Shaw. Lanham, MD: Rowman and Littlefield, 2001.
David B. Magleby, ed. *The Other Campaign: Soft Money and Issue Advocacy in the 2000 Congressional Elections*. Lanham, MD: Rowman and Littlefield, 2002.
National Democratic Committee Web site. http://www.democrats.org.
National Republican Committee Web site. http://www.rnc.org.
Barbara Sinclair. *Party Wars: Polarization and the Politics of National Policy Making*. Norman: University of Oklahoma Press, 2006.

NOTES

1. Christopher Lee and Jonathan Weisman, "House Passes Children's Health Bill," *Washington Post*, September 26, 2007.

2. James Bennet, "The Ad: Wew GOP Drive, New Finance Debate," *The New York Times*, May 31, 1996, A20.

3. Victoria A. Farrar-Myers and Diana Dwyre, *Limits and Loopholes: The Quest for Money, Free Speech, and Fair Elections* (Washington, DC: CQ Press, 2008), 143.

4. Ibid., 147.

5. David B. Magleby and Kelly D. Patterson, *War Games: Issues and Resources in the Battle for Control of Congress* (Provo, UT: Center for the Study of Elections and Democracy, Brigham Young University, 2007).

6. Ibid.

7. Marjorie Randon Hershey and Nicholas J. Clark, "The 2006 Indiana 9th Congressional District Race," in *War Games: Issues and Resources in the Battle for Control of Congress*, ed. David B. Magleby and Kelly D. Patterson (Provo, UT: Center for the Study of Elections and Democracy, Brigham Young University, 2007).

8. Lonna Rae Atkeson and Lorraine Tafoya, "The 2006 New Mexico 1st Congressional District Race," in *War Games: Issues and Resources in the Battle for Control of Congress*, ed. David B. Magleby and Kelly D. Patterson (Provo, UT: Center for the Study of Elections and Democracy, Brigham Young University, 2007).

9. Ibid., 145.

10. Eric Freedman and Sue Carter, "The 2000 Michigan Eighth Congressional District Race," in *Election Advocacy: Soft Money and Issue Advocacy in the 2000 Elections*, ed. David B. Magleby (Provo, UT: Center for the Study of Elections and Democracy, Brigham Young University, 2001), 195–97.

11. Bill Moore and C. Danielle Vinson, "The 1998 South Carolina Senate Race," in *Outside Money: Soft Money and Issue Advocacy in the 1998 Congressional Elections*, ed. David B. Magleby (Lanham, MD: Rowman & Littlefield, 2000), 99–100.

12. William H. Flanigan, Kathryn Pearson, and Nancy H. Zingale, "The 2006 Minnesota U.S. Senate Race and Minnesota 6th Congressional District Race," in *War Games: Issues and Resources in the Battle for Control of Congress*, ed. David B. Magleby and Kelly D. Patterson (Provo, UT: Center for the Study of Elections and Democracy, Brigham Young University, 2007), 114.

13. Kathleen Hall Jamieson, *Everything You Think You Know about Politics . . . And Why You're Wrong* (New York: Basic Books, 2000), 15.

14. Craig Wilson, "The 2006 Montana U.S. Senate Race," in *War Games: Issues and Resources in the Battle for Control of Congress*, ed. David B. Magleby and Kelly D. Patterson (Provo, UT: Center for the Study of Elections and Democracy, Brigham Young University, 2007).

15. Clyde Wilcox, *The Latest American Revolution? The 1994 Elections and Their Implications for Governance* (New York: St. Martin's Press, 1995), 2.

16. Karen Foerstel, "Parties, Interest Groups Pour Money into Issue Ads," *Congressional Quarterly Weekly Reports* (October 31, 1998): 2948.

17. Dana Milbank, "Democrats Meander in a New New Direction," *Washington Post*, September 15, 2006, A2.

18. Peter Marks, "The 2000 Campaign: The Ad Campaign," *The New York Times*, October 17, 2000, A1.

19. Ibid.

20. James W. Ceaser and Andrew E. Busch, *The Perfect Tie: The True Story of the 2000 Presidential Election* (Lanham, MD: Rowman and Littlefield, 2001), 224–26.

21. Douglas B. Harris, "Going Public and Staying Private: House Party Leaders' Use of Media Strategies of Legislative Coalition Building" (paper presented at the annual meeting of the Midwest Political Science Association, Chicago, IL, 2000).

22. Barbara Sinclair, *Party Wars: Polarization and the Politics of National Policy Making* (Norman: University of Oklahoma Press, 2006).

23. Patrick J. Sellers, "Leaders and Followers in the U.S. Senate" (paper presented at the annual meeting of the American Political Science Association, Atlanta, GA, 1999).

24. C. Danielle Vinson and Megan Remmel, "Congress Learns to Go Public: How Congress Uses the Media to Respond to the President" (paper presented at the annual meeting of the American Political Science Association, Chicago, IL, 2007).

25. Sellers, "Leaders and Followers."

26. Daniel Lipinski, "The Outside Game: Communication as a Party Strategy in Congress," in *Communication and U.S. Elections: New Agendas*, ed. Roderick Hart and Daron Shaw (Lanham, MD: Rowman and Littlefield, 2001).

27. Ibid.

28. Al Kamen, "In the Loop: The Sore Corps," *Washington Post*, May 16, 2001.

29. Tim Groeling and Samuel Kernell, "Congress, the President, and Party Competition via Network News," in *Polarized Politics: Congress and the President in a Partisan Era*, ed. Jon R. Bond and Richard Fleisher (Washington, DC: CQ Press, 2000), 95.

30. Vinson and Remmel, "Congress Learns to Go Public."

31. Timothy E. Cook, *Governing with the News: The News Media as a Political Institution* (Chicago: University of Chicago Press, 1998).

32. For examples of party and leadership Web sites, see http://www.rnc.org; http://www.dnc.org; http://www.youngrepublicans.com; http://www.yda.org; http://www.gop.gov; and http://www.house.gov/democrats/welcome.html.

33. Thomas E. Patterson, "Bad News, Period," *PS: Political Science & Politics* 29 (March 1996): 17–21.

34. Ibid.

35. L. Sandy Maisel, "Political Parties in a Nonparty Era: Adapting to a New Role," in *Parties and Politics in American History*, ed. L. Sandy Maisel and William G. Shade (New York: Garland, 1994), 275.

36. Darrell M. West, *The Rise and Fall of the Media Establishment* (Boston: Bedford/St. Martin's Press, 2001).

37. Roderick P. Hart, Sharon E. Jarvis, William P. Jennings, and Deborah Smith-Howell, *Political Keywords: Using Language that Uses Us* (New York: Oxford University Press, 2005), 192.

38. Darrell M. West, *Air Wars: Television Advertising in Election Campaigns 1952–1996*, 2nd ed. (Washington, D.C.: Congressional Quarterly, 1997).

8

Presidential Elections and the Media

Mary E. Stuckey and Kristina E. Curry

Research and commentary on the influence of the media in presidential elections have become a minor cottage industry.[1] Professionals and amateurs alike post and publish their opinions for the interested public to consider. The consensus of opinion is both clear and consistent: The media are responsible for the weakening of the national political parties and a simultaneous increase in the influence of journalists over that of professional politicians.[2] The media thus have contributed to the shallowness of political discourse, undue attention to "image" over "substance," and an impoverishment of our national politics generally. Like the aliens in *Independence Day*, the media are looming "out there," plotting the destruction of civilization as we know it. Their window of opportunity for the accomplishment of this destruction occurs with regularity, every four years. And with regularity, every four years, scholars and pundits appear—usually on national media—warning us that the sky is falling and that the polity cannot long sustain the potential damage. Miraculously, however, we manage to survive yet another election cycle, and although our politics are ever more wounded, still we struggle on.

This is, of course, hyperbole. But even so, it is not altogether inaccurate. Public discourse about the media tends toward the apocalyptic, and the media are convenient scapegoats for the myriad ills that are thought to assail us. Often, academics are little better, bringing judgment as well as analysis to the study of media influence in elections. There are three main areas of research on media influence in a presidential campaign: studies that focus on the structural aspects of campaigns and the media's influences on those structures; those that focus on the relative power of the media; and examinations of the content of campaign communication. In general, they are pessimistic, and in our view, are all based on common misperceptions about political communication in general and campaign communication in particular.[3]

The most important of these misperceptions are that when it comes to campaigns, the media matter more than anything else; that there was a golden age of political communication, and we have fallen from grace; that television is both different and separate from culture; and, finally, that voters are passive and imprisoned victims of television. All these perceptions have a grain of truth to them; this chapter is by no means a defense of the media. It is, however, an effort to put the media coverage of campaigns into a larger context. Consequently, we will discuss some of the trends of mediated campaigns, question the general understanding of how the media operate with reference to a broader context, look with particular attention at the last two presidential elections, and reflect on whether the events of the 2004 presidential election alter these trends and this understanding in significant ways.

COVERING PRESIDENTIAL CAMPAIGNS

Media organizations in the United States are businesses, and follow the dictates of business practice.[4] These dictates mean that the media will perform in predictable ways and will follow routines of newsgathering, production, and presentation. Successful campaigns are generally those that understand and use these routines and derive themes that resonate through them. These processes are not neutral; they are widely considered to have clear, often deleterious effects on campaigns and on politics in general.[5]

Campaigns are important elements of media political coverage. Since the 2002 midterm elections, a study by the Pew Internet and American Life Project released figures indicating that "69 percent of Americans cited television and 34 percent considered newspapers their leading choices for news; survey respondents could specify their top two. Radio and the Internet each got about 15 percent, while magazines had 2 percent."[6] While these figures show the increasing influence of the Internet, television "is still far and away the dominant channel of political information in this country, even for Internet users."[7] During an election year, campaign news comprises between 13 percent (newspapers) and 15 percent (television) of news stories,[8] and the content and style of such stories is remarkably uniform.[9] Such uniformity is the product of routines and incentives that demand exciting, dramatic events; change within a thematic context; and stories that can be presented in a "balanced" and "objective" manner. Thus, coverage of complicated issues and events is reduced to an easily dramatized conflict between personalities, and "both sides" are given equal time and roughly equal coverage.

Candidates, of course, play to these routines, and coverage is a major (if not *the* major) consideration of contemporary campaigns. Nearly everything candidates do is geared toward the media, especially television.[10] Not only have mediated events, such as the now obligatory appearance on *Larry King Live* and televised "town hall meetings" become campaign standards, but nearly all personal appearances are orchestrated with television in mind. For example, programs such as Jon Stewart's *The Daily Show* and Stephen Colbert's *The Colbert Report* are known as the "satire circuit"[11] and are important means by which a candidate sends her or his message to a particular demographic. In fact, one in five people under the age of thirty watches late-night programs for their political news.[12] Such shows appeal to younger audiences precisely because of their humorous style.[13] Lance Bennett writes that campaigns are mediated and, for that matter, "most campaign events . . . are dramatic productions: highly rule-governed, and carefully scripted, staged, and managed."[14] Thus, when candidates are prompted into straying from message—or do so accidentally—the media are right there to report the gaffes, and often in a negative way.[15] Even given these risks, campaign managers encourage candidates to visit such programs specifically to connect with younger voters.[16] Such "media events" are campaign staples, and a failure to respect these expectations—like a failure to honor deadlines, the need for interesting video, and the demand for fresh news—is certain to relegate a campaign to the status of "also-ran."

It is also problematic, however, for a campaign to engage in too much "news management." Events that are seen as too orchestrated, too contrived, too "unrealistic," do not receive much airtime. The political conventions are prime examples of this. When policy was actually made on convention floors—when controversy was possible—the conventions received "gavel-to-gavel" coverage. But the more the parties tried to control conventions—to present precise, clearly defined, and contrived images to the public through the media—the less coverage they received. Now, with the onset of cable as competition, the networks simply cannot afford to risk losing the audience; they provide coverage of key speeches and summaries of events, and leave the bulk of convention coverage to cable channels such as C-SPAN. The nostalgic may still visit C-SPAN online for in-depth details from the 2004 convention, including videos and transcripts of speeches, "convention events," and "candidate views" among a plethora of other election-related material.[17] In fact, C-SPAN's coverage of the 2008 campaign began well before the first series of primaries. People of all ages are being encouraged to learn about the process by means of C-SPAN's 2008 Campaign Bus, which is already "visiting communities, schools, and political events around the country to inform voters[,] empower teachers[, and] enrich civics education."[18] This is important because it reflects how the media, like the candidates themselves, are prepared to come to voters with well-prepared, scripted material, which further expands and deepens their influence.

The relationship between the media and political candidates has become so intertwined that veteran political journalist Robert Shogan asserts that the media "have been reduced to filling the role of enablers without fully realizing it or intending it, they allow and sometimes abet the abuse of the political process by the candidates and their handlers."[19] According to Shogan, the media need the candidates, the candidates need the media, and the political process is damaged by the relationship that therefore develops between them. This perspective, of course, rests on a somewhat rarefied notion of what the political process requires for its integrity and proper functioning.

The need for candidates to court the media is directly related to the phenomenon most often associated with the rise of the media, specifically television: the weakening of political parties. The media have, in many ways, replaced the parties as sources of political information, as providers of political ideology, and as winnowers of candidates.[20] Through both news and entertainment forums, the media are powerful sources of what issues are on the national agenda, and how those issues will be understood and framed. While this research overwhelmingly indicates that the media are important as sources of what the public will think about, there is also good evidence that they have little influence over specific positions on those issues. That is, the media tell us what to think about, but not what to think.[21]

This can, however, be taken too far. Voters rely on many sources for their political information, including peers and family,[22] and they process mediated information in a variety of ways, all of which lessen the media's ability to force an agenda on an unwilling public.[23] In addition, political parties remain the best predictor of the national vote, and of an individual voter's political preferences. Parties in the United States have always been weak, and the fact that they are further weakened may or may not be disastrous. Finally, the weakness of political parties is not solely the fault of the media; structural developments such as the reforms of the McGovern-Fraser Commission in 1968, which encouraged minority involvement and representation in government, and the consequent initiation of primaries[24] have had much to do with weakening the parties. It remains true, however, that in the absence of strong and popular parties, the media presently fill a void.

But they do not fill this void particularly well. As Tom Patterson insightfully notes,

> The proper organization of electoral opinion requires an institution with certain characteristics. It must be capable of seeing the larger picture—of looking at the world as a whole and not in small pieces. It must have incentives that cause it to

identify and organize those interests that are making demands for policy representation. And it must be accountable for its choices, so that the public can reward it when satisfied and force amendments when dissatisfied. The press has none of these characteristics. The media has its special strengths, but they do not include these strengths.[25]

The weakening of the political parties as organizing entities has contributed to the rise of candidate-centered campaigns.[26] Candidate-centered campaigns have contributed to the fragmentation and lack of coherence that characterizes our national politics, and that makes politics more difficult for citizens to assimilate and understand. The more confusing politics becomes, the more necessary are the media as interpreters. The cycle, once established, becomes self-reinforcing.

The media, especially cable and most especially the Internet, are also viewed as furthering the fragmentation of our national political life. The idea here is that there is—or once was—a common culture, and that cable and the Internet allow smaller, more fractured groups to participate in smaller, more narrow cultures. Consequently, the media further the interest group politics that are seen as increasingly dividing and not unifying the diverse groups that comprise the national polity.[27] For example, the liberal group MoveOn.org (which boasts of having 3.3 million members), is composed of the organizations MoveOn.org Political Action and MoveOn.org Civic Action. MoveOn.org Political Action is a political action committee (PAC) that "mobilizes people across the country to fight important battles in Congress and help elect candidates who reflect our values."[28] MoveOn.org Civic Action is a not-for-profit organization that "primarily focuses on education and advocacy on important national issues."[29] Conservative voters have choices too, such as Victory Caucus and MoveAmericaForward.org.[30] Whatever your special interest or political party, there is a group that wants and needs your support. With such wide and varied professional and homegrown sources of information to choose from, cable and the Internet are seen, on the one hand, as potentially enabling democracy,[31] and, on the other, as contributing to its demise as a viable form of political organization.[32] What we know about how the Internet and other forms of new media will affect our politics is that we do not yet fully know how the Internet will affect our politics.

In terms of the more traditional media, given the absence of strong partisan leaders, journalists and pundits have become the voice of political authority. Where the Sunday morning talk shows and other venues dedicated to political chat used to be devoted solely to interviews and discussions with political actors, they now also include analysis by journalists. Commentators often interview one another in the effort to derive political understanding. Whereas the point used to be exclusively to cover political events, there is increasing concern over journalists' tendency to become part of those events.[33] This self-referential tendency, disturbing in all political contexts, is particularly important in campaigns, in which voter information tends to be low (especially in the early stages) and in which such commentary can have correspondingly greater effects. Take, for instance, the example of Bill Clinton, in 1992 the undeclared winner of what political consultant turned commentator Paul Begala dubbed the "pundit primary."[34] Clinton benefited in numerous ways from the media's attention, not least of which was an increase in his ability to raise money, accompanied by a drop in the fundraising potential of his rivals.

Punditry is an increasingly visible element of the coverage of national campaigns, as once and future aides to officials and candidates take to the airwaves in what are supposed to be "objective" roles as analysts rather, than producers of policy. Often, as in the case of George Stephanopoulos, Clinton's former director of communications *cum* senior adviser for policy and strategy,[35] their role is to provide "inside" knowledge of the workings of the White House or the campaign. They fill airspace—often considerable amounts of airspace—but it is questionable whether they fill that space with politically meaningful information.[36] This assertion, of course, rests on the notion that only policy information is politically relevant, that gossip and process information are somehow less worthy than the "real" information we fondly suppose was once the province of political parties.

The media fill more than an informational void, however; as the Clinton example indicates, the media also have supplanted the political parties as winnowers and kingmakers. Surely the campaign coverage of "media darlings" like George W. Bush, Jimmy Carter, and Colin Powell would not have been likely in a context dominated by parties rather than journalists. Coverage of candidates like Joe Biden and Gary Hart has also contributed to this process by removing candidates from contention, often before primary voters are given an opportunity to express their preferences.

This phenomenon is most apparent in "frontloading," or disproportionate coverage given to early primaries.[37] As of June 1999, for instance, the electorally meaningless straw polls in Iowa were touted as the first salvo in the campaign wars, and their impact on the Elizabeth Dole and Pat Buchanan campaigns was thought to be all but definitive. For such a conclusion to be widely aired long before the election—and long before the majority of voters are even willing to begin thinking about starting to pay attention—would be laughable if it did not have such clear consequences. And as this is being written, the news has been full of information about candidate standings in Iowa and New Hampshire—months before a vote will be cast in either state.

Important among these consequences is the tendency to search for inconsistencies, which are then used to discredit a candidate in what is conventionally termed *"gotcha" journalism*. Consider, for example, the tendency of the Bush campaign to portray 2004 presidential contender John Kerry as a flip-flopper. Once such epithets are established in the public mind, they are hard to overcome.[38] This "need" to find flaws rather than focus on basic reporting of facts tends more often to eliminate potentially viable candidates than to uncover real malfeasance.[39]

A major instrument of such kingmaking/winnowing is the coverage of polling. Most often associated with "horse race" coverage,[40] polls tend to become benchmarks for campaigns; position in the polls is the definitive marker of the success or failure of a campaign. Certainly, they affected Elizabeth Dole's ability to garner funds and attention in the 2000 preprimary season. The effects of polls are not limited to the fates of particular candidates; they have policy implications as well.

Polls, as Kathleen Frankovic says, "not only sample public opinion, they define it."[41] While polls have long been an integral part of political coverage, they are now more necessary to the media than ever before,[42] and are thought to create rather than merely to define or report public opinion. Polls increase the attention reporters give the horse race and determine the nature and extent of candidate coverage. According to this view, polls deepen the debasement of political process.[43] Yet polls also underline the importance of public opinion, and in so doing, may actually increase voter interest and involvement in campaigns.[44] The cumulative effects of polls thus remain ambiguous.

Despite the fact—or because of it—that election 2000 was "too close to call" for weeks before the actual election, the polls became *the* story of the campaign, as "Americans were polled, polled, and repolled. And the media reported what were often two- and three-point statistically insignificant leads faithfully."[45] Because these polls carried no "news," they contributed nothing but tension and drama to the campaign—but tension and drama make for "good" stories, and so the polls were covered incessantly. Certainly, the influence of polls on election night 2000 created enormous difficulties, both for the candidates and for the political system.[46] We are so dependent upon the national media for our political information, the argument goes, and are generally so ignorant of how to interpret that information, that greater care in the use of polls is certainly called for.

Largely as a result of polling, but also because of the visual nature of television, modern campaigning is sometimes blamed for the further debasement of political discourse.[47] Despite the evidence that most presidential candidates make policy-oriented promises and, if elected, try to keep those promises,[48] scholars and pundits insist on the hollowness of candidate appeals, the shallowness of candidates themselves, and the emptiness of political discourse.[49]

Certainly, the tendency to cover events such as debates as if they are about performance rather than policy—focusing on sighs or stammers, shrugs or smirks[50]—while perhaps revealing something of candidate character, can hardly be said to contribute to public understanding of policy. Likewise, focus on candidate attire seems inconsequential, yet gets much coverage. Presidential candidate Hillary Clinton, for example, is consistently the subject of such absurd commentary.[51]

But some elections—1988 is a notable example—are simply empty of meaningful issue discussion, and the media cannot cover what is not there to begin with. Other elections—and 2000 is a good example—are notable for the amount of policy that is discussed. The 2000 election had enormous amounts of issue content, and was not reducible to jokes about "lock boxes"[52]—nor was it so reduced by the media. Similarly, the 2004 election was characterized by the focus on the highly controversial Iraq war. If there is substantive issue discussion, the media do cover it; they may do it in fragmented, personalized, and potentially trivializing ways, but it is also true that politics has always been full of the fragmented, the personal, and the trivial.

Nonetheless, the very fact of the media is considered to have an impact on the ways in which political communication is structured and presented,[53] an impact that is not necessarily positive if one wants a rational, well-informed electorate who are interested in issue-based information as a basis for making knowledgeable decisions.[54] Held up to anything approaching that standard, American election communication is woefully lacking. The question is whether or not that is either an appropriate or a realistic standard for political practice.

CAMPAIGNS IN CONTEXT

The crucial point made by critics of the media's roles in national elections is that media influence matters more than anything else as a determinant of the vote. There is considerable evidence that this is not the case. In his analysis of the 1980 campaign, for instance, journalist and former speechwriter Jeff Greenfield details the shattering of various myths about election coverage. He concludes that "television and the media made almost no difference in the outcome of the 1980 presidential campaign. The victory of Ronald Reagan was a political victory, a party victory, and victory of more coherent—not necessarily correct, but more coherent—ideas, better expressed, more connected with the reality of their lives, as Americans saw it, than those of Reagan's principal opponent, a victory vastly aided by a better-funded, better-organized, more confident and united party."[55] In Greenfield's view, while the campaign was transmitted through the media, the campaign, not its mediation, determined the winner and loser.

Yet the idea of media dominance is still very much with us, and still hampers our understanding of elections. No campaign can succeed without the media, just as no campaign can succeed without organization, money, some semblance of issue positions, and a host of other factors. But the media are not the sole determinant of campaign success. They may not even be the primary determinant. That we often talk as if they are is a tribute to the self-referential nature of election coverage, which tends to place the media in the center of campaigns, not to the actual processes of campaigns and elections.

Voters, for instance, have myriad and important resources. Selective exposure affects how voters get information and selective perception helps to determine how that information will be processed.[56] Predispositions, the opinions of peers, social status, race, gender, and other demographic considerations are significant indicators of how mediated information will be received.[57] Voter indifference to media may also be an important filter; there is considerable evidence that voters do not agree with what the media consider important issues, the Clinton/Lewinsky scandal being an obvious example.

In at least one area, the voters are influenced by the media without agreeing with them. If nothing else, we know that voters do not like negative campaigning—but that it works.[58] Negative campaigning does not only separate voters from the opposition, however; it may also separate voters from the political process, and may be related to the increase in voter disenchantment with the electoral process.[59]

The assumption that the media have contributed to the demise of substantive political communication in campaign contexts is based, however implicitly, on the notion that there was a golden age of political communication and that political discourse has since been on a long, downhill slide. This tendency is most notable in Roderick Hart's work, in which he urges citizens to "just say 'No'" to television,[60] but it is a prominent strain throughout media research.[61] The problem is that, in its simplest form, the assumption is simply not accurate. Not only is it difficult to make clear distinctions between "symbol" and "substance," but campaign communication has always relied on image, and has often been trivial, prurient, and downright shallow. There was, for instance, little substance in torchlight parades,[62] campaigns based on whiskey jugs in the shape of log cabins,[63] or slogans such as "Tippecanoe and Tyler too."[64]

Negative campaigning is also not a recent phenomenon. While it is often argued that negative politics are either a relatively new development[65] or at least a qualitatively different one,[66] there is considerable evidence that "going negative" has been around for some time, and that the practice has long involved personalization, distortion, and misinterpretation of issues. In 1864, for example, a variety of racist themes were conflated into accusations that Republicans advocated miscegenation, which would "be of infinite service to the Irish." Democrats labeled Abraham Lincoln "the widowmaker," and referred to him as "Abraham Africanus the First," implying that he was "tainted" with "negro blood."[67] Next to this, claims concerning Grover Cleveland's illegitimate child, not to mention Jimmy Carter's alleged "meanness," seem trivial.

Furthermore, the assumption that television has demeaned and trivialized politics erroneously treats the influence of television as unprecedented in the history of popular culture. Historically, the dominant media (from books to vaudeville to movies to television and computer games) have always been blamed for the deterioration of popular culture.[68] It is probably more sensible to understand television's place in popular culture in more restrained terms. The media alone are neither panaceas for our political ills nor the causes of them.

Blaming the media is also tantamount to arguing that voters are somehow dupes, incapable of recognizing the efforts to manipulate them that are so obvious to scholars and to media critics. This argument gives the image of voters trapped in "news prison,"[69] unable to break free (or able to do so only with great difficulty) of the ideological and informational chains with which the media bind them. As media critic Bonnie Dow notes in a different context,

> [V]iewers are likely to interpret television according to the dominant codes available to them as members of American society and as consumers of American media. This perspective assumes that viewers outside the white, middle-class, heterosexual "mainstream" to whom television always presumes it is speaking still understand the "rules" for preferred readings, even as they might work to deconstruct them.[70]

Voters, in other words, may know little about American politics, about the prevailing issues, or about the process of campaigns—but they are very smart about what makes "good" television, and are capable of interpreting it in terms of what makes "good" politics. That voter turnout continues to decline[71] is, at least potentially, evidence that voters are also capable of discerning the difference. They may watch so-called trash television, and they may vote for empty candidates, but it is at least possible that in doing so they are responding to the trivialization of politics by politicians and those who cover them, not failing to recognize that politics is, to many of them, trivial. What does not matter may as well be entertaining.

This is not to deny that the media have important effects on campaigns. It is to argue that we need to be more careful about analyzing the nature of those effects. For instance, it is likely that, as Greenfield argues, the content and nature of media coverage contribute to voter apathy.[72] The reluctance of pundits to believe what candidates say, their pervasive (if entirely reasonable) cynicism, their unwillingness to attribute to political action motives that transcend the purely opportunistic, and their fascination with the "game" elements of politics strip, in Greenfield's words, the voter of reasons to care about election outcomes.

Given the prevailing politics (candidate centered rather than party oriented), it falls to the media to explain the actual differences among and between candidates, and the implications that those differences hold for individual voters. It is this that media singularly fail to do, focusing instead on style, on political tactics and strategy, and—to the extent that issues are covered—on issues as a reflection of that style and/or those strategies and tactics.

REFLECTIONS ON CAMPAIGN 2000

Out of the myriad possibilities for analysis that stem from the 2000 presidential election, two things are particularly relevant to this discussion: Ralph Nader's campaign and its attacks on the political parties and the coverage of election night. Nader's third-party challenge to the major parties was premised on the notion that the prevailing processes of campaigning are corrupt, mostly because of the infusion of money into politics, but also because of the media that money can be used to buy.[73] The coverage of Nader's campaign focused, predictably enough, on the effect it would have on the Bush and Gore campaigns,[74] on the novelty of the challenge,[75] and on the personalities of those involved.[76] Thus, this coverage was pretty much what we would expect, emphasizing the horse race, personalizing issues, and contributing to the sense of electoral politics as trivial.

Equally predictable, the coverage of the 2000 election revealed many of the problems with media coverage of campaigns. Throughout the campaign, there were the usual charges of shallow coverage that trivialized the campaign and biased reporting that skewed voter perceptions.[77] These perennial problems, however, paled in comparison to the election night fiasco.

During election night, described by journalist Terence Smith as "a nightmare,"[78] news anchors and commentators became increasingly confused and incoherent amid the various projections, retractions, and apologies.[79] Television news has rarely looked worse than it did that night. As Marvin Kalb noted, "Television news, like all of contemporary journalism, is supposed to cover the news fairly and accurately. It is not supposed to be the news or make the news."[80] Yet that is exactly what happened.

The network news predictions for the pivotal state of Florida, based on a combination of statistical machinations and exit polling, proved to be considerably more accurate in terms of voter intention than in terms of voter behavior, as problems with ballots led numerous Gore supporters to vote for Pat Buchanan instead. The situation was further complicated by some bad data and misjudgments about how those data should be interpreted.[81] In essence, each network wanted to be the first to call Florida—and thus the election—and sacrificed accuracy for immediacy.[82]

Analyst Robert Kuttner had this to say about the media performance on Election Day:

> I don't just mean miscalling Florida twice. The aftermath was even worse. The networks and most print analysts convinced themselves that Al Gore had lost, that he was a sore loser, that the public was panicking, that a perilous interregnum was at hand, that court involvement would mean a constitutional crisis, and that an instant resolution was necessary for the good of the Republic. But each of those conceits was proven overheated and wrong. . . . The voters turn out to be more mature than the media. . . . Far from panicking, the voters are getting a fascinating civics lesson. Anyone who thinks this is just O.J. all over again is a vidiot, so media-besotted as to be unable to distinguish spectacle from substance.[83]

Perhaps only the American media can by comparison render the American voter a model of democratic virtue.

No media analyst, of course, could have foreseen the legal complications that, after five tortuous weeks, finally dragged the election to the United States Supreme Court. There is also little chance that the coverage of the events of those five weeks affected the results in any significant way.[84] But the on-air chaos did much to undermine the credibility of the national media, and will doubtless lead to reforms and changes in the processes of media coverage of national elections.[85]

What cannot be changed, however, is the pressure, exacerbated by the Internet, to be first with the news.[86] What will not be changed are the organizational and structural factors and incentives that cause news to be produced as it is currently produced. Looking into the future, things are likely to continue very much the same.

REFLECTIONS ON CAMPAIGN 2004

In 2004 George W. Bush was again the Republican candidate for president, along with Vice President Dick Cheney. Bush began the 2004 campaign by playing *Top Gun*, writes Lance Bennett. His "flight-suited jet landing aboard the aircraft carrier *Abraham Lincoln* on May 1, 2003 (declaring the end to major combat operations in Iraq) was successful as a pseudo event largely by journalistic proclamation. Reporters and pundits referred to it as a Hollywood moment, 'the greatest photo op of all time,' and as an unbeatable, iconic launch to the 2004 election campaign."[87] Bush's opponent, Vietnam War veteran John Kerry, declined to respond to the event. Among other credentials making him well suited to the presidency, John Kerry had served a long career in the Senate prior to securing the Democratic nomination with fellow senator John Edwards as his running mate.[88]

Like the 2000 election, 2004 was rife with controversy. This time, however, the state in question was Ohio. Various news outlets charged the Republican Party with preventing people from voting and/or having their votes counted.[89] Furthermore, companies associated with the paperless voting machines, Diebold and Triad Systems, were accused of election fraud.[90] There is even an Internet site devoted to this election and its plentiful problems.[91] In the end, Bush was awarded 62,040,606 votes, or 51 percent, to Kerry's 59,028,109 votes, or 48 percent. Independent candidate Ralph Nader got 411,304 votes, or 1 percent of the total votes cast.[92] Reporter John King says that the 2004 election was particularly contentious "after the last one in 2000 when the country was split right down the middle. The courts decided the election. You have an incredibly polarized public."[93] This is more than reflected in the actual vote count.

Since the 2004 election, scholars have investigated media effects on that tumultuous election and others in an effort to delineate those effects. In his article about media influence on voters, James Druckman writes that while newspapers and television programs may have different amounts of coverage (newspapers typically have more than television shows), the content of the reports is essentially the same.[94] Even so, Druckman writes, "a number of recent studies suggests that the unique contribution of newspapers in creating an informed electorate is minimal at best."[95] Limitations of the newspaper medium and the television medium necessarily influence how campaign information is received by the audience. That is, newspapers may devote more space to discussing the issues, whereas a television segment is more time constricted. Furthermore, television has the added burden that viewers must be present at the time the program runs (unless one has recorded it).[96] This is important because in today's multitasking 24/7 environment, voters need convenience in their coverage as well as accurate information. In his final analysis, Druckman finds that it is indeed newspapers that may have more influence in teaching the electorate about the issues than television.[97]

In contrast, in a document called *Election Focus 2004,* the U.S. Department of State asserts that "[a]mong the various mass media, television is the most important provider of election media coverage," and this is due to the fact that a whopping 98 percent of Americans have at least one television set.[98] Presumably, the number has remained steady, if not increased, since CNN conducted that poll in 2000. While Americans might gain more knowledge from newspapers, "[t]elevision has become the dominant source of political news for the American public."[99] Regardless of the traditional news source, the goal is the same. John King, a reporter for groups such as CNN and the Associated Press, was questioned about the media's role in presidential elections. He responded, "The most important role is to objectively observe and report on the positions the candidates take in the election, and hopefully as well, to report fairly on what voters view as the biggest issues."[100] Those issues are increasingly addressed in various formats posted on the Internet.

Of course, the Internet was a major source for voters to learn about election 2004—online magazines, blogs, forums, databases, and the like still lurk there, seemingly frozen in time. Groups of all kinds rushed to get candidate and opponent information posted for their readers. Still, says King, while the Internet can be "overrated," it does provide access to candidate information that might otherwise be unavailable to voters.[101] The fact that live coverage and cable news have made way for around-the-clock news coverage means that the media must consistently keep up with current election-related events.

Not only are the media pressed to consistently report new and interesting tidbits, they are increasingly monitored by nongovernmental organizations, many of which use the Internet extensively to communicate with voters.[102] Groups such as MoveOn.org, MediaChannel.org, and FactCheck.org investigate candidate claims and publish corrections, where necessary. That is, "some of these organizations closely monitor mainstream news coverage of their findings in an attempt to hold news executives to higher standards of coverage."[103] In addition, the less the major news organizations cover the issues and policies, the more candidates are forced to pay to get their messages out to the public.[104] This is important because candidates with plentiful coffers may blanket their chosen market with strategic information in the form of direct-mail pieces, rallies, television commercials, and radio interviews, to name just a few means.

CAMPAIGN 2008 AND INTO THE FUTURE

The media are responsible for presenting the public with accurate and timely information precisely because they are so instrumental in forming public opinion about the candidates. As we near the 2008 election, media outlets are already wooing candidates to appear on to their shows.

Beyond such standard appearances as the Sunday morning political programs, the candidates are also getting exposure to the voters through televised debates. For example, CNN and YouTube joined to produce a unique debate featuring voter "video questions in all forms."[105] During this debate, the Democractic candidates addressed thirty-nine out of the three thousand questions submitted.[106] Of course, traditional media outlets such as MSNBC and PBS have also sponsored candidate debates and aired them during prime time. In fact, the Web site You Decide 2008 lists thirteen Democratic candidate debates in 2007 and eleven Republican candidate debates in the same time period.[107] These debates are captured on video and, once complete, routinely posted on the Internet so that voters may access those shows at a convenient time.

In general, we can expect that the media will continue to act in ways that insure audiences, ratings, and profits. When the audience for PBS's highly regarded *NewsHour* exceeds that of the *Jerry Springer Show*, and when viewers demand issue-laden content, political candidates will respond with that sort of information. Until then, we can expect dramatization, personalization, emphasis on the horse race, and an overall trivialization of electoral processes.

As candidates still appeal to lessons learned during and in the aftermath of 9/11, the next election will be a difficult one in which to campaign and a difficult one to cover, as themes of patriotism appropriate to a nation at war are uneasy companions to the sorts of scandal-ridden, sensationalized coverage of the horse race that characterize election news. We cannot expect either the candidates or the media to find comfortable ways of dealing with this dilemma quickly. We can, however, expect a plethora of self-referential stories detailing how these themes and issues are covered; we can also expect stories about how the media are too powerful, too determinative, and too likely to focus on all of the wrong things. Much of this coverage can be safely ignored—and, from the evidence of past elections, voters will indeed ignore most of this coverage.

The media do matter. But they matter within a specific context, and without due attention to that context, the roles of the media will not be properly understood. The most important role the media occupy is that of winnower, for they have tremendous influence on the viability of campaigns, especially early in the process. This is particularly important when one examines the tendency for the media to equate fund-raising with political success, especially in the primaries. Despite evidence (such as the campaigns of John Connally and Michael Huffington) that campaigns are not bought and that money does not guarantee success, the media's equation between fund-raising and political viability is disturbing.

The media are also important as agenda setters. The media not only exercise influence over who will survive the election, but also over which issues the election will turn. Agenda setting is a complicated business, however, for the media and the candidates will focus on the issues that seem to resonate with voters. There is a reciprocity here that is often overlooked in popular discussions of media influence.

That influence relies on standardization, on what is often referred to as *pack journalism*, the tendency of all members of the media to cover the same story in the same way. There is some question as to whether this standardization is threatened by the growth of the Internet, which is radically decentralized, and which, it is often thought, will be taking on increasing influence in future campaigns.[108]

Three things bear noting here: The first is that those who use the Internet as a source of information seem to avail themselves of electronic access to mainstream news sources. That is, instead of reading *The New York Times* or watching NBC, they access the *Times*'s Web page or log on to MSNBC.com. Thus, the sources of news remain substantially the same, although the means of accessing those sources are different.

Second, those who use the Internet as a news source seem to be adding it to their other media. That is, they are not exchanging *The New York Times* for news.com; they are adding Internet sources to *The New York Times*. This means that those people who are already information rich, who follow politics consistently, and who are interested in and likely to participate in politics are likely to become even more aware, with more information and more up-to-the-minute news. Those who are indifferent to politics or who are only marginally interested in and involved in political processes are not likely to become more involved or interested simply because they have a computer in their home. To the extent that they use that computer to access the Internet, it will most likely be to find information on the things that interest them, not to become more aware of or knowledgeable about politics.

Finally, there is considerable overlap between the Internet and "mainstream" news. As Matt Drudge—"old-time gossip hound with a cyber-edge"[109]—and the tabloids have made clear, what appears first in an "illegitimate" venue will quickly be reported in the more "legitimate" news. There is no evidence that this process will work to improve the coverage of issues above symbols or of "legitimate" versus "illegitimate" or tabloid news.

In sum, the future of campaigns looks much like the past. Issue information is out there for those who seek it; the candidates will dedicate themselves to mediated campaigns, and there will be much wailing and gnashing of teeth (especially in the mainstream media) about the debasement of our politics. There will also be considerable speculation about and scholarly attention to the effects and impact of new communication technologies. And the result of the next election may be much like those in the past: Fewer people will vote; they will be disproportionately middle-aged, middle-class, white, and educated; and the media will be blamed for the downward spiral of our politics as we wait to be rescued by a president or presidential candidate who can save the world like movie presidents so often do. It will be a long wait.

DISCUSSION QUESTIONS

1. Much of the criticism of the media assumes that political debate was once "better" than it is now. How do these critics define "better," and when was this golden age of political debate?
2. Why do media scholars insist that mass-mediated argumentation is bad for democracy?
3. Are voters simply passive receivers of media messages?
4. Why is it important to understand media routines, and to understand media as a business?
5. How would elections be different if the media were overtly partisan rather than objective?
6. What is the relationship between media strength and the declining importance of political parties?
7. Why are polls so important to the coverage of elections?
8. How has the Internet changed your own involvement in politics? Do events such as the YouTube/CNN debates make you more receptive to election politics or less so?

SUGGESTIONS FOR FURTHER READING

Stephen Ansolabehere and Shanto Iyengar. *Going Negative: How Political Advertisements Shrink and Polarize the Electorate*. New York: Free Press, 1995.

Robert Entman. *Democracy without Citizens: Media and the Decay of American Politics*. New York: Oxford, 1989.

John G. Geer. *In Defense of Negativity: Attack Ads in Presidential Campaigns*. Chicago: University of Chicago Press, 2006.

Roderick P. Hart. *Seducing America: How Television Charms the American Voter*. New York: Oxford, 1995.

Thomas Patterson. *Out of Order*. New York: Alfred A. Knopf, 1993.

Michael Pfau and Henry Kenski. *Attack Politics: Strategy and Defense*. Westport, CT: Praeger, 1990.

NOTES

1. A quick search on Amazon.com revealed more than 320,000 books on the media—up from 14,000 five years ago. This number, of course, does not include the plethora of academic and journalistic articles on the subject.

2. See, for example, Robert Entman, *Democracy without Citizens: Media and the Decay of American Politics* (New York: Oxford University Press, 1989); Garret J. O'Keefe, "Political Malaise and Reliance on the Media," *Journalism Quarterly* (1980): 122–28.

3. Some of Mary E. Stuckey's work falls into this category.

4. Ben H. Bagdikian, *The Media Monopoly* (Boston: Beacon Press, 2000).

5. Edward S. Herman and Noam Chomsky, *Manufacturing Consent: The Political Economy of the Mass Media* (New York: Pantheon, 2002); Robert Waterman McChesney, *Corporate Media and the Threat to Democracy* (New York: Seven Stars, 1997); Darrell West, *The Rise and Fall of the Media Establishment* (New York: St. Martin's, 2001).

6. Associated Press, "More Go To Web for Political Campaign News," *Editor & Publisher*, January 17, 2007, http://www.editorandpublisher.com/eandp/departments/online/article_display.jsp?vnu_content_id=1003534131 (accessed October 27, 2007).

7. Ibid.

8. Doris Graber, *Mass Media and American Politics*, 5th ed. (Washington, DC: Congressional Quarterly Press, 1987), 244.

9. James Druckman reaches a similar conclusion, that campaign coverage in newspapers and television does "not drastically differ in terms of content." James N. Druckman, "Media Matter: How Newspapers and Television News Cover Campaigns and Influence Voters," *Political Communication* 22 (2005): 363–481.

10. David Paletz, *The Media in American Politics: Contents and Consequences*, 2nd ed. (New York: Longman, 2001); Martin Plissner, *Control Room: How the Media Calls the Shots in Presidential Elections* (New York: Free Press, 1999).

11. Michael Learmonth, "The Lure of Latenight," *Variety* (September 4, 2006– September 10, 2006): 17, LexisNexis Academic, October 28, 2007, http://www.lexisnexis.com/us/lnacademic/.

12. PBS, "More Americans Log On For Campaign News, Study Finds," *PBS Online NewsHour*, January 12, 2004, http://www.pbs.org/newshour/media/media_watch/jan-june04/campaignpew_01–12.html (accessed October 27, 2007).

13. See, for example, IU News Room, "It's No Joke: IU Study Finds *The Daily Show with Jon Stewart* to Be as Substantive as Network News," News Release, October 4, 2006, http://newsinfo.iu.edu/news/page/normal/4159.html (accessed October 27, 2007).

14. W. Lance Bennett, "News as Reality TV: Election Coverage and the Democratization of Truth," *Critical Studies in Mass Communication* 22, no. 2 (June 2005): 171–77.

15. Ibid.

16. Michael Learmonth, "The Lure," 17.

17. As of October 2007, details about the 2004 Republican National Convention may be still be found on C-SPAN at http://www.cspan.org/2004vote/convention.asp?Cat=Special_Topic&Code=GOP&Rot_Cat_CD=GOP. The 2004 Democratic National Convention is similarly detailed on C-SPAN at http://www.c-span.org/2004vote/convention.asp?Cat=Special_Topic&Code=DEMS&Rot_Cat_CD=DEMS.

18. The C-SPAN 2008 Convention Bus Web site is located at http://www.c-span .org/schoolbus/index.asp.

19. Robert Shogan, *Bad News: Where the Press Goes Wrong* (New York: Ivan R. Dee, 2001), as quoted in *NewsHour with Jim Lehrer* transcript, August 21, 2001.

20. Anthony Broh, "Polls, Pols, and Parties," *Journal of Politics* 45 (1983): 732–44.

21. On agenda setting, see Shanto Iyengar, "Television News and Citizens' Explanations of National Affairs," *American Political Science Review* 81 (1987): 815–31; Shanto Iyengar, *Is Anyone Responsible: How Television Frames Political Issues* (Chicago: University of Chicago Press, 1991); Russell J. Dalton et al., "A Test of Media-Centered Agenda Setting: Newspaper Content and Public Interests in a Presidential Election," *Political Communication* 15, no. 4 (October–December 1998): 463–481; Maxwell McCombs, "A Look at Agenda-Setting; Past, Present and Future," *Journalism Studies* 6, no. 4 (November 2005): 543–557; Young Jun Son and David H. Weaver, "Another Look at What Moves Public Opinion: Media Agenda Setting and Polls in the 2000 U.S. Election," *International Journal of Public Opinion Research* 18, no. 2 (Summer 2006): 174–97. On framing, see Robert Entman, "Framing: Toward Clarification of a Fractured Paradigm," *Journal of Communication* 43 (1993): 51–58; Doris Graber, "Framing Election News Broadcasts: News Context and Its Impact on the 1984 Presidential Election," *Social Science Quarterly* 68 (1987): 552–68; Henry Kenski, "From Agenda Setting to Priming and Framing: Reflections on Theory and Method," in *The Theory and Practice of Political Communication Research*, ed. Mary E. Stuckey (Albany: State University of New York Press, 1996), 67–83; Mark M. Miller, Julie L. Andsager, and Bonnie P. Riechert, "Framing the Candidates in Presidential Primaries: Issues and Images in Press Releases and News Coverage," *Journalism & Mass Communication Quarterly* 75, no. 2 (Summer 1998): 312–24; and Julie Yioutas and Ivana Segvic, "Revisiting the Clinton/Lewinsky Scandal: The Convergence of Agenda Setting and Framing," *Journalism & Mass Communication Quarterly* 80, no. 3 (Autumn 2003): 567–82.

22. Pamela Johnston Conover and S. Feldman, "Candidate Perception in an Ambiguous World: Campaigns, Cues, and Inference Processes," *American Journal of Political Science* 33 (1989): 912–40; Doris Graber, *Processing the News: How People Tame the Information Tide* (New York: Longman, 1984); Marion Just et al., *Crosstalk: Citizens, Candidates, and Media in a Presidential Election* (Chicago: University of Chicago Press, 1996).

23. R. Behr and Shanto Iyengar, "Television News, Real-World Cues, and Changes in the Public Agenda," *Public Opinion Quarterly* 49 (1985): 38–57; Diana Owen, *Media Messages in American Political Elections* (New York: Greenwood, 1991).

24. In the 2008 election cycle, primary dates in some key states are being adjusted to occur earlier than they have in the past. Andrew Romano refers to this phenomenon as "super duper Tuesday" with the inclusion of states such as California. With a large and diverse electorate, states like California will likely have an effect on the front-runner status of candidates in the early primaries. Andrew Romano, "Here Comes 'Super Duper' Tuesday," *Newsweek*, March 26, 2007, 30, LexisNexis Academic, http://www.lexisnexis.com/us/lnacademic/ (accessed October 28, 2007).

25. Thomas Patterson, *Out of Order* (New York: Alfred A. Knopf, 1993), 36.

26. Scott Keeter, "The Illusion of Intimacy: Television and the Role of Candidate Qualities in Voter Choice," *Public Opinion Quarterly* 51 (1987): 344–58.

27. For examples, see W. Lance Bennett and Robert M. Entman, eds., *Mediated Politics: Communication in the Future of Democracy* (New York: Cambridge University Press, 2000); Trudy Lieberman, *Slanting the Story: The Forces That Shape the News* (New York: New Press, 2000); Norman Miller, *Environmental Politics: Interest Groups, the Media, and the Making of Policy* (New York: Lewis, 2001); West, *Rise and Fall.*

28. MoveOn.org, "About the MoveOn Family of Organizations," http://www.moveon.org/about.html (accessed October 29, 2007).

29. Ibid.

30. David Weigel, "I'm in the Mood to MoveOn," *Reason*, June 29 2007, http://www.reason.com/blog/show/121139.html (accessed October 28, 2007).

31. Thomas Benson, "Desktop Demos: New Communication Technologies and the Future of the Rhetorical Presidency," in *Beyond the Rhetorical Presidency,* ed. Martin J. Medhurst (College Station: Texas A&M University Press, 1996); David Brin, "Disputation Arenas: Harnessing Conflict and Competitiveness for Society's Benefit," *Ohio State Journal on Dispute Resolution* 15 (2000): 587–617; Dan Johnson, "Politics in Cyberspace," *Futurist* 33, no. 1 (January 1999): 14.

32. See, for example, Hal Berghel, "Digital Politics," *Association for Computing Machinery* 39 (October 1996): 19; Dana Milbank, "Virtual Politics," *New Republic* 221 (July 5, 1999): 22–27.

33. The most glaring example of this in recent times is *Newsweek* reporter Michael Isikoff's relationship with Linda Tripp. Michael Isikoff, *Uncovering Clinton: A Reporter's Story* (New York: Crown, 1999), 58–60, 168.

34. Jack Germond and Jules Witcover, *Mad as Hell: Revolt at the Ballot Box, 1992* (New York: Warner Books, 1993), 103.

35. In his review of George Stephanopoulos's book *All Too Human: A Political Education,* John Pitney writes that there was a good deal of confusion over what, specifically, was Stephanopoulos's role in the Clinton White House. John J. Pitney Jr., *"All Too Human: A Political Education*—Review," *Reason* (July 1999), http://findarticles.com/p/articles/mi_m1568/is_3_31/ai_55015505 (October 27, 2007).

36. On punditry in general, see Eric Alterman, *Sound and Fury: The Meaning of Punditocracy* (Ithaca, NY: Cornell University Press, 2000).

37. David Castle, "Media Coverage of Presidential Primaries," *American Politics Quarterly* 19 (1991): 33–42.

38. John F. Harris, "Despite Bush Flip-Flops, Kerry Gets Label," *Washington Post,* September 23, 2004, http://www.washingtonpost.com/wp-dyn/articles/A43093–2004 Sep22.html (October 29, 2007).

39. Marvin Kalb, "The Rise of the 'New News': A Case Study of Two Root Causes of the Modern Scandal Coverage" (discussion paper D-24, presented at the Joan Shorenstein Center for Press, Politics, and Public Policy, October 1998); *NewsHour with Jim Lehrer* transcript, August 21, 2002.

40. In her article about the effects of horse-race news coverage, Diana C. Mutz describes it as "news emphasizing who is ahead or behind, or gaining or losing ground, [and] is the primary means by which people develop perceptions of the extent of mass public support for candidates" (1015). Diana C. Mutz, "Effects of Horse-Race Coverage on Campaign Coffers: Strategic Contributing in Presidential Primaries," *Journal of Politics* 57, no. 4 (November 1995): 1015–42.

41. Kathleen Frankovic, "Public Opinion and Polling," in *The Politics of News, The News of Politics*, ed. Doris Graber, Daniel McQuail, and Pippa Norris (Washington, DC: Congressional Quarterly Press, 1988), 150–70.

42. Frankovic, "Public Opinion," 156; Owen, *Media Messages,* 89.

43. Owen, *Media Messages.*

44. Frankovic, "Public Opinion," 167.

45. Lori Robertson, "Polled Enough for Ya?" *American Journalism Review* (January/February 2001): 29–33.

46. *NewsHour with Jim Lehrer* transcript, November 8, 2000.

47. Frankovic, "Public Opinion," 167.

48. Jeffrey Fishel, *Presidents and Promises* (Washington, DC: Congressional Quarterly Press, 1985).

49. Roderick P. Hart, *Seducing America: How Television Charms the Modern Voter* (New York: Oxford University Press, 1995); Roderick P. Hart, *The Sound of Leadership: Presidential Communication in the Modern Age* (Chicago: University of Chicago Press, 1987); Kathleen Hall Jamieson, *Eloquence in an Electronic Age: The Transformation of American Political Speechmaking* (New York: Oxford University Press, 1988).

50. *NewsHour with Jim Lehrer* transcript, August 21, 2001.

51. See, for example, Media Matters, "Ignoring Her Extensive Record of Bright Colors and Big Smiles, Fox's Cameron said Clinton Wearing Both to Solve 'Likability Problem,'" May 10, 2007, http://mediamatters.org/items/200705100008 (accessed October 29, 2007); Robin Givhan, "Hillary Clinton's Tentative Dip Into New Neckline Territory," *Washington Post*, July 20, 2007, http://www.washingtonpost.com/wp-dyn/content/article/2007/07/19/AR2007071902668.html (accessed October 29, 2007). For commentary on the relative importance of candidate appearance in general, see Maria Puente, "Candidates' Appearance Never Goes out of Fashion in Politics," *Tennessean*, October 18, 2007, http://www.tennessean.com/apps/pbcs.dll/article?AID=/20071018/FEATURES08/710180303/1005/RSS04 (accessed October 29, 2007).

52. During the 2000 presidential election, Democratic candidate Al Gore repeatedly referred to a "lockbox," even an "ironclad lockbox" designed to protect funds set aside for Social Security and Medicare. See, for example, the transcript of Al Gore and George W. Bush's first debate on October 3, 2000. Commission on Presidential Debates, "CPD: 2000 Debate Transcript," October 3, 2000, http://www.debates.org/pages/trans2000a.html (accessed October 28, 2007).

53. Mary E. Stuckey, *The President as Interpreter-in-Chief* (Chatham, NJ: Chatham House, 1991).

54. Jamieson, *Eloquence in an Electronic Age.*

55. Jeff Greenfield, *The Real Campaign: How the Media Missed the Story of the 1980 Campaign* (New York: Summit Books, 1982), 15.

56. Gina M. Garramone, "Motivation and Selective Attention to Political Information Formats," *Journalism Quarterly* 62 (1985): 37–44.

57. Samuel Popkin, *The Reasoning Voter: Communication and Persuasion in Presidential Campaigns* (Chicago: University of Chicago Press, 1991).

58. Michael Pfau and Henry Kenski, *Attack Politics: Strategy and Defense* (New York: Praeger, 1990).

59. Larry Sabato, *Feeding Frenzy: How Attack Journalism Has Transformed American Politics* (New York: Free Press, 1991), 26.

60. Hart, *Seducing America.*

61. Entman, *Democracy without Citizens*; Kathleen Hall Jamieson, *Dirty Politics: Deception, Distraction, and Democracy* (New York: Oxford University Press, 1992); Jamieson, *Eloquence in an Electronic Age*; Joshua Meyrowitz, "Visible and Invisible Candidates: A Case Study in 'Competing Logics' of Campaign Coverage," *Political Communication* 11 (1994): 145–64; William L. Rivers, *The Other Government; Power and the Washington Media* (New York: Universe, 1982); Sabato, *Feeding Frenzy.*

62. In the presidential contests of the mid-1800s, torchlight parades were considered "a highlight of every election." Candidates used these events "to inspire the most apathetic of voters" in the days before critical elections. History Wired, "A Few of Our Favorite Things," http://historywired.si.edu/detail.cfm?ID=384 (accessed October 29, 2007).

63. The SMU News writes that "Philadelphia distiller E.G. Booz put his whiskey into log cabin-shaped bottles for the 1840 campaign of William Henry Harrison, who was called the 'Log Cabin Candidate.' Thus the word 'booze' entered the American language." SMU News, "From George to George Test Your Campaign Trivia I.Q.," http://www.smu.edu/smunews/george/trivia.asp (accessed October 29, 2007).

64. This slogan was also tied to the 1840 presidential campaign. Harrison was considered a hero because of his role in the Battle of Tippecanoe, where he defeated Shawnee Indians. Also, his Vice President was John Tyler (i.e., "Tyler too"). Presidents of the United States, "1840 Presidential Campaign Slogans," 2002, http://www.presidentsusa.net/1840slogan.html (accessed October 29, 2007).

65. Sabato, *Feeding Frenzy.*

66. Jamieson, *Dirty Politics.*

67. James M. McPherson, *Battle Cry of Freedom: The Civil War Era* (New York: Oxford University Press, 1998), 789–90.

68. See, for example, Clement Greenberg, "Avant-Garde and Kitsch," *Partisan Review* 6 (Fall 1939): 34–49.

69. W. Lance Bennett, *News: The Politics of Illusion* (New York: Longman, 1988).

70. Bonnie Dow, *Prime-Time Feminism: Television, Media Culture, and the Women's Movement Since 1970* (Philadelphia: University of Pennsylvania Press, 1996), 18.

71. The presidential election of 2004 may be an exception. The U.S. Census Bureau reports that in the 2004, 64 percent of eligible citizens older than eighteen cast a vote. That figure was up slightly from 60 percent in the election of 2000. U.S. Census Bureau, "U.S. Voter Turnout Up in 2004, Census Bureau Reports," May 26, 2005, http://www.census.gov/Press-Release/www/releases/archives/voting/004986.html (accessed October 29, 2007).

72. Greenfield, *Real Campaign,* 27.

73. See, for example, Angie Cannon and Roger Simon, "The Making of a Political Spoiler," *U.S. News & World Report* 129 (November 6, 2000): 20; John Colapinto, "Ralph Nader Is Not Sorry," *Rolling Stone* 887 (September 13, 2001): 64.

74. See, for example, Jackie Calmes, "Nader Not Likely to Reach 5% Threshold," *Wall Street Journal*, November 8, 2000, A17; Cannon and Simon, "Political Spoiler."

75. See, for example, James Bradley, "Nader, Schmader," *Village Voice*, November 7, 2000, 28.

76. Most of the coverage was concerned with issues of personality. See, for example, Geoffrey Leon, "Blame Ego-Politics, Not Eco-Politics" *New Statesman* 130 (July 16, 2001): 22; Paul Magnusson, "The Punishing Price of Nader's Passion," *Business Week* 3708 (November 20, 2000): 44; Godfrey Sperling, "Mystery Men," *Christian Science Monitor*, November 7, 2000, 9; Lenora Todaro, "Ralph Nader Lashes Back," *Village Voice*, December 26, 2000, 29.

77. Daphne Eviatar, "Murdoch's Fox News: They Distort, They Decide," *Nation*, March 12, 2001; Alicia C. Shepard, "How They Blew It," *American Journalism Review* 23 (January/February 2001): 20–28; Sharyn Wizda, "Playing Favorites?" *American Journalism Review* 22 (January/February 2000): 34–39.

78. *NewsHour with Jim Lehrer* transcript, November 8, 2000.

79. Robert Kuttner, "Two Bad Calls: The Faulty Ballots, The Bumbling Press," *Boston Globe*, November 19, 2000, C7; *NewsHour with Jim Lehrer* transcript February 13, 2001.

80. Marvin Kalb, "Election 2000: What Does It All Mean? A Big Loss for Network News," *Boston Globe*, November 9, 2000, A19.

81. *NewsHour with Jim Lehrer* transcript, February 13, 2001.

82. Shepard, "How They Blew It."

83. Kuttner, "Two Bad Calls."

84. *NewsHour with Jim Lehrer* transcript, February 13, 2001.

85. Associated Press, "Voter News Service Opts to Carry On, but Revamp," *Washington Post*, June 1, 2001, A4. Since that election, changes have been made. CNN, for example, released a report detailing its new policies, including discontinuing the use of exit polls to project close races and discontinuing projection of the winner in a state until the polls have officially closed. CNN.com, "CNN Announces Election Night Coverage Change, Following 'Debacle,'" February 2, 2001, http://archives.cnn.com/2001/ALLPOLITICS/stories/02/02/cnn.report/index.html (accessed October 28, 2007). See also, CNN.com, "Statement of CNN Regarding Future Election Night Coverage," February 2, 2001, http://archives.cnn.com/2001/ALLPOLITICS/stories/02/02/cnn.statement/ (accessed October 28, 2007).

86. On the continuing importance of such pressure, see remarks by news anchors that appear in *NewsHour with Jim Lehrer* transcript, February 13. 2001; and in Kathy Kellogg and Terry Frank, "Media Fixture Finds Much to Say about the Election," *Buffalo (NY) News*, November 30, 2000, 3B.

87. W. Lance Bennett, "News as Reality TV: Election Coverage and the Democratization of Truth," *Critical Studies in Mass Communication* 22, no. 2 (June 2005): 171–77.

88. John Kerry won his Senate seat for the state of Massachusetts in 1984. PBS, "Online NewsHour Vote 2004 I Candidates I John Kerry I Political Career," http://www.pbs.org/newshour/vote2004/candidates/can_kerry-career.html (accessed October 29, 2007). John Edwards had been a senator for North Carolina for just one term when he became Kerry's running mate. Prior to that, he had been a successful trial lawyer. Nevertheless, Kerry eagerly endorsed him for the position of vice president

because of his skill and rigor to "think, argue, advocate and legislate." CNN.com, "Kerry Names Edwards His Running Mate," July 6, 2004, http://www.cnn.com/2004/ ALLPOLITICS/07/06/kerry.vp/ (accessed October 29, 2007).

89. For example, *Rolling Stone* reported that that amount would have made Kerry the victor in the election. Robert F. Kennedy Jr., "Was the 2004 Election Stolen?" *Rolling Stone*, June 1, 2006, http://www.rollingstone.com/news/story/10432334/was _the_2004_election_stolen (accessed October 29, 2007).

90. William Rivers Pitt, "Proof of Ohio Election Fraud Exposed," *t r u t h o u t*, Report, December 15, 2004, http://www.truthout.org/docs_04/121604Z.shtml (accessed October 29, 2007).

91. See http://www.electionfraud2004.org.

92. CNN.com, "Election 2004—U. S. President," 2005, http://www.cnn.com/ ELECTION/2004/pages/results/president/ (accessed October 29, 2007).

93. U.S. Department of State, "Presidential Election Media Coverage: An Interview with John King," *Election Focus 2004* 1, no. 11 (May 21, 2004): 4.

94. James N. Druckman, "Media Matter: How Newspapers and Television News Cover Campaigns and Influence Voters," *Political Communication* 22 (2005): 463–81.

95. Ibid., 463.

96. Ibid., 464.

97. Ibid., 476. While this may be a generalizable result, mind the fact that Druckman's analysis is based on one campaign, albeit with rigorous control mechanisms. The campaign he used in analysis was for a Minnesota Senate seat in 2000. Furthermore, the "standard length of a political spot in 2004 [was] 30 seconds." U.S. Department of State, "Media and the 2004 Election," *Election Focus 2004* 1, no. 11 (May 21, 2004): 2.

98. Ibid., 1.

99. Ibid.

100. U.S. Department of State, "Presidential," 1, 3.

101. Ibid., 4.

102. U.S. Department of State, "Monitoring Media Coverage of Elections," *Election Focus 2004* 1, no. 11 (May 21, 2004): 5.

103. Ibid.

104. Ibid.

105. CNN, "Questions, Not Answers, Highlight YouTube Debate," July 27, 2007, http://www.cnn.com/2007/POLITICS/07/23/debate.main/ (October 27, 2007).

106. Ibid.

107. You Decide 2008, "Full 2008 Debate Schedule from DNC and GOP— Updated 10/20/07," October 20, 2007, http://www.youdecide 2008.com/2007/06/13/ full-2008-debate-schedule-from-dnc-and-gop/ (accessed October 28, 2007).

108. Benson, "Desktop Demos."

109. Jeffrey Zaslow, "Matt Drudge," *USA Weekend*, July 3–5, 1998, http://www .usaweekend.com/98_issues/980705/980705talk_drudge.html (accessed October 27, 2007).

INTERVIEW: DAVID MARK,
SENIOR EDITOR, *POLITICO*

Why journalism?

Journalism was an outgrowth of my interest in politics. I really got into it during my freshmen year in college, in 1992. I started following the presidential race very closely. That extended to the congressional races. After the election was over I started watching C-SPAN, watching what was going on in Congress and I found myself essentially following the news all the time, kind of a classic news junkie, and I realized when I was trying to figure out whether I wanted to go to law school or academia for politics, I realized that I might as well get paid for doing what I would be doing anyway with my free time—that's what made me want to go into news.

Ever think about becoming a politician?

Not seriously. I realized you have to have a certain kind of personality for that. . . . I like being objective. I thought very seriously about academia, going for my PhD in political science and then teaching. What I really like to do is kind of be dispassionate and look at it from the sidelines and even though I might have opinions on certain issues. . . . I like more the process of it and being able to observe it from the sidelines.

Path to your current job?

I started out at a local paper in Southern California, where I'm from, in Pasadena, California. I worked my way then to the Associated Press where I worked in Tallahassee, Florida, covering the state legislature and Gov. Jeb Bush. I knew that I eventually wanted to come to Washington, I was always watching C-SPAN and my eyes were on Washington. I got an offer to join *Congressional Quarterly*. . . . I worked on covering Capitol Hill for two years or so and moved on over to *Campaigns and Elections* magazine, where, through a strange set of circumstances, I ended up as the editor when I was about thirty years old. And then, since October 2006, I've been at the *Politico*, where I'm a senior editor.

What is the Politico *and what do you do there?*

Politico is a nonpartisan newspaper and Web site. It's published in print three days a week and on the web all the time. It covers campaigns, lobbying, and Congress. . . . The print version is much more aimed at Capitol Hill insiders along the lines of *Roll Call* or the *Hill*, while the Web site is for a national political audience.

I am senior editor at the *Politico*, meaning probably about 70 percent of my job is doing the ideas, the opinion op-ed section, so I am responsible for soliciting articles from outside contributors, and having them write it along our guidelines and editing them and making sure they conform to *Politico* stan-

dards. I also line edit other reporters' articles, particularly on weekends. We ro-
tate who edits on weekends, and often these are some very odd hours. I write
and report a fair amount still. I was in Minnesota recently covering a congressional race out there. And then I do some strategic planning for the publication's future. . . Fifty to sixty hours a week or so.

Liberal bias in the media?
I don't think most reporters consciously are biased in favor of Democrats and
liberals. I don't think most journalists wake up in the morning and say, "How
are we going to help the Democrats get the Republicans?" Instead it's more
how issues are framed and what stories are done in the first place. The fact that
you see many stories repeatedly on the growing wealth gap. That's a legitimate
story to a point, but in a sense it's a reflection of free-market economics and
that's always going to take place. You see it on the abortion issue many times,
where if you are antiabortion you are often just labeled as wrong or strange or
out of the mainstream. In fact you rarely hear stories about how big of a bite
taxes take out of people's paycheck, how hard it is to raise a family when your
getting 30 percent of your income or more confiscated by the government.
That's a story you rarely see done. You often hear stories about what the government isn't doing for people rather than questioning whether it is the responsibility of government. I think in the recent debate over SCHIP, the children's health spending bill—not even getting into the merit of the
legislation—I think much of the coverage seemed to suggest that the government owed this kind of health expansion coverage to children and other young-
sters, and maybe it should, maybe it doesn't—not my place to say—but I didn't
see the other side of the argument presented very well, suggesting why is the
government in this kind of business in the first place.

I wouldn't say that it is a consistent problem at *Politico*. I think most of the
reporters are pretty mainstream, down the middle. You do see it occasionally;
it's a choice of words. You see it on the abortion issue often . . . on gay rights
. . . someone'll say someone is "against gay rights" and that's kind of a loaded
question because you can be not in favor of hate crimes legislation but not be
antigay as well. It's those kind of touchstone cultural issues where bias plays
itself out most frequently.

In your experience, is the journalistic profession liberal?
I would say it is overwhelmingly liberal, more like 89 to 90 percent liberal or
so. . . . I think a lot of journalists are pretty careful to register as independents.
If you register with a party it's public information and sources can go use that
against you, and say, "Oh, why should you believe that story, he's a registered
Democrat or Republican"—but just knowing the kind of people who get into
it. You see, many people get into journalism because they want to change the
world, they want to comfort the afflicted and afflict the comfortable. . . . I don't

have any problem with that, but for me it was more selfish reasons it was my own curiosity. I'm a voracious reader, I always want to find out more . . . and that's why I got into [it], not for ideological reasons.

Your politics?
I keep that very quiet. I don't even tell my girlfriend or most of my family. I won't say how I vote. The great thing about our system is it is a secret ballot. . . . I do have opinions; I do vote. I'm a taxpaying citizen; I have just as much right to have a statement about who is going to lead our country as anybody else, but when you are a journalist you kind of lose that right to go off and spout off about your opinions.

Some people think that I'm a flaming liberal, some people think I'm a paleoconservative, some people think that I'm a moderate . . . and that's just the way I like it.

How has the Internet changed the media?
It's driven up the metabolism exponentially. There was a time in the not-too-distant past when you basically had one news cycle a day at a newspaper, you did one story a day or so. Now we are constantly trying to pound news out. We're not just breaking our own stories but competing with other news outlets as well. So it has just quickened the metabolism many times over.

How is broadcast journalism different from print?
Much of it is about pictures, to be honest—it's what images you can use on the screen as opposed to the content of what you're saying. When I've done television . . . I won't say anything on television that I not willing to say in print. I won't speculate beyond what I know. Anything I'd be ashamed to say in print, I don't want to say on television either. But clearly television is very much about pictures. I see this every day because *Politico* is owned by the local news station, the local ABC affiliate, and I see how they put together their packages and it's all about images . . . rather than ideas.

Biggest interviews?
Vice President [Dick] Cheney. . . . He's very short and to the point, he's not Mister Talkative, he's very careful what he says, but he gave us some information.

Gov. Jeb Bush of Florida, Gov. [Arnold] Schwarzenegger of California, Senate Majority Leaders Harry Reid and Bill Frist before him, many other congressional leaders, Dennis Hastert and Nancy Pelosi, the Speakers of the House.

Proudest moments as a journalist?
In terms of covering news, when I was working for the Associated Press in Tallahassee, there was an overnight sit-in in the office of Gov. Jeb Bush by a couple of African American lawmakers [who were] protesting his executive order

banning affirmative action in state contracts, state's hiring, education, university systems, etc. They went up to his office, they staged a sit-in and they literally just camped out in his office. Bush, minding public appearances, was loath to have state troopers evict a couple of African American lawmakers from his office. . . . They were very savvy about getting press attention; we were tipped off about twenty minutes before that they were going to be going up there. A bunch of journalists collected in the office and we were told by the state troopers, "You're welcome to stay here all night but once you step out of the office you're gone, you can't come back in." So we were faced with the choice of essentially staying all the way through the night. We did that, we stayed overnight with these state lawmakers, got the story, stuck to them like glue until we were eventually tossed out by the Florida Department of Law Enforcement—but actually sticking to that story through the night and making sure we got it was my proudest moment in daily journalism.

My other proudest professional accomplishment is my book, *Going Dirty: The Art of Negative Campaigning*. The thing about writing articles, everyday journalism, is that it is fleeting. Even if you do a really great, in-depth piece, people read it and say, "Oh, that's great!" and then they move on. But if you do a book, it's remembered. It got a fair amount of commercial acclaim, I got to go on *The Daily Show with Jon Stewart*, and it's being picked up in courses in academia. And most importantly, it's lasting—it's on the shelves. I still hear from campaign consultants and other folks, academics, who've read it and know who I am.

What ethical dilemmas have you faced as a journalist?
Running the op-ed section, people want to curry favor and they want sometimes to buy you gifts or take you to a ball game and certain questions about whether I should accept this or that. . . . I've had cash offers. Somebody said, "We really need to get this op-ed placed, it's about this certain legislative issue that's coming up before Congress, it would really help our client, would $200 do?" Of course I said, "Absolutely not, get out of my face."

To be honest, it really makes me question when I read op-eds now in a lot of very reputable publications—I really wonder where a lot of them are coming from.

What don't most people know about media politics that would surprise them?
I would just say it is amazing how many times politicians are able to get their viewpoints across without being questioned very aggressively. Just go up and recite their talking points without a journalist questioning them, . . looking at their motivations and just kind of rewriting their press releases. Not to say that I'm always perfect in that regard. I would just say that anybody who wants to get involved in journalism, when a politician volunteers information like, "Hey I'm sponsoring this bill" or "I'm going to take this action," question why they

are doing it. It doesn't mean that it is an illegitimate story, but you have to look at their motivation for bringing it forward.

Advice for young people thinking about going into journalism?
It's the kind of thing to do only if you're very, very attracted to it. There are a lot of downsides to it. At least early in your career, the pay isn't nearly what it would be compared to other industries. The hours can be extreme. To really work your way up sometimes you have to go to odd markets. You might have to go out to rural Mississippi or Nebraska—I don't mean to criticize those places, fine places, but they're not necessarily Manhattan or Washington or Los Angeles; they aren't epicenters of activity in the country sometimes, so there are a lot of sacrifices to be made. The upside is you get to interview a lot of interesting people. I'm heading out on the road to Iowa shortly to cover the presidential race. You come into contact with people you probably would not otherwise. I interview members of Congress . . . activists, policy makers, other folks like that. Basically if you're a curious person, if you really enjoy learning, reading, educating yourself, there's no better way to make a living.

9

The News Media and Organized Interests
in the United States

Ronald G. Shaiko

The relationship between the American news media and organized interest groups and their lobbyists in Washington is a schizophrenic one—simultaneously antagonistic and symbiotic; it is also qualitatively different from the relationships between the media and the institutions of governance in Washington discussed in earlier chapters. In the American political system, the news media and organized interests are components of civil society, serving as institutional intermediaries in the political space between the citizens and the state. While both the media and organized interest groups are regulated, to a limited extent, by the federal government, they are autonomous institutions, constitutionally protected from excessive interference by the government. As such, both the news media and interest groups may serve as institutional checks on the political system and as institutional advocates for democratic governance. Nonetheless, neither the news media nor organized interests have responsibilities for governance in the American political system. Therefore, the political accountability of the news media and of organized interest groups is less clear. In theory, interest group leaders are accountable to their members, whether employees and stockholders in corporations, union members, or citizens who join collective action groups. The news media, in the twenty-first century are increasingly accountable to the corporate conglomerates that own the media outlets, and, secondarily, to the readers, listeners, and viewers who consume their news products.

MEDIA CONCENTRATION AND ITS CONSEQUENCES

Twenty-five years ago, Ben Bagdikian wrote about the "media monopoly" that was emerging in the industry. At the time, he found roughly fifty media conglomerates dominating the media market.[1] In the 2000 edition of *The Media Monopoly*, Bagdikian lowered the figure to around ten mega media companies and another dozen conglomerates as second-tier competitors.[2] In his most recent revision, Bagdikian adapted his title to reflect the changes that have occurred in the early years of the twenty-first century: *The New Media Monopoly*. By 2004 Bagdikian had cut the number of globally dominant media conglomerates to just five corporations—Time Warner, Walt Disney Company, Viacom, News Corp., and Bertelsmann.[3] Each of these media conglomerates has grown exponentially over the past two decades. In 1988 Time and Warner Communications generated revenues of $4.2 billion and $3.4 billion, respectively. By 2006 Time Warner produced $44.2 billion in revenues, with $6.6 billion in profits. Disney grew from a $2.9-billion company to a media conglomerate generating $34.3 billion in revenues during the same time frame. In 1988 Viacom was a $600-million company; by 2006 it generated more than $11 billion in revenues. News Corporation and Bertelsmann, a German media conglomerate, each produced more than $20 billion in revenues in 2006. The second-tier media corporations include the large newspaper-based conglomerates such as Gannett, Knight-Ridder, and the New York Times Company, along with cable conglomerates Comcast and Cox Enterprises and CBS, a broadcast corporation. These second-tier corporations, while not as comprehensive in media scope, witnessed similar profits during the decade of the 1990s and into first decade of the twenty-first century. In fact, Cox Enterprises rivals the top five global media conglomerates, with annual revenues in 2006 of more than $20 billion.[4]

The paradox of such financial profitability in the media sector is what Penn Kimball has labeled the "downsizing of the news."[5] With the concentration of the media in the hands of a relatively few corporate giants, the value of news gathering and dissemination is now counterbalanced by the value of corporate profitability. As a result, the major television networks as well as the large newspaper chains have cut back significantly on news-reporting workforces. Kimball found that "the drastic budget cuts experienced by the three networks since being taken over by new corporate management in 1986 have hit the Washington bureaus substantially, but less drastically than elsewhere. NBC, CBS, and ABC have all closed down or downsized most of their bureaus overseas and across the country."[6] These cutbacks, along with the proliferation of alternative information sources via cable outlets and the Internet, have produced a qualitatively different media system for the twenty-first century, one Bill Kovach and Tom Rosensteil identify as "the new Mixed Media Culture." This culture has five major characteristics, each of which has consequences for the relationship between the news media and organized interests in the United States: (a) never-ending news cycles that make journalism less complete, (b) sources gaining power over journalists, (c) no more gatekeepers, (d) argument is overwhelming reporting, and (e) the "blockbuster" mentality.[7]

Instant journalism, as practiced by the twenty-four-hour cable networks, produces a never-ending news cycle that influences the decisions of television network executives and newspaper editors. Journalism-on-the-cheap, a result of paradoxical staff cutbacks at the major networks and on newspapers in the face of huge corporate profits, has made journalists far more reliant on sources as *the* primary means of developing stories. Due to the proliferation of media alternative outlets, there is no longer a journalistic consensus regarding "newsworthiness," resulting in lowest-common-denominator reporting.

Related to these changes in the media culture, the culture of argument has supplanted the culture of news gathering and verification: "The economics of these new media, indeed, demand that this product be produced as cheaply as possible. Commentary, chat, speculation, opinion, argument, controversy, and punditry cost far less than assembling a team of reporters, producers, fact checkers, and editors to cover the far-flung corners of the world."[8] And, finally, the *big* story sells!

MEDIA COMPETENCE AND INTEREST GROUP INFLUENCE

Each of the characteristics outlined above offers an avenue for organized interests and their representatives to influence the news media in ways that benefit the organized interests, often at the expense of the collective interests of the general public. These changes in the media culture have also affected the relationship between organized interests and the news media. This love-hate relationship has developed over time and has become even more complex in recent years. In the past, one would be hard-pressed to characterize news media portrayals of interest groups and lobbyists as anything other than negative. Phrases such as "special interests," "hired guns," and "influence peddlers" are widely used to characterize interest groups and lobbyists. Jeffrey Birnbaum—*Washington Post* columnist, political analyst on Fox News, and author of two books on lobbyists and lobbying—when asked to characterize the relationship between the news media and the lobbying profession at a meeting of the American League of Lobbyists in Washington, D.C., replied, "[I]n general, it is antagonistic."[9]

On one level, the antagonism is mutual. Lobbyists and leaders of interest groups, particularly those not held in high esteem by the journalistic community (e.g., corporate representatives, conservative group leaders), feel as though the news media do not present a fair and accurate portrayal of interest groups and lobbyists in general and in their specific roles in the public policymaking process. In a 1998 membership survey conducted by the American League of Lobbyists, a national association of government relations and public affairs professionals, 76 percent of the lobbyists sampled responded negatively to the question "Do you believe that the press generally portrays lobbying and lobbyists fairly?" Only 19 percent felt that the press is fair in its coverage of lobbyists and lobbying activities. When asked which publication generally portrays the lobbying profession the most objectively, only *National Journal*, a weekly politics and policy magazine, garnered more than 25 percent of the responses. Conversely, while most respondents reported reading the *Washington Post* and *The New York Times* on a daily basis, fewer than 5 percent of the respondents selected either newspaper as the most objective portrayer of the lobbying profession.[10]

Journalists tend to view lobbyists as easy targets for derision. Unlike policy makers in Congress or in executive agencies, lobbyists have little recourse against attacks by journalists. Since members of Congress as well as presidents often use "special interests" as scapegoats in the policymaking process, journalists are free to follow the lead of government officials in targeting organized interests and their representatives as part of the problem rather than part of the solution. No president in modern history was as inextricably linked to organized interests and their political contributions as President Bill Clinton, yet that did not stop him from lamenting the ills of special interests in the nation's capital. So if the president can do it, why not the press?

Despite the negative characterizations often presented by the media of interest groups and lobbyists, the general public perceives journalists as too often influenced by such groups. In a 1997 national survey conducted by the Roper Center/Gannett Newseum, 63 percent of the respondents believed that the news media are too manipulated by special interests.[11] In many ways, such findings fuel the antagonism between these two institutional intermediaries.

Yet, on another level, there is a growing symbiotic relationship between interest groups and the media. The events of the last fifteen years in Washington, D.C., have injected a dose of pragmatic compromise to this otherwise hostile relationship. Thomas Boggs, one of the elder statesmen of the lobbying industry, identified three important occurrences that have led to a greater willingness on the part of organized interests to engage the press in policy dialogues.[12] First, in the early 1990s, Congress, with the assistance of President George H. W. Bush, passed the Budget Enforcement Act (BEA), creating a pay-as-you-go mechanism in the budget process. The BEA, you may recall, broke the Bush "read my lips, no new taxes" pledge and likely assisted in his defeat in 1992. Its longer-term impact was to pit interest group against interest group. Advocates for Group X had to defend their existing government program from attack by advocates of Group Y, who wished to kill the Group X program and use those saved revenues to fund the Group Y program. While the battle for policy ground continued as usual within the halls of Congress, interest groups began to take their messages to the media to articulate the comparative advantages of their programs. So after decades of giving the press the silent treatment for their negative characterizations, interest group leaders and lobbyists began to contact journalists with new information on ongoing policy issues.

Second, the 1994 elections and the ensuing Republican revolution in Congress so changed the balance of power and upset the internal lobbying relationships between lobbyists and policy makers that interest group leaders and lobbyists had to develop new lines of communication to members of Congress and their staffs. The subsequent recapturing of the House and Senate by the Democrats in 2006 once again upset the balance of power in Washington, D.C., causing organized interests and their lobbyists to rethink their strategies. As a result of these two significant power shifts, almost two-thirds of the current members of Congress were not in Congress in 1990; old lines of communication would not work with new occupants of the House and Senate. For lobbyists, the media served as an important new conduit through which issues could be communicated. And third, related to the first two occurrences but broader in scope, was the emergence of grassroots lobbying as one of the key elements in any interest group strategy. Organized interests must demonstrate to policy makers that policy proposals or changes to existing policies have demonstrably positive or at least no detrimental impact on the folks back home. To the extent that the news media can assist in delivering such a message, organized interests will engage the media to serve their ends. Rarely do contemporary interest group strategies not include a media or "outside lobbying" component.[13]

From the media perspective, the pragmatic compromise and engagement with organized interests comes out of necessity, for all of the reasons outlined above regarding increasingly limited resources and the proliferation of alternative media. Journalism-on-the-cheap requires a reportorial shorthand. Just as members of Congress and their staffs rely on interest groups for information and, more important, intelligence (information in political context), so too must the news media. But, as with institutions of governance and interest groups, there is a potential danger with an increased media engagement with organized interests.

More than a half century ago, Jesse Unruh, the architect of the modern California legislature, reached the following conclusion regarding the relationship between organized interests and the legislature: Lobbyists and interest group leaders "have influence in inverse ratio to legislative competence. It is common for a special interest to be the only source of legislative information about itself. The information that a lobbyist presents may or may not be prejudiced in favor of his client, but if it is the only information that the legislature has, no one can really be sure. A special interest monopoly of information seems to be more sinister than the outright buying of votes that has been excessively imputed to lobbyists."[14] In constructing the modern legislature in California, Unruh sought to build a competent institution, one that would not be solely reliant on information generated by organized interests. As a result, the California legislature is a full-time, professionalized, fully staffed institution capable of generating its own information and able to check the validity of information provided by organized interests.

Today, the same relationship exists between the news media and organized interests—*interest groups and lobbyists have influence in inverse ratio to media competence.* To the degree that the news media, through both newspapers and local, network, and cable news reporting, are institutionally ill equipped to analyze and verify information independent of outside sources, the influence of organized interests and their representatives will grow significantly in years to come. And, in many ways, the stakes are higher for the media than they are for modern legislatures. For in the legislative setting, organized interests are far more constrained in presenting information to policy makers than they ever will be in presenting information to journalists. There is an old adage among lobbyists in Washington, D.C.—"You can't make the same mistake once." That is, you cannot afford to give a member of Congress, congressional staffer, White House staffer, executive official, or any other policy maker a single piece of untruthful information. The second a member of Congress uses that information in the policymaking process and the information is found to be erroneous, the lobbyist who provided the information might as well pack his or her bags and leave town, because his or her lobbying career is over. Do lobbyists advocate for particular positions? Yes. Do they present their position in the best light possible? Yes. But the best lobbyists present all sides of the issue, including the strengths and weaknesses of their positions and the potential positive and negative consequences of the support of a member of Congress. In the relationship between organized interests and their representatives and journalists, there are no such constraints placed on lobbyists. Lobbyists are free to spin journalists, but lobbyists spin policy makers at their peril.

SPIN AND NEWS MEDIA SOURCES

Spin is a word that has crept into the American political vernacular only in recent years, yet the idea of spin has been around for a long time. The idea of spin was articulated by George Orwell in his classic *1984,* in the form of "newspeak." In Orwell's totalitarian state, those in power controlled thought by controlling language. Today, signs of political language control are everywhere. We don't have pro-abortion or antiabortion groups in the United States; we have pro-choice and pro-life groups. Organizations on the left and the right battle for supremacy in issue framing; sometimes the left wins and sometimes the right—although in recent years, the political right has been a more dominant force in political rhetorical battles.[15] For example, a gold star should be awarded to the person who labeled the antiunion movement in the United States the National Right to Work Committee—brilliant. Who could be against the right to work? Interest groups of all political and ideological stripes seek to control the language of political debate, to force the opposition to use their words, and to convince the media to adopt their words as well.

In his book *Spin This!* Bill Press offers the following succinct definition: "Spin (n): something between truth and a lie."[16] Orwell, in his powerful essay "Politics and the English Language," offered a more nuanced approach to spin, arguing that "political language . . . is designed to make lies sound truthful and murder respectable, and to give the appearance of solidity to pure wind."[17] The final phrase is most appropriate to the contemporary political environment—spin as giving the appearance of solidity to pure wind. Under current conditions, the news media—and the broadcast and cable outlets in particular—are increasingly susceptible to being spun by interest groups and their lobbyists seeking to promote their own organizational agendas. With comparatively limited time, brought on by never-ending news cycles, and limited resources due to significant cutbacks in staffs, travel, and support, the news media have an increasingly difficult task of distinguishing facts from spin. And if the news media fail in discerning the difference, they are responsible for giving substance and legitimacy to pure wind.

Ultimately journalists must rely on sources to provide substance to stories and articles. Judgments made by journalists regarding the validity of sources are based on experience, verifiability, and corroboration, according to Jack Fuller, president and publisher of the *Chicago Tribune*, in his book *News Values.* But fundamentally, "the basis of news reporting is a kind of trust. It begins with trust between a journalist and his sources of information and from there builds to the trust he wants to establish with his audience. No rule of thumb can describe the complex factors that go into a judgment of trust."[18]

From the relationships between lobbyists and journalists presented thus far, it is difficult, at an institutional level, to identify any systematic pattern of trust established between these two elements of civil society. Rather, it is likely that relationships have developed and will continue to develop in a piecemeal fashion, with trust relationships forming in particular policy niches (e.g., between environmental lobbyists and environmental beat reporters or between defense lobbyists and Pentagon correspondents), with marriages (perhaps *trysts* is a better word) of convenience developing on an episodic basis. For if only one thing is true in Washington, D.C., from an interest group perspective it is this: There are no permanent friends and no permanent enemies, only permanent interests. As a result, interest groups and their lobbyists are primarily, if not solely, obligated to their own political interests and will use whatever means necessary to advocate those interests, including spinning the news media when it is useful in their advocacy strategies. To the degree that the news media are institutionally competent, they resist being spun and report the news in a balanced and accurate fashion. Of course, in the current media culture identified above, this is easier said than done.

FIVE CASES OF ADVOCACY IN THE MEDIA

Interest group advocacy through the media in the United States appears in two basic forms. First, organized interests may simply purchase commercial airtime on television or radio, or place advertisements in newspapers. This approach is often referred to as *paid media*—that is, interest groups craft the messages on their own and simply buy airtime or advertising space in order to disseminate their messages to wider audiences. For the most part, the news media have no part in such activities, although news media outlets have increasingly sought to perform a watchdog role on political advertising, particularly in the context of elections. A classic example of paid media campaigns is the series of "Harry and Louise" commercials aired by the Health Insurance Association of America (HIAA) during the debate over the Clinton Health Care Plan in 1993–1994. Expertly crafted, these "'issue advocacy" television commercials cut through the clutter surrounding the complex debate and drove home a message that resonated with citizens. The enduring legacy of "Harry and Louise" led to their resurrection in 2002 in the context of the congressional debate on cloning and fetal tissue research, much to the dismay of HIAA leaders, who did not take a position in the debate.

Second, interest groups and lobbyists attempt to persuade the news media that the issues that they are advocating are sufficiently newsworthy to warrant coverage in major newspapers and on network and cable news programs. This approach is referred to as *earned media* or *free media*—that is, interest groups receive news coverage and, as a result, have their messages disseminated to wider audiences at no cost to the organizations. If interest groups are really lucky, they can convert paid media into free media by packaging their issue or product in such a way that local news organizations will air the item as news, rather than as a paid "infomercial." Such packages, known as *video news releases* (VNRs), have become more prevalent in recent years.

CONVERTING PAID MEDIA INTO FREE/EARNED MEDIA—VNRS

Organized interests of all types seek to generate free or earned media as opposed to paying for airtime or advertising space. While VNRs are largely produced and disseminated to media outlets by economic interests—corporations and business/trade associations—the federal government produces VNRs in support of its programs and initiatives as well. Video news releases are prepackaged television spots that resemble news segments on daily newscasts. Organized interests send these segments to local network affiliates or cable outlets "with the hope that reporters will incorporate all or some of the footage into a news segment."[19] The issue, in the context of this chapter, is how such VNRs are identified to viewers and listeners. Are they presented as news, without attribution, or are they clearly identified as being produced by an organization unaffiliated with the news entity? The Federal Communications Commission (FCC) regulates the broadcast media in the United States, including the content of newscasts. It does not, however, regulate newspapers. As a result, there is no similar burden placed on newspaper editors in running press releases verbatim, without attribution. In its recent decision in September 2007 against a local cable operator for airing VNRs without attribution, the FCC ruled that Comcast and its affiliated cable network, CN8, was in violation of Section 76.1615 of FCC rules: "This rule generally requires cable operators engaged in origination cablecasting to make sponsorship identification announcements when presenting matter in return for money, service, or other valuable consideration. We find that Comcast cablecast portions of the video news release ('VNR') produced on behalf of 'Nelson's Rescue Sleep' without also airing required sponsorship identification announcements."[20] Comcast was fined $4,000 in this action. Currently there are dozens of additional cases pending before the FCC regarding VNR violations.

Two media watchdog groups, the Center for Media and Democracy (CMD) and Free Press, have spearheaded the campaign for VNR disclosure. It was the Center for Media and Democracy that first posited the "valuable consideration" argument against local television and cable outlets, which was adopted in the FCC ruling. To date, CMD has identified more than one hundred instances in which VNRs were run without attribution, including segments produced by Capital One, Harris Corporation, John Deere, General Mills, and Allstate Insurance.[21]

Beyond the distribution of VNRs by corporate interests seeking to gain free/earned media for their interests, the federal government spends significant amounts of money marketing its policies and programs. Overwhelmingly, the expenditures of federal funds for such marketing are legal and the federal government is properly identified as the source in VNRs. In addition, the federal government spends even more money on paid media. We are all familiar with the commercials for the armed services. These commercials are paid for with tax dollars and are aired nationally. In Government Accountability Office (GAO) analysis of seven federal departments from 2003 to mid-2005, expenditures to advertising agencies, public relations firms, and media organizations for public engagement campaigns totaled $1.6 billion. Expenditures by the Defense Department accounted for $1.1 billion of the total spending.[22]

The nation's largest public relations firms have benefited significantly from contracts with the federal government with such firms receiving $197 million in contracts during the two-and-a-half-year period analyzed by the GAO.[23] Ketchum, one of the leading global PR firms, earned more than $100 million during the past decade from federal government contracts to promote various government departments and agencies. PR giant Fleishman-Hillard received more than $75 million over the last ten years from various government agencies—including the Social Security Administration, the Environmental Protection Agency, and the Library of Congress—to produce VNRs and other marketing tools.

Both firms have been criticized by the Center for Media and Democracy for failing to disclose the federal government as the funding source for VNRs they produced. According to the CMD, Ketchum "produced a VNR for the Education Department that was widely criticized, as it 'comes across as a news story but fails to make clear that the reporter involved was paid with taxpayer money,' explained Associated Press. The VNR promoted tutoring programs under 'No Child Left Behind,' and included then-Education Secretary Rod Paige and PR flack Karen Ryan, who misrepresented herself as a reporter."[24] Fleishman-Hillard, in its work with the White House Office of National Drug Control Policy, sought to "'debunk the misconception that marijuana was harmless.' Part of that contract involved producing VNRs, which were later found to be covert propaganda, because ONDCP 'did not identify itself to the viewing audience as the producer and distributor of these prepackaged news stories.'"[25]

It is hard not to conclude that the news media outlets are guilty coconspirators, along with the corporations and the federal government, in producing VNRs without attribution. The news producers must have knowledge of the sources of the VNRs. Rather than disclose the sources, they would rather present the VNR as "news" in order to maintain the facade of ownership of the news content. It is not hard to imagine, in the Ketchum VNR produced for the Education Department, the local news anchor setting up the "news story" on tutoring programs and then introducing "our correspondent in Washington, D.C., Karen Ryan." The realities of news gathering and production in the early twenty-first century make VNRs an increasingly prevalent and controversial means of presenting the news to the American public.

INTEREST GROUP ADVOCACY—CONSUMERS UNION AND CHILD SAFETY SEATS

Many, if not all, public interest groups seek to market themselves and their activities to an audience broader than their membership bases in order to legitimize themselves and to attract potential new members. Members of the news media have the ability to facilitate this outreach by focusing on the activities of such groups and thereby demonstrating the newsworthiness of the interest group's endeavors. One would hope, however, that the news media outlets have some responsibility to serve not simply as conduits through which interest group information and research findings pass. The media should have some responsibility in vetting the information provided by organized interests. Unfortunately, the vetting process often comes down a process analogous to what, in social science methodological circles, is referred to as *face validation*—that is, does the journalist accept, on its face, the validity of the organization as a credible source of information, without any due diligence on the part of the journalist to check the facts herself? Consistently, public interest groups that wear the "white hats" (e.g., consumer groups, environmental groups, government reform groups) are accepted as credible sources, whereas organizations representing "black hat" interests (e.g., the tobacco industry, the alcohol industry, the gambling industry) are far more closely scrutinized when they put forth information for media consumption.

When the news media simply serve as conduits for information flow, they shirk their responsibility to assure that the news is accurate. On January 4, 2007, Consumers Union, a nonprofit membership organization that publishes *Consumer Reports*, held a press conference announcing that ten of the top twelve child safety seats sold in the United States, which they tested, had failed to meet federal government standards in crash tests at 38 miles per hour. Many daily newspapers as well as several television and cable networks ran the story as told by spokespersons from Consumers Union. CBS ran a four-minute segment on *The Early Show* the following morning, relating the findings as presented by Consumers Union. CNN ran it as a headline story. Within hours of the release of the findings by Consumers Union and prior to any broadcast segment on the topic, at least two independent organizations challenged the claims. Safe Kids Worldwide and its U.S.-based organization, Safe Kids USA (http://usa.safekids.org), and the Auto Channel (http://www.theautochannel.com) posted responses on their Web sites that sought to assure parents that the seats tested remain safe. "Safe Kids Worldwide wants to reassure parents and caregivers that the seats are safe and effective when used according to manufacturers' instructions. Parents should not fear for their children's safety in cars in response to a recent Consumers Union report raising questions about the performance of infant car seats."[26] None of the network or cable segments aired on January 5, 2007, mentioned these challenges to the Consumers Union claims, even though a quick Google search of "child safety seats" on January 4 would have generated the posted challenges. The news media took at face value the findings of Consumers Union.

As it turns out, the Consumers Union analysis was significantly flawed. Only after the National Highway Traffic Safety Administration reviewed the findings was it discovered that the testing was undertaken at 70 miles per hour, rather than the federal standard of 38 miles per hour. After further scrutiny, it was discovered that Consumers Union had contracted out the testing to a private testing laboratory. By January 18, 2007, Consumers Union had retracted its report: "We withdrew the report immediately upon discovering a substantive issue that may have affected the original test results. The issue came to light based on new information received Tuesday night and Wednesday morning from the National Highway Traffic Safety Administration (NHTSA) concerning the speed at which our side-impact tests were conducted."[27] Three months later, after a more detailed internal investigation, Consumers Union concluded that a "series of misjudgments and a key misunderstanding between *Consumer Reports* and an outside laboratory led to the publication of erroneous crash-test data in our recent report on infant car seats, an expert investigation and interviews with those involved has revealed."[28]

After the January 18 announcement by Consumers Union, CBS and other network and cable outlets reported on the retraction. CBS led with the following: "*Consumer Reports* on Thursday retracted a negative report on infant car seats that left many parents worried about their babies safety—an embarrassing revelation for the venerable magazine."[29] Consumers Union and the editors of *Consumer Reports*, while losing control over the testing process by contracting out the key component of the research, behaved responsibly by quickly addressing the issue and retracting their report. Interestingly, not a single news outlet apologized for running the story in the first place. The ultimate irony in this case is that it took a government agency, NHTSA, to discover the problem, rather than the consumer watchdog organization or the media.

GOVERNMENTS AS ADVOCATES—REVERSE LOBBYING BY THE BUSH ADMINISTRATION

As we read in the first case study, the federal government routinely spends tens of millions of dollars each year orchestrating "public engagement campaigns" with the help of large PR firms. In broad terms, these campaigns are legal in the sense that they are not specifically created to change the minds of citizens on particular policy issues. Reverse lobbying, or advocacy efforts on the part of a presidential administration to convince organized interests or the general public to support or oppose government policies, is regulated by federal law. The most relevant regulatory statute is the Anti-Lobbying Act of 1919 (18 U.S.C. § 1913). While the statute allows the president, the members of the cabinet, and other high-level executive branch officials to advocate for administration proposals without limit, the law does place limits on the amount of money the executive branch can spend on policy advocacy campaigns. While the law itself is vague in that it prohibits "substantial" grassroots lobbying campaigns by the White House that advocate for administration policies, the legislative history of the law provides a figure of $7,500 as the maximum amount to be spent. In current dollars, that would amount to roughly $70,000 in expenditures.[30] In addition, executive departments and agencies and their contractors are prohibited from engaging in "covert propaganda" (i.e., any entities outside the government contracted to provide support for or opposition to federal policies must disclose publicly their financial relationship with the federal government).

The current Bush administration has undertaken numerous public engagement campaigns during its eight years. Yet it is not alone in orchestrating elaborate reverse lobbying campaigns. The Clinton administration, for example, invested significant resources in mobilizing police associations to support the Clinton Crime Bill and the COPS Program.[31] In an effort to compare the public engagement efforts of presidents Bill Clinton and George W. Bush, the minority staff of the House Committee on Government Oversight analyzed the executive branch contracts with public relations firms in 2000 and 2004 and found that spending had increased from $39 million in 2000 to $88 million in 2004.[32] Beyond this increase, the Bush administration has taken reverse lobbying to a new level as it sought to engage media commentators as part of its public engagement campaigns on the Bush Marriage Initiative in 2002 and on No Child Left Behind (NCLB) in 2003.

"In 2002, syndicated columnist Maggie Gallagher repeatedly defended President Bush's push for a $300 million initiative encouraging marriage as a way of strengthening families. 'The Bush marriage initiative would emphasize the importance of marriage to poor couples' and 'educate teens on the value of delaying childbearing until marriage,' she wrote in *National Review Online*, for example, adding that this could 'carry big payoffs down the road for taxpayers and children.'"[33] The problem with this advocacy on behalf of the president was that Maggie Gallagher failed to disclose to *National Review* or any of the other media outlets through which she was publishing at the time that she had received a $21,500 contract from the Department of Health and Human Services to promote the Bush Marriage Initiative for the White House. When *National Review* editor Rich Lowery was informed of the contract, he replied, "We would have preferred that she had told us, and we would have disclosed it in her bio."[34] Gallagher also received $20,000 from the Justice Department in 2002 and 2003 to write a report for a nonprofit organization, the National Fatherhood Initiative, called *Can Government Strengthen Marriage?* Responding to media criticism when these contractual relationships came to light, Gallagher responded, "Did I violate journalistic ethics by not disclosing it? I don't know. You tell me." When asked if she should have disclosed the relationship with the Bush White House, she said that she would have "been happy to tell anyone who called me. Frankly, it never occurred to me."[35]

While the Maggie Gallagher incident caused a bit of a stir in Washington, D.C., politics, a much larger firestorm erupted with it discovered that conservative media commentator Armstrong Williams failed to disclose that he had signed a $241,000 contract with the Department of Education (DoED), through the PR firm Ketchum, to promote No Child Left Behind, the Bush administration's education initiative, in 2003. Williams had signed a contract with the Department of Education through his firm, the Graham Williams Group (GWG), as part of a larger contract with Ketchum to promote NCLB. Specifically, Williams was contracted to promote the NCLB policy to minority audiences through his various media enterprises.

The fallout from this revelation was far-reaching. The Federal Communications Commission issued a citation against Williams and GWG, finding that the explanation regarding the lack of disclosure on the part of Williams was not terribly convincing: "We find that GWG's explanation that its monthly reporting efforts, made over a year-long period, 'were incorrect in listing all of [Williams's] media interviews and activities and automatically includ[ing] them' or that Williams only 'realized for the first time' such significant reporting errors in January 2005, after this matter was disclosed by the national press to be unpersuasive."[36] The FCC citation concludes with the following: "[T]he record here establishes that Williams and GWG received more than nominal consideration from DoED to include particular material in programming supplied to and intended for transmission by broadcast stations and that the material was, in fact, aired by various broadcast stations. In these circumstances, Williams and GWG were obliged under Section 507(c) to disclose to the licensees receiving programming that the NCLB-related broadcast material was sponsored by DoED. The record also establishes that such disclosure was not provided by either Williams or GWG. We conclude that GWG and Williams violated Section 507 of the Communications Act."[37]

In addition to the FCC citation, Williams reached a settlement with the Department of Education, agreeing to repay $34,000, which was determined to be an overpayment in the $241,000 contract, without admitting any wrongdoing. The FCC did levy fines of $76,000 relating to the broadcasting of Williams programming by two broadcast companies—Sunshine Family Television, Inc. ($40,000) and Sinclair Broadcast Group ($36,000).[38] The biggest hit to Williams, however, came when Tribune Media Services, syndicator of his weekly newspaper column, severed its ties with Williams in January 2005. At that point Williams expressed regret for his actions: "It's important that I have a credible voice and that I'm not perceived as being paid for what I say. This is my responsibility. I blame no one. I get the message and I will be better."[39]

FOUNDATION ADVOCACY—NPR, PBS, AND NEWS COVERAGE

In the United States, public television (Public Broadcasting System, PBS) and public radio (National Public Radio, NPR) are often viewed as separate and distinct from commercial broadcasting. After all, they are supported by viewers and listeners like you. In part, they are unique in the media. Nonetheless, they are not "public" in the sense that they are immune to economics. For more than thirty years, public television and public radio have functioned with the limited assistance of the federal government through the Corporation for Public Broadcasting ($30 million to PBS and $2 million to NPR in 2004).[40] Roughly 2 percent of NPR funding and 6 percent of PBS funding is derived from the federal government. Mainly, NPR and PBS rely on contributions from citizens and corporations across the nation, revenues generated from the contracting of programming to local public television and radio stations, and, in recent years, the support of a growing number of foundations. Support from the government, corporations, and citizens comes with virtually no strings attached. But while some foundations provide financial assistance without linking such support to specific policy concerns, a growing number of foundations are providing support to public television and radio in exchange for specific news coverage—whether health policy, children's issues, the media itself, or coverage of specific regions of the world.

For fiscal year 2003, PBS received more than $1 million in support from each of the following foundations: Alfred P. Sloan Foundation, American Legacy Foundation, Annie E. Casey Foundation, Arthur Vining Davis Foundation, Charles H. Revson Foundation, the Ford Foundation, the Henry Luce Foundation, the John D. and Catherine T. MacArthur Foundation, the Kohlberg Foundation, Luesther T. Mertz Charitable Trust, the Pew Charitable Trusts, the Picower Foundation, the Robert Wood Johnson Foundation, and the Walter and Shirley Wang Foundation. Fifteen additional foundations, including the Andrew W. Mellon Foundation and the John M. Olin Foundation, each gave between $500,000 and $1 million to PBS in 2003, and fifty-four other foundations gave between $100,000 and $500,000.[41] For fiscal year 2006, PBS received approximately $72 million in foundation grants. With an operating budget of about $490 million, this amounts to roughly 15 percent of its annual funding.[42] While some of these foundations provide truly philanthropic support in the form of unrestricted grants for public television and radio (e.g., the recent three-year, $10-million Ford Foundation grant to the Corporation for Public Broadcasting), a significant minority of foundation supporters link contributions to specific activities or coverage to be delivered by PBS.

Foundation support for public radio is equally significant. In fiscal year 2000, NPR received 22.9 percent of its support from foundations; when one includes support from its own NPR Foundation, NPR received more than one-third of its annual funding from foundations, more than three times the national average for foundation support of nonprofit entities.[43] More recent NPR annual reports merge contributions, sponsorships and foundation grants. For fiscal year 2005, these revenue sources totaled $57.6 million, or roughly 33 percent of annual revenues.[44] The percentage of the budget supported only by foundation grants is a bit skewed due to a monumental influx of revenue several years ago. In late 2003 NPR received more than $225 million from the estate of Joan B. Kroc, widow of McDonalds Corporation founder Ray Kroc; this bequest amounted to the largest monetary gift ever to a cultural institution in the United States.[45] At the time, NPR had an annual operating budget of $101 million; today it stands at $170 million. As a result of this significant increase in operational budgeting after the Kroc gift, the relationship between foundation support and the overall budget has declined in recent years, but its impact still remains significant.

From 1993 to 2005, NPR and the NPR Foundation received more than $5 million from the John D. and Catherine T. MacArthur Foundation; between $1 million and $5 million from the Ford Foundation, Doris Duke Charitable Foundation, and the Kresge Foundation; and between $500,000 and $1 million from the Abramson Foundation, the Horace W. Goldsmith Foundation, the Overbrook Foundation, William U. and Lia G. Poorvu Foundation, and the Rockefeller Brothers Fund. Twenty additional foundations gave between $100,000 and $500,000 during the thirteen-year period.[46] As with public television support, many foundation supporters of NPR provide assistance for targeted activities. According to an analysis of NPR contributors conducted by the Foundation Center, a national clearinghouse for foundations, "National Public Radio received 36 separate foundation grants of $10,000 or more in 1998. That included $200,000 from the W.K. Kellogg Foundation 'to cover stories on issues currently of interest and importance to philanthropy and the nonprofit world and particularly those related to Kellogg Foundation programming.' (An NPR spokesperson disputed that the grant was actually used that narrowly)."[47]

Kellogg is not the only foundation to provide support to NPR with strings attached. The Annie E. Casey Foundation provides support only for news coverage of issues affecting children; the Pew Charitable Trusts supports arts and religion reporting; the Soros Foundation/Open Society Institute and the Ford Foundation support news coverage of central and eastern Europe; the Robert Wood Johnson Foundation and the Henry J. Kaiser Family Foundation support health policy reporting; and Pew also supports coverage of the media. NPR devotes several pages of its news policy manual to the issue of foundation-supported journalism, including "Restricted grants must not be so narrow in concept as to coincide with the donor's area of economic or advocacy interest." Even so, it is difficult to miss the agenda-setting function served by targeted foundation support to NPR.[48]

PBS has actually gone a step further than NPR in intermixing the agendas of foundation supporters with news reporting. According to Rick Edmonds of the Poynter Institute (a nonprofit journalism-training entity and owner of the *St. Petersburg Times*), the *NewsHour with Jim Lehrer* "inconspicuously crossed the line: It accepted explicit foundation sponsorship of two reporting units."[49] Health reporting is no longer sponsored by viewers like you; rather, Susan Dentzer and her team of health reporters, originally sponsored by the Kaiser Family Foundation, are now sponsored by the Robert Wood Johnson Foundation. Similarly, media reporting by Terence Smith and this research unit, originally brought to you by the Pew Charitable Trusts, is now sponsored by the Knight Foundation.

Many foundations have clearly defined policy agendas; as such, they closely resemble interest groups. Perhaps their methods of influencing public policy are more subtle and indirect. Nonetheless, to the extent that they have infiltrated public radio and television and have significantly altered the issue agendas of the news-gathering and reporting operations to reflect their internal policy priorities, rather than those of the general public, they have made public radio and public television a little less public.

ADVOCACY JOURNALISM—HOMELESSNESS IN AMERICA

Beyond being influenced by outside interests or private foundations, the news media have their own journalistic values and issue agendas. Former CBS reporter Bernard Goldberg, in his book *Bias*, provides an uneven accounting of the biases he encountered during his three decades of reporting at CBS. One of the strongest cases he presents, supported by empirical evidence, is his argument regarding advocacy journalism in the national news media. He focuses his attention on the issue of homelessness and its coverage by the major newspapers and television networks over the past two decades. Goldberg addresses the issue of the number of homeless in America and compares government and reputable think tank figures with those presented by the media. In the 1980s and early 1990s, the U.S. Census Bureau set the number of homeless in the United States at 230,000. The Government Accountability Office, a support agency of the U.S. Congress, found that there were between 300,000 and 600,000 homeless persons; the Urban Institute, a Washington think tank specializing in urban public policy, estimated the number of homeless to be between 355,000 and 462,000 people nationwide.[50] For the sake of argument, 500,000 homeless persons in America would seem to be a fair estimate.

The national news media arrived at very different figures. In 1989 on CNN, Candy Crowley reported that "winter is on the way and 3 million Americans have no place to call home." In 1993 on NBC, *Weekend Today* anchor Jackie Nespral found that "nationally, right now, 5 million people are believed to be homeless." Finally, Charles Osgood of CBS was willing to predict the future of homelessness: "It is estimated that by the year 2000, 19 million Americans will be homeless unless something is done, and done now."[51] While advocates for the homeless had a hand in skewing the numbers dramatically upward, the media willingly accepted the figures and even went a step further to advance the cause. Beyond the wild numbers presented by the media, the face of homelessness was skewed as well by the media.

According to Goldberg, the network news media framed the issue of homelessness around two themes: (1) the homeless are just like us, and (2) they are homeless because of cutbacks in government programs previously in place under Democratic administrations, but cut by the Reagan administration in favor of increased defense spending. He makes a good case for both themes. Advocates for the homeless were less comfortable with these approaches than they were with fudging the numbers of homeless. Consistently the media sought out a sanitized version of homelessness: "White was better than black. Clean was better than dirty. Attractive was better than unattractive. Sane was better than insane. And sober was better than addicted. So when the TV people went looking for just that right kind of homeless face to put on their news programs, they went to people like Robert Hayes, who ran the National Coalition for the Homeless in New York. In 1989, Hayes told *The New York Times* that when congressional committees and TV news producers contact him, 'they always want white, middle-class people to interview.'"[52]

S. Robert Lichter of the Center for Media and Public Affairs, a Washington, D.C., think tank focused on the media, analyzed more than one hundred stories on homelessness in the late 1980s aired by ABC, NBC, and CBS, as well as twenty-six stories written in *Time, Newsweek,* and *U.S. News & World Report.* Lichter concluded that the findings "provide a blueprint for advocacy journalism. . . . Only one source in twenty-five blamed homelessness on the personal problems of the homeless themselves, such as mental illness, drug and alcohol abuse, or lack of skills or motivation. The other 96 percent blamed social or political conditions for their plight. The primary culprit cited was the housing market, including forces like high mortgage interest rates, high rents, downtown redevelopment, etc. Next in line was government inaction, especially the government's failure to provide adequate public housing."[53]

The timing of such media accounts also drew the attention of Goldberg. Again, empirical evidence supports his claim that the homelessness advocacy of the media has been targeted at Republican administrations. Journalist Philip Terzian reported in a 1999 column in the *Village Voice* that *The New York Times* ran fifty stories on homelessness, including five on page one, in 1988. A decade later, in 1998, only ten stories on the homeless appeared in the newspaper, with none appearing on page one. The Media Research Center, a conservative media watchdog group, found a similar pattern of coverage. In 1990, when George H. W. Bush was president, ABC, CBS, NBC, and CNN ran seventy-one homelessness stories on evening newscasts; by 1995, when Bill Clinton was president, the number had dropped to only nine stories.[54] With these findings and the patterns cited earlier, Goldberg sarcastically titled the chapter dealing with advocacy journalism "How Bill Clinton Cured Homelessness."

THE MEDIA AND ADVOCACY: THE MISGUIDED INSTITUTION?

More than a decade ago, Thomas Patterson, in his cogent analysis of the role of the media in the American electoral process, *Out of Order*, concluded that the news media are a "miscast institution," ill equipped to assist citizens in their electoral choices. "The problem of the modern presidential campaign," he wrote, "lies in the role assigned to the press. Its traditional role is that of watchdog . . . . This vital function, however, is different from the role that was thrust on the press when the nominating system was opened wide in the early 1970s. The new role conflicts with the old one. The critical stance of the watchdog is not to be confused with the constructive task of the coalition-builder. The new role requires the press to act in constructive ways to bring candidates and voters together."[55]

Outside of the electoral context, the news media are performing an even wider variety of roles: signaler, alerting the public to important political developments; common carrier, channeling messages from policy makers to the public; watchdog, protecting the public from government and its occupants; and public representative, spokesperson for and advocate of the public. The media are increasingly susceptible to the influence of organized interests in the performance of each of these roles.[56] To the extent that the influence of organized interests in news gathering and reporting is significant, the news media in the United States will become an increasingly *misguided institution*.

Historically, the news media have performed the first three roles outlined above fairly well. Yet even in these instances, the influence of organized interests on news gathering and reporting raises some question as to the capacity or competence of the media to perform these tasks. Regarding the first role of signaler, the case of government advocacy through media commentators highlights the circumstances under which the media might be signaling in a rather peculiar way. In addition, the transformation of paid commercial spots into video news releases and the subsequent airing of VNRs as news calls into question the ability of the news media to signal the "newsworthiness" of such an advertisement, giving credence to the subject matter. Performing the common-carrier role necessitates conscious resistance to spin, both from policy makers and from organized interests likely to be brought into the news stories. In the Consumers Union child safety seat case, the news media passed on erroneous information to the general public without any effort to check the validity of the claims being made by the interest group.

Regarding the media's watchdog role, the agenda-setting efforts of foundations in public radio and television bring into question the policy priorities of these media; as a result the watchdog function may be skewed toward (or away from) the policy domains funded by these outside sources of support. It should be noted that foundations have not limited their support efforts to PBS and NPR. To the contrary, foundations are providing support with strings attached to newspapers, commercial television stations, magazines, and even the *Columbia Journalism Review.*[57] Finally, the news media have taken on the role of public representative virtually on their own. Traditionally, elected officials, political parties, and the institutions of governance performed the public representative role. Vietnam and Watergate changed the political equation, at least for the news media. Since that time, journalists have viewed themselves, at least in part, as advocates for their versions of good public policy. The homelessness in America case lays bare the shortcomings of such a role being performed by the news media.

Interest groups and their representatives view the news media as useful tools in their advocacy strategies. To the extent that their causes and issues will be well served by positive media or their opponents will be ill served by negative media, they will engage the necessary media outlets to serve their purposes. Spin is more than fair game for organized interests. Given the myriad outlets from which to choose and the shrinking resources available to the news media, burning a media bridge with orchestrated spin has few negative consequences. Only an increasingly competent news media in the United States will be equal to the challenge of the ever-growing barrage of organized interests seeking to use the institution for their own purposes. Without such redoubled efforts to perform the first three roles—signaler, common carrier, and watchdog—and perhaps to jettison the fourth role of public representative, the news media will be destined to become more than a miscast institution; it will become a misguided institution.

DISCUSSION QUESTIONS

1. How does the concentration of media outlets in the hands of a few media conglomerates affect the ability of organized interest groups to influence the reporting of political news?
2. Can a streamlined, downsized media remain "competent" to gauge the veracity of interest group information sources? If so, how? If not, what recourse do media outlets have in dealing with interest groups as sources?
3. How can media outlets protect themselves from "spin" by organized interest groups?
4. What should the role of the media be in covering interest groups engaged in political campaigning?
5. Should public television and public radio outlets accept foundation support for specific types of news reporting? Why? Why not?
6. How might the media prevent themselves from becoming a "misguided" institution?

SUGGESTIONS FOR FURTHER READING

Ben Bagdikian. *The New Media Monopoly*. Boston: Beacon, 2004.
C. Edwin Baker. *Media, Markets, and Democracy*. New York: Cambridge University Press, 2002.
Allan J. Cigler and Burdett A. Loomis, eds. *Interest Group Politics*, 7th ed. Washington, DC: CQ Press, 2006.
Paul S. Herrnson, Ronald G. Shaiko, and Clyde Wilcox, eds. *The Interest Group Connection: Electioneering, Lobbying, and Policymaking in Washington*, 2nd ed. Chatham, NJ: Chatham House, 2003.
David Lowery and Holly Brasher. *Organized Interests and American Government*. Boston: McGraw-Hill, 2004.
Robert W. McChesney. *Rich Media, Poor Democracy: Communication Politics in Dubious Times*. Urbana: University of Illinois Press, 1999.
Bartholomew H. Sparrow. *Uncertain Guardians: The News Media as a Political Institution*. Baltimore: Johns Hopkins University Press, 1999.

NOTES

1. Ben H. Bagdikian, *The Media Monopoly* (Boston: Beacon, 1983), 4.
2. Ben H. Bagdikian, *The Media Monopoly*, 6th ed. (Boston: Beacon, 2000), 5.
3. Ben H. Bagdikian, *The New Media Monopoly* (Boston: Beacon, 2004), 3.
4. Robert W. McChesney, *Rich Media, Poor Democracy: Communication Politics in Dubious Times* (Urbana: University of Illinois Press, 1999), 19–20; see also Dean Alger, *Megamedia: How Giant Corporations Dominate Mass Media, Distort Competition, and Endanger Democracy* (Lanham, MD: Rowman & Littlefield, 1998); Bartholomew H. Sparrow, *Uncertain Guardians: The News Media as a Political Institution* (Baltimore: Johns Hopkins University Press, 1999); C. Edwin Baker, *Media, Markets, and Democracy* (New York: Cambridge University Press, 2002). Corporate revenues for 2006 were found in the Fortune 500 index. Bertelsmann revenues for 2006 were $19.3 billion.
5. Penn Kimball, *Downsizing the News: Network Cutbacks in the Nation's Capital* (Baltimore: Johns Hopkins University Press, 1994).
6. Ibid., 23.
7. Bill Kovach and Tom Rosenstiel, *Warp Speed: America in the Age of Mixed Media* (New York: Century Foundation, 1999), 6–7.
8. Ibid., 7.
9. "Lobbying and the Media" (American League of Lobbyists Forum, Washington, DC, 1998, C-SPAN Videotape 115402). Birnbaum's personal antagonism toward the lobbying profession was made evident by the title of his second book on the subject—*The Lobbyists: How Influence Peddlers Get Their Way in Washington* (New York: Times Books, 1992). The subtitle on the softcover edition was changed by the publisher after lobbyists complained that the substance of the book was not

reflected in the title. Lobbyists who were subjects in the book rightly argued that, in many instances, they did not "get their way" on the issues portrayed in the book. Hence, the subtitle for the paperback version became: *How Influence Peddlers Work Their Way in Washington.* The lobbyists remained influence peddlers, much to the dissatisfaction of the lobbying community, but the change was made regarding their relative success.

10. American League of Lobbyists, *1998 Membership Survey* (Alexandria, VA: American League of Lobbyists, 1998), 6–7.

11. Cited in Sparrow, *Uncertain Guardians*, 120.

12. "Lobbying and the Media."

13. See David Lowery and Holly Brasher, *Organized Interests and American Government* (Boston: McGraw-Hill, 2004), 108–47; William P. Brown, *Groups, Interests, and U.S. Public Policy* (Washington, DC: Georgetown University Press, 1999), 95–102; Ken Kollman, *Outside Lobbying: Public Opinion and Interest Group Strategies* (Princeton, NJ: Princeton University Press, 1998), 27–57.

14. Cited in William K. Muir Jr., *Legislature: California's School of Politics* (Chicago: University of Chicago Press, 1982), 136.

15. See George Lakoff, *Don't Think of an Elephant! How Democrats and Progressives Can Win: Know Your Values and Frame the Debate: The Essential Guide for Progressives* (New York: Chelsea Green, 2005) for an attempt to organize liberal/progressive rhetoric to compete with the conservative movement in the United States.

16. Bill Press, *Spin This! All the Ways We Don't Tell the Truth* (New York: Pocket Books, 2001), xxiii.

17. Cited in ibid., xvii.

18. Jack Fuller, *News Values: Ideas for an Infomation Age* (Chicago: University of Chicago Press, 1996), 39.

19. Kara Rowland, "FCC Fines Use of VNRs," *Washington Times*, October 3, 2007, B1.

20. Federal Communications Commission, "In the Matter of Comcast Corporation, Notice of Apparent Liability for Forfeiture" (47 C.F.R. § 76.1615), File No. EB-06-IH-3723, September 21, 2007, 1–2.

21. Diane Farsetta, "Know Fake News: Summary," Center for Media and Democracy, October 11, 2007, http://www.prwatch.org/fakenews3/summary.

22. United States Government Accountability Office, "Media Contracts: Activities and Financial Obligations for Seven Federal Departments," GAO-06-305, 1.

23. Ibid.

24. Diane Farsetta, "Desperately Seeking Disclosure: What Happens When Public Funds Go to Private PR Firms?" Center for Media and Democracy, March 9, 2005, http://prwatch.org/node/3348.

25. Ibid.

26. "Child Safety Experts Reassure Parents that Car Seats are Safe and Effective When Correctly Used," The Auto Channel, January 4, 2007, http://www.theautochannel.com/news/2007/01/04/033020.html.

27. Consumers Union, "*Consumer Reports* Withdraws Infant Car Seat Report," *Consumer Reports*, January 18, 2007, http://www.consumerreports.org/cro/babies-kids/baby-toddler/travel-gear/car-seats/car-seats-2–07/overview/0207_seats_ov.htm.

28. Consumers Union, "How Our Car Seat Tests Went Wrong," *Consumer Reports*, May 2007, http://www.consumerreports.org/cro/babies-kids/baby-toddler/travel-gear/car-seats/how-our-car-seat-tests-went-wrong-5–07/overview/0507seat.htm.

29. "Child Safety Seat Warning Withdrawn," CBS News, January 18, 2007, http://www.cbsnews.com/stories/2007/01/18/tech/main2371839.shtml?source=search_story.

30. Ronald G. Shaiko, "Reverse Lobbying: Interest Group Mobilization from the White House and the Hill," in *Interest Group Politics*, 5th ed, ed. Allan J. Cigler and Burdett A. Loomis (Washington, DC: CQ Press, 1998), 256–57.

31. Ibid., 259–66.

32. Minority Staff, Committee on Government Reform, "Federal Public Relations Spending," U.S. House of Representatives, January 2005.

33. Howard Kurtz, "Writer Backing Bush Plan Had Gotten Federal Contract," *Washington Post*, January 26, 2005, C1.

34. Ibid.

35. Ibid.

36. Federal Communications Commission, "Citation: File No. EB-05-IH-0031: The Graham Williams Group," FCC-DA 07–3351, 3.

37. Ibid., 4.

38. Diane Farsetta, "Time to Pay for Payola Pundit Armstrong Williams," Center for Media and Democracy, 2, http://www.freepress.net/news/27201.

39. Judy Keen and Jim Drinkard, "Media Distributor Severs Ties with Commentator," *USA Today*, January 9, 2005, http://www.usatoday.com/news/washington/2005–01–09-williams_x.htm.

40. Paul Farhi, "PBS Scrutiny Raises Political Antennas," *Washington Post*, April 22, 2005, C1.

41. Public Broadcasting Service, "Our Supporters: FY 2003 Underwriters of PBS National Programming, http://www.pbs.org/aboutpbs/content/annualreport/2003/FY03NPSUnderwriters.pdf. Note: PBS has not posted its supporter lists on its website since FY 2003.

42. Public Broadcasting Service, "Public Broadcasting Service and Subsidiaries: Consolidated Financial Statements and Independent Auditors' Report, Years Ended June 30, 2006 and 2005," (Washington, DC, 2006), 5, 10, http://www-tc.pbs.org/aboutpbs/content/annualreport/2006/FullFinancialHighlights.pdf.

43. National Public Radio Financials, "Financials," 2002, http://www.npr.org/about/place/corpsupport/Financials.html.

44. National Public Radio, "Annual Report 2005," 5, http:/npr.org/about/annualreport/2005_Annual_Report.pdf.

45. National Public Radio, "NPR Receives a Record Bequest of More Than $200 Million," press release, November 6, 2003, http://npr.org/about/press/031106.kroc.html.

46. NPR, "Annual Report 2005," 10.

47. Rick Edmonds, "Special Issue: Foundations' Role in Journalism," *Poynter Report* (Spring 2001): 14.

48. Ibid., 24.

49. Ibid., 18.

50. Bernard Goldberg, *Bias: A CBS Insider Exposes How the Media Distort the News* (Washington, DC: Regnery, 2002), 66.

51. Quoted in ibid., 66–67.

52. Quoted in ibid., 65.

53. Quoted in ibid., 69.

54. Ibid., 73.

55. Thomas E. Patterson, *Out of Order* (New York: Knopf, 1993; Vintage, 1994), 51.

56. See Thomas E. Patterson, *We the People: A Concise Introduction to American Politics*, 7th ed. (Boston: McGraw-Hill, 2008), 345–54.

57. Edmonds, "Foundations' Role in Journalism."

ASSIGNMENT: THE POLITICAL MESSAGE
OF YOUR FAVORITE MOVIE

When political scientists study the media, we typically limit our study to traditional news sources such as newspapers and television news broadcasts. But some scholars include entertainment media such as movies, television shows, and novels.

Some movies are explicitly political, such as Michael Moore's *Fahrenheit 9/11*, an angry documentary against the Bush administration, or *V for Vendetta*, an exploration of the ethics of violent resistance to a tyrannical government. But even movies that appear entirely nonpolitical inevitably contain political messages. A shallow teen sex comedy like *American Pie* conveys messages about gender roles, family life, and other topics. A movie that is supposed to be about "typical" American life but has no positive black characters also conveys a political message by its omission.

For this assignment, you are tasked with examining the political messages embedded in your favorite movie.

There are several theories about Hollywood's politics. Perhaps the most popular is that Hollywood is *liberal* and puts liberal ideas into its movies. In his book *Hollywood vs. America*, conservative film critic Michael Medved gives many examples of liberal bias in Hollywood movies. Movies such as *Platoon* are highly critical of American foreign and military policy. Medved and others have noted how often corporations and government officials are villains in such movies as *Erin Brockovich* and *Patriot Games*. Other critics note that most prominent actors tend to be liberals when they get involved in political campaigns.

Another way of looking at Hollywood is that it is inherently *conservative*. The major studios are gigantic global corporations. They have made many movies that support the American capitalist system and American foreign policy. Movies such as *Pretty Woman* support the idea that good people eventually get rich in America, and that shopping on Rodeo Drive in Beverly Hills is the greatest pleasure imaginable. Very few Hollywood movies ask radical questions about the nature of American capitalism, such as why citizens in poorer European countries have universal health care for all citizens but poor people in America often lack access to basic health care. Movies like *Top Gun* portray America's military and its global role in a very positive light. The studio that made the movie needed the permission of the military to get access to locations and expertise. Some believe it resulted in a recruitment surge for the Navy. If the movie had been critical of the military, it could not have been made. More recently, other studios have been accused of avoiding topics that might anger powerful governments like China.

Another way of looking at Hollywood is that, with notable exceptions, it has few consistent political positions. The studios simply seek to make as much money as possible. If that means making movies that praise capitalism and the market system or traditional religious values, they will happily do so, but if the public seems to want movies that praise working-class values and unions, or argue against nuclear power, or simply sell sex, that's what they will give. This "give the people what they want" explanation for the politics of Hollywood is the most flexible.

Of course, these three theories are not mutually exclusive. They could all be true to some degree. Individual directors, writers, and actors may seek to put out liberal messages in their movies. Studios, by contrast, may prefer more conservative movie scripts that portray American capitalism and foreign policy in a positive light. And at the same time, most actors, writers, directors, and studio heads in Hollywood want to make as much money as possible.

Why should we care if Hollywood has a point of view about politics? Consider that the favorite movie of Oklahoma City bomber Timothy McVeigh was *Star Wars*. In that movie, a group of brave and outnumbered rebels fight against an all-powerful evil government, ultimately winning by exploding the enemy's headquarters. Is it just a coincidence that McVeigh saw himself as part of a rebellion against a dictatorial national government and decided to blow up a federal building? Also, movies may be much more powerful in the long run than news broadcasts at shaping our deeper attitudes about society and politics. Perhaps the growing acceptance of homosexuality in American life has been partially caused by the number of movies in which gay characters are portrayed in a positive fashion.

So, now that you understand a bit more about the politics of Hollywood and its impact, analyze the politics of your favorite movie. Answer the following questions in a three-page essay:

- Are the politics of this film explicit or implicit? In other words, is politics one of the main topics, such as with a movie about a politician or an election, or is about a nonpolitical subject like sports or science fiction?
- Do you think the movie has an overall liberal or conservative message?
- Does it uphold traditional family values such as heterosexual marriage and respect for parents, or does it portray homosexuality in a positive way?
- Does it portray the government or government officials as helpful or as villainous?
- What does it say about poverty in America, if anything? What about racial problems?
- This is your favorite movie. Do you find its overall political message agrees with your basic views? If yes, do you think this is a coincidence? If no, why do you think you like a movie that has a differing view about politics?

10

The Media and Public Opinion

Stephen K. Medvic and David A. Dulio

Poll, poll, poll. Try reading a news story or watching one aired on TV without encountering the word.

—Christopher Hitchens, "Voting in the Passive Voice"[1]

There is little doubt that the media's reliance on public opinion as a source of news has exploded in the last quarter century. One can hardly turn on a network news broadcast, open a newspaper, or look at an online news source without seeing or hearing about "the latest survey" or "the most recent polling data." The near-omnipresent nature of public opinion in the media's reporting of news depends on continuous measures of public sentiment in the form of public opinion polls. In this chapter we address issues and concerns related to public opinion in the media. We examine the sources of public opinion that the media rely on for news, and the role of that information in news stories. We also critically evaluate the news media's reporting of public opinion data in terms of information the public needs in order to be good consumers of the news. In addition, we consider the range of topics on which poll results are reported, from individuals and institutions to issues and elections. We conclude with a discussion of one specific measure of public opinion—exit polling—that has caused a great deal of controversy after recent elections, especially on Election Day 2000 and 2004. As exit polls may be the most significant measure of public opinion the media take, the circumstances surrounding how they are conducted and reported deserve careful attention.

In 2006, major network and cable news broadcasts (ABC, CBS, NBC, PBS, CNN, Fox, MSNBC, and CNBC) included more than 280 separate stories that referenced or referred to a "poll" or "polls" and reported results. This was an increase from fewer than 230 stories in 2005, but a sharp decrease from 2004, when nearly 400 poll-related stories were aired. For further comparison, in 2000, 230 separate stories on polls were reported, while only about 150 aired 1999.[2]

The same reliance on polls can be found in print media sources. For example, one "examination of the stories featured on the covers of the three leading U.S. newsmagazines—*Time*, *Newsweek*, and *U.S. News and World Report*—between 1995 and mid-2003 reveals that about 30 percent of them cited public opinion polls."[3] The range of topics on network news programs for which poll results were used during 2006 varied from the nomination of Samuel Alito to the Supreme Court, the death penalty, terrorism, and global warming, to video games, Mardi Gras, gas prices, and Brad Pitt and Angelina Jolie's adoption of a baby from an African nation. Of course, the frequency with which public opinion data is reported is only heightened during an election year. The focus on polls during a campaign is more pointed than ever. The result of this, however, is that "[p]olls are not only part of the news today, they are news."[4]

This raises a number of important issues with regard to the nature of the media's use of public opinion. The first pertains to the role that the information plays in the news broadcast. As Kathleen Frankovic hints, public opinion data can either be used by the news media to *report* news, or it can be used to *create* news.[5] The second relates to who conducts the opinion polling. In the modern context of public opinion and news coverage, there are two main sources of surveys and polls for the media to tap—the major news outlets and media organizations themselves (internal) and academic or commercial polling outfits (external). These two issues—the role of public opinion in the news and its source—are intimately intertwined. In utilizing either type of source (internal or external) the media can either simply report a newsworthy story or create a news story.

SOURCES AND FUNCTIONS OF PUBLIC OPINION IN THE MEDIA

Increasingly, media outlets rely on their own internal abilities to construct, conduct, analyze, and report survey research on the public's attitudes. Each of the major broadcast television networks has created a mutually beneficial partnership with a print source to sponsor and conduct polling that both can use to generate news stories. These affiliations include ABC News and the *Washington Post*, NBC News and the *Wall Street Journal*, and CBS News and *The New York Times*. When major news services couple their resources, they are often able to support an independent polling entity that handles all aspects of the survey research process. This is in contrast to other news outlets, which rely on outside firms to conduct their polls. For example, on the television and radio side of the media, Fox News retains Opinion Dynamics as its survey research partner, CNN uses Opinion Research Corporation, and National Public Radio uses both Public Opinion Strategies (a political polling firm often hired by Republican candidates) and Greenberg Quinlan Rosner Research (a Democratic firm). In addition, on the print side, *Newsweek* frequently uses the services of Princeton Survey Research Associates, Reuters retains Zogby International, *USA Today* employs the Gallup organization, and *U.S. News & World Report* has used the Democratic political consulting firm Lake Research Partners and the Republican firm the Tarrance Group. The difference between these relationships and the partnerships between major news networks and print sources is that the latter control the polling process from start to finish, while the former contract their polling work out to a firm.

That said, those outlets that contract polling out to a separate firm still control the topics of surveys that are done, as well as the ever-important question selection. This gives the media a great deal of power in terms of what stories come out of their research. But the major partnerships created by the networks and newspapers go one step further. The dissemination of survey results that come from a network/newspaper poll not only give a great deal of visibility to both outlets, but the networks' print partners lend credibility and prestige to a poll and can also keep the results in the public eye for an extended period of time.[6] In the era of a twenty-four-hour news cycle, if a network relied only on its own broadcast to report its survey findings, the story would quickly come and go. But with a newspaper also reporting the same findings, the story has more staying power and can be reported in much more detail, as the time and space constraints for a print outlet are less strict than those for a network news program.

A media outlet that conducts or commissions its own polls can either report or create news with its survey research. Major issues and events are often the impetus behind network stories focusing on public opinion. The economy, abortion, tax cuts, foreign policy, presidential nominations, and especially elections are topics often covered by media polls that are done in-house. In these cases the issue or event is already on the national agenda; here, news networks add value to the story by reporting the public's views on important issues.

Networks and print sources can also create news by producing their own measures of public opinion. Many times this is in the context of an election when their polling shows a slight change in the public's evaluation of one or more candidates. Even the slightest change in a candidate's standing in the polls over the course of a few days or a week is sometimes taken as a sea change in the public's attitudes. For instance, a *USA Today* headline in 2004 announced, "Kerry Lead Fades in Two Battleground States."[7] While this would seem to indicate an important shift in public attitudes toward the presidential candidates, Kerry support remained within the margin of error of the poll (see below). Similarly, if the president's job approval is shown to slip even slightly, the media may take this as an opportunity to reinvestigate the progress of an administration or how the president is performing generally. As will be discussed later, in many cases like these, the media are "making mountains out of molehills" and may be inaccurately reporting the actual meaning of poll results.

"The proliferation of polls corresponds to the proliferation of available information generally and to the ever-faster news cycle."[8] While television news programs, newspapers, and magazines all look to their own polling or their contracted polls for stories, they dispense a voluminous amount of information focusing on the public's attitudes and beliefs that they themselves do not collect. The availability of information is supplemented by sources that are not affiliated with any news organization, but instead are organizations looking to gain some attention or increased visibility for their own reasons. The use of external public opinion polling by media outlets can also either simply report newsworthy information or it can create news for the benefit of both the news organization and the sponsor of the poll. The media, in fact, must rely on some outside surveys in order to fully report on influential and important events and issues. For example, an outlet like the *Washington Post* or CNN is not likely to devote its own resources to conduct a poll on Kenyan or Australian elections, the approval ratings of Pakistan's president Pervez Musharraf in his home country, or British citizens' views of terrorism within their borders. Instead, they rely on other sources for the information and report that to the public in the United States.

However, many media outlets do not stop there. Because there is fierce competition between news organizations for their audience, keeping the public's attention is at a premium.[9] Many news organizations rely on external sources to provide interesting survey results to their audience. The potential sources of public opinion data are literally endless. For instance, in the last year newspapers have relied on sources ranging from the National Retail Federation (*St. Louis Post Dispatch*),[10] AAA (*Philadelphia Inquirer*),[11] and the British government (*The New York Times*),[12] to the condom manufacturer Durex (*Washington Post*)[13] and SnagAJob.com (*Boston Herald*).[14] Academic institutions are also often cited. The information included in this type of survey result can deliver much sought-after attention and focus on a particular issue or organization. For instance, when its survey is reported on network news, the National Retail Federation not only connects with its current members but it gets media attention that may attract new members. A poll by a corporate entity such as Durex is likely done to try to increase sales of a product.

REPORTING ON POLLING METHODOLOGY

With the use of outside and external sources also comes another set of issues centering on both sponsorship and quality of the opinion polling. The partnerships between network and print media outlets add some credibility to the results of a poll, but not all media-sponsored polls are the same. This is also true for surveys done by organizations external to the media organization that is running the story. While we can be relatively confident in the procedures and practices of polls done by ABC News/*Washington Post*, NBC News/*Wall Street Journal*, and CBS News/*The New York Times*, other polls found in the media may not be so credible. This is because many times the proper techniques, methods, and standards are not applied to what the media may call public opinion.

While most polls done by media organizations are scientific in nature, pseudopolls are becoming more prevalent.[15] Pseudopolls are not really polls at all, but rather are "straw polls" of opinion that are gathered when a media organization invites viewers, listeners, or readers to call or write with their opinion. In the era of twenty-four-hour news cycles and cable news channels, interest in immediate reaction to an event, such as a presidential debate or a politician's press conference, has increased dramatically. The use of call-in or online polls can seriously mislead news audiences as to the true opinions of their fellow citizens, since the "polls" were not conducted scientifically—that is, they are not random samples of the public and therefore are not likely to be representative of the general population.

Additionally, journalists often make reference only to "the polls" when reporting a story, with no mention of any specific aspects of the survey that was conducted. A study by the Annenberg School of Communication found that in the 1988, 1992, and 1996 election cycles, the generic term *polls* was cited as evidence more frequently than any specific measure of public opinion done by a news organization or an external group.[16] Clearly, not all polls reported by the media are created equal.

Because the media do rely on external sources for a good portion of the polling data that they report, and because the general public is not well versed in the intricacies of statistical sampling, question wording and ordering, or data analysis, some basic information must be identified before any trust or confidence can be put into a poll done by a media organization or a news story that reports polling data. Fortunately, three major professional organizations of pollsters and survey research—the American Association for Public Opinion Research (AAPOR), the National Council on Public Polls (NCPP), and the Council of American Survey Research Organizations (CASRO)—provide a number of guidelines for both the press and the public.

Both journalists and the public must take care in evaluating the quality of a survey that reports public opinion before considering the results of that survey. The general public should be aware of certain aspects of opinion polls because they are the consumers of information and are the targets of poll sponsors. Journalists, too, must be aware of some polling intricacies if they are going to accurately interpret poll results in a story.

The NCPP has published "20 Questions a Journalist Should Ask about Poll Results" to aid reporters and editors in deciding what poll results are worthy of being reported on television or in newspapers. The NCPP guidelines are designed to help journalists weed out unscientific polls that are conducted by nonmedia sources that are simply looking to gain some visibility by reporting bogus or unreliable poll results. By asking themselves these questions, "the journalist can seek the facts to decide how to handle every poll that comes across the news desk each day" (see table 10.1).[17] These guidelines focus on the who, what, where, when, and why of polling and are the bare essentials of what to look for in the results of public opinion research. By paying attention to these issues that are at the heart of quality public opinion research, the polls that do get reported will be of high quality and will be of use to the general public.

While the NCPP list focuses on the polls that come to media outlets from external sources, the AAPOR "Standard for Minimum Disclosure" applies to what the media report from their own internal polls as well as those external polls they cover (see table 10.2). These few criteria represent a selection of the most critical and essential elements of public opinion research that can verify and validate the credibility of a poll that is reported on television or in a newspaper. They are designed to help journalists "present material so that readers and viewers have the necessary information to evaluate the quality of the poll results being reported."[18] AAPOR has even gone so far as to censure one pollster, Republican Frank Luntz, because he failed to provide thorough background information on survey research he did for the Republican Party's Contract with America, which received a great deal of media attention prior to the 1994 midterm elections.[19]

These guidelines can also be seen as a check to be used by the general public on how a media organization reports public opinion polls. In other words, they can help the viewer or the reader decide whether to believe what is being reported and can help the public be critical consumers of public opinion research that is reported in the media: "Just as customers in a supermarket of-

Table 10.1. National Council on Public Polls—20 Questions a Journalist Should Ask about Poll Results

1. Who did the poll?
2. Who paid for the poll and why was it done?
3. How many people were interviewed for the survey?
4. How were those people chosen?
5. What area (nation, state, or region) or what group (teachers, lawyers, Democratic voters, etc.) were these people chosen from?
6. Are the results based on the answers of all the people interviewed?
7. Who should have been interviewed and was not? Or do response rates matter?
8. When was the poll done?
9. How were the interviews conducted?
10. What about polls on the Internet or World Wide Web?
11. What is the sampling error for the poll results?
12. Who's on first?
13. What other kinds of factors can skew poll results?
14. What questions were asked?
15. In what order were the questions asked?
16. What about "push polls?"
17. What other polls have been done on this topic? Do they say the same thing? If they are different, why are they different?
18. What about exit polls?
19. What else needs to be included in the report of a poll?
20. So I've asked all the questions. The answers sound good. Should we report the results?

Source: National Council on Public Polls, "20 Questions a Journalist Should Ask about Poll Results," http://www.ncpp.org/?q=node/4 (accessed November 6, 2007).

ten inspect the list of ingredients in a product, so too should consumers of public opinion question what went into a poll before accepting its results."[20] By knowing what to look for in a news story that uses polling results, the public can become active rather than passive consumers of public opinion and make an informed judgment on the quality of a poll. "In the course of becoming better consumers of public opinion research, citizens need not become experts at drawing samples, constructing questionnaires, and analyzing data."[21] Rather, individuals simply need to be aware of some of the different criteria that constitute a sound and scientific poll.

However, the question becomes: How well do the media provide this type of information when they report either the results of polls they have conducted themselves or those that come from external sources? The short answer to this is not very well. Several studies have shown that neither newspapers nor television news programs do a very good job of reporting the criteria set forth by AAPOR.[22] In reporting of some aspects of the AAPOR standards, news outlets usually do better when they cover election polls versus nonelection polls,[23]

Table 10.2. American Association for Public Opinion Research, Standard for Minimal Disclosure

- Exact question wording and response options, including any instruction and explanation texts that might reasonably be expected to affect the response.
- Definition and description of the sampling frame used to identify this population.
- Method by which respondents were selected.
- Size of sample and, if applicable, information on eligibility criteria, screening procedures and completion rates.
- Method, location, and dates of interviews.
- When results are based on parts of the sample, instead of the whole.
- Who sponsored and conducted the poll.
- Information about the precision of the findings, including, if appropriate, estimates of sampling error, and a description of any weighting or estimating procedures used.

Source: American Association for Public Opinion Research, "Standard for Minimal Disclosure," http://www.aapor.org/disclosurestandards (accessed October 20, 2007).

and newspapers are usually more complete than television news programs in their reporting of polling intricacies.[24] The difference in reporting practices between television stations and newspapers is likely due in part to the fact that newspapers have less stringent time and space constraints than do television programs to report factors such as question wording, sample size, the sampling procedure, and the selection criteria.

Herbert Asher contends, however, that not all the blame should be placed at the feet of news organizations. He points out that the AAPOR and the NCPP standards are aimed at the "survey organizations and pollsters who release the results rather than to the media that are covering the results."[25] While national news organizations do have their own in-house polling operations, many of the polls they report still come from external sources, which may or may not provide the requisite information. Additionally, Asher argues that some of the standards are unclear and subjective. For example, "different polling organizations might very well disagree about the meaning of 'instruction or explanation . . . that might reasonably be expected to affect the response'" (see table 10.2).[26]

THE CONTENT OF PUBLIC OPINION COVERAGE

While the issues raised above focus on *how* the media report public opinion and the care they take to make sure their audiences are properly informed, another concern is *what* they report and whether it is an accurate representation of public opinion. If the results of a poll are taken out of context or are presented in a misleading way, it makes no difference how well a survey is conducted or how much a newspaper or television program reveals about the details of the poll. These concerns apply to whatever the media are reporting on, whether it be an issue like abortion, a political actor or institution such as the president or Congress, or an election campaign.

A full discussion of the complexities and issues of question wording in polling is beyond the scope of this chapter.[27] However, as both the AAPOR and NCPP standards indicate, public opinion can be misrepresented if the full wording of the question is not reported. Furthermore, public opinion can be misunderstood if the media selectively interpret findings from a poll.

Very often a survey—whether conducted or commissioned by a news organization, or from an external source—asks a number of different questions about the same topic. In asking about the same issue or phenomenon multiple ways, there may be multiple sets of results that can indicate different things about the public's beliefs and attitudes. The leeway this gives the media can cause difficulties for both reporters and editors (and producers in the case of television) in that they are constrained by the space and time limitations of modern journalism as well as the intense competition among news organizations today; they all worry about ratings or the number of papers they sell. As Asher points out, "Even simple description can pose a problem if a news story covers only a subset of the items on a topic because there is insufficient time or space."[28] Does the reporter write the story that is most memorable, or does he/she report each of the different sets of results? The logic of space and time constraints and competitive pressures would say that the most alluring and captivating of the results will be reported.

As an example of the power and force of question wording in a poll, one has to look no further than a 2007 *USA Today*/Gallup survey that asked a sample of 1,009 adults a number of questions about the State Children's Health Insurance Program. For one question, half the sample got a general question about who the respondents trust to handle SCHIP and the other half got a more specific question detailing the two sides' positions on the issue (see table 10.3). The results indicate that a majority of the public trusts Democrats more than President Bush on SCHIP generally; however, when the details of the two positions are provided, a majority backs Bush's approach to the issue.

These data represent two important points. First, question wording can influence the responses to a survey item. Second—and more important for our purposes—the results from a poll with diverging responses like those in this *USA Today*/Gallup survey can create a dilemma for reporters and editors. Should a story discussing the poll rely on the general conclusion that Democrats are trusted more on SCHIP, or should it only refer to the results of the specific question offering the positions of the Democrats and Bush? In fact, *USA Today* mentioned both: "[A] USA TODAY/Gallup Poll this week showed

Table 10.3.   Alternative Wording of Questions from a *USA Today*/Gallup Poll on SCHIP

"Based on what you have heard or read about this bill, who do you have more confidence in to handle this issue: George W. Bush or the Democrats in Congress?" Options rotated. N = 507 adults, MoE ± 5 (Form A).

Bush	Democrats	Neither (vol.)	Unsure
32%	52%	10%	5%

"As you may know, the Democrats want to allow a family of four earning about $62,000 to qualify for the program. President Bush wants most of the increases to go to families earning less than $41,000. Whose side do you favor?" Options rotated. N = 502 adults, MoE ± 5 (Form B)

Bush	Democrats	Neither (vol.)	Unsure
52%	40%	3%	4%

USA Today/Gallup Poll, October 12–14, 2007. N = 1,009 adults nationwide; MoE ± 3 (for all adults).
Source: PollingReport.com, http://www.pollingreport.com/health3.htm (accessed October 28, 2007).

Democrats are trusted more to handle the issue. But slim majorities in that poll want the program to focus more on low-income, uninsured children, as Republicans have demanded."[29] Not all media outlets can be expected to be as responsible in reporting the results of polls.

PUBLIC OPINION AND ELECTION COVERAGE

From nearly the beginning of any campaign until the final weekend before Election Day, the media report preelection polls that ask potential voters about their choice of candidates. Whether it be a generic ballot (i.e., "If the election were held today, would you vote for the Democratic candidate or the Republican candidate?") or a question that names specific candidates, the media seems to have a fascination with polls that try to assess who is ahead and who is behind at a certain point in a campaign. The fixation on the "horse race" aspect of a campaign has led to a great deal of criticism of the media.

Critics argue, among other things, that there is a lack of attention to issues in modern campaign coverage. Thomas Patterson argues that the media use a *game schema* when reporting on elections—that is, the media cover elections as if they are a game, where strategy and the score (i.e., poll results) are more important than issues and "candidates play the game well or poorly."[30] The game schema is opposed to the *governing schema*, in which policies matter and candidates or parties are judged according to their issue positions.[31]

The media's use of the game aspect of public opinion returns us to some of the concerns mentioned at the beginning of this chapter. Asher points out that this is another way in which the media can create news rather than simply reporting it.[32] Again, this stems from the constraints media outlets operate under—both space limitations and the competitive market they face. The horse race aspect of election coverage allows any media outlet to quickly gain attention in very little space or time. In addition, the results may have what appear to be tantalizing characteristics if new data show any change from the last poll that was done. Even the slightest shift from one candidate to another or from one party to another seems to elicit great reactions from even the most respected media outlets. But this type of reporting can be suspect in that the "shift" in public opinion may not be a shift at all but merely the result of sampling error. If, for example, the margin of error in a poll is ±3 percentage points and the media report a shift in support that is only 2 percentage points, there are no statistical grounds to assume that there has been a significant change in support for either candidate.[33]

Despite the fact that preelection polls are often reported in a somewhat misleading way, the accuracy of those polls is usually quite impressive. Even in the close election of 2004, the results of the final preelection polls fell within the margin of error, with the exception of the *Newsweek* poll (which, we should note, stopped interviewing before any of the other polls; see table 10.4). The underestimation of each candidate's final percentage of the vote is, in part, due to the fact that some voters have not made up their minds before Election Day and do not report a decision to pollsters; fewer voters will fail to make a choice on Election Day. Of course, media polling does not stop before votes are cast. Polls are also conducted in key precincts on Election Day.

Exit polls are self-administered questionnaires given to voters as they leave the polling place. The precincts in which exit polls are conducted are chosen based on "past voting behavior, geographic regions (within or across states), urban vs. rural counties, percent foreign stock, type of voting equipment, or poll closing times."[34] Specific voters are selected at random according to a "sampling interval"; for example, every twentieth person might be asked to participate.[35] In recent years, exit polls have been conducted for the media in every state and the District of Columbia (in addition to separate national exit polls),[36] except for the state of Oregon, whose voters cast ballots entirely by mail.

The results of exit polls are used for two purposes. First, demographic information can be coupled with vote choice to explain which groups voted for which candidates and to what extent. Questions that tap the reasons for a person's vote choice can also help explain why an election turned out as it did. Second, the results of the election can often be determined from the results of the exit poll. When entered into a statistical model along with actual vote counts throughout the day (as well as other variables), the exit poll results make it possible to project the winner of the election. The use of exit polling on Election Day means that the media change course from trying to *predict* what will happen to *explaining* what did happen. Arguably, exit polls are the most important measure of public opinion the media conduct because of the uses of that information.

Table 10.4.   Final Poll Results from Various Media Outlets for the 2004 Presidential Election

Question[a]: If the presidential election were held today, would you vote for Democrat John Kerry or Republican George W. Bush, or someone else?

	Kerry	Bush	Bush Lead
FOX News			
{10/30–31; 1200; ±3}[b]	48	46	–2
CBS News			
{10/29–11/1; 1125; ±3}	47	49	2
CNN/*USA Today*/Gallup			
{10/29–31; 1573; ±3}	47	49	2
NBC News/*Wall Street Journal*			
{10/29–31; 1014; ±3.1}	47	48	1
ABC News[c]			
{10/28–31; 2904; ±2}	48	49	1
Washington Post			
{10/28–31 2904; ±2}	48	49	1
Newsweek			
{10/27–29; 882; ±4}	44	50	6
TIPP			
{10/30–11/1; 1284; ±2.8}	45	47	2
Average	46.75	48.37	1.61
Actual Results	48.3	50.7	2.4

[a] Question wording varies slightly from poll to poll. For example, some mention vice presidential candidates, while others do not. Furthermore, some polls give the respondent an option of being "unsure," while others only record uncertainty if it is volunteered by the respondent.
[b] Numbers in brackets represent the dates of the poll, the number of likely voters surveyed, and the margin of error.
[c] ABC News and the *Washington Post* shared data collection, then independently applied their own models to arrive at likely voter estimates.

The failure of the media to accurately make projections based on exit polls has caused a great deal of consternation in recent years, especially on election night in both 2000 and 2004. It should be noted, however, that while anger about exit polls might be justified with respect to election projections, the other purpose of exit polling is to help us understand the complex dynamics surrounding elections. To that end, we need careful thought about how to improve the reporting of exit poll results, not sweeping condemnation of the use of exit polls generally.

EXIT POLLING AND ELECTION NIGHT COVERAGE

Exit polls have become essential to election night reporting. When coupled with actual election returns, they provide the media with the information necessary to project winners in the most closely watched races. They also give reporters and other election analysts important data for understanding why people voted as they did. But exit polling is a complicated process and there have been numerous problems with exit polls in recent election cycles.

The problems with using exit polling to report on elections and their outcomes—or at least the problems with the way the media currently use exit polling—became patently obvious on election night 2000. Media projections that Vice President Al Gore had won the state of Florida, and their subsequent retractions, along with further proclamations of a Bush win in Florida (including the designation of the Texas governor as "President-Elect Bush") and the retraction of those projections, combined to give the media the biggest collective embarrassment they have, perhaps, ever faced. But as we will see, 2000 was not the only time exit polling caused consternation toward the media. Problems and controversy also occurred in 2002 and 2004.

Mistakes made by the media as a result of polling were not unprecedented before 2000. In 1936, after four stunningly correct presidential election predictions, the *Literary Digest* blundered by forecasting a landslide for Republican Alf Landon (who lost by more than 23 percentage points to President Franklin Roosevelt).[37] Similarly, but for different reasons, pollsters incorrectly predicted a victory for Thomas Dewey over President Harry Truman in 1948.[38] The assumption that Dewey would win handily led to a headline in the *Chicago Daily Tribune*—captured in a famous photograph of Truman holding the paper next to his smiling face—that read "Dewey Defeats Truman." Yet what makes these cases different from the 2000 election is that the media used exit polls to make the call in the latter, whereas the previous mistakes were based on preelection polls.

While one might assume that exit polls are more accurate than polls taken before the election (since the former measure how people report having voted versus what they claim are their voting intentions), exit polls themselves have been wrong before. In 1989, Douglas Wilder won the Virginia gubernatorial election by less than 1 percentage point though exit polls suggested a 10-point win; in 1992, exit polls indicated that Patrick Buchanan would finish just 6 points behind President George H. W. Bush in the New Hampshire republican primary, but he lost by 16 points; and in 1996, Sen. Bob Dole was projected to come in third in the Arizona primary, behind Steve Forbes and Pat Buchanan, when, in fact, he finished a close second to Forbes.[39] In each case, it should be noted, the eventual winner had been correctly projected, a fact that helps erase from memory the mistaken margins of victory. Given the importance of the race and the magnitude of the errors, however, few will soon forget the media blunders of election night 2000.

The story actually begins a decade earlier, in 1990, when Voter Research and Surveys (VRS) was formed by CNN and the network news organizations for the purpose of conducting exit polls for the member organizations. To the extent that they used exit polls at all to that point, individual media outlets had conducted their own polling. Most election night coverage relied on actual election returns gathered by News Election Service (NES). Any projections news organizations might make would be based on their own calculations. In 1993, however, VRS and NES were combined to form a new entity called Voter News Service (VNS). VNS would conduct exit polls, collect election returns from around the country, and analyze the data to provide member organizations (which would eventually include Fox News) with projected winners in key races.

Projections based on VNS analyses had been relatively accurate for the election cycles leading up to 2000. But the polls—and the media's use of those polls—led to significant errors that year. The details of election night 2000 are worth recalling. NBC was the first to project a Gore win in Florida, at 7:48 P.M. EST, based on the VNS "CALL GORE" determination.[40] "Call" status "is not yet an actual projection of a . . . victory by VNS, but is an alert to its clients to examine the data and to consider whether they wish to call the state."[41] CNN and CBS (who used a joint "decision team" to evaluate VNS results) followed NBC minutes later, and just before 8:00 P.M. VNS moved Florida to the "WIN GORE" category. This was clearly a significant development in that most observers knew going into the election that Florida would be close and that the winner of that state would be in a commanding position to capture the White House. Of course, there were other states that would be central to a winning combination of electoral votes. Michigan and Pennsylvania were among those, and Gore was called the winner of those states at 8:00 P.M. and 8:47 P.M., respectively.[42] At that point, had the Florida projection been accurate, it would have been nearly impossible for Bush to win.

At 9:38 P.M., however, "VNS sent a message [to its clients] that read, 'We are canceling the vote in Cnty 16—Duval Cnty, FL—vote is strange.'"[43] CNN and CBS retracted their calls for Gore in Florida at 9:54 P.M., and by 10:16 P.M. VNS had retracted its decision to place Florida in the "WIN GORE" category.[44] Interestingly, just as VNS was reversing itself on the Florida call, it was awarding New Mexico to Gore; hours later, New Mexico would again be considered "too close to call," only to end up in Gore's column weeks later. Similarly, VNS projected a victory for Maria Cantwell in the Washington Senate race when, in fact, the election was not decided until December 1 following a recount. Though some of the hasty calls made by VNS were "correct" to the extent that the eventual winner had been projected, it would be hard to say those calls were "accurate," at least at the time they were made.[45] In the end, VNS exit poll results for the presidential race were incorrect in eight states and VNS calls were wrong in three.[46]

For nearly four hours, the nation waited as real votes were tallied in Florida. At 2:08 A.M. on November 8, VNS determined that Bush had a 51,000-vote lead in Florida with roughly 180,000 votes left to count. According to VNS calculations, Gore would need 63 percent of the remaining votes to win Florida. Fox News gave Florida—and the presidency—to Bush at 2:15 A.M., followed by NBC at 2:16 A.M., CNN and CBC at 2:17 A.M., and ABC at 2:20 A.M. Interestingly, VNS and the Associated Press never officially made the call for Bush in Florida.[47]

At around 3:00 A.M., Gore phoned Bush to congratulate him on his victory. Yet the actual vote count was showing an incredibly close election. Apparently, Bush's supposed 51,000-vote lead had been based, in part, on erroneous information from Volusia County.[48] By 3:15 A.M., sources began to tell reporters that there would likely be an automatic recount of the Florida vote. Less than forty-five minutes after conceding to Bush, Gore called Bush again to retract his concession. Shortly after 4:00 A.M., those networks that had made a second projection in the Florida presidential race retracted their call once again.[49]

The question, of course, is why did these mistakes occur? Many of the errors on election night stem from the fact that each of the news organizations relied on the same source for data and primary analysis. Among the specific problems at VNS, according to a report commissioned by CNN, were a serious lack of communication between VNS and the member news organizations, and poor quality control of the data, allowing multiple errors in vote counting to enter the VNS system.[50] Generally speaking, however, the problem was that only one source gathered and had primary responsibility for analyzing the data. "The simple fact," argued Steven Brill, publisher of the media watchdog magazine *Brill's Content*,

> is that the news media's election-night fiasco happened because the press seems to have violated antitrust laws by organizing a cartel called Voter News Service that was guaranteed to eliminate competition for a quality product—and, therefore, destined one day to produce a defective product that no one could tell was defective because there would be no alternative products to compare it to.[51]

Ultimately, however, the news organizations themselves are responsible for making a call on the air. In fact, they all hire their own teams of analysts to double-check the conclusions made by VNS. As the authors of the CNN report note, "[A]fter ABC used its own personnel during the 1994 congressional elections to make calls, sometimes ahead of VNS and thus ahead of its competitors, the other networks created their own decision desks or decision teams to analyze data received from VNS on Election Night."[52] Thus, despite the lack of competition with respect to data gathering and primary analysis, there remained fierce competition between the networks to be first in calling an election. As the CNN report concludes, "a news environment that cultivates the urge to a definitive conclusion impelled CNN, and the other networks, in such a way as to contribute to the inaccuracy of the reporting that evening and the resulting confusion that followed the election."[53] Indeed, VNS never made a second call in Florida; the networks made that decision themselves, though admittedly it was based on what seemed like fairly solid evidence from VNS. Nevertheless, some argue that it was precisely the desire to avoid being "scooped," or beaten to a story, that forced the networks to quickly follow Fox's lead once it projected a Bush win.[54]

Exit polls are very difficult surveys to administer. Though many of the mistakes made on election night 2000 were specific to that particular evening, there are many sources of error that plague exit polls, and their use to project outcomes in general. Sampling error, which exists in all polls and surveys, increases with exit polls because the sampling design is more complicated than the simple random sample typically used in telephone polls.[55] Nonresponse poses another problem for exit polling. Potential respondents may either refuse to participate or may simply be missed by the interviewer (because, for example, the respondent does not leave the polling place in the area where the interviewer is stationed). While some research suggests that exit poll respondents do not differ significantly from nonrespondents, the potential for bias does exist, particularly because older voters have been found to refuse more than younger voters.[56] Similarly, some voters may be systematically excluded from exit polls (that is, there is "coverage error") either because they voted early or by absentee ballot or because they voted during a part of the day when the exit poll was not being conducted.[57] Indeed, VNS estimated that 7.2 percent of the total 2000 Florida vote would be absentee ballots, whereas such voters actually accounted for 12 percent of the votes cast.[58] As more and more voters choose to vote in ways that make them physically absent at the polls on Election Day—as in Oregon, for instance—exit polls will become increasingly difficult, if not impossible, to undertake. Finally, at least with respect to the administration of exit polls, measurement error—or the amount of error caused by things like question wording, format, and order—must be considered.[59]

Once obtained, exit poll data are used in models that project election outcomes. The development of these models requires a sophisticated understanding of both elections and statistics. Because the assumptions used to construct an election night model are based, in part, on a previous, comparable election, the choice of the comparison election is crucial to the success of the model. In 2000 VNS used the 1998 Florida gubernatorial election as the comparison election. As it turns out, according to an analysis by VNS, the 1996 presidential race in Florida or the 1998 Florida Senate election would have been better comparisons for 2000.[60]

For the 2002 elections, VNS revamped its computer system and the software it used to make projections. Despite the changes, significant errors in the exit polls and the vote tabulations occurred on election night. In fact, the errors were so grave that the exit poll data from 2002 were never released. As a result of this additional round of mistakes, VNS was disbanded the following year.

In its place, the major news organizations formed the National Election Pool (NEP) to conduct exit polling under the direction of two veteran pollsters. According to the new arrangement, the Associated Press would continue to tabulate votes based on official returns and would provide that data to its subscribers and the other consortium members. However, if the media hoped to avoid further controversy by dissolving VNS and creating NEP, they were undoubtedly disappointed in 2004.

As had been the practice at VNS, NEP gave the members of the consortium exit poll data at regular intervals throughout Election Day. Though consortium members agreed not to release such information, it was inevitably leaked to a number of outlets outside the consortium. Having never agreed to honor an embargo of such data, some Internet sites published the early results, which showed John Kerry with a lead in most of the key states. This information spread rapidly via bloggers. Though none of the consortium members openly referred to the exit polls on the air, the idea that Kerry was headed to victory subtly influenced early characterizations of the election. Some reporters, for example, suggested the mood in the Bush White House had been downcast late into the afternoon.[61]

Unlike in 2000, no incorrect projections were made in 2004. Nevertheless, the exit polls were once again inaccurate. As a report by the NEP pollsters concludes, "The exit poll estimates in the 2004 general election overstated John Kerry's share of the vote nationally and in many states."[62] There were numerous methodological reasons for the errors, but the most likely cause was "Kerry voters participating in the exit polls at a higher rate than Bush voters."[63]

Exit polls are typically reliable sources of information about election outcomes. In fact, they are thought to be so reliable that some have concluded it was the election returns themselves—and not the exit polls—that were inaccurate in 2004. That is, only vote fraud could explain why the exit polls were off the mark: a statistically unlikely event, according to those alleging malfeasance.[64] Few observers take this possibility seriously since it would require an even more unlikely conspiracy to stuff ballot boxes while leaving behind no evidence of such activity.

Keep in mind that while the exit polls may have been inaccurate in 2004, the media did not rush to judgment in calling the election. If nothing else, they appear to have learned patience from their experience in 2000. To further reduce the chance of error, however, NEP did not provide exit poll results to consortium members in 2006 until 5:00 P.M. EST. This eliminated the possibility of leaks and made it impossible for reporters to offer even subtle clues about potential outcomes. In 2006 the media were cautious in their use of exit polling, and once again no incorrect projections were made. Whether this will be true on election night 2008—an evening that is sure to be characterized by high drama—remains to be seen.

CONCLUSION

This chapter has examined the media's role in measuring, reporting, and interpreting public opinion. We have argued that the media no longer simply report the news; they can also create it. They do so, by and large, by conducting public opinion polls, the results of which become news in and of themselves; the media also rely on external sources for public opinion data that may or may not be newsworthy. Yet reporting on poll results often falls short of the ideal set by professional polling associations. Critical consumers of the news should be able to determine the credibility of a poll or survey based on basic information provided by the media (e.g., the sample size, the dates a poll was conducted, the question wording, the margin of error, etc.).

When it comes to covering elections, the media rely extensively on public opinion. Polls are ubiquitous in election reporting, and "horse race" coverage now predominates over policy considerations. Indeed, polling continues into Election Day in the form of exit polls. But exit polls are subject to various forms of error, and in close elections those errors can lead to mistaken projections of the winner. That is precisely what happened in the historic election of 2000. Though we may never know exactly what went wrong, we can reform the Election Day reporting process so as to never face a disaster like that again.

DISCUSSION QUESTIONS

1. What sources of polling data are more reliable, valid, and/or credible— external polls or internal media polls? Why?
2. What are pseudopolls and how useful are they in gauging public opinion on a given topic? Why do you think the media relies on them so much?

3. Scan today's newspaper or television news for stories that cite public opinion data. How were poll results used (e.g., was it the focus of the story or did it support a conclusion)? How much information about the methodology was reported? Did you have enough information to evaluate the credibility of the poll?

4. Thomas Patterson says the media uses a game schema for election coverage. What is the game schema and in what ways is such coverage problematic?

5. What lessons should the media have learned from what transpired on election night 2000? Have they, in fact, learned those lessons?

6. Ultimately, does a heavy reliance on public opinion polling (and the media's reporting of it) enrich our democracy or damage it? Explain.

SUGGESTIONS FOR FURTHER READING

Paul J. Lavrakas and Michael W. Traugott, eds. *Election Polls, the News Media, and Democracy*. New York: Chatham House/Seven Bridges Press, 2000.

Thomas E. Mann and Gary R. Orren, eds. *Media Polls in American Politics*. Washington, DC: Brookings, 1992). National Council on Public Polls. http://www.ncpp.org.

"Polls and the News Media: A Symposium," *Public Opinion Quarterly* 44, no. 4 (Winter 1980): 567–71.

Matthew Robinson. *Mobocracy: How the Media's Obsession with Polling Twists the News, Alters Elections, and Undermines Democracy*. Roseville, CA: Forum/Prima, 2002.

Tom Rosenstiel. "Political Polling and the New Media Culture: A Case of More Being Less." *Public Opinion Quarterly* 69 (2005): 698–715.

NOTES

1. Christopher Hitchens, *For the Sake of Argument* (London: Verso, 1993).

2. The Vanderbilt Television News Archive is the source of information on news story topics discussed in this paragraph. For news references to polls, a simple search on the archive's Web site (http://tvnews.vanderbilt.edu/) for the term "poll" produced the results. Separate searches for "survey research" or "polling data" did not produce a significant increase in stories from the numbers reported above.

3. Herbert Asher, *Polling and the Public: What Every Citizen Should Know*, 7th ed. (Washington, DC: CQ Press, 2007), 4.

4. Kathleen A. Frankovic, "Public Opinion and Polling," in *The Politics of News*, ed. Doris Graber, Denis McQuail, and Pippa Norris (Washington, DC: CQ Press, 1998), 150.

5. Ibid.

6. Ibid.

7. Susan Page, "Kerry Lead Fades in Two Battleground States."*USA Today*, August 30, 2004, 4A.

8. Frankovic, "Public Opinion and Polling," 163.

9. Ibid.

10. Gail Appleson. "Many Shoppers Stuff Their Own Stockings," *St. Louis Post-Dispatch*, December 17, 2006, E1.

11. Paul Nussbaum, "Polls Find Most Drivers Oppose Leasing Roads," *Philadelphia Inquirer*, March 27, 2007, B3.

12. Alex Berenson, "Sending Back the Doctor's Bill," *The New York Times*, July 29, 2007, WK-3.

13. Laura Sessions Stepp, "How's Your Love Life? 60 Years after Kinsey, Americans Remain Shy about Answering," *Washington Post*, May 22, 2007, HE01.

14. Darren Garnick, "The Water Cooler; The Working Stiff; Take Heart! Celeb Valentines On Way," *Boston Herald*, February 7, 2007, 22.

15. Barry Orton, "Phony Polls: The Pollster's Nemesis," *Public Opinion* 5 (June/July 1982): 56–60; Asher, *Polling and the Public*.

16. Annenberg School of Communication, "Using the Annenberg Presidential Campaign Discourse Archive," Version 1.0 (Philadelphia: Annenberg School for Communication, Annenberg Public Policy Center, 1997).

17. Sheldon R. Gawiser and G. Evans Witt, "20 Questions a Journalist Should Ask about Poll Results," National Council on Public Polls, 3rd ed., http://www.ncpp .org/?q=node/4 (accessed January 23, 2008).

18. Michael Traugott and Elizabeth C. Powers, "Did Public Opinion Support the Contract with America?" in *Election Polls, the News Media, and Democracy*, ed. Paul J. Lavrakas and Michael W. Traugott (New York: Chatham House, 2000), 101.

19. Richard Morin, "A Pollster's Peers Cry Foul," *Washington Post*, National Weekly Edition, April 28, 1997, 35; see also Traugott and Powers, "Contract with America."

20. Herbert Asher, *Polling and the Public: What Every Citizen Should Know*, 4th ed. (Washington, DC: CQ Press, 1998), 15.

21. Asher, *Polling and the Public*, 4th ed., 15.

22. M. Mark Miller and Robert Hurd, "Conformity to AAPOR Standards in Newspaper Reporting of Public Opinion Polls," *Public Opinion Quarterly* 46 (1982): 243–49; Michael B. Salwen, "The Reporting of Public Opinion Polls During Presidential Years, 1968–985," *Journalism Quarterly* 62 (1985): 272–77; David L. Paletz et al., "Polls in the Media: Content, Credibility, and Consequences." *Public Opinion Quarterly* 44 (1980): 495–614.

23. Miller and Hurd, "Conformity to AAPOR Standards."

24. Paletz et al., "Polls in the Media."

25. Asher, *Polling and the Public*, 7th ed., 121.

26. Ibid., 122.

27. See, for instance, ibid.; Earl Babbie, *The Practice of Social Research*, 9th ed. (Belmont, CA: Wadsworth, 2000); Pamela L. Alreck and Robert B. Settle, *The Sur-*

vey Research Handbook, 2nd ed. (Burr Ridge, IL: Irwin, 1995); Floyd J. Fowler, *Survey Research Methods*, 2nd ed. (Newbury Park, CA: Sage, 1993).

28. Asher, *Polling and the Public*, 7th ed., 127–28.

29. Richard Wolf, "House Fails to Override Veto of Insurance Bill," *USA Today*, October 18, 2007, http://www.usatoday.com/news/washington/2007-10-18-schip_N .htm (accessed October 28, 2007).

30. Thomas E. Patterson, *Out of Order* (New York: Vintage, 1994), 57.

31. Ibid., 59.

32. Asher, *Polling and the Public*, 7th ed.

33. As Election Day approaches, most media outlets conduct tracking polls. Such polls are conducted daily with 250 to 500 people. The responses of those 250 to 500 individuals are then added to those from the previous two days. In other words, tracking polls are rolling polls that drop one-third of the respondents every day but add another third to the total. Thus, a 2 percentage point change in each of three consecutive days would, in fact, signal a significant change in opinion.

34. Mark R. Levy, "The Methodology and Performance of Election Day Polls," *Public Opinion Quarterly* 47 (1983): 56; see also Daniel M. Merkle and Murray Edelman, "A Review of the 1996 Voter News Service Exit Polls from a Total Survey Error Perspective," in *Election Polls, the News Media, and Democracy*, ed. Paul J. Lavrakas and Michael W. Traugott (New York: Chatham House, 2000).

35. Levy, "Methodology and Performance of Election Day Polls," 59; Merkle and Edelman, "1996 Voter News Service Exit Polls," 69.

36. Merkle and Edelman, "1996 Voter News Service Exit Polls," 69.

37. For an examination of the problems in the 1936 *Literary Digest* poll, see Peverill Squire, "Why the 1936 *Literary Digest* Poll Failed," *Public Opinion Quarterly* 52 (1988): 125–33. Incidentally, the *Literary Digest*, once a very popular magazine, went out of business the year following its election poll mistake. Susan Herbst, *Numbered Voices: How Opinion Polling Has Shaped American Politics* (Chicago: University of Chicago Press, 1993), 70.

38. Robert S. Erikson and Kent L. Tedin. *American Public Opinion*, 5th ed. (Boston: Allyn and Bacon, 1995), 31.

39. Asher, *Polling and the Public*, 7th ed., 152. The Wilder mistake stems from the willingness of white respondents to say they voted for Wilder, a black candidate, when in fact they did not. Michael W. Traugott and Vincent Price, "Exit Polls in the 1989 Virginia Gubernatorial Race: Where Did They Go Wrong?" *Public Opinion Quarterly* 56 (1992): 245–53. In the Republican Primary cases, it appears that Buchanan voters were more willing to participate in exit polls than Bush or Dole supporters. Asher, *Polling and the Public*, 7th ed., 152; Warren J. Mitofsky, "What Went Wrong with Exit Polling in New Hampshire," *Public Perspective* 3 (March/April 1992): 17; Richard Morin, "This Time in New Hampshire, A Somewhat More Graceful Exit," *Washington Post*, National Weekly Edition, February 24–March 1, 1992, 37.

40. Though most of the polling places in Florida closed at 7:00 P.M. EST, those in the Florida Panhandle, which are in the Central Time Zone, did not close until 8:00 P.M. EST. Many felt that the premature call for Gore may have discouraged turnout in the Panhandle, which is solidly Republican. That charge seems dubious, given that the

call was made only twelve minutes before the polls closed. Nevertheless, the networks say they do not call an election before the polls close in a state, and this was a clear violation of that policy. In the weeks following the election, the Panhandle dispute would fuel much of the Bush supporters' anger about the Gore call.

41. Joan Konner, James Risser, and Ben Wattenberg, "Television's Performance on Election Night 2000: A Report for CNN," 2001, http://a388.g.akamai.net/f/388/21/1d/ www.cnn.com/2001/ALLPOLITICS/stories/02/02/cnn.report/cnn.pdf, 11 (accessed November 1, 2007).

42. Ibid., appendix 4, i.

43. Seth Mnookin, "It Happened One Night." *Brill's Content*, February 2001, 150.

44. Konner, Risser, and Wattenberg, "Television's Performance," 13.

45. Mnookin, "It Happened One Night," 150–51.

46. Konner, Risser, Wattenberg, "Television's Performance," appendix 3, ii; Mnookin, "It Happened One Night," 151.

47. Konner, Risser, Wattenberg, "Television's Performance," 16; Mnookin, "It Happened One Night," 151.

48. There were, in fact, even more inaccuracies. Nearly 400,000 votes—not 180,000—remained to be counted at the time of the Fox News call for Bush. Furthermore, Brevard County was showing a vote total that undercounted the Gore vote by 4,000. Thus, what had appeared to be a 51,000-vote Bush lead was actually a 27,000-vote lead, with 400,000 votes to be counted—including many in the heavily Democratic counties of Broward, Miami-Dade, and Palm Beach. Konner, Risser, and Wattenberg, "Television's Performance," 15.

49. Ibid., 16–17.

50. Ibid., 18.

51. Steven Brill, "Fixing Election Night," *Brill's Content*, February 2001, 26.

52. Konner, Risser, and Wattenberg, "Television's Performance," 19.

53. Ibid., 19.

54. Adding yet another bizarre twist to the story, John Ellis, the head of Fox's decision desk and a cousin of George W. Bush, was responsible for Fox's call for Bush. Needless to say, that fact angered Gore supporters, even though decision makers at other networks vehemently deny simply jumping on Fox's bandwagon; see Mnookin, "It Happened One Night," 152.

55. Merkle and Edelman, "1996 Voter News Service Exit Polls," 72.

56. Ibid., 74.

57. Ibid., 80; Asher, *Polling and the Public*, 7th ed.

58. Konner, Risser, and Wattenberg, "Television's Performance," 19.

59. Merkle and Edelman, "1996 Voter News Service Exit Polls," 87.

60. Konner, Risser, and Wattenberg, "Television's Performance," 20.

61. Michael W. Traugott, Benjamin Highton, and Henry E. Brady, "A Review of Recent Controversies Concerning the 2004 Presidential Election Exit Polls," National Research Commission on Elections and Voting, March 10, 2005, http://elections.ssrc .org/research/ExitPollReport031005.pdf (accessed October 29, 2007).

62. Edison Media Research and Mitofsky International, "Evaluation of Edison/Mitofsky Election System 2004." National Election Pool, January 19, 2005,

http://msnbcmedia.msn.com/i/msnbc/Sections/News/A_FOR%20EDIT/Evaluation of Edison Mitofsky Election System January 19 2. .pdf, 3 (accessed October 21, 2007).

63. Edison Media Research and Mitofsky International, "Evaluation of Edison/ Mitofsky Election System 2004," 3.

64. See Steven F. Freeman and Joel Bleifuss, *Was the 2004 Presidential Election Stolen? Exit Polls, Election Fraud, and the Official Count* (New York: Seven Stories Press, 2006).

11

The New Bully Pulpit

Global Media and Foreign Policy

Maryann Cusimano Love

While the cameras rolled the Irish rock star Bono held forth, circled by the president of the United States and heads of state from other countries, U.S. legislators, and other political leaders, all eager to hear his views on international debt relief, aid and trade to Africa, and public health programs aimed at the world's poorest countries. "It's not about charity, it's about justice," Bono said.[1] "6,500 Africans are still dying every day of a preventable, treatable disease, for lack of drugs we can buy at any drugstore. This is not about charity, this is about Justice and Equality."[2] Whether speaking to three thousand attendees (plus additional television viewers) at the National Prayer Breakfast in Washington, D.C., or speaking to 3 billion people who watched the Live 8 concerts July 2, 2005, Bono stays on message.

This message—and the activism of nongovernmental organizations (NGOs) on these issues—is yielding results. Nearly half the world's population watched the Live 8 concerts to Make Poverty History; more than a million music fans packed ten concerts on four continents, another 2 billion watched on television, and the remainder tuned in online. The concerts were designed to pressure world leaders assembling for the G-8 meetings in Gleneagles, Scotland, to aid to the world's poor, especially in Africa, by increasing development assistance, funding for HIV/AIDS prevention and treatment, and debt relief.[3] The efforts largely succeeded. The G-8 leaders committed to double aid to Africa (an increase to $25 billion now and $50 billion by 2010), cancel the debt of some of the world's poorest countries, provide greater access to HIV/AIDS treatment drugs, and work to reform trade practices that hurt the world's poor. The movement continues to pressure world leaders to keep and expand upon these promises.[4]

How is an Irish musician able to help change the foreign policies of governments and intergovernmental organizations like the World Bank and International Monetary Fund (IMF) on a range of issues affecting Africa? Bono and the NGOs he works with have a number of tools in their arsenal. Chief among them is using the media to draw international attention to glaring policy problems—and to shame and name and inspire policy makers to address these issues. When Bono traveled with then-U.S. treasury secretary Paul O'Neil to Africa in 2002, the media chronicled their every move, which was a major purpose of the trip. "We created dozens of hours for CNN—a lot of which they showed to the world," O'Neill says. "I think they did it because of Bono's notoriety and fame and my title, which for me is exactly how these things can be used."[5]

NGOs and other nonstate actors are redefining the bully pulpit. Theodore Roosevelt first coined the term a hundred years ago, referring to his ability to use public office to focus attention on issues of interest to the president. "I suppose my critics will call that preaching," said Roosevelt, "but I have got such a bully pulpit!" Today the bully pulpit has changed. In an age of global and instant media, increasingly focused on entertainment and celebrity content, presidents and public officials are no longer the only ones with access to a bully pulpit. The twenty-four-hour news cycle creates a hunger for content, which is constantly needed for Web sites as well as traditional press and broadcast media outlets. Nonstate actors who can effectively figure out how to "feed the beast"—to give the media the content they need to fuel their media outlets—can now compete with the messages and media strategies of governments and official state actors.

"NGOs use media and communications power as a force multiplier for their values, ideas, and information power. [Although] NGOs vary in their skills and access to global media, they do have certain media advantages. Global media simplify issues to attract wider audiences [and] compete against ever-shorter sound bites . . . to sell their products. If NGOs often emphasize how policies or practices affect particular individuals or groups, or how global issues present clear moral choices, then they may be able to attract media attention. NGOs can use . . . media as a megaphone for their message if they understand the care and feeding of the [media and can] deliver compelling stories [and] good pictures [with] clear good guys and bad guys, in arenas where government, IGO, or corporate responses may . . . be slow or lack credibility . . . . Media and communications power are important to groups that trade in ideas. NGOs, like others who can persuade but [can]not compel, must be good salespeople as well as good preachers [to effectively] mobilize their ideas." Media attention also raises public attention and funding to NGOs. Compelling media coverage of the 280,000 killed in the tsunami in Southeast Asia brought record contributions. The International Red Cross discontinued fund-raising on January 26, 2005, because so much money (over

1.2 billion in contributions) had been pledged in the first thirty days.[6] The experience of antiwar groups who were not able to garner significant or favorable media coverage of their positions prior to the U.S. invasion of Iraq in 2003 shows that government officials still can control the bully pulpit, especially on issues in which they can claim exclusive access to critical information. Yet increasingly in other areas of foreign policy, nonstate actors can also effectively use global media.

However it is not only "the good guys"—such as antipoverty or pro-democracy activists or the Red Cross—who have access to the new bully pulpit. Illegal nonstate actors can also use global instant media. Al-Qaeda has developed a prolific media organization, the as-Sahab Institute for Media Production, which produces al-Qaeda TV ("The Voice of the Caliphate"), a "news and information" program detailing world events from a violent jihadist point of view. The institute also produces and distributes audio- and videotapes of Osama bin Laden and other al-Qaeda leaders for distribution and broadcast by other media outlets, from Al Jazeera to CNN. The year 2007 has been the most prolific to date for al-Qaeda media production, which released seventy-four tapes by September 9, 2007, a rate of one release every three days.[7] These efforts yield publicity for al-Qaeda's cause, one of the terrorist group's chief aims. According to Brigitte Nacos, Osama bin Laden and the al-Qaeda network receive extensive media coverage—at times more coverage than President Bush or official policy makers.[8]

Terrorist groups' access to the bully pulpit has led to a controversial debate over the impact of global media. Do the media affect foreign policy in a positive or negative direction—or not at all? Under what specific circumstances are the media more or less likely to impact foreign policy, and how? While globalization is not new, the speed, reach, and intensity of media coverage of foreign policy in the current period of globalization *are* new. News is instant and global, as fast and accessible as text and digital photos uploaded to the Internet and satellite-uplinked coverage broadcast in real time. The cheapness and wide dispersion of information technology means that a wider audience can access media products more quickly. Broadcasts and print reports are no longer national, and national governments have decreased control, with fewer state-owned media outlets.

THE POSITIVE VIEW: THE MEDIA AND DEMOCRACY

There are now more democracies than ever before, at the same time that free media are accessible in more parts of the globe than before. Many argue that this correlation equates to causation: that global media help democratization by giving citizens access to information by which to access their governments, serving a "watchdog" and public forum role, and helping to create a space for civil society. During the Cold War, when Germany was divided, approximately 90 percent of East German households tuned into free television and radio broadcasts from the democratic West. The people watched Soviet leader Mikhail Gorbachev enact his perestroika and glasnost reforms of greater openness, while their ruler in East Germany, Erich Honecker, steadfastly resisted any reforms to the failing communist system. In May 1989 Gorbachev announced that the Soviet Union would no longer use force to prevent democratic transitions in its satellite states, as it had done in the past. In Poland and Hungary, pro-democracy groups were negotiating transfers of power away from the Communists. On May 2, 1989, Hungary began taking down the barbed wire and guard towers that separated it from non-Communist Austria. East Germans followed these events closely through the Western media, and over the summer thousands traveled to Hungary, Poland, Czechoslovakia, and to West German diplomatic posts, attempting to flee to the West. On September 10, Hungary announced it would no longer stop East Germans from leaving to the West; the Czech and West German consulates soon followed suit, allowing more than one hundred thousand East Germans to emigrate to the West. Gorbachev arrived in East Berlin on October 6, to celebrate the fortieth anniversary of the establishment of East Germany. He warned Honecker to change with the times, but still Honecker resisted. Thousands of protesters took to the streets, and their cries of "Gorby, save us!" could even be heard on state-controlled East German television, which was unable to filter out the sound on its broadcasts. This emboldened the resistance. Peaceful demonstrations at St. Nicholas Lutheran Church in Leipzig grew from a few thousand to more than three hundred thousand. Honecker, whose health was failing, was forced to resign. By November 4, a million East Germans protested in the streets. At 7:00 P.M. on November 9, 1989, Politburo member Guenter Schabowski made an offhand announcement in his nightly news briefing that reforms would allow East Germans to travel freely to the West. The news spread instantly, and huge crowds gathered at the wall, demanding their right to leave. Caught unaware, the guards initially resisted, but as the numbers swelled the Politburo did not want a bloody battle. The Berlin Wall fell, and shortly thereafter, so did East Germany and the Soviet Union.

Poland provides another example: Foreign journalists and international media broadcasts into Poland helped to feed the Solidarity movement's underground newspapers and opposition to the Communist regime, in what William Hachten and James Scotton notes as a triangular information flow.[9] Lech Walesa, leader of Solidarity and the first leader of democratic Poland after the fall of communism, believes the impact of foreign media on Polish democratization was crucial: "Would there be an earth without the sun?"[10]

Did the global media cause the fall of the Berlin Wall and the end of the Soviet Union's control over other countries? Some argue yes. British scholar Anthony Giddens believes that "[t]he ideological and cultural control upon which communist political authority was based could not survive in an era of global media. The Soviet and the East European regimes were unable to prevent the reception of Western radio and television broadcasts. Television played a direct role in the 1989 revolutions, which have rightly been called the first 'television revolutions.' Street protests taking place in one country were watched by television audiences in others, large numbers of whom then took to the streets themselves."[11]

According to this argument, real-time media broadcasts directly affected public opinion and public action. Cheap access to technologies such as radio, television, and the Internet make possible easy and cheap access to information that is not censored or controlled by governments. The information revolution, which the media facilitate, are empowering individuals and making it harder for oppressive regimes to manipulate information and perceptions, and thereby to control their citizens. Groups as ideologically diverse as the American Civil Liberties Union, the Committee to Protect Journalists, the Heritage Foundation, and Freedom House all encourage freedom of the press internationally as a means to expand and protect personal liberties and democratic, limited governments:

> The information revolution is thus profoundly threatening to the power structures of the world, and with good reason. In Prague in 1988 the first protesters in the streets looked into CNN cameras and chanted at the riot police, "The world sees you." And it did. It was an anomaly of history that other Eastern Europeans watched the revolution on CNN relayed by a Russian satellite and mustered the courage to rebel against their own sovereigns. All this had confirmed Abraham Lincoln's sentiment, expressed on his way to his first inauguration, that the American Declaration of Independence "gave liberty not alone to the people of this country, but hope to all the world, for all future time." At the time Lincoln spoke, his words were heard by only a handful of people. It is a testament to his prescience that changes he could not have imagined have brought his words, and freedom itself, to unprecedented portions of humanity.[12]

Following this logic, the spread of a free and independent press is important to secure the democratic transitions now taking place around the globe. Since established democracies tend not to go to war with one another,[13] the spread of free media not only help to depose autocratic regimes but may also increase the chances for peace as the world witnesses a rising number of democratic states. Independent media may help the growth of civil society, an important component of democratization. Globalization is marked by an increase in the number and power of civil society NGOs, some of which are devoted to furthering the spread of independent media, such as the National Press Institute, which focuses on assisting the development of independent media in the former Soviet Union.

Finally, media coverage may help states to publicly debate and assess foreign policy, the very hallmarks of democratic process. The idea is that foreign policy is improved by transparency, accountability, legislative scrutiny, and public debate.[14] If the legislature and the public are divided about a foreign policy initiative (such as a military intervention), better to know this at the outset than attempt to conduct foreign policy in secrecy, without public and legislative support. In the United States this is especially true, since congressional approval is needed for all foreign policy expenditures. Many military leaders, such as Caspar Weinberger, Reagan's secretary of defense, and his assistant, Colin Powell, felt strongly that these were some of the clearest lessons learned from the U.S. intervention in Vietnam. In articulating the Weinberger/Powell Doctrine—now taught at all U.S. military academies—they advised that there be strong public and congressional support (among other preconditions) before committing U.S. troops abroad. Since it is difficult to gauge public and congressional support for foreign policies conducted in secret, media coverage is an important component of conducting a successful, publicly supported military intervention.

Yet Pippa Norris offers a caveat to this positive view of global media's impact on democratization: For the media to serve the watchdog and public forum roles that aid democratization, citizens must have widespread access to coverage by free media outlets.[15]

THE NEGATIVE VIEW: THE MEDIA AND A LOSS OF FOREIGN POLICY CONTROL

Others disagree with the argument that free, independent media may encourage positive foreign policy developments, such as the spread of democracies and thereby the spread of the democratic peace. These skeptics point out that the media can influence foreign policy in a negative way—by hijacking the foreign policy agenda around whatever issues are in the media's spotlight, by forcing policy makers into ill-advised foreign policies the media favors, by decreasing the secrecy needed for delicate foreign policy initiatives, and (in state-controlled media) by being a tool of carrying out war or genocide.

According to this argument, the media shape public opinion in ways that decrease public support for key foreign policy objectives. This makes the conduct of foreign policy by experienced foreign policy experts more difficult. Many members of the U.S. military used this reasoning and blamed the media for the U.S. public's declining support of the Vietnam War in the late 1960s and early 1970s, which led to the withdrawal of U.S. troops from Vietnam. According to this view, the media were not patriotic, presenting distorted images of U.S. casualties, losses, and war atrocities in order to deliberately end the U.S. presence in Vietnam, or at least to increase their own ratings. Reporter Morley Safer broke a story about the U.S. Marines burning civilian villages in Vietnam in an attempt to flush out supporters of the Communist Vietcong guerrilla group. Secretary of State Dean Rusk criticized Safer for supposedly inventing the story and bribing marines to lie on camera—and for insufficient patriotism since he was a Canadian citizen. According to Safer, Rusk's untrue criticism is an example of blaming the messenger for telling unpleasant truths about failed foreign policies.[16] The United States was not able to prevail in a violent civil war in Vietnam at a cost that was acceptable to the American Congress and public, just as the French had failed before. The media did not create this situation; they merely reported it.

But what about when media coverage creates the conditions for failure— specifically, when media coverage erodes the secrecy needed for delicate foreign policy negotiations? During the Iranian Revolution in 1979, the U.S. Embassy compound was taken over by student extremists loyal to the Ayatollah Khomeini, and sixty-six U.S. citizens were taken hostage. U.S. diplomat Ramsey Clark headed to Iran for secret negotiations through back channels to come up with a face saving release for the hostages. Instead, NBC broke the news of the supposed-to-be-secret negotiation mission, and—in the glare of the television cameras—the Iranians broke off the talks. Would Clark have been able to broker a deal to release the U.S. hostages if the press had not exposed the behind-the-scenes negotiations? While some hostages were released or escaped, fifty-two hostages were held for 444 days, a story the media covered nonstop using their newly acquired satellite technologies. The three major television networks devoted about one-third of their weeknight news programs to the hostage story. Every night ABC ran a thirty-minute program on the situation, *The Crisis in Iran: America Held Hostage*, which launched the career of Ted Koppel and was later renamed *Nightline*. The intensity and volume of media coverage made government efforts to release the hostages difficult. Generally, terrorists commit actions in order to gain publicity for their causes. While the media were giving the hostage takers ample free publicity for their concerns, what incentive did they have to release the hostages?[17] After the exposure of the Clark mission, the Carter administration believed it could not expect secrecy for its foreign policy initiatives. It wanted to conduct a military rescue operation, but fear of media exposure led it to cancel any practice training and rehearsal exercises for the military operation. The military rescue effort failed, and eight U.S. servicemen died in the Iranian desert. Did the media coverage contribute to these failed U.S. foreign policy efforts?

In countries where the media are state controlled, they may bear particular responsibility for foreign policies of war or genocide. During the wars over the breakup of the former Yugoslavia, local television stations often inflamed war fever, presenting those on the other side of the conflict not as former neighbors and friends, but as barely human murderers. In Rwanda, radio was skillfully used as an integral part of carrying out genocide. Radio broadcasts not only incited people to violence generally, but also announced specific lists of people to be killed and instructions for doing so. Shutting down the hate media can be an important step in stemming conflict.

In privately owned Western media, the role in foreign policy failures is of particular concern since the end of the Cold War. Without the Cold War conflict as a guiding star to foreign policy, it is argued that the media have an increased ability to set the foreign policy agenda through their coverage of international affairs. Dubbed the *CNN effect*, the concern is that extensive media coverage of foreign human rights abuses forces governments into ill-advised military interventions (such as Somalia or Bosnia). After troops are committed abroad, press coverage then changes to focus on the body bags created by the conflict, thus undermining public support for the very intervention the media initially forced.[18]

Since the world watched the Gulf War live on CNN in 1991, the rise of CNN and other twenty-four-hour news networks (and Internet sites) has intensified debates over the media's effect on foreign policy. People and policy makers sense CNN and the new real-time media are important, but they are not sure exactly how important. Different definitions also complicate the debate. Some define the CNN effect as public diplomacy; for example, during the Gulf War presidential press secretary Marlin Fitzwater used CNN to speak directly to both Saddam Hussein and coalition allies in real time, using television broadcasts to try to influence their positions. Others use the term to denote the smaller time frame for government reaction forced by the real-time reporting of an event. Some, such as former assistant secretary of state Rozanne Ridgway, speak of "a 'CNN curve,' which she describes as CNN's ability to prompt popular demands for action by displaying images of starvation or other tragedy, only to reverse this sentiment when Americans are killed while trying to help."[19] This is similar to another use of the term by veteran U.S. diplomat George Kennan, suggesting "a loss of policy control on the part of government officials supposedly charged with making that policy," in which control is wrested by the media or likewise by the public.[20]

THE SKEPTICAL VIEW: MEDIA EFFECTS WHEN FOREIGN POLICY IS ILL-DEFINED OR CONTESTED

A third view critiques both previous arguments on the power of the media to affect foreign policy either positively or negatively. The skeptics point out that these events are overdetermined; many other factors brought about the end of the Soviet Union, the fall of the Berlin Wall, and the end of the Vietnam War. In Russia free media tended to follow, not lead, the democratic transition; conflict continues today in Russia over media independence.[21] In the late 1960s press coverage of the Vietnam War followed congressional and public opinion; it did not lead it.[22] Only after Congress and the public became more skeptical and outspoken against the war in Vietnam did the media cover these viewpoints and actions, but the press coverage followed, and therefore did not cause the change.[23] A scant 2 percent of television coverage showed actual bloodshed, so media pictures were not predominantly bloody, and thus graphic pictures could not have caused the decline in public and Congressional resolve to fight the war. [24]

And as for the so-called CNN effect, studies suggest these media effects in foreign policy are overstated.[25] Most publics abroad don't have access to television (let alone CNN); therefore they do not see or understand the English-language broadcasts. Further, media coverage tends to follow rather than precede troop deployments. Media coverage does not guarantee a policy response. For example, despite media coverage of the genocide in Rwanda, none of the major Western powers intervened. The media showed Bosnian atrocities on television for years with no international response.[26] When the United States did finally intervene late in the conflict, the response was limited and reluctant. The studies suggest that when the government has a clear policy in place, the media will not be able to force an easy policy reversal or loss of government control over the policy; instead the government may be able to use the media to gain free "advertising time" to support its policies to the public. If, however, a policy vacuum exists—as is often the case when crises arise in less powerful and less important countries in the developing world in the post–Cold War period—the media can, in the absence of another position, exert an influence to raise an issue to the foreign policy agenda or to frame the issue.[27] According to this argument, any media effects during the Vietnam War were caused by the Johnson administration's failure to explain to the American public and Congress why U.S. troops were fighting in Vietnam, and to clearly convince them of what was at stake. In the vacuum created by an administration's failure to set and explain its policy, the media may be able to affect the foreign policy agenda. The media cover the viewpoints of government foreign policy elites; news coverage is heavily indexed to official conflict. If officials agree about foreign policy, the media cover that unity and public opinion tends to agree with that official consensus. If officials are in conflict about foreign policy, the media cover that conflict among foreign policy elites, and public opinion becomes more split over foreign policy options. Thus the media can communicate and amplify either the existing unity or disunity, creating openings for foreign policy shifts or closing ranks around existing policy. Media effects may be shown in specific cases to influence public opinion, agenda setting, and framing of an issue,[28] but media coverage alone does not guarantee a particular effect on foreign policy. In practice, it depends on the content and context of the coverage.

However, regardless of how or whether the media affect mass public opinion, the media may exert a direct effect on policymaking elites, both at home and abroad.[29] Thus media coverage can influence foreign policy independent of whether the public is mobilized on particular foreign policy issues. For example, President George H. W. Bush was affected by media coverage of the famine in Somalia. After reading a *New York Times* story on the humanitarian crisis there, he wrote in the margins of the article, "This is terrible. Isn't there something *we can do*?" and passed this note along to the State Department. For months electoral concerns prevented Bush from acting. But after he lost the 1992 presidential election to Bill Clinton, Bush intervened, sending over twenty thousand U.S. troops into Somalia in his last days in office. There was no loud outcry of public or congressional concern over Somalia. Foreign policy was barely a factor in the 1992 election, and Congress was in recess when the president initiated the troop deployment. But Bush admits that the media coverage of Somalia alerted him to the problems there and mobilized his action.[30] Thus, media effects may occur independent of public opinion or mass mobilization.

Further, many of the arguments concerning media effects are inconsistent and self-serving. Reporters who claim credit for bringing about democratic transitions abroad also claim to have little effect on the foreign policy process at home. The media minimize their own effect, claiming that they merely report on the foreign policy process; they do not affect it. Policy makers, in contrast, tend to exaggerate media effects, blaming the media for foreign policy failures (for example, the Vietnam War, the failed Iranian hostage rescue attempt). But government officials do not credit the media for rallying public support around successful foreign policies, such as the media's role in rallying allied, legislative, and public opinion behind the first Gulf War. Further,

while Western policy makers decry irresponsible media coverage of government policy here, they suggest that foreign governments should open themselves up to greater media scrutiny abroad.

Media effects can be difficult to prove empirically, since correlation is not
causation. Showing that media coverage occurred before a foreign policy action does not mean the media coverage caused the foreign policy action—just
as the fact that you brushed your teeth this morning may not have caused the
events that followed in your day. Since general laws are difficult to posit (i.e.,
media coverage may affect foreign policy differently depending on the type
of coverage and the context of other intervening variables, such as elite consensus), those on all three sides continue to make their arguments, while
scholars sort out the mixed evidence for and against the various claims, although more scholars hold to the skeptical view of limited effects in specific
circumstances.

PERCEPTIONS MATTER

While scholars debate under which specific circumstances the media may exert particular influences, leaders believe that the media affect foreign policy
and act accordingly to try to influence media coverage of international affairs.
Whether or not the media affect the content or conduct of foreign policy, they
can affect the image and perception of foreign policy. Governments, NGOs,
intergovernmental organizations (IGOs) and corporations believe that media
coverage of international affairs matters, and thus devote significant resources toward media management strategies. Why? With global media, images spread far and quickly, and perceptions matter. Sixty percent of the
world's countries are now ruled by democratic governments, meaning that
perceptions of a ruling regime's efficacy can now influence whether the rulers
will remain in office. More of the world's economies are market-oriented,
capitalist systems than ever before. This means that private investors and individual consumers decide where to put their money, and their perceptions of
international affairs affects those investment decisions. As the Asian financial
flu showed in 1997, investors may pull their monies out of sound and weak
economies alike if they perceive their investments to be at risk. Advances in
information and communications technologies allow the media to broadcast
information instantly around the globe. Thus, images can be passed to a wide
audience quickly and cheaply. As democracy spreads around the globe,
greater freedom of the press has spread also, while government ownership
and censorship over the media declines. The spread of capitalism also brings
more private ownership of the media. Together these trends—of more open

societies, economies, and technologies—mean that governments no longer have a monopoly on information about foreign policy, while media images move quickly and globally.

Even nondemocratic states are now more concerned about international perceptions and are more vulnerable to Western media reports, given the increased importance of international investors in a globalized economy and the fluidity of global financial markets in which investors can easily pull their capital out of a country. Thus, while Chinese leaders may not be interested in their own public's opinions, they are interested in courting foreign investors and thus are more attentive to Western media reports and public relations than they were when their economy was not linked to the global economy.

Besides economic investing, media-generated perceptions can also affect military policies. For example, the media proclaimed the Patriot missile defense system a success in the Gulf War,[31] lending momentum to the push in the U.S. Congress to spend more money on missile defense systems and to scuttle the Anti-Ballistic Missile (ABM) Treaty.[32] The fact is that not a single attacking Iraqi Scud missile was intercepted by the Patriot system,[33] but the media perception still stands. As Lt. Gen. William Odom noted,

> A key debate emerging from the Gulf War [and in the military generally] is the familiar one over the possibility of "victory through air power" alone . . . . The image of the war conveyed by the media has left this [pro-air power/surgical bombing] impression in the public mind, but appearances do not square with realities . . . the number of tanks, artillery, and infantry fighting vehicles destroyed as the war progressed from the air phase to the land-air phase in Kuwait . . . were not very high until the ground component of the war began . . . clearly ground forces destroyed the majority . . . the issues are complex, and the television images from the war can be misleading.[34]

Similarly, media accounts continually refer to the U.S. intervention in Somalia as a failure because of the deaths of eighteen U.S. Army Rangers, supposedly due to the failures of UN foreign commanders. But it was Adm. Jonathan Howe and Gen. Colin Powell—not foreign UN commanders—who sent the Rangers on their ill-fated mission,[35] and this small number of U.S. casualties saved the lives of more than a quarter million Somalis.[36] But since most viewers do not have the chance to directly experience the foreign policy in question, media images matter. Since speed is of great importance in the information age, it often does not matter if an organization is later able to put out a finely argued briefing explaining why the initial pictures and perceptions of an incident were wrong.

MEDIA COVERAGE OF FOREIGN POLICY

Leaders believe and act as if media coverage matters. But how do the media cover foreign affairs? There are nearly two hundred countries in the world. Each day events occur in every country that affect their relations with other states and nonstate actors, and vice versa. Clearly, limitations on broadcast time and print space mean that not all events that happen internationally each day receive media coverage. Despite its motto, *The New York Times* does not publish "all the news that's fit to print," but rather, "all the news that fits." How do reporters and media organizations select which events receive coverage, construct "stories" from the barrage of data, and how do these decisions, patterns, or "biases" of media coverage affect foreign policy?

Two parameters influence media coverage of foreign policy. One is that reporters are professionals. What and how they report on foreign policy is influenced by their professional training and the "industry standard" practices of their peers. We never see all the news on foreign affairs; we see all that reporters believe is newsworthy, based on their judgments as influenced by what they were taught in journalism school or learned from their peers (including cultural blinders as well as their personal knowledge base). The second parameter is that media organizations are businesses. They do not exist to discover and disseminate "truths"; they exist to turn a profit. If news organizations cannot earn enough money by selling their product and selling advertising space to sponsors, they close their doors. Therefore news coverage is influenced by what editors believe will sell, by what reporters believe their readers and viewers want to know, and even by what the owners of media organizations believe should and should not be broadcast.

Reporters learn basic definitions of what is news in journalism school. One popular definition contends that news events impact many people or prominent people; the events are proximate to the broadcast area, bizarre, timely (especially occurring within the last news cycle), or at least currently being talked about. Reporters learn to follow the inverted pyramid concept that the lead, or beginning of a story, should contain answers to the basic questions "who, what, when, and where?" The "why and how?" information—as well as further elaboration of the story—follow, and may be cut due to space constraints. Since reporters do not know how much space or broadcast time their editors will grant them, following this basic formula is a standard way to construct news stories and makes editing easier, as the most vital information will be in the first sentences.

Given these standard practices, how do reporters tend to cover foreign affairs? Who is covered? Government sources top press coverage. Heads of state are covered automatically, with the U.S. president receiving round the clock coverage by the U.S. media, whether or not he is acting in official capacity. The practice is called *horizontal coverage*, or "covering the body," and includes reporting information about the president's vacation, shopping, birthday parties, and doctor's appointments. After the U.S. president, which heads of states receive U.S. media coverage varies by country. The French media tend to cover the heads of major parties, whereas the U.S. media tend to focus coverage on the "Golden Triangle"—sources from the White House, Pentagon, and State Department.[37] Each country covers the activities of government officials in its own state, neighboring states, and key allies or adversaries. Former imperial states cover events in their former colonies, and vice versa. In developed countries, the activities and statements of the heads of the richest G-8 countries receive more media coverage than events in poorer and less powerful states. Following heads of states, most coverage goes to other government officials, the head of the United Nations and other important IGOs, and known actors (often former government officials), individuals, or organizations to whom reporters have the easiest access. In his studies of who gets media coverage, Herbert Gans found stories about "known" actors such as government officials to outnumber stories about "unknown" people four to one.[38]

People not in government or powerful positions, poor people, women, and nonwhites tend not to be covered. People in poor countries generally receive coverage in the media of rich countries only when there is war, famine, or disaster to report. In practice these trends also translate to gender and racial biases. Ninety-two percent of U.S. media sources are white, 85 percent are men, and where political party was identified, 75 percent were Republican. More than two-thirds of experts quoted are "baby boomers," although the 1945–1960 generation makes up less than one-third of the U.S. population.[39] Only 17 percent of news stories feature women at all, while women make up the majority of the world's population. The stories that do cover women are more likely to be arts and entertainment or celebrity news features; women rarely appear as news subjects in stories on politics (12 percent), international crises (11 percent), or national defense (6 percent). Internationally, women are portrayed as victims nearly three times more frequently than men.[40]

The exception to the bias in coverage of government officials is celebrity coverage. Presidents and heads of state are not the only public figures to attract constant "coverage of the body," and celebrities who take up political causes may be able to use that media coverage to draw considerable attention to particular issues. Shrinking coverage of hard news and foreign news, while soft news and entertainment stories receive greater attention, gives greater opportunities for media coverage of NGOs and celebrity activism.[41]

What gets covered? In general, the media cover what they think their audiences will be interested in and buy. The media cover dramatic actions: War, conflict, disasters, and things that go boom receive media coverage—the foreign policy equivalents of car chases and Arnold Schwarzenegger films. Not all wars or terrorist actions are covered due to space and broadcast time limitations, creating a dynamic in which conflicts and terrorist attacks compete against each other for coverage. In the United States, conflicts that involve U.S. troop deployments, key allies, or neighbors receive more coverage than conflicts in poor and distant countries (especially African states). Terrorist actions that affect U.S. citizens receive steady coverage. Middle Eastern terrorists are more likely to be covered than other terrorists, due the importance of Middle Eastern oil reserves; the importance of religious and cultural sites there to Jewish, Muslim, and Christian news consumers; and cultural misconceptions about the Middle East. Colombia, Greece, and India have significant terrorist incidents, but terrorist acts and victims there receive little coverage. Because most conflicts since the end of the Cold War are civil wars, and since most poor countries receive little media attention except when there is conflict or disaster, the media present a false impression that all poor countries are marked by unending war and natural disasters. Peace and reconciliation are underreported in the media. Unexpected events and events that provide dramatic pictures receive media coverage, whereas expected events that do not lend themselves to photos do not get covered (which is why we don't read headlines such as "International Law Is Obeyed"). Western media show pictures of volcanic explosions in Sicily and of children with their limbs hacked off in Sierra Leone, but do not show pictures of advancements against AIDS in Brazil or of improvements in the Italian legal system. This leads to an underreporting of "good news" in international affairs and a persistent media bias toward cynicism.

Events reporters have access to cover, that can be simplified to clear good guy versus bad guy storylines, and that affect the media outlet's target audience receive top billing.[42] This can lead to nationalism and ethnocentrism in news reporting. As Associated Press reporter Mort Rosenblum explains, "The closer news is to home, the greater its import. A British press lord once tacked up a memo in his Fleet Street newsroom: 'One Englishman is a story. Ten Frenchmen is a story. One hundred Germans is a story. And nothing ever happens in Chile.' The old Brooklyn Eagle had it: 'A dogfight in Brooklyn is bigger than a revolution in China.'"[43] Globalization has changed some of these trends; now that they are key Western trading partners, China and Chile receive more news coverage than they did earlier this century. But the underlying dynamic remains true if you were to substitute an African state in the statement. For example, when the U.S. Embassy complexes in East Africa were bombed in August 1998, U.S. media coverage focused more on the 12 dead U.S. citizens than the 289 African fatalities and more than 5,000 African casualties from the explosions. Similarly, when Pan Am flight 103 was downed by terrorists over Lockerbie, Scotland, on December 21, 1988, the local media in New York State focused more on the 34 Syracuse University students on board the plane than the other 270 victims.

Primarily, the media cover what is easy to cover and what they have always covered, which leads to a status quo bias in media coverage and a repeat of similar stories. This is very economical and conservative, the argument being that if the public bought these news products before, they will buy them again. However, it can lead to familiar scripts that present distorted images of the world. For example, when the Murrah Federal Building in Oklahoma City was bombed on April 19, 1995, the media immediately reported that Middle Eastern terrorists were likely to blame. Shortly after the bombing, CBS featured a terrorism "expert" who speculated that the bombing bore all the earmarks of Middle Eastern terrorism. *The New York Times*, hypothesizing why terrorists would have struck in Oklahoma City, noted that the city is home to three mosques. Syndicated call-in radio personality Bob Grant declared on his show that Muslims were responsible for the bombing and that Islam is a "violent" religion; when a caller suggested he was rushing to judgment, he said he wanted to shoot the caller.[44] *Chicago Tribune* syndicated columnist Mike Royko advised that the United States should retaliate in the Middle East by bombing "a country that is a likely suspect." If it happened to be the wrong country, he added, "well, too bad, but it's likely it did something to deserve it anyway."[45] The Oklahoma City bombers turned out to be entirely homegrown. Timothy McVeigh and Terry Nichols were U.S. born and bred and served in the nation's military together. McVeigh's car bore a bumper sticker that read "American and proud of it. Distorted press coverage concerning the Middle East and Muslims can add friction to the conduct of U.S. foreign policy. Many Middle Eastern and Muslim states are important U.S. allies (Egypt) and control strategic oil reserves (Saudi Arabia, Kuwait), and Islam is one of the fastest-growing religions in the world. Regardless of how the distortions emerged originally, overplayed and flawed—but familiar—media scripts make media innovation difficult.

In answering the question "when?" the increasing speed and number of global media outlets, including the Internet, means that reporters face a shrinking time horizon for coverage of foreign affairs. Reporters have always reported on events they could cover by their deadlines. Generally, stories tend to focus on events that happened within the last news cycle (since the last product was offered—the last broadcast, newspaper, or magazine edition). But the Internet and real-time media outlets like CNN are further shrinking the news from the typical twenty-four-hour news cycle, giving reporters even shorter deadlines. This leads to an underreporting of long-term trends, events that happen gradually, and historical perspective in foreign policy news stories such as immigration trends or global warming. Current anniversaries of past historical events are one way reporters compensate for the media's bias toward the present tense.

"Where" do the media cover? Concerns for keeping costs down have led to more stories being filed from capital cities, which intensifies the focus on heads of government and stories featuring government sources rather than the perspective found in reporting from other areas. For example, most reporters filing stories on the conflict in Northern Ireland are based in London, a fact that may affect the way they cover the story and their access to information. The *Irish Times* has one reporter charged with covering all of North America. He is based in Washington, D.C., which affects his coverage of events outside of Washington, especially in Mexico and Canada. Generally, the "where" in foreign affairs coverage is affected by where reporters can access, which increasingly means where their editors and bosses will allow them to go, based on how much it will cost. Cost consciousness has led to a decrease in the number of foreign-based reporters, an increase in reliance on wire service reports, and an increase in *parachute journalism*—stories filed by reporters flown in to cover a particular story who may have little feel or knowledge about the story and few contacts in the country. As ABC News executive Paul Slavin put it, "I don't need a bureau in Africa. I am much better off with David Wright getting there for three weeks. I don't need a bureau in Afghanistan, but I am sending Bob Woodruff. That is a more efficient use of resources."[46] This leads to more stories written in hotel compounds frequented by other reporters or based on conversations with cab drivers or other reporters, on people who can speak English, rather than stories benefiting from a reporter's more in-depth knowledge of a place and its language. The media are also constrained by where it is safe for them to operate and where governments will allow outside reporters. Coverage of many conflicts around the world has suffered for these reasons.

The questions "why?" and "how?" are the most difficult ones for the media to answer, and require the most expertise, knowledge, experience, and time to construct. Reporters' time is in especially short supply in the Internet age. For these reasons, and reasons of cost and space, they are the most frequently cut components of news coverage.[47] Why and how may also be given less emphasis because of reporters' fears that answering these questions borders on offering their own opinions and analysis, rather than merely describing empirical data. Answering these questions is harder to do, and the media usually focus on covering what's easy. So "why?" and "how?" perspective stories are generally done in feature stories or news series, but are often cut from the regular news stories, significantly watered down, or reduced to familiar—but flawed—scripts. For example, explaining why and how genocide broke out in Rwanda in April 1994 required an explanation of the political, economic, and historical distinctions between the Tutsi and Hutu groups, the dynamics of "divide and conquer" practiced during French colonization, and the ramifications of those divisions in Rwandan society today. Instead, most explanation of why and how was omitted from media coverage of the dramatic bloodletting. When U.S. media outlets did offer an explanation. it was an erroneous, ethnic script: "'Pure tribal enmity' (4/18/94) was *Time* magazine's explanation for the 'tribal carnage' (4/25/94)."[48] This explanation was false (the divisions between Hutus and Tutsis are not tribal or ethnic in nature), and had policy consequences, suggesting the situation would be resistant to any foreign policy initiatives, since the "cause" was unalterable, ancient, ethnic animosity. The media have erroneously applied the same flawed script to describe conflict in Bosnia and Somalia. Yet even in countries where conflict does correlate to ethnic or racial identities, those identities are constructed and manipulated by leaders to bring about conflict. Past civil conflict does not make future violence inevitable.[49] Especially in coverage of foreign policy, which by its very nature is often less familiar to audiences, cutting the "why and how" questions damages the public's ability to glean meaning from the rush of daily description.

Perspective and context for the dizzying list of daily actions is often lost, leaving the public not only wondering why certain foreign policy actions were taken, but also why the story is important, and why they should care. This can lead to a vicious circle in U.S. reporting on foreign policy. Poor or spotty media coverage of foreign policy, which focuses on the same "bad news" stories and presents the world as a hostile and hopeless place, may make the public less likely to tune in to foreign news reporting. Did the news stories cause the public apathy, or is public apathy the reason many editors and media owners are unwilling to devote greater resources to media coverage of foreign policy? This "chicken or egg" question vexes citizens and journalists interested in understanding and improving media coverage of foreign affairs.

WHO MANIPULATES WHOM? STRATEGIES TO MANAGE MEDIA COVERAGE AND SELL FOREIGN POLICY

Feeling that media image matters and knowing how the media typically cover foreign policy, governments, NGOs, IGOs, and corporate leaders try to influence media coverage of international affairs to sell their foreign policy preferences. The media, in turn, try to use government, NGO, IGO, and corporate news briefings and press releases for their own purposes: to try to produce and sell their product. Picture blank newspaper pages or empty broadcast time, with each party jockeying over how to fill that space. While often presented as a conflictual relationship, it is also symbiotic. The media could not exist without information. The more media budgets are cut and owners scrutinize the bottom line, the more the media rely on actors' press releases and briefings for their stories. Governments, NGOs, IGOs, and corporations need to disseminate information in order to generate support for their activities. Governments, NGOs, IGOs, and corporations provide information to the media, but they try to do so in a way that privileges their interests and sells their foreign policy viewpoints. The media choose and use information, using foreign policy stories to sell their own news products. As Michael Deaver, chief "image maker" in the Reagan White House, describes it,

> We don't have news in television. This is entertainment. This is commercial. That's entertainment, what I was a part of . . . . I had a commodity to sell, Ronald Reagan, and the media needed me at least as much as I needed them and often more, because I provided them with good pictures for their programming which were also good for myself and the president.[50]

While agreeing that at times the White House spin may have been "over the top" in terms of shading the truth, Deaver finds no fault with trying to spin or manipulate press coverage, because the news outlets at any time could have decided not to air his "product":

> You guys [the media] have a job to do and so do I. My job is to sell my President and your job is to sell your product. What you are upset about is that I beat you at your own game. There was nothing stopping the media from not showing these pictures and instead going out and making their own. But reporters are lazy.[51] I was doing my job and the media was airing my PR wholesale and often without question. Not much of my stuff ever ended up on the cutting room floor. Nobody ever said, "This is bullshit." Instead, they wrote it down and shipped it off to New York! We need more good, investigative reporting. In the Persian Gulf War, this brilliant PR effort by the Pentagon, where was the media questioning how many of these superbombs do we have, and how effective are they? The truth as it turns out is that these "surgical bombs" are not very effective. But no one was saying that. They just consumed the Pentagon's PR info wholesale. They rolled the video tracks of the perfect bombing runs, often without any sound accompaniment at all . . . . In the Reagan White House, we were constantly looking for venues that were visual. This is Disneyland, that's the bottom line.[52]

Who will prevail in this tug of war for releasing and shaping information varies by situation and issue. In general, for any topic over which one party has a monopoly or can control the information flow, that party will have the advantage in how information is released or presented to the public. For any situation in which the media has independent access to information or can easily and cheaply access reliable information from many separate sources, the media will have greater choice and control over what, when, and how information is presented.

For example, the U.S. government exhibited great skill in shaping media coverage during the Gulf War. It used several means to do so. Reporters were restricted to the pool system, meaning the government chose which reporters and news organizations had access to battlefield coverage. The government escorted the media to sites of the government's choosing, and even then the media had to submit their reports to government censorship. Most of the media spent most of the Gulf War in hotel rooms in Dhahran, Saudi Arabia, reporting on government press briefings, and rebroadcasting the Pentagon's footage of perfect bombing runs and surgical air strikes. The media had no independent ability to confirm or deny these rosy pictures and reports, and no ability to track down stories the government did not want shown, such as those about Iraqi casualties, civilians dead or injured, missed bombs, or failures to strike Saddam Hussein.

Not surprisingly, the media complained loudly about the pool system restrictions. Yet the major media organizations all volunteered to abide by these restrictions. Why? Because from a media organization's viewpoint, the only thing worse than restricted access to an important story is no access at all. The media feared that if they did not voluntarily agree to the restricted access of the pool system, the government would shut them out of the news flow entirely, as the Reagan and Bush administrations had done in Grenada and Panama. The media also agreed to the pool system in the Gulf War because they had been led to believe they would have greater autonomy and access to information than actually turned out to be the case. Objections to the Bush administration's use of the pool system to deny reporters access during the first three days of the U.S. invasion of Panama was met with a series of negotiations between the media and the Pentagon. The media said they were given assurances of reforms to the system that did not materialize in the Gulf War. The Pentagon argued that in wartime national security concerns led them to release information as they believed it advisable. They believed they offered a great deal of information and access to the media, and that security concerns overrode any public right to know information other than what the government chose to release. Reporters who chose not to abide by the pool system risked arrest by the U.S. military and the Saudi and Iraqi governments.

In response to critiques of the pool system, following the 2003 U.S. invasion of Iraq reporters were "embedded" with military units, so they would be able to report from the battlefield. This did not lead to a more independent or critical voice for the media than in the pool system. Instead, reporters sympathized and identified with the military units to which they were assigned, often filing stories that "*we* were attacked by enemy fire today." Reporters' self-censorship replaced overt government censorship, leading to an even more complete victory for government media and information strategies. In the run-up to the Iraq invasion, most major U.S. media outlets gave extensive coverage to the views of administration officials, who argued that (1) Saddam Hussein possessed large arsenals of newly developed weapons of mass destruction that posed an imminent threat to the United States and thus needed to be eliminated, and that (2) Hussein was cooperating with or in some way connected to the al-Qaeda terrorists who attacked the United States on 9/11. None of these claims were true, but U.S. media coverage reinforced the administration's arguments in favor of the war. While some major media outlets produced stories critical of the administration's views (*Washington Post*, PBS), the critical stories were often posted later in the newspaper or broadcast, whereas pro-administration stories were given higher billing.[53]

Clearly, in these examples the U.S. government controlled the battle space and therefore could control the information flowing from that space. If the media wanted to cover the story easily, cheaply, and reliably, they had to play by the government's rules. Since war sells, market dynamics made the media vulnerable to elite manipulations and framing of the story.

In contrast, in other situations when the media is in place before conflict breaks out, they are less dependent on the government for access to the story. Also, where elite opinion is divided, the media will cover the conflict among officials, limiting the government's ability to manage the news.[54] For example, the conflict in Vietnam broke out in successive stages over the course of decades. First the French fought and were pushed out in Vietnam in the 1950s. U.S. forces slowly replaced the French in the 1960s, first as advisers to the South Vietnamese forces; then in increased numbers as war fighters, as the South Vietnamese army was unable to prevail over the Communist north alone. Reporters were in Vietnam before U.S. troops were. Since the battle space was broad, changing, and never sealed off or controlled by only one party; because the conflict was never officially declared a war and occurred over a longer time span; and because U.S. government officials were themselves divided over the war, the government was not able to manage media reports as it did during the Gulf War.

During wartime governments have greater control over information if the conflict is confined in time and space, if one side controls the battle space, and if official debate is limited. Then independent access to the battlefield may be too expensive or risky, or simply unavailable to the media, and they may therefore have to content themselves with weaving their news products from unified official press briefings and government-supplied film footage. In situations where the conflict takes place over time or in a wide swath of space over which no one side has total control and where official opinion is divided, the media will be more able to present information which differs from government reports.

As the ease and cheapness with which the media can access information on a story independent of government briefings increases, governments will have less ability to control the flow of information. Thus during peacetime, government news briefings generally face greater competition from information from other sources. Similarly, democratic governments face more competition in shaping the news on foreign policy than nondemocratic governments. The media are generally state-owned or state-controlled in nondemocracies, and even private media from democratic states may have difficulty garnering information to verify or contrast nondemocratic governments' releases of information. For example, in democracies, the media have access to at least the opposition party's critique of any government foreign policy or economic report. The media may often have easy access to several critical voices and sources of alternative information on events. But when autocratic China reports a healthy 7 percent economic growth rate, who can the media consult to check this story? It can be dangerous, expensive, and impossible to contact opposition sources of information within China. The media may raise skepticism about the government figures by noting that economic growth has been stagnant or declining over the last decade in neighboring Japan and Russia, and that the rest of Asia has experienced difficult economic circumstances since the Asian financial crisis of 1997. But the Chinese government figures could be true, as China has a vast and growing domestic market and increasing rates of foreign direct investment into China, which could be buoying the Chinese economy while all around them stumble. It is more difficult for reporters to access information challenging the Chinese government's economic forecasting than it is for them to compare and contrast the economic figures released by open democratic states.

There are two exceptions to this generalization concerning the media in democracies. One is that emerging democracies fall in between this continuum of more and less government control. Emerging democracies with longer traditions of independent media and with media that have greater access to financial backing (such as Poland and Hungary) will have stronger media outlets less subject to government control than transition states with no history of independent media and where the media have less secure financial standing (such as Russia).

The second exception is reporting on terrorist incidents. The laws in democratic states vary widely over how much the media are censored in their coverage of terrorist incidents. Britain has very strong censorship laws, which, for example, severely limited the media's coverage of the conflict in Northern Ireland. Until the Good Friday Agreement mellowed the conflict in 1998, British media were not allowed to broadcast the voices of Irish Republican Army (IRA) leaders or even the leaders of the political party Sinn Féin, which is affiliated with the IRA. Viewers of U.S. media broadcasts could listen to the voice of Gerry Adams, while British viewers listened to the voices of actors or media anchors giving voiceovers to the words of the Sinn Féin leader. In some countries, such as Japan and Israel, self-censorship and cultural and market considerations may constrain media coverage of terrorist acts more than legal restrictions.

Governments are not the only actors trying to influence media coverage of foreign policy. NGOs, IGOs, and corporations also devote considerable time, money, and attention to media management strategies. Just as governments in certain wartime situations may have a greater ability to control the flow of information from the battle space, there are rare situations in which NGOs, IGOs, or corporations may be able to control the information space. For example, on February 16, 1995, the British government approved Shell Oil's plans to dump the Brent Spar floating oil storage platform in the North Sea. The plan was greeted with opposition from neighboring states and environmental groups. On April 30, 1995, thirty members of the environmental NGO Greenpeace boarded the Brent Spar platform, raised a banner that read "Save the North Sea," and organized an all-out media campaign to discourage ocean dumping of the platform. Shell responded in the courts, trying to obtain a legal injunction against the group for trespassing. Greenpeace used sophisticated satellite-to-digital video feeds to provide the media with pictures of their "David versus Goliath" story, which met many of the media's criteria for newsworthiness (it was a dramatic conflict with eye-catching pictures that could be simplified into good guys and bad guys). BBC News editor Richard Sambrook

estimated that Greenpeace spent $2 million dollars on the Brent Spar campaign, of which some $540,000 was spent on TV equipment and feeds. Greenpeace's media operation was headed by Richard Titchen, an ex-BBC journalist who was Greenpeace International's Director of Communication and one of seven executive directors. He worked with a staff of 29 and an annual budget of $1.5 million (about 4.5 percent of the organization's total budget). In addition to the video feeds supplied by protesters, independent journalists covering the incident at sea were "forced" to report from the Greenpeace ship, as it was the only available point of access. Shell never offered to supply journalists with either ships or aircraft.[55]

Opposition to Shell and Britain's plan grew throughout Europe, especially in Germany. Shell Oil products were boycotted, and "[i]n Berlin, Shell service stations reported a 30 percent fall in sales in the first two weeks of June. German mothers sent Shell hundreds of letters with pictures of their babies urging them to stop the planned sinking."[56] Shell and Britain abandoned the plan to dump the Brent Spar at sea, and neighboring countries enacted a ban on sea disposal of decommissioned oil installations throughout the North Atlantic and the North Sea. Later disclosures indicate that Greenpeace scientists miscalculated the environmental danger from dumping the Brent Spar, and Shell scientists were closer to the mark in estimating the environmental impact. But in this incident Greenpeace had considerable control over the broadcast space (in part because Shell did not pursue an effective media strategy) and was able to prevail to change foreign policy. To a lesser degree, in some humanitarian crises, if NGOs control the communications infrastructure reporters need to send their stories back home (i.e., the NGOs have landlines, satellite phones, or satellite uplinks, whereas the media outlets do not), the NGOs may have more access to reporters as they cover events. NGOs often rely on attracting media coverage of humanitarian emergencies to help in their private fund-raising efforts as well as in their struggle to mobilize government resources.[57]

In practice, media access may be difficult for NGOs to leverage into influence because the NGO community is diverse and pluralistic; since there is often no NGO "consensus" on an issue, the media will find diverging viewpoints and information within the NGO community. Of course, the same may be true of government, IGO, or corporate viewpoints, depending on the issue. Since the media cover conflict, internecine disputes will likely attract media attention, thus fracturing an actor's ability to bring attention to its cause.

Corporate control of media outlets have led many to question whether media reporting on foreign affairs can be unbiased, or whether corporate interests will always shape media coverage of foreign policy due to the bottom-line business concerns for media outlets to sell their products. This concern is nothing new. In the early days of television news, Camel cigarettes sponsored the CBS evening news. Edward R. Murrow had to have a Camel cigarette burning at all times during the news broadcast and interspersed coverage of the Korean War with announcements that Camel was supporting U.S. troops abroad by giving them cartons of free cigarettes (the broadcasts never noted that these "contributions" were creating lifetime customers by addicting soldiers to nicotine). Reporters had to ask permission from the tobacco companies to show film footage of Winston Churchill, who habitually smoked a cigar, not cigarettes. What is new today is the concentration of corporate control in a very few hands, due to mergers and acquisitions. While the advent of new technologies (cable and satellite television, the Internet) appear to have opened up new media venues, in fact, many of these various stations and publications are owned by the same companies and carrying the same news products. For example, in 1945, 80 percent of American newspapers were independently owned. By 1982, fifty corporations owned almost all of the major media outlets in the United States, including 1,787 daily newspapers, 11,000 magazines, 9,000 radio stations, 1,000 television stations, 2,500 book publishers, and 7 major movie studios. Today, five corporations own it all.[58]

How might corporate ownership patterns affect foreign policy coverage and influence foreign policy? Corporate concern for profits has cut the number of foreign correspondents and made news organizations rely more heavily on news services and stringers. This creates more repetition of fewer views. All the major U.S. television networks are owned by multinational corporations that benefit from globalization and institutions such as the World Trade Organization, NAFTA, and other free-trade regimes. Simultaneously, their coverage of globalization has tended to be positive, while coverage of antiglobalization protestors has been negative. Representatives of labor receive minuscule coverage, and then only when there is a strike or labor unrest, whereas representatives of corporations regularly appear as experts on a wide variety of topics.[59] When networks such as NBC are owned by major defense contractors, can the media be unbiased in their coverage of the Iraq war, which funnels billions of dollars their way?[60] Corporations that do not own media outlets can also exert influence by threatening to pull advertising dollars from programs or news products they find objectionable. The attention to independent Internet reporters and bloggers has led many to argue that new media outlets create opportunities to break the gatekeeping function and corporate control of traditional media outlets.

However, in practice these new media outlets tend to rebroadcast or lengthen the attention given to stories first broadcast or reported by traditional media. At this point, these new outlets don't have much capacity for independent reporting of new information, instead repeating or refocusing the news cycles on stories first broken elsewhere. While governments try to control the information flow to shape media coverage of foreign policy, and NGOs and IGOs try to tempt the media with attractive stories, corporations can get the media where it counts: in their purse strings.

In general, governments, NGOs, IGOs, and corporations practice similar strategies in trying to control or manage media coverage of foreign affairs. If the actor can control the information space and the media cannot independently access the story or information, the actor has greater control in shaping the media coverage. If the actor can provide the media with compelling pictures and emotional stories the media judges would help sell news products, the media are more likely to air the actors' images. The media are more likely to air the views or information provided by government officials (those in power and key opposition leaders), celebrities, powerful or moneyed organizations or individuals (generally men), and groups located in capital cities or who make media access easy. If the actor can corroborate its views or information with those of other key groups or institutions, the media may pay more attention to it. If courted, local media may ask less difficult questions and be more likely to run favorable coverage than national media outlets, but local media outlets devote less coverage overall to foreign affairs than to local news. Actors' abilities to get their message across externally are compromised by divisions internally. If the actor cannot "speak with one voice," media coverage will focus on the internal conflicts and muddy the external message the actor seeks to project.

Timing is crucial. The media have broadcast and print space to fill each day—but only a finite amount. Thus on "slow" news days, actors will have an easier time placing stories with the media than on "heavy" news days (during crises, wars, or elections, for example). Actors savvy and responsive to what the media wants and tends to cover will be more successful in using the media to disseminate their views and information. Actors who do not make themselves accessible to the media or do not understand how to make their information "fit" media parameters will be more likely to find their views and information on the cutting room floor.

Who manipulates whom in coverage of foreign policy in the post–Cold War world? On the one hand, the globalization of the media means that stories travel farther and are rebroadcast more widely than when there were fewer media outlets and more state-controlled media. More media and fewer state controlled media make a more complex target for government media management strategies. Additionally, the greater importance of economic, environmental, and humanitarian foreign policy stories, and the lessening of international wars, means that the issues over which governments have more opportunities for censorship or control (wartime coverage) are not the only salient foreign policy issues today. Nonstate actors offer competing views, information, and foreign policies to government views, information, and foreign policy. These trends may undermine states' ability to influence media coverage of foreign policy.

On the other hand, even in military affairs, the change from the larger draft army of the World War II, Korea, and Vietnam eras to today's smaller, all-volunteer U.S. armed forces means fewer U.S. reporters have military experience than in previous decades. The same is true internationally, as an era of downsized militaries and democratic peace means fewer reporters have military experience. Reporters with less military experience may have difficulty critiquing government information on military affairs, and may thus be more subject to government manipulation. The strongest critics during the Gulf War and Iraq war were reporters with military experience, whereas the most malleable reporters were those without it.

Ironically, due to global market dynamics, more media outlets does not mean more news, and fewer state-controlled media means more market-controlled media. More centralized media ownership patterns, fewer foreign reporters, more reliance on pooled news service reports, and an overall smaller news "hole" (meaning more time for entertainment, sports, lifestyle, business coverage, and advertising) may translate into greater media reliance on press releases and more opportunities for savvy actors to influence media coverage of foreign policy. Actors compete to influence media coverage because they believe that whoever can impact the coverage of foreign policy can impact the shape of foreign policy.

DISCUSSION QUESTIONS

1. There are two ideas presented in the chapter about media concentration. One is that fewer and fewer international corporations control major media outlets, and so information is more subject to elite control now than ever before. The other is that the Internet allows for greater global communication by individuals without governmental or corporate supervision. Which idea do you think is more accurate as a description of the global media?

2. Do you feel that the American media cover war well and fairly? Do you think it is a problem that fewer journalists have military backgrounds now than in the past? Do you think the American media should cover war from an American perspective even in this new global environment?

3. Do you share the author's concern about parachute journalism? Would you be willing to pay more for a newspaper that operated many offices in foreign countries?

4. Do you think the CNN effect and the CNN curve are worrisome developments? Are elitist critics like George Kennan right to worry that our foreign policy, if guided by media and public opinion, is likely to shift rapidly and become less coherent and effective? Or should we want a foreign policy that responds to people's changing preferences, as directed by the media?

5. The chapter tells us that many things affect whether a foreign policy development overseas receives domestic media coverage, such as the

presence or absence of conflict or violence; proximity to the United States; media campaigns by NGOs, IGOs, corporations, and governments; the presence of sympathetic victims; and even the role of international celebrities. Which of these should the media follow as they set the nation's foreign policy agenda? Are there some that you wish were not on the list?

SUGGESTIONS FOR FURTHER READING

W. Lance Bennett and David L. Paletz, eds. *Taken by Storm: The Media, Public Opinion, and U.S. Foreign Policy in the Gulf War*. Chicago: University of Chicago Press, 1994.

Margaret Gallagher and the Global Media Monitoring Project. *Who Makes the News? The Global Media Monitoring Project 2005*. London: World Association for Christian Communication (WACC), 2005. http://www.whomakesthenews.org/.

Jonathan Mermin. *Debating War and Peace: Media Coverage of U.S. Intervention in the Post-Vietnam Era*. Princeton, NJ: Princeton University Press, 1999.

Larry Minear, Colin Scott, and Thomas Weiss. *The News Media, Civil War, and Humanitarian Action*. Boulder, CO: Lynne Rienner, 1996

Warren Strobel, *Late Breaking Foreign Policy: The News Media's Influence on Peace Operations*. Washington, DC: United States Institute of Peace, 1997.

NOTES

1. Bono, "Transcript of Bono's Remarks to the National Prayer Breakfast," *USA Today*, February 2, 2006, http://www.usatoday.com/news/washington/2006-02-02 -bono-transcript_x.htm.

2. Ibid.

3. Michael Warner, "2 Billion Unite to Help the Starving," *Herald Sun*, July 4, 2005.

4. Maryann Cusimano Love, *Beyond Sovereignty*, 3rd ed. (New York: Thomson/ Wadsworth, 2007), 68–69; The One Campaign, "ONE Reaction to G-8 Communiqué," July 8, 2005, http://www.one.org/g8countdown.html.

5. Sridhar Pappu, "Bono's Calling: The Irish Rocker Has a Mission: To Fight Poverty, and Enlist the Powerful in the Battle," *Washington Post*, November 26, 2007, C01.

6. Maryann Cusimano Love, *Beyond Sovereignty*, 74.

7. Intel Center, "Al-Qaeda Messaging Statistics," 3, no. 3 (September 9, 2007), http:// www.intelcenter.com/QMS-PUB-v3-3.pdf.

8. Brigitte L. Nacos, *Mass-Mediated Terrorism: The Central Role of the Media in Terrorism and Counterterrorism* (Lanham, MD: Rowman & Littlefield, 2002).

9. William A. Hachten and James F. Scotton, *The World News Prism* (Blackwell, 2007), 69.

10. Lee Edwards, *Mediapolitik* (Washington, DC: Catholic University of America Press, 2001), 1.

11. Anthony Giddens, *Runaway World: How Globalization is Reshaping Our Lives* (New York: Routledge, 2000), 32–33.

12. Walter B. Wristen, "Bits, Bytes, and Diplomacy," *Foreign Affairs* (September/ October 1997): 175–76.

13. Michael Brown, Sean Lynn Jones, and Steve Miller, eds., *Debating the Democratic Peace* (Cambridge, MA: MIT Press, 1996).

14. Benjamin Page and Robert Y. Shapiro, *The Rational Public* (Chicago: University of Chicago Press, 1992).

15. Pippa Norris, "Giving Voice to the Voiceless: Good Governance, Human Development and Mass Communications," 2004, 1, http://ksghome.harvard.edu/ pnorris/Acrobat/pfetsch%20chapter.pdf.

16. Morley Safer, interview, *From Newsreels to Nightly News: A History*, part 4 (New York: History Channel, 1997).

17. Raphael F. Perl, "Terrorism, the Media, and the Government: Perspectives, Trends, and Options for Policy Makers," Washington, DC: Congressional Research Service, October 22, 1997, http://www.fas.org/irp/crs/crs-terror.htm; Michael A. Leeden, "Secrets," in *The Media and Foreign Policy*, ed. Simon Serfaty (New York: St. Martin's Press, 1991), 121–23; John P. Wallach, "Leakers, Terrorists, Policy Makers, and the Press," in *The Media and Foreign Policy*, 81–93; Robert B. Oakley, "Terrorism, Media Coverage, and Government Response," in *The Media and Foreign Policy*, 95–107.

18. Larry Minear, Colin Scott, and Thomas Weiss, *The News Media, Civil War, and Humanitarian Action* (Boulder, CO: Lynne Rienner, 1996).

19. Warren Strobel, *Late Breaking Foreign Policy: The News Media's Influence on Peace Operations* (Washington, DC: The United States Institute of Peace, 1997, 4.

20. Warren Strobel, *Late Breaking Foreign Policy: The News Media's Influence on Peace Operations.* Washington, DC: United States Institute of Peace, 1997), 4.

21. Freedom House, "Freedom of the Press 2007," http://www.freedomhouse.org/ template.cfm?page=362; Robert Karl Manoff, testimony on the Russian Media Crisis before the House Foreign Operations, Export Financing, and Related Programs Subcommittee of the House Appropriations Committee, Washington, DC, March 4, 1999; David Hoffman, "Russian Media Fight to Live," *Washington Post*, June 28, 2000, A16; Sharon LaFraniere, "Russian Media Fear for Their Independence: Under Putin, Journalists Feel Increasingly Misused, Mistreated," *Washington Post*, February 21, 2000, A19.

22. John E. Mueller, *War, Presidents, and Public Opinion* (Lanham, MD: University Press of America, 1985), 107; Strobel, *Late Breaking Foreign Policy*, 30–37.

23. Jonathan Mermin, *Debating War and Peace: Media Coverage of U.S. Intervention in the Post-Vietnam Era* (Princeton, NJ: Princeton University Press, 1999); Daniel C. Hallin, *The Uncensored War: The Media and Vietnam* (New York: Oxford University Press, 1986).

24. James F. Hoge Jr., "Media Pervasiveness," *Foreign Affairs* (July 1994): 141; Strobel, *Late Breaking Foreign Policy*, 30.

25. Johanna Neuman, *Lights, Camera, War: Is Media Technology Driving International Politics?* (New York: St. Martin's Press, 1996); Strobel, *Late Breaking Foreign Policy*; Nik Gowing, "Real Time TV Coverage from War: Does It Make or Break Government Policy?" in *Bosnia by Television*, ed. James Gow, Richard Paterson, and Alison Preston (London: British Film Institute Publishing, 1996), 81–91.

26. James Gow, Richard Paterson, and Alison Preston, eds., *Bosnia by Television* (London: British Film Institute, 1996).

27. Strobel, *Late Breaking Foreign Policy*; Ted Koppel, "The Global Information Revolution and TV News," address to the U.S. Institute of Peace, Managing Global Chaos Conference, Washington, DC, December 1, 1994.

28. Shanto Iyengar and Adam Simon, "News Coverage of the Gulf Crisis and Public Opinion: A Study of Agenda-Setting, Priming, and Framing," in *Taken by Storm: The Media, Public Opinion, and U.S. Foreign Policy in the Gulf War*, ed. W. Lance Bennett and David L. Paletz (Chicago: University of Chicago Press, 1994).

29. Michael Dobbs, "The Amanpour Factor: How Television Fills the Leadership Vacuum on Bosnia," *Washington Post*, July 23, 1995, C2.

30. "Operation Restore Hope: The Bush Administration's Decision to Intervene in Somalia," by Maryann Cusimano, Case Study 463 (1995, Georgetown University's Institute for the Study of Diplomacy).

31. Simon Serfaty, ed., *The Media and Foreign Policy* (New York: St. Martin's Press, 1991); John R. MacArthur, *Second Front: Censorship and Propaganda in the Gulf War* (Berkeley and Los Angeles: University of California Press, 1993).

32. John D. Steinbruner, "Unrealized Promise, Avoidable Trouble," *Brookings Review* (Fall 1995): 8–13; Lawrence J. Korb, "Who's in Charge Here? National Security and the Contract With America," *Brookings Review* (Fall 1995): 4–7.

33. Steinbruner, "Unrealized Promise, Avoidable Trouble"; MacArthur, *Second Front*.

34. William E. Odom, *America's Military Revolution: Strategy and Structure after the Cold War* (Washington, DC: American University Press, 1993), 56–57.

35. Kenneth Allard, *Somalia Operations: Lessons Learned* (Washington, DC: National Defense University Press, 1995); Korb, "Who's in Charge Here?"; Cusimano Love, "Operation Restore Hope."

36. Chester A. Crocker, "The Lessons of Somalia," *Foreign Affairs* (May/June 1995): 2–8; Cusimano Love, "Operation Restore Hope."

37. Timothy E. Cook, "Domesticating a Crisis: Washington Newsbeats and Network News After the Iraqi Invasion of Kuwait," in *Taken by Storm: The Media, Public Opinion, and U.S. Foreign Policy in the Gulf War*, ed. W. Lance Bennett and David L. Paletz (Chicago: University of Chicago Press, 1994).

38. Herbert Gans, *Deciding What's News* (New York: Vintage, 1980), 8–10.

39. Ina Howard, "Power Sources," Fairness and Accuracy in Media, June 2002, http://www.fair.org/index.php?page=1109; Margaret Gallagher and the Global Media Monitoring Project, *Who Makes the News? The Global Media Monitoring Project 2005* (London: World Association for Christian Communication [WACC], 2005), http://www.whomakesthenews.org/; Andrew Tyndall, "Who Speaks For America? Sex, Age and Race on the Network News," 10th Annual Women, Men and Media

Study, conducted by ADT Research in conjunction with The Freedom Forum, October 20, 1998, Washington, DC.

40. Gallagher, *Who Makes the News?*

41. John Stacks, "Hard Times for Hard News," *World Policy Journal* (2004), http://www.worldpolicy.org/journal/articles/wpj03-4/stacks.html.

42. Carlin Romano, "The Grisly Truth about Bare Facts," in *Reading the News*, ed. Robert Karl Manoff and Michael Schudson (New York: Pantheon, 1986).

43. Mort Rosenblum, *Who Stole the News? Why We Can't Keep Up with What Happens in the World, and What We Can Do about It* (New York: John Wiley & Sons, 1993), 9.

44. Jeff Cohen and Norman Solomon, "Knee-Jerk Coverage of Bombing Should Not Be Forgotten," *Media Beat*, April 26, 1995.

45. Mathieu Deflem, "The Globalization of Heartland Terror: The Oklahoma City Bombing," paper presented at the annual meeting of the Law & Society Association, Toronto, ON, June 1995.

46. Lucinda Fleeson, "Bureau of Missing Bureaus," *American Journalism Review* (October 2003): 3, http://www.ajr.org/articles.asp?id=3409; Sherri Ricchiardi, "The Limits of the Parachute," *American Journalism Review* (November 2006); Daniel C. Hallin, "Where? Cartography, Community, and the Cold War," in *Reading the News*, ed. Robert Karl Manoff and Michael Schudson (New York: Pantheon, 1986); Rosenblum, *Who Stole the News?*

47. James W. Carey, "Why and How? The Dark Continent of American Journalism," in *Reading the News*, ed. Robert Karl Manoff and Michael Schudson (New York: Pantheon, 1986).

48. Jane Hunter, "As Rwanda Bled, Media Sat on Their Hands," *Extra!* (July/August 1994).

49. Cusimano Love, *Beyond Sovereignty*.

50. Michael Deaver, address to Johns Hopkins University class on Politics and the Media, March 26, 1991. Many of these themes are also reflected in Michael Deaver's memoirs, *Behind the Scenes* (New York: William Morrow, 1987).

51. Of course, laziness is only one possible reason why stories fed to the networks by the government often are used. Another important reason is the downsizing of news staffs as newspapers struggle to stay alive and network news teams have to pay close attention to their bottom lines given increases in competition and in corporate buyouts. Without adequate resources or staffs, the media may be increasingly vulnerable to running prepackaged government story suggestions. See Penn Kimball, *Downsizing the News: Network Cutbacks in the Nation's Capital* (Baltimore: Johns Hopkins University Press, 1994).

52. Michael Deaver, address to Johns Hopkins University class on Politics and the Media, March 26, 1991. Many of these themes are also reflected in Deaver's memoirs, *Behind the Scenes*.

53. PBS, "The Press' Reporting on WMD: Who Got It Right, Who Got It Wrong, and How Frontline Fared," *Frontline* "News Wars" series, February 13, 2007, http://www.pbs.org/wgbh/pages/frontline/newswar/part1/wmd.html; Tom Regan, "Media Knocked for Iraq war coverage," *Christian Science Monitor*, February 11, 2004.

54. W. Lance Bennett, "The News about Foreign Policy," in *Taken by Storm: The Media, Public Opinion, and U.S. Foreign Policy in the Gulf War*, ed. W. Lance Bennett and David L. Paletz (Chicago: University of Chicago Press, 1994); John Zaller, "Elite Leadership of Mass Opinion: New Evidence from the Gulf War," in *Taken by Storm*.

55. Samuel Passow, "Sunk Costs: The Plan to Dump the Brent Spar," Cambridge, MA: Harvard University, Kennedy School of Government Case Program, Case Number CR1–97–1369.0, 1997, 9.

56. Ibid., 11.

57. Minear, Scott, and Weiss, *The News Media*.

58. Ben Bagdikian, *The New Media Monopoly* (Boston: Beacon Press, 2004); Media Reform Information Center Corporate Ownership, http://www.corporations.org/media/; Corporate Media Ownership Chart, http://www.mediachannel.org/ownership/moguls-printable-150dpi.pdf; Robert W. McChesney, *Rich Media, Poor Democracy: Communication Politics in Dubious Times* (Urbana: University of Illinois Press, 1999); Eric Barnouw and Todd Gitlin, *Conglomerates and the Media* (New York: New Press, 1998).

59. Robert McChesney, "The Problem of the Media: U.S. Communication Politics in the Twenty-First Century," *Monthly Review Press*, 2004, p.71; Fairness and Accuracy in Reporting, "Media Distortion of World Bank/IMF Protests Starts Early," April 11, 2000, http://www.fair.org/activism/world-bank-protests.html. Corporate bias is not the only explanation for proglobalization media coverage; unity among official sources in favor of globalization policies limits media coverage of opposition viewpoints, since the media tend to cover government sources and intragovernment conflicts.

60. Michelle Ciarrocca, "Holes in the Coverage: What's Left Out of Reporting on Missile Defense," *Extra!* (November/December 2000); Mark Crispin Miller, "Free the Media," in *We the Media: A Citizen's Guide to Fighting for Media Democracy*, ed. Don Hazen and Julie Winokur (New York: New Press, 1997).

ASSIGNMENT: PLAYING POLITICS
ON SOCIAL NETWORKS

Have you ever gotten into an argument about politics online with someone you are linked to through a Web site like Facebook? One of the most exciting and least understood new developments in media politics has been the influence of social networking sites like MySpace, Facebook, Friendster, and others.

This is a short project that you could complete as a class assignment, working in small groups or even with the whole class. Consult with your professor as to whether this project can fulfill one of the course requirements.

Question: Do birds of a political feather flock together on social networking sites? Most people on social networking sites are not there to network about politics. Some MySpace profiles include political content, or the profile of a favorite politician will be among a member's friends, but the main focus of the members is seldom politics. Although some candidates and political movements have used mainstream networking sites to rally supporters, and some political sites (like Daily Kos) resemble social networking sites in some ways, the world of social networks tends to remain distinct from the world of politics.

One of the questions political scientists have studied for more than half a century is the influence of peers (friends, acquaintances, and co-workers) on our political views. Two factors have prevented peers from being as influential as family or the media in shaping our political views. First, for whatever reason, people tend to have fairly similar political views to their friends, and some researchers think this effect is increasing. Second, the topic of politics seldom comes up in most conversations between friends. People who like to talk about politics a lot are not common, and they are often good friends with similar people.

But what about the Internet? Does the Internet give us "friends" who are diverse in their views? Is a liberal from Berkeley, California, likely to become Facebook friends with a gun-owning conservative from Abilene, Texas? Or do we still largely group together, so that the liberals from California will befriend the rare liberal from rural Texas, while the conservatives from Texas will find the lonely conservative in Berkeley?

Here's a way you and your classmates can research this question. Find at least one classmate with political views that are quite different from yours but who is on the same social networking site as you (it doesn't matter which one, so long as it has many members). You are now coresearchers on the politics of social networking sites.

Now, prepare a very short survey on political views. Here are some questions to consider:

• In politics generally, do you think of yourself as a liberal, a conservative, a moderate, or don't you think of yourself in these ways?

- Do you generally think of yourself as a Democrat, a Republican, an independent, some other party, or don't know/other?
- Do you approve of the job the president is doing as president?

Feel free to add a few questions of your own that you would find particularly interesting, but remember that your survey must be very short to be successful. The longer the survey, the fewer respondents you will have. You will want to add at least a few demographic questions, such as age, gender, race, and religion. Remember that many online friends are citizens of other nations, so you will want to include a question about nationality and location.

Once you have finished your short survey, you and your coresearcher(s) should post it as an announcement to all of your networked friends, asking them to fill it out. Do not use e-mail or personal contact to encourage friends to fill it out—it is important to just use the social networking site's interface.

Of course, all the researchers need to fill out the survey, with some additional questions about their usage of the site. For example, all researchers should answer questions like these:

- How often do you talk about politics with friends at (the social network site you are studying)?
- How closely do you follow politics, generally? Very closely, somewhat closely, not that closely, not at all.

Feel free to create some more questions for your research team that you think would affect the outcome. If you are the leader of the campus Republicans who uses Facebook to stay in touch with conservative activists around the country, and your coresearcher is a fairly inactive Democrat, we would expect to find tremendous differences in your set of online friends.

Decide in advance how many reminders, if any, you want to send out, and make sure all the researchers send out similarly worded reminders. Your results will be less valuable if one researcher sends out twenty reminders and one sends out none.

Collect all the responses and examine how they differ. First, calculate your response rate. The response rate can be calculated by taking the number of survey responses a research team member has and dividing it by the number of online friends he has at the networking site. If you have twenty-five friends and get five responses, your response rate was 20 percent. The response rate is a rough measure of both political interest and the closeness of the friendship. Some profiles have thousands of friends who may be less likely to respond to a personal appeal to fill out a survey, whereas if you are linked to just a few close friends and relatives, you may get close to 100 percent response.

Now compare the responses of each researcher's friends to the researcher's own answers. What percent of the researcher's friends are of the same political party? What percent are of the same political ideology? Do conservatives have a higher percentage of friends who agree with them? Do Democrats? Do you see any patterns when you look at the demographics like race and sex?

What do your results tell you about the political influence of friends on social networking sites? Is it very different from how peers affected political views before the Internet?

Feel free to adapt this assignment to a particular interest or topic, so long as it is okay with your professor. You could examine whether opinions among online friends are different for one particular cultural issue, like gay rights or abortion, or look at attitudes on foreign policy.

12

The Central Role of Media and Communication in Terrorism and Counterterrorism

Brigitte L. Nacos

In early 2006 Jarret Brachman and William McCants of the Combating Terrorism Center at the United States Military Academy at West Point published a scholarly article entitled "Stealing al-Qa'ida's Playbook" that examined the writings of several prominent jihadi scholars, among them Ayman al-Zawahiri, al-Qaeda's second in commend. In response, al-Zawahiri released a videotape in which he responded to the article in some detail. Originally posted on an extremist Internet site, the video was in due course available on Google Video as well.[1] Commenting on Zawahiri's response to a review of his writings, Brachman said that "postmodern doesn't quite capture it."[2] Perhaps not. But the exchange illustrated how today's terrorists, even those hiding in the most remote places, can and do exploit global information and communication networks to promote their causes—and most of the time not by engaging in scholarly discourse.

In essence, contemporary terrorists follow the path of their predecessors, who understood all along that their violent deeds were a sure means to publicize their existence and their causes. For this reason, nineteenth-century anarchists explained their violence as "propaganda of the deed." Long before Johannes Gutenberg invented the printing press, terrorists assured themselves the greatest amount of publicity by striking in crowded places so that a large number of eyewitnesses spread the news among their families, friends, and neighbors. The emergence of the press and each new communication technology thereafter expanded terrorists' ability to spread their propaganda via the news media. However, whenever possible terrorists have not relied solely on the gatekeepers of the traditional media (newspapers, newsmagazines, radio, and television) but tried to circumvent them. For example, the Brazilian revolutionary Carlos Marighela wrote in the *Minimanual of the Urban Guerrilla* that the modern mass media were important instruments of propaganda but that this opportunity should not prevent his comrades from utilizing their own presses and copying machines.[3] In addition to their own printing presses and copying machines, more recent terrorists have used on- and offshore radio transmitters, satellite telephones, and their own television channels. The Lebanese Hezbollah expanded its originally very modest local Beirut TV station into a regional player and eventually into a global satellite TV network. Today, Hezbollah's Al Manar is the preferred TV network of millions of Muslims around the world and especially in the Muslim diaspora in the West. In early 2006 the Palestinian Hamas add a television station, Al Aqsa TV, to its radio station Voice of Al Aqsa. Both are located at secret locations in the Gaza strip.

Videotapes, audiocassettes, and DVDs have been used by al-Qaeda and like-minded groups in the Middle East, Europe, and elsewhere to spread propaganda and condition teens and young adults for recruitment. Hamdi Issac, who was one of the participants in the failed London bombing attacks on July 21, 2005, told Italian interrogators after he was arrested in Rome that he had been recruited by another would-be bomber, Said Ibrahim. According to Isaac,

> We met each other at a muscle-building class in Notting Hill and Muktar (Said Ibrahim) showed us some DVDs with images of the war in Iraq, especially women and children killed by American and British soldiers.
>
> During our meetings we analyzed the political situation and the fact that everywhere in the West Muslims are humiliated and that we must react.[4]

Video games, such as Umnah Defense I and Umnah Defense II, are advertised and sold on the Internet. The description of the scenario for Umnah Defense I explains that it is "the year 2114 and the Earth is finally united under the Banner of Islam." Some of these video games are made in the United States and sold mostly to customers abroad. There is also a lucrative international music scene that produces white supremacist rock music that advocates hate and violence against nonwhites and non-Christians; most of these products are distributed via Internet sites. While Islamic fundamentalists condemn Western popular culture as decadent, "radical Islamic groups have harnessed the influence of Hip Hop in American and Western culture by producing their own [Hip Hop] bands" that try to indoctrinate young listeners.[5] According to Madeleine Gruen, "The most extreme militant Islamic Hip Hop is known as 'Terror Rap.' The video 'Dirty Kuffar' by the British Hip Hop group Soul Salah Crew features a masked 'Sheik Terra' dancing in front of the camera with the Quran in one hand and a gun in the other."[6] The lyrics glorify terrorist groups (i.e., Hezbollah and Hamas) and terrorist idols (most of all Osama bin Laden) and vilify countries (i.e., the United States and the United Kingdom) and leading enemies (most of all George W.

Bush and Tony Blair). The same group produced a shocking rap video titled "Dirty Kuffar Murder Iraqi Civilians."[7] These and a number of similar terror rap videos by this group are not hard to find—they are available on the most popular sites on the Internet, such as YouTube, Goggle Video, and Yahoo! Video. The same is true for videos that celebrate suicide bombers and attempt to recruit "martyrs"—even from the ranks of children. Thus, after Hamas's Al Aqsa TV aired a children's program that depicted the real-life story of a female Palestinian suicide bomber and the reaction of her little daughter, who—in the television version—pledged to follow her mother's example, a video clip of the scenes was posted on YouTube by Palestinian Media Watch.[8] While meant to expose the brainwashing of Palestinian children, the video was nevertheless widely accessible for replays—and not only to critics of such propaganda. Similarly, when the Hamas television network aired *Tomorrow's Pioneers*, a children's program starring Farfour, an Arabic version of Mickey Mouse, video clips were easily accessible on Internet sites. The propaganda show ended with Farfour's heroic death as a "martyr" for the Palestinian cause—killed by Israeli "terrorists."[9]

Finally, books—even when veiled as fiction—serve as powerful propaganda tools and how-to-commit-terrorism guides. For example, William Pierce, founder of the neo-Nazi/white supremacist organization National Alliance, provided blue prints for big style terrorism in *The Turner Diaries* and *Hunter*, published under the pseudonym Andrew MacDonald. As he planned the 1995 Oklahoma City bombing, Timothy McVeigh followed the prescriptions in *The Turner Diaries*. A copy of *Hunter* was found in the possessions of McVeigh's accomplice, Terry Nichols. Headquartered in the United States, the National Alliance still has followers in North America and abroad, and then there are many "do-it-yourself" manuals—many available on Internet sites—that contain detailed instructions on how to build bombs or otherwise commit acts of terrorism.

Yet when everything is said and done, the traditional news media remain for the time being central to the terrorist publicity scheme—in spite of the Internet and other communication vehicles that allow terrorists to communicate directly with the audiences they target.

TERRORISM AND POLITICAL COMMUNICATION

In liberal democracies, modern-day politics comes mostly down to mass-mediated communication, because personal encounters between citizens, government officials, and other political actors are the exception, not the rule. Thus, political communication occurs mostly within what I call the triangle of political communication, in which the mass media, the public, and governmental decision makers as well as other mainstream political players form the three corners. The media gatekeepers control not only access to the news, but access to the general public and to government officials as well. Unless they are well funded and well connected, peaceful groups with extremist agendas rarely get access to the mainstream media. However, when extremists resort to political violence—terrorism, in other words—the media gates open up for the "propaganda of the deed" and spread the terrorist messages to the general public and the political elite.

Apart from working in the domestic setting, there is a global or international triangle of communication that works along the lines of the domestic triangular links: Continents, countries, policies, movements, religions, and so on, which normally get spotty international news coverage, instantly receive a great deal of attention by the international media when terrorists stage major acts of political violence. Today, people around the world can receive and watch news that not long ago was disseminated to domestic and perhaps regional audiences. As figure 12.1 shows, the Internet encircles the triangles of communication, allowing terrorists to circumvent the gatekeepers of the traditional media and communicate with audiences in literally all parts of the world.

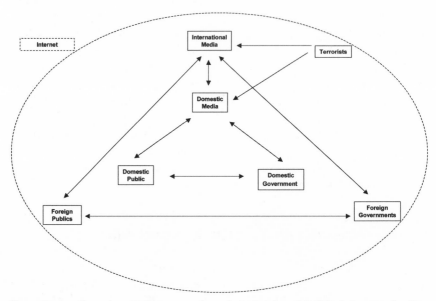

Figure 12.1.   Terrorism, Counterterrorism, the Triangles of Political Communication, and the Internet.

Source: Author.

THE GOALS OF TERRORIST PROPAGANDA

All terrorist organizations' objectives are ultimately political, even if they are promoted as religiously motivated. Some want national independence, others vie for regime change, and some demand the withdrawal of foreign powers from countries or regions. Whatever their ultimate goals may be, terrorists know that publicity and propaganda are necessary means to their larger ends. Without making friends and foes aware of their existence, their motivations, and their objectives, terrorists would not see a chance to further their political agenda. Thus, when Abu Musab al-Zarqawi was the leader of al-Qaeda in Iraq, he had all terror strikes by his group filmed because he recognized that the video camera was a weapon of war. Al-Zarqawi was convinced that his organization had to prove its lethal attacks against U.S. troops and Shia enemies, and could do so by showing them on Internet sites and distributing them in form of DVDs. After al-Zarqawi was killed by U.S. troops, his successors continued this practice and were able to beam these videos "across Iraq and much of the Middle East 24 hours a day, broadcast by a banned Iraqi satellite television station," as *The New York Times* reported in early 2007.[10]

When it comes to propaganda, terrorists have the following very specific objectives in mind:

- First, terrorists want the awareness of various audiences inside and outside their target societies and thereby condition their targets for intimidation.
- Second, terrorists want the recognition of their motives, their grievances, and causes. They want people to ask: Why do they hate us? Why do they attack innocent civilians?
- Third, terrorists want the respect and sympathy of those in whose interest they claim to act.
- Fourth, the upper echelon of terrorist organizations aims for a quasi-legitimate status among friends and foes and the media attention that legitimate political actors receive.

In view of these objectives, the question is whether and to what extent news coverage furthers one, several, or all of these imperatives.

AWARENESS/INTIMIDATION GOALS

Thomas Friedman has suggested that Osama bin Laden "is not a mere terrorist" but a "super-empowered" man with geopolitical aspirations who does not seek news coverage but wants to kill as many Americans as possible.[11] The idea that there is no longer a need for publicity on the part of terrorists in the age of catastrophic attacks is shared by others, who argue that the new "terrorism of expression" speaks for itself and does not need explanations or claims of responsibility. I disagree with this assessment. Just think of al-Qaeda's media-savvy operations, which include a propaganda/media arm and the production group Al Sahab, which by 2007 had improved the quality of its productions and increased the quantity of its audio- and videotape output to one new release every three days.[12] Moreover, a training manual that was used in al-Qaeda's training camps in Afghanistan advised recruits to target "sentimental landmarks" such as the Statue of Liberty in New York, Big Ben in London, and the Eiffel Tower in Paris, because their destruction would "generate intense publicity."[13]

In terms of getting the attention of friends and foes, the terror strikes of September 11, 2001, in the United States; March 11, 2004, in Spain, and July 7, 2005, in the United Kingdom were more successful in terms of publicity than any previous terrorist deed—including the brutal attack on Israeli athletes at the Munich Olympic Games in 1972 by Black September terrorists. In 1972 the Palestinian terrorists calculated correctly that they would get worldwide attention because they struck at a place where the international media had gathered to cover a premier sporting event. As for the attacks on the London's transit system, while certainly well planned in advance, the architects of the quadruple bombing picked a date that coincided with an important G-8 summit in Scotland. By striking at the outset of that meeting, the terrorists hijacked the news and swept the leaders of the eight most powerful countries off the television screens and front pages. Just take *The New York Times* the day after the London bombings as a typical example: The front page was mostly devoted to the 7/7 attacks, and the execution of the Egyptian ambassador to Iraq by terrorists made page one as well—but the G-8 summit did not. What a publicity success for the perpetrators of terror! In the weeks thereafter, refueled by the failed follow-up attack in London, the terrorist threat continued to dominate the news, as did counterterrorist measures in the United Kingdom, United States, and elsewhere. But it does not take major terrorist strikes for the press to report extensively and prominently. Even groups such as the Earth Liberation Front and Animal Liberation Front, which thus far have not injured or killed persons, receive plenty of publicity after each of their strikes against buildings and other sites.

Closely tied to the terrorist goal of dominating (and even dictating) the content of breaking news is the desire to intimidate a targeted population, spread fear, and undermine the declared values of the targeted political system by pushing a frightened society and government into overreaction. The propaganda of fear has proven to be quite successful. In the days and weeks after 9/11, public opinion polls revealed that many Americans were traumatized: They suffered from sleeplessness, felt depressed, and feared that they or their loved ones could become the victims of future terrorist attacks. While these feelings subsided, many people—especially in New York and Washington, as well as other places considered to be likely targets—continued to be very concerned about more terrorist attacks. Moreover, heavy news consumers were more plagued by fear of terrorism than those who did not follow the news closely.[14]

This is precisely the reaction that terrorists desire. Certainly bin Laden and his associates aimed for such effects. Speaking about the impact of 9/11 on the American people, bin Laden remarked with obvious satisfaction, "There is America, full of fear from north to south, from west to east. Thank God for that."[15]

RECOGNITION OF GRIEVANCES AND GOALS

Once they have the attention of their target audiences, terrorists want to inform them about their motives. On this count, too, bin Laden and his comrades in arms have been quite successful. Before 9/11, the American news media did not report a great deal about the growing anti-American sentiments among Arabs and Muslims in the Middle East and in other parts of the world; this changed after 9/11 in that they expanded their reporting from these regions. Suddenly, there were many stories that pondered the question President George W. Bush had posed shortly after the attacks: Why do they hate us? The focus of this sort of reporting was not simply on the motives of the terrorists themselves, but also on the vast majority of nonviolent Arabs and Muslims who resented the United States. As mentioned above, Internet sites—especially chat rooms and message boards—as well as CDs and DVDs were instrumental in spreading al-Qaeda's (and like-minded groups') version of its cause in particular and the Muslim and Arab world's grievances in general. This propaganda went into a higher pitch once U.S.-led coalition forces attacked the Taliban and al-Qaeda in Afghanistan, and even more so in response to the invasion of Iraq and the years of occupation thereafter. As al-Qaeda and similar groups exploited traditional and new media to showcase their versions of the U.S.-led coalition's attacks on innocent Muslims, they referred to this material to emphasize what they described as mounting grievances of the whole Arab and Muslim world.

Or take the 7/7 bombings in London that resulted in an avalanche of reports on the sentiments and grievances of Muslims in the United Kingdom and elsewhere in Europe and on the role of the Iraq war in the recruitment of homegrown British subjects. The news media carried stories on the radicalization of young Muslims in the European diaspora before the London attacks, but this coverage paled in comparison to far more in-depth reporting by domestic and global media about grievances among a growing number of Muslims in western Europe and their possible vulnerability to be recruited into extremist and terrorist groups. Whenever al-Qaeda leaders or those in like-minded circles followed up by reciting a growing list of Western, American, and British "sins," they did so not to convince targeted societies to change their ways but instead renewed their efforts to persuade Muslims and Arabs everywhere to join their causes.

Eventually, al-Qaeda and like-minded groups began to produce their own propaganda material that explained their cause and grievances and targeted westerners in particular. For example, a new English-language bin Laden video released in mid-September 2007 was produced with subtitles in many languages—among them German, French, and Danish—and available on various Web sites. According to one account, "Al Qaeda and its followers have used the Internet to communicate and rally support for years, but in the past several months the Western tilt of the message and the sophistication of the media have accelerated."[16]

RESPECT AND SYMPATHY GOALS

In spite of the dramatic increase in their direct appeals to Westerners, Osama bin Laden and like-minded terrorists did not win the respect of the American, Spanish, or British people by committing catastrophic anti-American terrorism in those countries. On the contrary, for many Americans, Spaniards, and the British, the architects and actual perpetrators became the personification of evil, and bin Laden the villain-in-chief. This reaction did not come as a surprise to bin Laden and his kind. After all, when international terrorists strike abroad, they do not strive to be loved by their target audiences; they want to be feared. But at the same time, they aim for increased respectability and sympathy among those people on whose behalf they claim to act. This is precisely what bin Laden, his closest aides, and the network of supporters and sympathizers were after in the post-9/11 years. According to cross-national polls in a number of Muslim countries, the confidence in bin Laden to do the right thing as world leader was highest in 2003 and declined significantly in the following years. By 2007 the majority (57 percent) of respondents only in the Palestinian territories expressed such trust in the al-Qaeda leader, whereas support elsewhere had fallen in comparison to 2003 surveys to 41 percent in

Indonesia, 38 percent in Pakistan, 20 percent in Jordan, 13 percent in Kuwait, 5 percent in Turkey, and 1 percent in Lebanon.[17] One wonders, however, to what extent the question wording influenced the encouraging trends. Instead of simply asking whether or not respondents supported bin Laden or not, pollsters asked the following question: "Now I'm going to read a list of political leaders. For each, tell me how much confidence you have in each leader to do the right thing regarding world affairs—a lot of confidence, some confidence, not too much confidence, or no confidence at all?" Besides bin Laden's name, the names of legitimate leaders, such as the U.S. president, the French president, the British prime minister, and the secretary general of the United Nations were read.

QUASI-LEGITIMATE ACTOR GOALS

The mere fact that these surveys included bin Laden's name in a list of the most influential leaders of states in the Middle East and elsewhere in the world is hardly surprising in view of news media's and political actors' long-standing practice of treating terrorist leaders like legitimate political actors.

Wittingly or not, the news media bestow a certain status upon terrorist leaders. When reporters or anchors interview and present leading terrorists like legitimate political actors, they elevate their status and play into their hands. For example, during the buildup phase to the first Gulf War, Ted Koppel of ABC News interviewed Dr. George Habash of the Popular Front for the Liberation of Palestine (PFLP) during a *Nightline* program. Habash repeated and expanded on his threats of violence against Americans in case of military actions against Iraq and its occupation of Kuwait, and spoke about Arab grievances against the United States. Saudi Arabia's ambassador to the United States was a guest on the same program and topic. More recently, Koppel devoted a full *Nightline* program to an interview with the Chechen "rebel leader" Shamil Basayev, who claimed responsibility for two of the most deadly terrorist incidents in Russian history: the takeover of a Moscow theater in the fall of 2002 and the Beslan school siege in September 2004, which resulted in the death of hundreds of innocent people—in the latter case mostly children.[18] While the interview was conducted by a Russian reporter, Koppel nevertheless provided a public stage to an unapologetic terrorist leader who used the opportunity to explain Chechen grievances against Russia. As with Habash's earlier Koppel interview, the Russian terrorist leader was treated like a legitimate political actor. While this did not justify a move by the Russian government to deny ABC News access to its Defense Ministry or other official sources, officials in Moscow were not the first to protest the legitimization of terrorists by granting them access to and equal opportunities in major news media. When appalled by American and Western journalists' presence at a press conference held by the Lebanese hijackers of a TWA airliner in 1985, then Secretary of State Alexander Haig warned, "when TV reporters interview kidnappers, it risks making international outlaws seem like responsible personalities. Television should avoid being used that way."[19]

A few weeks after the 2004 train bombings in Madrid, bin Laden offered to halt terrorism in European countries if they withdrew their military forces from Muslim lands. In a message first aired on the Arab television network Al Arabiya, bin Laden said, "The door to a truce is open for three months. The truce will begin when the last soldier leaves our countries."[20] This message was the predominant news story in Europe, where it was aired frequently, prominently, and extensively. Within hours high-ranking officials in several Western European countries went public with their respective governments' responses. Although all of these governments rejected the truce offer categorically, their immediate reaction was a testament to bin Laden's quasi-legitimate status. It is indeed very likely that the legitimate leaders of many countries around the world would have gotten neither such media attention nor these immediate highest-level public responses. However, in this particular case government officials were prompted by the high degree of attention the European media paid to bin Laden's tape. As German TV commentator Elmar Thevessen noted, "I think it would be better not to react to the tape in the way many governments did today. Of course, one shouldn't keep quiet about it, but by talking about bin Laden's message all the time, we are upgrading him to a global player."[21] In the United States, there were also high-level reactions to literally any statement by bin Laden and eventually to communications by his right-hand man al-Zawahiri and others in al-Qaeda Central and al-Qaeda in Iraq. For example, in the summer of 2005, al-Zawahiri starred in an al-Qaeda-produced videotape and threatened more terrorist attacks against the United Kingdom and the United States. Unlike Prime Minister Tony Blair, who had stopped commenting on al-Qaeda communications the previous year, Bush's widely reported response proved once again that when leading terrorists speak, the news media report, and even the most influential world leaders listen—and respond.[22]

Even when individuals and groups that monitor terrorist Web sites pick up announcements of soon-to-be-released statements by al-Qaeda leaders, the media report this as "breaking news," and terrorism analysts, experts, and public officials comment on this "news" before it actually had occurred.

When it comes to their four publicity goals, terrorists have always been quite successful in achieving them, but never more so than in recent times, thanks to the dramatic growth of domestic and global media and communication means.

TERRORIST PROPAGANDA AND THE CONTEMPORARY MEDIA

While the press has always been interested in reporting violence, the proliferation of television and radio channels and the emergence of megamedia organizations has resulted in greater competition and insatiable appetites for shocking, sensational infotainment that is believed to keep audiences captivated and boost ratings and circulation, and, most importantly, increase profits. Few events fulfill the requirements of gripping infotainment as acts of terrorism and the plight of terrorist victims. To be sure, the most fundamental function of the free press is its responsibility to fully inform the public. Thus, terrorism must be reported; the question is how and how much to report on this sort of political violence.

Is it in the public interest to play every act of terrorism as the day's leading news? In questioning the news judgment of editors, critics complain that the threats against and the murder of hostages are presented as lead stories in TV and front-page stories in newspapers. As Mark Bowden put it,

> What disturbs me is the way terrorists use sensationalism to vastly amplify their message. They know that horror and drama capture the media's attention so they manufacture them. This is why instead of merely executing their victims, they cut off their heads on camera and broadcast videos. When that gets old, which it will, they will come up with something even more awful.[23]

Bowden is not the only one who fears that terrorists will think of and commit ever more outlandish acts of violence precisely because they know that the news media will cover "never before" horror news most prominently.

Regardless of the media's preferences, one must ask whether it is in the public interest to replay the shocking images of deadly attacks over and over again, or whether it is responsible journalism to show the victims of terrorism regardless of the horror of such images. Should the news media display visual images of victims regardless of their condition?

In the case of 9/11, the published images of people jumping to their death from the highest floors of the World Trade Center come to mind. Equally unsettling were the emotionally wrenching videotapes that depicted hostages begging for their lives in Iraq and Saudi Arabia. Even without the visuals of actual beheadings, detailed textual accounts of the victims' predicament can cross the line of what is ethical. Consider, for example, the following description of an American civilian's decapitation by his terrorist kidnappers, as published in a leading U.S. newspaper:

> As the insurgent speaks, the gray-bearded man identified as Mr. Armstrong appears to be sobbing, a white blindfold wrapped around his eyes. He is wearing an orange jumpsuit. The masked man then pulls a knife, grabs his head and begins

slicing through the neck. The killer places the head atop the body before the video cuts to a shot of him holding up the head and a third, more grainy shot showed the body from a different angle.[24]

There is no need to provide such graphic details to fulfill the free media's responsibility to inform the public; nor is there a need to critique the videotape scenes of hostage ordeals and executions as if they were parts of Hollywood movies. One such newspaper account first described a video released by a militant group in Iraq that showed "insurgents slicing off the head of a man identified as Kenneth Bigley, the British engineer who was kidnapped here last month."[25] Then, mentioning an earlier video by the same group that showed the same hostage in distress, the reporter wrote,

> The captors have shown a cold cinematic flair. At the end of the 11-minute video, they showed a series of title cards in Arabic and English on a black screen in which they asked whether a British civilian was worth anything to Blair. The last screen read, "Do leaders really care about their people?"[26]

By referring to the "cold cinematic flair" of these terrorist productions, this description read more like the review of a well-done motion picture than the report of a cold-blooded real-life murder.

DOMESTIC AND INTERNATIONAL MEDIA

Not so long ago, the news media operated mostly within national borders, despite foreign correspondents, international wire services, and broadcast networks that reached beyond the domestic spheres. The international media and communication nets of the past pale in comparison to today's global communication systems. Moreover, satellite television networks like Al Jazeera, Al Arabiya, or Al Manar challenge the international dominance of the American and Western media. Add to this the reach of the Internet! In short, today's global communication and media networks overshadow the domain of national media. This point was driven home in the fall of 2002, when Chechen terrorists seized a theater crowded with Russians. As soon as the Chechens controlled the hostage situation, their comrades outside delivered to the Moscow bureau of Al Jazeera—not Russian TV—a preproduced videotape on which the terrorists articulated their demands and their willingness to die for their cause. Within hours, the clip was aired by television networks around the world. It did not matter that the Russian government censored their own broadcast stations' reporting of the hostage situation, because interested Russians were able to get information on the video tape and the hostage drama via CNN and other global TV networks. This case demonstrated the limits of domestic media censorship by governments—which is, of course, incompatible with the values of liberal democracies. But the incident also illustrated the limitations of sensible self-restraint on the part of domestic news media with respect to covering terrorism. Even if national media organizations agreed to follow a set of guidelines, it would not prevent the public from accessing foreign media without such self-imposed reporting limits.

But most of all, the Internet allows terrorists to circumvent the traditional media—national and global—to communicate with each other and reach audiences around the world independent of media gatekeepers and filters.

Terrorists and the Internet

Contemporary terrorist groups have communication experts among their members and work with sophisticated computers and video-recording and editing equipment; they also hire media experts. In October 2005, for example, the pan-Arab daily newspaper *Asharq al-Awsat* reported that al-Qaeda placed a "help wanted" ad on an Internet site that described job openings in the communication field. Al-Qaeda looked for a person to compile material on Iraq, including audio and video clips, and an editor with excellent English and Arabic grammar skills.[27] Around the same time, the Global Islamic Media Front, an al-Qaeda mouthpiece, inaugurated *The Voice of the Caliphate*, a weekly television broadcast on the Internet. The first newscasts featured an anchor and propaganda reports from various countries and regions, among them Iraq, Afghanistan, Gaza, and Sudan.

Today's terrorists perpetrate violence and, if they choose, report on their own deeds themselves. This was certainly the practice in Pakistan, Iraq, and Saudi Arabia when terrorists beheaded their victims and then posted videotapes of their murderous actions on Internet sites. Here the terrorists were the sources and the reporters of terrifying news. The traditional media were left to report on what terrorists had reported about their own murderous acts.

Referring to the news media's massive coverage of suicide bombings in Iraq, *The New York Times* columnist John Tierney wrote, "I am still puzzled by our zeal in frantically competing to get the gruesome pictures and details for broadcasts and front pages."[28] He concluded, "For some reason, their [suicide terrorists'] media strategy still works."[29] Tierney was certainly right. Yet the communication scheme behind suicide bombings and other terrorist deeds would continue to work for the architects and perpetrators of such violence even if the traditional media did not report them at all—simply because terrorist groups use their own Web sites or those of sympathizers to report their brutal deeds.

The Internet has many qualities that serve terrorists well: It is a global means of communication and an unprecedented source of information; it is easily accessible, inexpensive, and mostly unregulated; it allows users to remain anonymous; and it gives them access to potentially huge audiences and the ability to target specific groups. These characteristics are utilized by terrorists and those who encourage terrorism in several respects:

- As a carrier of propaganda, psychological warfare, and hero worship that allows terrorists to circumvent the traditional media's gatekeepers and pursue the publicity goals described above.
- As a means of planning and coordinating terrorist operations. Thus, the 9/11 terrorists and al-Qaeda's operational boss Khalid Shaikh Mohammed communicated via the Internet during the months preceding their strikes.
- As a source for the retrieval of valuable information. Computers left behind in Afghanistan by al-Qaeda revealed that they were extensively used to access open sources for all kinds of information—site maps, antisurveillance methods, and so on. Whether international or domestic terrorists, they get a great deal of information—including on terrorist methods, weapons, explosives, bomb making, and so forth—from the Internet.
- As a virtual classroom for teaching terrorists how to carry out violence, how to acquire explosives, and how to build their own bombs.
- As a tool for the recruitment of new members. While personal contacts were traditionally most successful in efforts to win new recruits, the Internet has proved more recently instrumental in this respect. Internet chat rooms have become meeting places of all kinds of extremists.
- As a vehicle for fund-raising—often in concert with selling merchandise. Both domestic and international organizations make efforts to raise funds via the Internet, and most groups have been quite successful on this count.

THE MEDIA AND COUNTERTERRORISM

Just as terrorists utilize and exploit the domestic and international triangles of political communication, government officials take advantage of this form of mass communication as well. Indeed, whereas terrorists must resort to violence or make credible threats to be admitted to the triangle of political communication by the gatekeepers of the traditional media, highly placed public officials do not have to unleash violence to gain such access because they form one corner of the domestic communication triangle and are part of the international triangular communication linkages as well. From this position of strength, governmental sources tend to dominate reporting on foreign and security policy—especially when this involves military conflict or the likelihood of military deployment. In the United States these dominant news sources are typically situated in the White House, the State Department, and the Pentagon.

Freedom of the press is a fundamental right in liberal democracies, because only a media free from governmental control can function as a check on government in the interest of its citizens. However, just as during wartime and other serious international crises, the press may become part of a national outburst of patriotism in reaction to terrorist attacks at the expense of its watchdog responsibilities. Whether this change from watchdog to lapdog is the result of self-censorship or of intimidation by governments and their supporters—or both—does not matter, since the results are the same: Docile media organizations allow governmental decision makers far more latitude to enact emergency policies and enlist support for military actions in response to major terrorist strikes and threats than they would in times of normalcy. While this "rally 'round the flag" phenomenon occurs frequently in reaction to foreign crises, it is also common in the immediate aftermath of significant international terrorist incidents. Thus, the Iranian hostage crisis (1979–1981) during the presidency of Jimmy Carter; the TWA hijacking/hostage crisis (1985) and the bombing of Pan Am flight 103 (1988) during the Reagan presidency; and the Oklahoma City bombing (1995) and the USS *Cole* bombing (2000) during Bill Clinton's presidency resulted in significant gains in these presidents' public approval that qualified as strong rallies 'round the flag.[30]

But none of these previous gains in public approval came close to the jumps in favor of President George W. Bush immediately following the attacks of 9/11, when his approval increased from 51 percent in the last pre-9/11 poll to 86 percent in the first post-9/11 survey and an additional 4 percent—to 90 percent approval—in the following poll. To put it differently, within a few days the president's approval rating increased by 39 percentage points![31] While this record approval declined gradually, it was not a short-term expression of support: It took two years before the presidential approval rating returned to the pre-9/11 level. And even when Bush's general approval ratings fell below the pre-9/11 marks, majorities or pluralities of Americans continued to approve of his handling of the terrorist threat and the war on terror for years.

Since leaders with solid public approvals are in excellent positions to lead public opinion to begin with, they are likely to succeed in enlisting their compatriots' support for their counterterrorist policies in the aftermath of major terrorist attacks. One reason for this advantage is the press's tendency to pay extraordinary attention to the utterings of heads of governments and states during crisis situations. As a result, presidents and prime ministers are in excellent positions to affect and even set the media agenda with respect to a perceived crisis. Not surprisingly, in the months immediately following 9/11, when the U.S. president and members of his administration were most vocal about their efforts to hunt down Osama bin Laden as the head of al-Qaeda, this emphasis was reflected in the news.

But when efforts to catch the number one on the FBI's list of most-wanted persons proved unsuccessful and Bush and other administration officials focused on what they deemed as major threat posed by Iraq's president Saddam Hussein, this shift was clearly reflected in the media's agenda. Table 12.1 demonstrates that bin Laden was mentioned far more often than Saddam Hussein in the news coverage of major American news organizations in the first half of 2002, and that there was far more media attention to Saddam Hussein in the second half of 2002, when the Bush administration's public statements had singled out Iraq and the Iraqi leader as the most dangerous terrorist threat. To be sure, the news media in democratic and nondemocratic settings are expected to report extensively on politics, policymaking, and thus on their government leaders' views and actions. But one would nevertheless expect that the media do not simply reflect their governments' agenda, but report independently as well.

Given the contemporary news media's insatiable appetite for what Sissela Bok has called "violence as public entertainment" and "media violence,"[32] the press tends to pay far more attention to military responses and the preparations for military actions than to nonviolent counterterrorist measures designed to prevent terrorist attacks and prepare for adequate response in case of future terror strikes. Thus, while paying little attention to the comprehen-

Table 12.1.   News Stories Mentioning Osama bin Laden and/or Saddam Hussein

	Period I		Period II	
	Saddam Hussein	Bin Laden	Saddam Hussein	Bin Laden
	(N)	(N)	(N)	(N)
ABC News	83	372	791	311
CBS News	115	438	595	298
NBC News	123	293	581	220
NPR	93	260	604	212

N = Number of Stories
Period I = January 1–June 30, 2002; Period II = July 1–December 31, 2002

sive and far-reaching antiterrorism legislation proposed by the Bush administration shortly after 9/11 and adopted by Congress in record time as the Patriot Act, the American media was far more interested in the first military phase of Bush's declared "war on terror" in Afghanistan. And although the new law expanded the federal government's surveillance and intelligence gathering powers, the news media failed to inform the public fully about the hastily written and adopted legislation's potential impact on civil liberties. Except for mentioning in passing the adoption of the legislation by the House of Representatives and the Senate or the president's signing of the bill, the major television networks (ABC, CBS, and NBC) completely ignored the far-reaching legislation. CNN, NPR, and the print media did not fare much better in this respect. In the face of strong support for the antiterrorism measures in Congress and elsewhere, news organizations were neither informing the public nor questioning the wisdom of some of the antiterrorism measures.

It was a very different story several years later, when a number of important provisions in the Patriot Act were set to expire unless reauthorized by Congress. This time around there was opposition to renewing certain provisions in its original form on both sides of the aisle in both legislative chambers. Moreover, many news organizations were less inclined to forfeit their watchdog role than they had been in the months and indeed years immediately following the 9/11 attacks. In a far cry from the noncoverage or spotty coverage of the original Patriot Act, each of the three major television networks carried more than seventy segments, NPR and *The New York Times* close to two hundred items, and CNN more than four hundred stories about the renewal process.[33] Whereas the media did not inform the public about the trade-offs between security and civil liberties in the original Patriot Act, they provided ample information about the pro and con arguments in the reauthorization debate.

But good reporting occurred only after most news organizations covered the buildup period to the Iraq war heavily in favor of pro-war sources and pro-war arguments, at the expense of voices that raised important and probing questions. Pointing to news organizations' belated criticism of the Bush administration's prewar disinformation campaign, media critic Michael Massing wrote,

Watching and reading all this, one is tempted to ask, where were you [people in the media] all before the war? Why didn't we learn more about these deceptions and concealments in the months when the administration was pressing its case for regime change — when, in short, it might have made a difference? Some maintain that the many analysts who've spoken out since the end of the war were mute before it. But that's not true. Beginning in the summer of 2002, the "'intelligence community' was rent by bitter disputes over how Bush officials were using the data on Iraq. Many journalists knew about this, yet few chose to write about it."[34]

The New York Times in an editorial and the *Washington Post* in an investigative report admitted flaws in their prewar reporting.[35] As the *Post*'s executive editor, Leonard Downie Jr., put it: "[W]e were so focused on trying to figure out what the administration was doing that we were not giving the same play to people who said it wouldn't be a good idea to go to war and were questioning the administration's rationale. Not enough of those stories were put on the front page. That was a mistake on my part."[36] For Orville Schell, "[i]t is understandable that governments would want to limit dissent within their own ranks and to avoid embarrassing disclosures. Less understandable, however, is that an independent press in a 'free' country should allow itself to become so paralyzed that it not only failed to investigate thoroughly the rationales for war, but also took so little account of the myriad other cautionary voices in the on-line, alternative, and world press."[37]

Why was the British fourth estate less compliant than the American press, even though the Blair government also engaged in a questionable pro-war propaganda campaign to justify the deployment of British troops in the U.S.-led Iraqi invasion? The difference was probably that members of the American press, unlike their British counterparts, were deeply affected by the events of 9/11—the most lethal terrorist attack in Western history. While the bombing raids on London during World War II are part of the collective memory in Great Britain, the attack on Pearl Harbor was less traumatic in the minds of mainland Americans. For precisely that reason, Americans were far more traumatized by the events of 9/11 than were the British by the quadruple suicide attacks on their London transit system on 7/7—and people in the media were no exception.

In the American setting, most news media became the carriers of propaganda messages by the Bush administration and its supporters in Congress and elsewhere who directly or indirectly linked Iraq's ruler to al-Qaeda and the 9/11 attacks—while ignoring completely or mostly that there was no credible evidence for such claims. Moreover, while it was widely believed in the United States and elsewhere that Iraq possessed weapons of mass destruction (WMD), there were also credible voices that questioned the so-called WMD evidence. Since the media reflected overwhelmingly or exclusively the arguments of the pro-war side, the vast majority of the American public believed—before, during, and after the invasion of Iraq—that there were links between Saddam Hussein, al-Qaeda, and 9/11, and that Iraq possessed lethal WMD.

These attitudes were so deeply seated that a vast majority of the public stuck to these views even when information to the contrary was widely disseminated in the media. In March 2006, three years after the Iraq war began, 23 percent of Americans still believed that before the war, Iraq actually had weapons of mass destruction and 18 percent that the country had had a major WMD program at the time, whereas 42 percent thought that Iraq had limited WMD activities and only 12 percent believed that there had not been WMD activities at all.[38] On the other hand, a clear majority of Americans (57 percent) believed by March 2006 that the United Nations and its weapons inspectors "have been vindicated in their prewar insistence that there was no clear evidence that Iraq had a WMD program." Yet, although no WMD were found in Iraq to this day, 40 percent of Americans insisted three years after the invasion of Iraq that the UN and its agencies had been proven wrong on this point.[39]

In its "Statement of Principles," the American Society of Newspaper Editors (ASNE), a pioneer in the establishment of journalistic ethic rules, offers an excellent explanation of the news media's responsibilities in the service of the public good. Of particular importance here is the following sentence in ASNE's ethics rules:

> The American press was made free not just to inform or just to serve as a forum for debate but also to bring an independent scrutiny to bear on the forces of power in the society, including the conduct of official power at all levels of government.[40]

In the post-9/11 years, the American press did not live up to these ideals. The point here is not that the news media should have taken a stand against the war, but rather that all Americans would have benefited from comprehensive, balanced, probing reporting and editorializing so that individuals would have had the chance to make well-informed decisions for or against the Iraq war, for or against the Patriot Act, and for or against other issues arising from terrorism and counterterrorism.

CONCLUSION

Given the centrality of publicity in terrorism and counterterrorism, the traditional gatekeepers of the "old" media have a particular responsibility to exercise their considerable influence carefully and guided by the highest journalistic standards. But even when the news media manage to report according to their professional ideals, terrorists have proven very savvy in circumventing the old media by exploiting a variety of new entertainment and news media for their purposes—from DVDs to the Internet. Governments, on the other hand, have been less successful in utilizing those new media for effective counterterrorist propaganda campaigns.

DISCUSSION QUESTIONS

1. Why did nineteenth-century anarchists define terrorism as "propaganda by deed"?
2. What is meant by "triangles of communication" in the context of terrorism?
3. Why is the Internet so attractive to terrorist organizations?
4. How can governmental leaders utilize the triangles of communication as they fight global terrorism?

SUGGESTIONS FOR FURTHER READING

A Odasuo Alali and Kenoye Kelvin Eke, eds. *Media Coverage of Terrorism: Methods of Diffusion*. Newbury Park, CA: Sage, 1991.
Brigitte L. Nacos. *Mass-Mediated Terrorism: The Centrality of the Media in Terrorism and Counterterrorism*, 2nd ed. Lanham, MD: Rowman & Littlefield, 2007.
———. *Terrorism and the Media: From the Iran Hostage Crisis to the World Trade Center Bombing*. New York: Columbia University Press, 1996.
Pippa Norris, Montague Kern, and Marion Just. *Framing Terrorism: The News Media, the Government, and the Public*. New York: Routledge, 2003.
Philip Schlesinger, Graham Murdock, and Philip Elliott. *Televising "Terrorism": Political Violence in Popular Culture*. London: Comedia, 1983.
Alex P. Schmid and Jenny de Graaf. *Violence as Communication: Insurgent Terrorism and the Western News Media*. Beverly Hills, CA: Sage, 1982.
Gabriel Weiman and Conrad Winn. *The Theater of Terror: Mass Media and International Terrorism*. New York: Longman, 1994.

NOTES

1. See http://video.google.com/videoplay?docid=-1172754576785196282&hl=en (accessed May 20, 2007).
2. Brachman made this comment in an e-mail to the author.
3. Carlos Marighela, *Minimanual of the Urban Guerrilla* (Abraham Guillen Press, 2002).
4. "Italy Arrests Another Brother of London Bomb Suspect," Agence France Presse, July 31, 2005, http://news.yahoo.com/afp/20050731/wl-uk-afp/britainattack-sitaly-050731153552&prin (accessed July 31, 2005).
5. Madeleine Gruen, "Innovative Recruitment and Indoctrination Tactics by Extremists: Video Games, Hip Hop, and the World Wide Web," in *The Making of a Terrorist*, vol. 1, ed. James Forest (Westport, CT: Praeger, 2005).
6. Ibid.

7. See http://video.google.com/videoplay?docid=9083681522527526242&q=Sheikh+Terra+and+the+Soul+Salah+Crew (accessed June 15, 2007).

8. See http://www.youtube.com/watch?v=cqHUdwePfbM (accessed June 1, 2007).

9. See "Palestinian Mouse Martyred!" http://www.youtube.com/watch?v=Fkvbln 1ORk0 (accessed July 2, 2007).

10. Marc Santora and Damien Cave, "On the Air, the Voice of Sunni Rebels in Iraq," *The New York Times*, January 21, 2007, 8.

11. Thomas L. Friedman, "No Mere Terrorist," *The New York Times*, March 24, 2002, 4-15.

12. For more on al-Qaeda's propaganda see Michael Moss and Souad Mekhennet, "An Internet Jihad Sells Extremism to Viewers in the United States," *The New York Times*, October 15, 2007, 1.

13. Hamza Hendawi, "Terror Manual Advises on Targets," http://story.news.yahoo .com/news?tmpl=story&u+/ap/20 . . . /afghan_spreading_terror_ (accessed February 11, 2002).

14. For example, see Andrew Kohut, "Washington 2002: Attitude Adjustment— The 9/11 Effect is Starting to Fade," *Columbia Journalism Review* 5 (September-October, 2002), http://www.cjr.org/issues/2002/5/wash-kohut.asp.

15. "Text: Bin Laden Statement," *Guardian*, http://www.guardian.co.uk./waronterror/ story/0,1361,565069,00html (accessed April 7, 2002).

16. Moss and Mekhennet, "An Internet Jihad."

17. Indonesia was the only country in which trust in bin Laden increased from mid-2005 to mid-2007 (by 6 percent). Surveys were conducted for the Pew Global Attitudes Project of the Pew Research Center for the People and the Press in 2003, 2005, and 2007. See http://www.people-press.org.

18. The *Nightline* program was aired on July 28, 2005. The Russian Foreign Ministry tried to convince ABC News not to broadcast the interview and protested against the program after it was aired.

19. Haig was quoted by Brigitte L. Nacos, *Terrorism and the Media* (New York: Columbia University Press, 1994), 67.

20. Richard Bernstein, "Tape, Probably Bin Laden's, Offers Truce to Europe," *The New York Times*, April 16, 2004, 3.

21. Ibid.

22. Al-Zawahri's video message was aired and reported on July 4, 2005, and within hours Bush responded during a meeting at his ranch at Crawford, Texas, with Colombian president Alvaro Uribe.

23. Mark Bowden, "News Judgment and Jihad," *Atlantic Monthly* (December 2004): 41.

24. Neil MacFarquhar, "Acting on Threat, Saudi Group Kills Captive American," *The New York Times*, June 19, 2004, 1.

25. Edward Wong, "Video Shows Beheading of Kidnapped British Engineer," *The New York Times*, October 9, 2004, 6.

26. Ibid.

27. "Al Qaeda Posts 'Help Wanted' Ad on Website: Report," *Khaleej Times*, October 3, 2005.

28. John Tierney, "Bombs Bursting on Air," *The New York Times*, May 10, 2005, 17.

29. Ibid.

30. Brigitte L. Nacos, *Mass-Mediated Terrorism*, 2nd ed. (Lanham, MD: Rowman & Littlefield, 2007).

31. The record approval ratings cited were taken from surveys conducted by the Gallup organization for CNN/*USA Today* on September 7–10, September 14–15, and September 21–22, 2001.

32. Sissela Bok, *Mayhem: Violence as Public Entertainment* (Reading, MA: Perseus Books, 1998).

33. From July 2005, when the reauthorization process began in Congress, to mid-March 2006, when Bush signed the revised Patriot Act, ABC News and CBS News carried 71 pertinent items each, NBC 76, CNN 457, NPR 175, and *The New York Times* 201. These were the results of a search of the LexisNexis database covering the period from July 1, 2005, to March 15, 2006, and using the search term "Patriot Act."

34. Michael Massing, *Now They Tell Us: The American Press and Iraq* (New York: New York Review Books, 2004), 25, 26.

35. "From the Editors: The Times and Iraq," *The New York Times*, May 26, 2004, 10; Howard Kurtz, "The *Post* on WMDs: An Inside Story," *Washington Post*, August 12, 2004, A1.

36. Kurtz, "The *Post* on WMDs."

37. Massing, *Now They Tell Us*, iv.

38. According to surveys conducted by WorldPublicOpinion.org and Knowledge Networks, March 1–6, 2006.

39. Ibid.

40. ASNE Statement of Principles are published on the organization's Web site: http://www.asne.org/kiosk/archive/principl.htm.

INTERVIEW: ED MORRISSEY, POLITICAL BLOGGER

Captain's Quarters (http://www.captainsquartersblog.com/mt) is one of the most popular conservative blogs in the country, ranked number ten among all political blogs by the Truth Laid Bear (http://truthlaidbear.com), which measures active links from other blogs. Morrissey has become an influential voice in conservative politics through his Web site, which mixes political commentary and media analysis.

How did you start out as a blogger?
I started in October 2003 as a way to develop more discipline as a writer. I just decided to sign up for a TypePad account and start writing with the first word, and after taking a few weeks to find my voice, kept going. It never even occurred to me that blogging would bring this kind of notoriety. I expected to use this as an alternative to getting into verbal debates with friends and family, and to give myself a record of the issues. At best, I expected to be a known entity in a very small pond.

First time you realized how big it was getting?
Probably the first time I got invited as a guest on a nationally syndicated talk radio show, with Hugh Hewitt. That came about two months after I started. Blogs had already had an impact before that, as they had forced the Trent Lott comments about Strom Thurmond to the national media. The Dan Rather memo scandal came after that and really showed how blogs could challenge even the media giants.

The effect of blogs on media coverage?
I think that blogs make it more immediate. Analysis follows within seconds of events, sometimes even while events unfold. It gives them more visibility — and it makes it harder for politicians to talk regional in national campaigns. What's said in Virginia becomes relevant in California.

Contact with politicians and campaigns?
I have had a lot of direct communication, both with the blog and my Internet radio show. I have interviewed presidential candidates, senators, congressmen, and cabinet officers. I even got to interview Afghanistan's ambassador to the United States from his Washington, D.C., office and have the best iced tea I have ever tasted. Campaigns are especially accessible, for obvious reasons. It's very heady stuff, and it's hard to keep perspective on the fact that everyone in these transactions wants and needs something, and bloggers have to develop some objectivity to keep from being used.

Are blogs causing an increase in personal attacks in media politics?
I'd agree that personal attacks and rumors are always a problem, one that existed well before blogging. I think it was a bigger problem before blogging, when e-mail smear campaigns gave very little opportunity for the victims to rebut them. Blogs may repeat these smears, to the erosion of their credibility, but blogs can provide a platform for high-visibility debunking and accountability for the purveyors of such attacks.

Are blogs parasites on the mainstream media, robbing them of readers but dependent on newspapers for the quality reporting that bloggers use each day?
I think this is a false argument to a large extent. Bloggers don't take readers away from media outlets; they *are* the readers. They're the MSM's [mainstream media] best customers, and they direct their readers to those outlets they follow. I have to read dozens of media outlets every day to keep up with my blogging, and when I analyze and criticize coverage, I'm linking back to these outlets. The bloggers provide a feedback loop for the mainstream media, a focus group to determine whether they perform well or poorly. Good sources of news will prosper even more from the vetting process that blogs provide, while poor sources will get ignored. It's free-market economics, and the market will make those determinations.
    I'd say that the bigger problem facing the media is declining readership and advertising revenue for newspapers and their need to shift to an online model that makes money. That has little to do with bloggers, and represents a much greater threat to resources at the moment.

Proudest moment as a blogger?
My work on the Canadian AdScam scandal. The American media barely even noticed it, and the Canadian media were barred legally from reporting what I could. It forced the judge to end his gag rule in the case and made it possible for Canada's press to freely report the wrongdoing by its government—and the whiff of the forbidden made AdScam much more interesting to Canadians.

Biggest mistake?
It might be answering this question! Any time I haven't done my research properly and publish erroneous information is an embarrassment. I've run corrections every time I've done this. I once made a factual error in a column I wrote for a newspaper that came from work done on my blog, which forced the paper to print a partial retraction, about three years ago. That's the worst, because I put someone else other than me in an uncomfortable position, and I stopped doing work for that newspaper as a result. That was my decision, not theirs.

Bloggers you respect?
I respect a wide variety of bloggers, including conservatives such as Hugh Hewitt, the entire crew at *National Review*, Power Line, Mitch Berg, the Anchoress

(who mostly blogs on spiritual matters), Michael Yon, Michael Totten, J. D. Johannes, Daniel Glover, Michelle Malkin, and many more. Joe Gandelman has done remarkable work as the proprietor of the Moderate Voice, an indispensable centrist blog. Flash at Centrisity would be another.

Left-wing bloggers you respect?

While not agreeing with their politics, I respect the ethics and talent of a number of progressive bloggers. Jeralyn Merritt of TalkLeft, Chris Bowers of OpenLeft, Michael Stickings at the Reaction, Shaun Mullen at Kiko's House and TMV. John Amato at Crooks and Liars is a good guy who sometimes has just a little too much fun for his own good. John Aravosis sometimes crosses the line at AMERICAblog, but he's a good guy in "real life." Ezra Klein is a very good writer at the *American Prospect*, but also sometimes crosses the line into invective. I'm sure there are more, but I'd rather people read conservative bloggers!

Advice for a young person thinking of blogging?

It would depend on what kind of interest they have in politics. If they want to run for office someday, I might discourage them from blogging. The act of committing opinion to paper tends to make it more difficult to change one's position later, even for the best of reasons. Otherwise, I'd encourage them to jump in with both feet and enjoy one hell of a ride. Be certain of your facts and refrain from letting personal invective cloud your postings. The one currency that matters the most in the blogosphere is credibility, and it's a lot more difficult to earn than it is to lose.

13

The Internet and the Future of Media Politics

Jeremy D. Mayer and Michael Cornfield

Political communication is undergoing a transformation arguably as important as the shift from writing to printing from the fifteenth to seventeenth centuries and from print to broadcast media in the twentieth century. The current transformation centers on the rise of the Internet.[1] By the end of 2006, more than 230 million Americans age twelve and older were going online, with the average time each person spent there increasing to more than one hour a day.[2] Trend studies by the Pew Research Center show that the Internet is the only medium in which political communication rose in the last decade. Campaigners are expanding their reliance on it to impress voters, donors, and other supporters. The news media are embracing blogs, videos, interactive databases, and other online formats as legitimate and important, if not yet profitable, means to deliver their products. Today, while television remains the most influential medium in American politics, in terms of number of consumers and campaign dollars spent, it is clear that television has a new challenger on the scene.

The Internet facilitates back-and-forth communication between citizens and media/political elites. Individuals reached as the members of mass and targeted audiences are taking advantage, using the Net to reach back. Online political advertisements acknowledge the fact and value of this backflow; they routinely contain links for viewers to click through to a Web site where they can find more information and opportunities for comments, donations, and volunteering. Internet users are also talking media and politics among themselves, from e-mail and instant messaging to consumer-generated Web content. Through these two-way and lateral channels, citizens get more involved in activities previously restricted to consultants, journalists, and officials. The proliferation of "feedback" and "peer-to-peer" alternatives to "top-down" messaging has made the Internet a locus not just for revolutionary hopes and fears, but for demonstrable changes in power relations as well.

If we pull back from the bursts of innovation, we can see patterns in the attributes the Internet brings to the public fore. This essay discusses four positive online infusions: creativity, interactivity, independence, and depth. Then it turns to five mostly negative implications of the Internet for political communication in America: inequality, filterlessness, blurring, surveillance, and cocooning. Think of these terms as qualities to watch for, reflect upon, and — given the Internet's capacity to enhance public participation — get involved in as online politics unfolds.

CREATIVITY

Technologically, the Internet is an unusually dynamic medium. It took decades for color television to replace black and white, whereas the Internet has rapidly evolved from a text-dominated medium accessed by telephone dial-up to a video-dominated medium accessed through high-speed, high-volume "broadband" technology. Internet innovations emerge quickly and constantly from Silicon Valley and other information technology (IT) industry centers. Innovations also arise from users: for example, the WikiScanner, which identifies contributors to the online encyclopedia Wikipedia, was developed by someone with no connection to the enterprise.

One series of innovations has been dubbed *Web 2.0*. The term refers to the streaking popularity of Web sites where consumers generate the bulk of the content. Tens of millions of Internet users are posting their own content via such Web 2.0 or "social media" sites as Flickr (photographs), Digg (ratings), del.icio.us (classification categories), Wikipedia (encyclopedia entries), YouTube (videos), and MySpace (personal profiles). In response to the exuberant growth of Web 2.0, the old media and politics establishment, accustomed to thinking in terms of "paid" (advertising) and "earned" (journalistic) media, has developed its own favorite new online applications and practices to cope with — if not control — the strong growth in social media. The establishment's 2.0 toolbox includes microtargeting, in which survey and commercial data are studied to customize conversational outreach to individuals; reputation management, in which companies monitor the Internet for negative commentary and seek to answer critics in ways that lead to group outreach; and word-of-mouth marketing, in which people are given incentives to talk up a topic on behalf of a candidate, company, or product.

New ways of packaging information, gathering citizens, and persuading voters and other political decision makers surface continuously. Communications experimentation builds upon technological experimentation. Since some innovations and practices originate with individuals unaffiliated with existing power structures, the Internet can foster its own checks on the unaccountable powers inherent in the new media.[3] For example, the aforementioned WikiScanner hedges the capacity of people to shape opinions anonymously, and perniciously, by tracing entries to their computers of origin. Creativity also comes from social movements seeking to blunt established power. During the 2004 presidential campaign of Democrat Howard Dean, one supporter suggested via e-mail that other "Deaniacs" write handwritten letters to uncommitted voters in the early and crucial states of Iowa and New Hampshire. This was a tactic used to great success by the 1960 John F. Kennedy campaign, but the new twist was that it was put into effect via MeetUp.com, a Web site that promotes local meetings among people with shared interests.

Distributed journalism is another example of online creativity in public services. As described by Dan Gillmor in his book *We the Media*,[4] this Internet-enabled phenomenon taps the observational and research skills of nonjournalists to augment the reporting of social events. Like many other types of online communication, distributed journalism received a power boost from the advent of easily produced and published videos. Today, citizens can become eyewitnesses to history by being in the right place at the right time, pointing their camera/cell phones and shooting, and then pointing their computers to YouTube and other video repository sites and clicking to upload. Responding to the popularity of amateur videos and text posts, political bloggers, interest groups, and news media organizations alike have learned to solicit such contributions from their readers.

Creativity in communication enhances individual freedom and buoys the hopes of the underfranchised. It also places new and exacting pressures on established media and politics institutions. They often dismiss outsider innovations easily at first, but as the power and popularity of the user-generated content grows, established media that refuse to compromise will lose market share. Most news organizations now solicit videos from viewers, often paying a nominal fee for footage used on the air. The 2004 Bush campaign developed an in-house version of MeetUp known as the "House Party," to great success. Yesterday's innovation becomes today's familiar feature, awaiting tomorrow's improvement in another round of entrepreneurial activity.

The creativity of the Internet harnesses the ideas and suggestions of millions of people worldwide more rapidly than any previous medium has done. If a teenager in South Korea suddenly discovered a way to communicate with young people about politics using a simple new mobile technology, it could be adopted in just a month or two by dozens of American campaigns. And a programmer in Texas could come up with an improvement to the Korean's idea, which would get back to Korea even faster. The multiplication of creativity online means that this medium will change faster than anything the world has seen before. Already talk has begun in the IT industry about Web 3.0. We can only safely predict in the long run a rapidly changing technical environment for public affairs and further disruptions to expected courses of events as public affairs innovations catch the powerful by surprise.

INTERACTIVITY

Democratic politics—as it occurred in the New England town hall, Venetian palace, and *agora* or marketplace of classical Greece—allowed for fluid interactivity between governors and governed. Beyond direct conversation, citizens could affect the course of events through their audible and visible reactions. Mass media vastly expanded the number of citizens who could learn quickly about interactive public events, but they lacked the means to participate. Media executives gained "gatekeeping" powers to shape political perceptions, agendas, and moods through their decisions of what to include and not include in their widely seen representations of interactive scenes. Political professionals were also beneficiaries of mass media influence. When television ads and direct mail were the main channels for presidential campaigns and Americans gleaned information about candidates and issues only from candidate debates and news accounts, there were fewer opportunities for voters to feel involved than in the direct settings of the previous eras.

Today, the Internet revives the possibilities of democratic interactivity in public affairs. While reading a news story on the Net or watching a streaming video of a candidate making her case, citizens can register their reactions without actually being in the presence of the powerful. They can shoot off e-mails, give money, spread the word to friends, and engage in an electronic version of "standing up to be counted." The counting phenomenon works as follows: Web sites of mass media organs increasingly display the "most viewed" and "most emailed" stories of the day on their home pages. As Web users click around media offerings—consciously and unconsciously, spontaneously and sparked by online campaigns—they engage in a form of publicity through the aggregation of their choices. Audience input is even seeping into old media channels: Bill O'Reilly reads emails from viewers on his Fox News show, something broadcast anchors seldom did in the twentieth century. In these ways and others, consumers of online journalism interact with the subjects and narrators of political coverage.

Online interactivity ranges beyond communication into transactions. Donating money is one of the most important modes of participation American citizens can have in politics, for better and worse. Typically, donors of large sums of money procure direct access to political decision makers. They pay for "face time"—and are beseeched for it by solicitous campaigners. Now, thanks to the Internet, small donors have a greater say. Presidential candidates in 2008, notably Republican Ron Paul and Democrat Barack Obama, have seen tens of millions of dollars pour into their campaign accounts in $25 and $50 amounts.[5] The entire public square has taken notice of this fiscal *vox populi*. Online contributors do not have the chance to have in-depth conversations with their designated recipients, but their preferences become known symbolically.

Interest groups have learned to interact with officials online as well. In pluralist democracies, power is distributed unequally toward groups able to organize most effectively. The Internet diffuses that power to *ad hoc* groups, and abstract groups without formal memberships and agendas, notably the progressive antiwar operation MoveOn.org and the conservative hub FreeRepublic.com. Some think the Internet can, as deployed by new types of groups, overcome the chronic curse of collective action: the tendency for the many to stand by powerlessly while the well organized push their "special interest" preferences into office and law. By making timely information more available to all, lowering entry barriers to membership and participation, and bundling individual voices, dollars, and votes, the Internet has already led to several outcomes in American politics that would not have been predicted by collective action and pluralist theory. The defeat of the 2006 and 2007 immigration reform bills, backed by the White House, congressional leadership, and major business sectors, occurred because of a populist uprising spurred through talk radio and executed through e-mail and telephone petitioning.

The Internet has also brought about higher levels of interactivity between citizens and businesses and governments in terms of public services: paying taxes, filing for benefits, applying for contracts, complying with regulatory requirements, and so forth. Bureaucratic mazes have been shortened as users enter commonsense keywords and are delivered to the Web pages of the right office, whereupon they may download forms or enter data directly. It is a big leap from improved government service to enhanced citizen participation in government decision making, but the Internet at least makes that a plausible development.

INDEPENDENCE

The Internet weakens media and government controls over what citizens learn about politics. At the basic level, it affords people greater choice *not* to

Jeremy D. Mayer and Michael Cornfield

absorb information about public affairs. Mass media consumers often encounter political information whether they want to or not, because it has been marbled into the content of programs and publications they have chosen for other reasons. Viewers of broadcast television at certain hours of the day are most dependent on what has been programmed. Cable subscribers and owners of DVD players can abandon news programming for nonstop entertainment, much as newspaper and magazine readers can ignore news sections and publications. But Internet consumers exercise nearly complete control over information topics. Markus Prior argues that a fundamental (albeit not absolute) choice between news and entertainment consumption is a hallmark of "post-broadcast democracy," with important implications for voter knowledge and turnout.[6]

Those who elect to absorb news and politics online experience independence on a richer level. The Net provides direct access to news, discussion, and other political information sites around the world—it is truly the first global medium, in that people can readily procure streams of content emanating from nations other than their own. Even in the notorious case of China and other totalitarian regimes, access to outside information is more obtainable for more people online than through other channels. Smuggled pamphlets and cassettes, the modes used by dissidents of previous generations, are less detectable, but also less timely and available. Moreover, the Internet supplies information outside the control of the global corporations that dominate the media marketplace: News Corporation, Viacom, Google, Yahoo!, and the like. While the most popular sites on the Web in terms of raw traffic numbers are affiliated with these corporations, there are a profusion of alternative sources and interpretations—some of which are linked to or republished by the behemoths. Conversely, blogs and other sites run by individuals or small groups, such as Talking Points Memo (http://www.talking pointsmemo.com) and Drudge Report (http://www.drudgereport.com), link to editorial and political content supplied by established authorities and posted by the media giants. The end result of this elaborate ganglion is that Web users have gained some liberation from the media oligopoly, at least as far as the types and perspectives of information they can procure.

The Internet may also contribute to nonconformist thought having greater visibility, if not outright influence, in public affairs. During the height of television's media dominance, Elizabeth Noelle-Neumann discovered evidence of a "spiral of silence," where those with minority views would see no support for their opinions in public and consequently keep their views to themselves for fear of ostracism.[7] Today, almost no opinion is so eccentric that it cannot find at least one kindred spirit on the Web. The possibility of like-minded connectivity nourishes independence in political thought.

The same goes for political expression, thanks to the low cost of producing and distributing opinions, observations, and data, combined with the huge content capacity of the network and individual terminals. In the mass media era, publicly available messages about the United States Senate essentially came from Senate offices, registered lobbyists, and journalists with credentials to enter the Senate Press Gallery. Then came C-SPAN, which televises Senate proceedings, and then the Web. Today, anyone with something to say to the world about the Senate can upload a package of evidence and commentary—or just the latter. Such an expression will probably not be amplified by *The New York Times*, but it will be indexed by Google and other search engine portals.

The Internet has lowered the boundaries separating the playing fields of politics from its spectators. That is not the same as leveling the field; wealthy and official players still hold tremendous advantages in having their say heard in public. But most people online have more freedom than they did not to listen to the big players, to listen to others, and to talk back.

DEPTH

Lance Bennett has identified fragmentation and personalization as two key defects in modern media coverage of politics.[8] Journalists represent public affairs episodically, overdramatically, and slight historical and institutional forces in favor of clashes of personalities. This is particularly true of television news. Bennett contends that these journalistic biases threaten the health of our democracy. The Internet ameliorates the plight. It accommodates a rich and diverse amount of content, giving users the chance to deepen their understanding of current events.

The path to knowledge begins, of course, with the galactic-size, granular-scale system of keyword-organized searches of the Web that has made *Google* a common verb. The links on search engine return pages—some the result of mathematical calculations of previous searchers' preferences, some the result of advertising buys ("sponsored links")—are gateways to the kinds of intellectual activity previously concentrated in libraries and schools: browsing, researching, consulting experts, conversing with peers, calculating, comparing, analyzing, thinking.

For example, while video messages available on the Web through YouTube and other sites reproduce and arguably vitiate the fragmented and personalized coverage of televised journalism, the Internet surrounds those videos with captions, data, and, most importantly, links. The televised video is a drive-by experience, superficial at best and demagogic at worst. So is the Web video—but with the invaluable, universal, and habit-forming option to "drill down" on what has just been seen. Citizens can now more readily reflect on a video message by reviewing it multiple times. Fact-checks, disputations, gossip, dissections, and more are a click or two away, and the entirety is archived. Those in search of depth can also head to Project Vote Smart (http://www.vote smart.org) and Congress.org (http://www.congress.org), two civic-minded Web sites full of political documentation in helpful formats.[9] Voters trying to make up their minds among presidential candidates in 2007 could head to Vote Help (http://votehelp.org), where, in the style of find-a-date or find-a-music artist matching services, they could enter preferences into an interactive quiz and be presented with the candidate most suited to them.

The Internet adds depth to polities as well as individuals. James Surowiecki has detailed how the pooling of a great many people's "local knowledge" can, under the right circumstances and arrangements, yield smarter answers than a Nobel laureate.[10] The Internet is seemingly tailor-made for depth creation by social synthesis. To be sure, the public at large cannot be proven correct on most political questions, because those usually hinge on values and visions along with facts and empirically validated theories. But democracy is predicated, as E. B. White famously remarked, on "the recurrent suspicion that more than half the people are right more than half the time." Drawing on as many people as possible to deliberate on leaders and policies authenticates the resulting decisions and lends support to a pillar of Enlightenment thinking that free people can reason together and rule better as a result.

* * *

So there now exist easy routes to information and discourse that can compensate for the limits of journalism as well as those of campaigning, bureaucracy, and marketing. However, the paths to knowledge and political action based on knowledge remain as arduous as ever. In fact, the Internet has placed a few boulders in the way of civilized and just self-governance. We now turn to five of these negatives.

INEQUALITY

Although the Internet has lowered many costs associated with political communication, the price of adequate connectivity remains a threshold some have a difficult time crossing. The percentage of Americans online has remained in the 70 percent range for several years, and shows little sign of climbing into the practically universal stratum of telephones and televisions. That offline segment of the public embodies a democratic inequality. To the extent the demarcation persists because of class divisions, an inability to pay or to grasp the benefits of going online, the inequality is troublesome. It is less troublesome for those—primarily well-off and older—who choose to stay offline but know about and participate in public affairs through other media.

The class and education barrier was known as the *digital divide* in the 1990s. The term lost currency after the turn of the millennium, but the phenomenon remains significant, especially on a global scale. In the United States, according to the Pew Internet and American Life Project, only 55 percent of those with household incomes less than $30,000 a year were online in 2007, compared with 93 percent with household incomes above $75,000 a year. Only 40 percent of Americans with less than a high school education were connected, whereas 81 percent of those with some college education were.

A second technical stratification of significance concerns broadband. Home penetration of high-speed, high-volume connections doubled in the United States between 2004 and 2007, and it is now above 50 percent, with 30 percent of those with dial-up connections having access to broadband in the workplace. Such workplace access, it is important to note, may be constrained by those in charge; having a technical connection but being blocked, monitored, and otherwise deterred from accessing the digital public square is certainly inadequate access. Those who have limited access to the Internet at work tend to be in blue-collar and service occupations. Thus, the digital divide is reproduced in technical upgrades and workplace conditions.

It may also be reproduced in government and corporate policies. The issue of *network neutrality* refers to a proposal advanced by telecommunications companies to move to tiered service, in which those paying more would be able to receive and send information more quickly. The companies contend that such pricing differentiation is necessitated by the costs of improving and maintaining the infrastructure, and is no different than what is found in cable and airline service. Opponents argue that such an arrangement would only pad what are already healthy profits for a public good and introduce yet another inequality into society and public life.

FILTERLESSNESS

If the Internet grants us independence from the centralized power of the mass media, this independence is inextricably tied to the problem of filterlessness. Political, civic, and media institutions use filters to improve the quality of the information they depend on and release to the public. They check facts, revise sentences, rearrange photos, and so forth. The Internet's virtue of no authoritative control permits dissidents and eccentrics to promulgate their views to

the world, but this quality is also a significant weakness. A book that was released by a reputable academic press could be expected to have undergone
lengthy peer review by knowledgeable experts. A story printed in *The New
York Times* has undergone careful and redundant fact checking. The rapid
pace of the media in the era of cyberpolitics has removed much of the filtering process: Rumor, falsehood, and innuendo quickly move into public discourse. Matters about the private sex lives of public officials that would never
have been printed in previous eras are now fodder for Web gossips like Matt
Drudge.

One can point to examples of the media abusing its gatekeeping authority
in the past, such as its refusal to inform the nation of philandering presidents
whose preoccupation with illicit sex arguably raised questions about national
security and judgment.[11] However, the loss of gatekeeping power by the mass
media has made politics a less appetizing field of endeavor for both citizens
and politicians. The first story of the Monica Lewinsky affair appeared on
Drudge Report, because an "old media" editor at *Newsweek* refused to run it.
Similarly, during the ensuing impeachment, Drudge Report ran a controversial account of an alleged rape committed by Clinton decades ago, an account
no mainstream media outlet would cover because they did not believe it had
been fully sourced. Pressured by the coverage on Web sites and in chat rooms,
the mainstream media eventually ran both stories. It should be noted, however, that the gatekeepers of the mass media do retain some filtering power.
A lurid and false rumor about Clinton fathering an interracial child with a
prostitute circulated on the Web for years, but never broke into mainstream
media sources and remained unknown to most Americans.

Filterlessness also alters the nature of political campaigns. Television ads
that refer to major media outlets as sources have been shown to be more effective than those that simply make unsourced allegations.[12] Yet what if an attack was based on an anonymous Wikipedia post? In the 2006 congressional
campaign in South Dakota, incumbent Stephanie Herseth Sandlin was attacked by her opponent's staff based on an erroneous Wikipedia entry that alleged she was pregnant by her chief of staff. While Herseth Sandlin was able
to convince the local media that the story was a blatant lie and Wikipedia
quickly corrected the mistake, the incident demonstrates the danger of filter-
less media for campaigns.[13] Numerous emails have circulated passing along
false stories about Barack Obama's religious upbringing, for example. Of
course, in the past, rumors and whisper campaigns were a vibrant part of
American campaigns, but today the unfiltered Internet makes such campaigns
faster and easier.

Filterlessness has also produced an avalanche of information about politics. When there were only three television news networks and only a few

leading nationally influential newspapers, the major media outlets had tremendous power to focus the attention of citizens and elites on a given topic. Today, with so many diverse outlets, there may be far less of a sense of a unified national agenda to which politicians have to react and the public has to pay attention. The citizen, presented with the chaotic, shifting, and massive amount of political information available on the Web, may simply retreat from the overload of data. Too much political information might be almost as much of a problem as too little. Without the media filtering the important from the trivial, is the national agenda inevitably fragmented?

BLURRING—WHO IS A JOURNALIST IN THE INTERNET AGE?

The Internet has begun to alter political journalism in fundamental ways, most importantly by altering the definition of who is a journalist. In the past, a journalist was someone who worked for the established print or electronic media. Credentials to cover the White House or other major political institutions were granted on the basis of employment by a respected media outlet. Is someone who sets up a Web site that talks about politics a "journalist"? What if the Web site is basically a subsidiary of one of the political parties and covers only news that favors that party?

During President George W. Bush's first term, an obscure "news service," Talon News, which shared a Web site with a Republican group, hired a "journalist" by the name of Jeff Gannon, whose qualifications for journalism were, to be charitable, remarkably scant. Denied permanent press credentials by the White House press corps because he lacked any credible experience, he was mysteriously issued day passes to White House press briefings for months, asking questions that almost always reflected a pro-administration position. When one of his questions to the president was found to be factually incorrect—as well as taken directly from conservative radio host Rush Limbaugh's broadcast—reporters began to investigate Gannon and found that not only were his credentials thin, but his past employment included work as a prostitute. When politics and sex meet, a media firestorm predictably ensues, and such was the case here. Reporters wanted to know how an unqualified partisan with an extremely shady past had managed to get daily passes into one of the most secure sites on earth. But amid the scandal, a deeper question remains: Who exactly is a journalist?

The question of defining journalists affects campaigns. If a citizen is hired by a congressional campaign to write and distribute political leaflets, every dime spent must be reported to the Federal Election Commission (FEC). The author of the leaflets isn't a journalist, and no one reading them would think so. If a campaign hired a newspaper columnist to write for it, on the other hand, both the campaign and the journalist would be seen as violating the sanctity of elections and the free press. But when a campaign paid two political bloggers to secretly advocate on its behalf, as a Republican candidate did in a 2004 Senate campaign, most of the media ignored it.

If anyone can become a journalist just by paying a few dollars a month to have a Web site, then the privileges of the press such as immunity to campaign finance laws and the confidential source shield laws in forty-nine states will become cheapened by their universality. On the other hand, prominent political bloggers fear that government regulation of the Internet will kill its vitality and vibrant freedom. The FEC has so far chosen not to regulate the Internet in campaigns, except to require all expenditures by the campaign on the Internet be reported, as with any other expense. For now, the broader question of who is a journalist under the law and under custom remains blurred by the new force of the Internet.

CONSTANT SURVEILLANCE: THE END OF POLITICAL PRIVACY?

The rise of the Internet combined with miniaturization of video technology has changed the way American politics is conducted. When Larry Sabato wrote *Feeding Frenzy*, about how the media had taken over the presidential campaign, he outlined the media's endless appetite for scandal and negative information and images. But the Internet has made the surveillance of candidates even more constant and damaging. The contrast between today and 1968 is illustrative. On the campaign trail in 1968, film was shot of various candidates at most rallies. Film cameras were large and bulky, and so expensive that the ability to make quality images was largely limited to professionals. And news organizations had to rush the actual film to a studio for developing and then processing, and, later in that day or the next day, broadcasting. Today, an amateur with a $400 digital video camera can capture images as good as or better than the professional images of 1968. They do not need processing, and can be up on YouTube or another free video distribution service within moments.

In the 2006 Virginia Senate race, video technology combined with the Internet was responsible for the collapse of the campaign of a well-respected Republican incumbent, Sen. George Allen. Allen was expected to cruise to an easy reelection in his red state of Virginia, and was already making plans to run for president in 2008. The question among cognoscenti in Virginia was not whether he would win, but by how much. But then Allen was caught on camera mocking an opposition volunteer of Indian descent during a Republican rally in Virginia. Allen called him "macaca" and welcomed him to a nearly all-white rural crowd, which he labeled "the real Virginia, the real America." The racial implications were immediately obvious: Dark-skinned Asians were not real Americans or Virginians. Moreover, while *macaca* is not familiar as a racial epithet to most Americans, it is a derogatory term for blacks in parts of Northern Africa. Allen's campaign issued several different explanations for why the senator used that phrase—that it had been gibberish, that he had been trying to say "Mohawk" in reference to the volunteer's unusual haircut, or that he thought that was the man's name. The fact that Allen's mother had spent time in her childhood in Tunisia, where the word was common, was not one of the reasons offered by the campaign, but it did make it likely that none of the serial explanations offered was honest. The mainstream media, with its addiction to scandal and image, used the footage extensively. It is rare for a Senate campaign to make the nightly news, but this made all three networks. It even led to jokes on the major late night talk shows. Allen, after at first denying any problem, apologized profusely, both in public and to the young man personally. But it was never clear what he was apologizing for, since he had denied, implausibly, knowing what the word meant.

The Allen campaign never recovered from this gaffe, and, while it would be wrong to attribute his narrow and surprising defeat to this single mistake, in a previous era—before YouTube and ubiquitous video cameras—the incident would have barely been a story, let alone one that attracted national attention and changed the race.

The campaign worker singled out by Allen had been following the campaign for days, videotaping Allen at every opportunity. This has become standard practice in presidential and congressional campaigns. Campaigns send out volunteers to do opposition videotaping, hoping that a careless comment or a negative image will become powerful fodder for an election ad. What the macaca incident did was show how the Internet could make something newsworthy even before the mainstream media had the chance to decide. A campaign can post something on YouTube, and, if it gets enough hits, it may not even require the mainstream media to give it attention. In the 2006 Montana Senate race, the Democratic challenger posted clips of the incumbent snoring at a congressional hearing as well as calling firefighters "losers."

The constant monitoring of candidates adds an extraordinary unpredictability to politics. It could lead to the rise of "robo-candidates" who avoid all spontaneous interactions. It is worth noting that following the macaca incident, Allen's campaign kept their man as far from public interaction and media surveillance as possible. But even the most programmed candidate may be unable to avoid the nearly universal surveillance offered by the combination of the Internet and cheap video cameras.

COCOONING

> We live in self-imposed exile from communal conversation and action.
> The public square is naked. American politics has lost its soul. The repub-
> lic has become procedural, and we have become unencumbered selves. In-
> dividualism has become cancerous. We live in an age of narcissism and
> pursue loneliness.
>
> —Albert Borgman[14]

Although Borgman wrote these words while the Internet was in its infancy,
they capture many of the most far-reaching problems some see inherent in the
new medium. The growth of technology's role in American life may contribute to a sense of hyperindividualism, as we all cocoon ourselves away
from not only politics but real-world human connections. While champions
of the Internet's possibility rave about the potential for spatially separated individuals to form interest groups through the Web, perhaps such groups fail
to provide community, solidarity, and other group benefits that are necessary
to civil society. Consider the difference between a union hall gathering of
workers in 1950 and an Internet chat room on politics today. The union hall
meeting requires physical presence and interactions beyond the level of typ-
ing and reading. Those present see each other as complete beings who have
left their private domains to enter into public discourse. The patterns of listening and speaking, of debate and discussion, probably would not be unfamiliar to a colonial Virginian or an ancient Greek. By contrast, the denizens
of a chat room or the readers of a bulletin board may hide behind pseudo-
nyms; they may misrepresent their true selves or opinions with careless abandon. Most importantly, they may not feel the same sense of connection to
each other as do people who meet in the flesh.[15]

Thinkers as diverse as Alexis de Tocqueville[16] in the nineteenth century
and political scientist Robert Putnam in the late twentieth century have emphasized that America's civil society rests on the health of voluntary associations among citizens. Civic activities that build up "social capital" have been
declining rapidly in the last forty years, and this troubles many scholars,
politicians, and citizens. One of Putnam's more intriguing findings in his influential 2001 book *Bowling Alone* was that for every hour of newspaper
reading civic engagement increased, while for every hour of television watching it decreased.[17] While comparable data are not yet available for Internet usage, it seems plausible that local "real" activities decline as Internet usage expands. Thus, it becomes important to find out whether the "communal"
activities on the Web can produce the same connectedness that characterized

traditional groups. As one recent article asked: "When it comes to . . . building community, is the Internet more like a Girl Scout troop or a television set?" Unfortunately, given current patterns of usage, it seems that the Internet is far more similar to the dreaded idiot box than to a meeting with other citizens.[18]

Thus, "cocooning" may represent the most subtle and insidious danger in cyberpolitics. Even before the Internet, many worried that Americans were increasingly unconnected to each other. More and more of the upper classes live in gated communities, send their children to private schools, and fail to interact in any meaningful way with less wealthy Americans. Demonstrations and marches and rallies declined in effectiveness as Americans ceased congregating in public spaces, replacing downtowns with privately owned malls. With the dawn of Internet shopping, telecommuting, and Web-based entertainment, leaving home becomes almost superfluous. Perhaps the new media possibilities of the Web will provide Americans with access to new and unfiltered information about politics. But if we do not have a sense of community, of shared obligations and values, will we care about political news from home or abroad? Instead of "thinking globally and acting locally" will we now "entertain individually and disappear locally"? In this sense, the Internet may be the apotheosis of what America's first great media critic, Walter Lippmann, described as "pseudo-reality."[19] In Lippmann's original conception, the media provided the citizen with a useful simplification of the complex real world. His reaction to that pseudo-reality would eventually have real-world implications. However, the Internet may create a "virtual reality" all its own, in which behaviors and interactions that never leave cyberspace become an end in themselves.

Cocooning will surely be more of a threat tomorrow than it is today. The trend in the Internet is toward more and more integration, both of content and of methods of transmission. Broadband technology offers the potential for a grand unification of all media into a single giant data stream. The future American home may have one connection to the outside world, and through that broadband cable will stream news, movies, telephone, e-mail, Web sites, votes, political donations, shopping orders, bills, banking, and everything necessary for life save water, food, and air (and our orders for all those things may be encoded in the pipeline as well). The effects that this will have on America's political culture are incalculable at present. Perhaps the unified media will be more subject to centralized control. Perhaps the Web will retain the virtue of independence, and Americans will take advantage of greater choices in sources of political information. Whatever happens in this brave new world of unified media, the incentives to leave home will be lessened, and the tendency to cocoon in one's own space more common.[20]

CONCLUSION: THE INEVITABLE INTERNET
VERSUS THE RESILIENT STATUS QUO?

There is no way to unring the bell of technological change. The Internet has expanded by leaps and bounds during the last fifteen years because it filled needs that Americans had, even if they did not know they had them: interactivity, faster news, easier contacts, and greater independence. It has changed the way Americans learn about politics, and it has begun to change the way they participate in politics.[21] The ordinary citizen can now readily correct for media biases of many varieties as far as being able to see politics more fully than before the Internet arrived. But the improved capacity for political vision is not the same as an improved capacity for political action. Protesters, dissenters, opponents can get their message out, and the sympathetic can find it. But there's quite a psychological road to travel between perception and action: Viewers must believe they have a chance at victory before they will organize to act, and the Internet, through encouraging cocooning, may act as a barrier to political action. Furthermore, the Internet also has sinister implications for government and corporate surveillance of our actions and thoughts. Allied with video cameras, the Internet can be used to monitor citizens in public spaces. "Cookies" can track where viewers have browsed. Post-9/11 legislation gave the government new powers to read e-mails at home and abroad.

So again, we are left where we began: Will the Internet be a source for positive political change, or will it exacerbate existing ills in American media politics as well as adding its own? A third possibility suggests itself: Perhaps the Internet will not alter American politics all that much. The status quo has a resiliency that should not be underestimated. Television affected many aspects of American politics, but few would argue that politics and journalism changed beyond recognition. Such potentially isolating forces as "cocooning" do not alter the constitutional structure. So long as we remain in a winner-take-all system, a winner must get at least a plurality, and usually more—and this impels campaigners for office and for legislation to reach out via the Net and other media to form coalitions.

Similarly, those who speak of the "information revolution" happening as a result of the Internet are not looking carefully enough at the political situation into which the new media have been piped. For example, a fallacy in the information overload concept is that it is not automatic with the new technology, but set off by the need to absorb a lot of disorganized information in a short time. By one measure, there has been no information revolution because revolution denotes a swift redistribution of power, and the Internet has not done that yet—not even in the technical sense of power. Neil Postman, among others, argued that the invention of the printing press ultimately altered the power relationships between citizens and rulers, and made large-scale republican democracy possible. The most enthusiastic bloggers and Internet activists cannot yet make a similar claim about the Internet.

The Internet has clearly changed American media politics and altered not only the method of political communication but the content and direction of political information. However, even at the rapid pace with which the Internet is growing and evolving, it may be years or decades before we can know how or indeed whether it will alter American politics itself in a fundamental fashion.

DISCUSSION QUESTIONS

1. Compare a town hall meeting that takes place in person to a meeting that takes place over the Internet. Would we lose something if we shifted to "virtual" meetings to resolve local political disputes? Would we gain anything?
2. Should we worry about the "digital divide"? Should government take actions to make the Internet more available to all citizens?
3. Have your political views ever been changed by a Web site, as opposed to a newspaper or television broadcast?
4. Which has the most credibility with you: a fact reported on a Web site, on television news, or in a newspaper? Why? If you could get political information from only one of the three sources, which would you pick?
5. Select one of the institutions discussed in this text (the president, Congress, the parties, the Supreme Court, the bureaucracy) and assess how the Internet has changed the way it operates. Overall, do you think the effect has been more positive than negative?

SUGGESTIONS FOR FURTHER READING

Michael Cornfield. *Politics Moves Online: Campaigning and the Internet*. New York: Century Foundation, 2004.

Steve Davis, Larry Ellin, and Grant Reeder. *Click on Democracy: The Internet's Power to Change Political Apathy into Civic Action*. Boulder, CO: Westview, 2002.

Jeremy D. Mayer. *American Media Politics in Transition*. New York: McGraw-Hill, 2008.

Markus Prior. *Post-Broadcast Democracy: How Media Choice Increases Inequality in Political Involvement and Polarizes Elections*. New York: Cambridge University Press, 2007.

Diana Saco. *Cybering Democracy: Public Space and the Internet*. Minneapolis: University of Minnesota Press, 2002.

NOTES

1. By *Internet*, we mean the network of computerized-driven communication accessible by mobile and stationary terminals.

2. USC–Annenberg Digital Future Project 2007 Report,http://www.digitalcenter .org.

3. Yochai Benkler, *The Wealth of Networks: How Social Production Transforms Markets and Freedom* (New Haven, CT: Yale University Press, 2006).

4. Dan Gillmor, *We the Media: Grassroots Journalism by the People, for the People* (Sebastopol, CA: O'Reilly Media, 2004).

5. In 2007 Paul netted $13.6 million in contributions of $200 or less, much of it through the Net. Obama reaped $10.3 million in small donations. "Presidential Fundraising in 2007 Doubles 2003," Campaign Finance Institute news release, February 11, 2008, http://www.cfinst.org/pr/prRelease.aspx?ReleaseID=179.

6. Markus Prior, *Post-Broadcast Democracy: How Media Choice Increases Inequality in Political Involvement and Polarizes Elections* (New York: Cambridge University Press, 2007).

7. Elizabeth Noelle-Neumann, *The Spiral of Silence: Public Opinion—Our Social Skin* (Chicago: University of Chicago Press, 1984).

8. W. Lance Bennett, *News: The Politics of Illusion*, 4th ed. (New York: Longman, 2001).

9. Full disclosure: Cornfield works at the company that maintains Congress.org.

10. James Surowiecki, *The Wisdom of Crowds: Why the Many Are Smarter Than the Few and How Collective Wisdom Shapes Business, Economies, Societies, and Nations* (New York: Doubleday, 2004).

11. Thomas C. Reeves, *A Question of Character: A Life of John F. Kennedy* (Rocklin, CA: Prima, 1991).

12. Michael Geer, *In Defense of Negativity* (Chicago: University of Chicago, 2007).

13. Congresswoman Stephanie Herseth Sandlin, interview with Mayer, Washington D.C., December 2007.

14. Albert Borgman, *Crossing the Postmodern Divide* (Chicago: University of Chicago Press, 1992), 3.

15. It should be noted that at least one analyst worries that the Internet may actually provide a sense of connection to extremists and terrorists. In his 2001 book *Republic.com*, Cass Sunstein argued that the Internet could be used by terrorists to connect a far-flung conspiracy. Sunstein's warnings today look prophetic, now that it is known that the men who plotted the tragic attacks of 9/11 used the Internet to stay in touch. Had the terrorists been forced to meet in person or use more traditional forms of communication, it is possible that American intelligence would have detected their conspiracy.

16. Alexis de Tocqueville, *Democracy in America* (1840; reprint, New York: Signet, 2001).

17. Robert Putnam, *Bowling Alone: The Collapse and Revival of American Community* (New York: Touchstone, 2001).

18. Margie K. Shields, Susan E. Linn, and Stephen Doheny-Farina, "Connected Kids," *American Prospect*, December 26, 2000.

19. Walter Lippmann, *Public Opinion* (1922; reprint, New York: Free Press, 1997).

20. Cocooning can be exaggerated as a threat. The Internet can be a medium for civic connection in which two or more people come to see the world from each other's perspective, and so mature, as classic liberal Enlightenment theory would have it. On-line communities can promote dialogue between citizens of differing views. Additionally, they can knit families and other necessary social groupings closer together. A Harris poll found that 48 percent of American Net users said they communicate more often with family and friends than before. Michael J. Weiss, "Online America," *American Demographics* (March 2001).

21. The Internet has also changed the way scholarship is conducted. The two authors of this piece, in addition to using the Internet extensively for research, never met before they wrote the version printed in the first edition, and met only once before revising for this edition. Most of our collaboration was online. All of us can collaborate with colleagues and anchor our imaginations in the work of others far more readily and expansively, if not more competently, than before the medium arrived.

Index

About the Editors

Mark J. Rozell is professor of public policy at George Mason University and the author of four books on media and U.S. politics.

Jeremy D. Mayer is associate professor of public policy at George Mason University and director of the Master's of Public Policy program. He is the author of *Running on Race: Racial Politics in Presidential Campaigns 1960–2000*.